אִיּוֹב

JOB

SONCINO BOOKS OF THE BIBLE

EDITOR: REV. DR. A. COHEN M.A., Ph.D., D.H.L.

Job

HEBREW TEXT & ENGLISH TRANSLATION
WITH AN INTRODUCTION
AND COMMENTARY

by

RABBI DR. VICTOR E. REICHERT
B. LITT., D.D.

THE SONCINO PRESS

LONDON . JERUSALEM . NEW YORK

FIRST EDITION 1946
SECOND IMPRESSION 1958
THIRD IMPRESSION 1960
FOURTH IMPRESSION 1963
FIFTH IMPRESSION 1965
SIXTH IMPRESSION 1967
SEVENTH IMPRESSION 1970
EIGHTH IMPRESSION 1974
NINTH IMPRESSION 1976

PUBLISHERS' NOTE

*Thanks are due to the
Jewish Publication Society of America
for permission to use their very beautiful
English text of the Scriptures*

PRINTED IN GREAT BRITAIN BY
THE WHITEFRIARS PRESS LTD
LONDON AND TONBRIDGE

DEDICATION

This Commentary on the Book of Job is dedicated in love to Rabbi Dr. Henry Cohen, renowned Rabbi of Galveston, Texas, whose matchless ministry has been the visible rhetoric of the inspiring ethical idealism of Job.

Born in London, England, 1863, Henry Cohen's adventurous path of life led him in 1888 to Galveston, Texas, where for more than half a century, as the Rabbi of Temple B'nai Israel, he has lit and kept burning a far-shining lamp of love. Unique shepherd of souls, friend in need, a preacher who ministers rather than a minister who preaches; familiar with many tongues, ancient and modern; lover and patron of Jewish lore whose mind and heart have encompassed not only the heaped-up treasures of his people but the spiritual wealth of mankind; scholar and sage, without false pride or vanity;—his whole life has been tirelessly filled with the translation of noble Jewish precept into helpful human practice.

Already in his life-time, Henry Cohen has become a legend and a figure of folk-lore. Presidents of the United States have been his friends. Woodrow Wilson called him 'the First Citizen of Texas.' He has helped Jew, Gentile, white, coloured, the great and the lowly alike.

'A father to the needy' (Job xxix. 16) אב לאביונים

May this Commentary on the Book of Job, an ancient hero of righteousness, help to build a bridge of better understanding and of brotherhood among men, and be the means, in humble measure, of perpetuating in the great Libraries, Colleges and Seminaries of our land, the image of Rabbi Dr. Henry Cohen who, like the hero of this Book, has ever served God in reverence and love!—V.E.R.

Cincinnati
April 24, 1946

CONTENTS

FOREWORD BY THE GENERAL EDITOR

WITH this volume, the whole of the 'Wisdom Literature' has now been included in THE SONCINO BOOKS OF THE BIBLE. It will be succeeded by the Pentateuch (with the Haphtaroth), and then the Prophetical Books will follow.

The series is distinctive in the following respects:

(*i*) Each volume contains the Hebrew text and English translation together with the commentary. (*ii*) The exposition is designed primarily for the ordinary reader of the Bible rather than for the student, and aims at providing this class of reader with requisite direction for the understanding and appreciation of the Biblical Book. (*iii*) The commentary is invariably based upon the received Hebrew text. When this presents difficulties, the most probable translation and interpretation are suggested, without resort to textual emendation. (*iv*) It offers a *Jewish* commentary. Without neglecting the valuable work of Christian expositors, it takes into account the exegesis of the Talmudical Rabbis as well as of the leading Jewish commentators.

All Biblical references are cited according to chapter and verse as in the Hebrew Bible. It is unfortunate that, unlike the American-Jewish translation, the English Authorized and Revised Versions, although made direct from the Hebrew text, did not conform to its chapter divisions. An undesirable complication was thereby introduced into Bible study. In the Hebrew the longer headings of the Psalms are counted as a separate verse; consequently Ps. xxxiv. 12, e.g., corresponds to verse 11 in A.V. and R.V. It is also necessary to take into account a marginal note like that found against 1 Kings iv. 21, 'ch. v. 1 in Heb.', so that the Hebrew 1 Kings v. 14 tallies with iv. 34 in the English.

It is hoped that this Commentary, though more particularly planned for the needs of Jews, will prove helpful to all who desire a fuller knowledge of the Bible, irrespective of their creed.

A. COHEN

ix

PREFACE

AN ancient teacher in Israel once said: 'I have learnt much from my teachers, and from my colleagues more than from my teachers, but from my disciples more than from them all.'

This Commentary on *Job* bears on every page the visible and invisible evidence of my obligations to all three sources of illumination. My inspiring teacher, Dr. Moses Buttenweiser, of sacred memory, has stood before me as I toiled in the early dawn or late at night on this volume. A large part of my inward satisfaction in contributing to THE SONCINO BOOKS OF THE BIBLE has been the feeling that I have performed a pious act of homage towards my consecrated teacher of Bible at the Hebrew Union College who first opened to me the vistas of this immortal Book.

I gratefully record here, too, my appreciation to my students at the University of Virginia where, in the summer of 1938, I first taught *Job* to an alert group of College students. Since then, I have been privileged to unfold the spiritual grandeur of this classic to my classes in the Literature of the Old Testament at the University of Cincinnati. To these young men and women, my disciples, my fond thanks for many rewarding hours of discussion together.

Nor am I unmindful of my obligation to my Congregation, the Rockdale Avenue Temple, where for twenty years I have been privileged to serve as Rabbi. I value more than I can say their encouragement, understanding and support of the best Rabbinic traditions of scholarship.

To the learned and gracious Rev. Dr. A. Cohen, the Editor of THE SONCINO BOOKS OF THE BIBLE, I owe an immeasurable debt. His deep erudition and wise judgment have unquestionably improved the manuscript I sent to England. I feel honoured and privileged to link my name with his in the Commentary on *Ecclesiastes* in this series and now to have the benefit of his discriminating scholarship in preparing my Commentary on *Job* for the press.

Finally, to Mr. J. Davidson, Director of the Soncino Press, my affectionate thanks for the honour of having invited me as the first American to participate in the distinguished work of the Soncino Press, and my gratitude for his great patience with me as well as for the meticulous care with which he has produced this Book.

VICTOR E. REICHERT

In the City of Cincinnati
April 24, 1946

INTRODUCTION

GREATNESS OF THE BOOK

THE criteria of greatness of any literary product and the canons of judgment by which it wins its way into the ranks of world masterpiece are three:

It must have the dimension of height—that upreaching unto the sublime that brings one nearer to the eternal stars of light.

It must possess the dimension of breadth—that spacious universal quality that can leap over barriers of creed, colour, rank, and race and reveal the shared humanity that makes the whole world kin.

It must know the dimension of depth—that dive into the soul of man where, as in a well of living waters, surge the profoundest tensions of the heart, its pain no less than its peace, its torment but also its triumph.

The Book of Job fulfils these standards of excellence. Unnumbered scholars, poets, philosophers, critics in generation after generation have delighted to bestow upon this product of the Hebrew religious genius the accolade of reverent homage. Professor George Foot Moore of Harvard University summarizes the universal testimony in these comprehensive and superlative words: 'The Book of Job is the greatest work of Hebrew literature that has come down to us, and one of the great poetical works of the world's literature.' 'The Matterhorn of the Old Testament,' says Professor Charles Foster Kent in unfeigned astonishment.

What a noble mountain peak it is that rises in majestic grandeur out of many promontories of revelation to be found in the Sacred Scriptures of Israel! As spacious, too, as the broad vistas of our American prairies, or the wide Arabian deserts traversed by the caravans of Tema of which the Book speaks. For depth, compare it with the springs of the sea and the recesses of the deep or the awesome Grand Canyon, that miraculous fissure in the earth that confronts the beholder with millennium piled upon millennium in spectacular array.

Profuse have been the praises heaped upon the Book of Job by men themselves richly endowed with spiritual perception. Tennyson and Carlyle spoke of it with bated breath: 'Great as the summer midnight, as the world with its seas and stars! There is nothing written, I think, in the Bible or out of it, of equal merit. . . . A noble Book; all men's Book. It is our first, oldest statement of the never-ending Problem—man's destiny, and God's ways with him here in this earth.' William Blake drew from its lines the inspiration for his mystic art. A. D. Lindsay, the Master of Balliol College, Oxford, finds in its 'rare combination of unflinching truthfulness and religious reverence,' which he links with the Ethic of Spinoza, 'no small part of the legacy of Israel.' Mary Ellen Chase calls it 'the incomparable literary masterpiece of our Bible.' And most recently, Robert Frost, America's leading

poet, demonstrated anew the unimpaired vitality of its meanings in his *Masque of Reason.*

A DRAMA OF THE HUMAN SOUL

We stand, then, before one of those massive monuments of genius that rank in men's minds with the classics of first magnitude: Homer's *Odyssey* and Vergil's *Æneid*, with Dante's *Divine Comedy*, Milton's *Paradise Lost*, Goethe's *Faust*, and the great tragedies of Shakespeare. Though dating from the fourth century before the Christian era, this masterpiece, characterized by Professor R. G. Moulton as 'a magnificent drama' seems to have been written with uninked fingers. Who that author was is lost in the mists of time. He remains a great unknown.

There is a flash in the fourteenth chapter of Ezekiel (verse 14) that supplies us with an elusive clue for the bare name of the hero of the Book. There we find Job's name linked with those of Noah and Daniel as a paragon of piety. (For new light on the ancient Canaanite background of this passage, cf. Shalom Spiegel, *Noah, Daniel, and Job touching on Canaanite Relics in the Legends of the Jews* in Louis Ginzberg Jubilee Volume.) Aside from this thread of the memory of a man of exemplary righteousness, there is no evidence to support the conclusion that the author of the Book of Job had other materials at hand save his daring imagination and consummate art upon which to weave the rich tapestry of plot he has set before us.

Those who crave neat categories and pigeon holes will be satisfied with the identification frequently made, with large measure of justice, that the Book of Job belongs to the Wisdom Literature of the Bible, and is the work of the ancient wise men of Israel described by Dr. A. Cohen, the editor of this Soncino Series of Bible Commentaries, in the Introduction to *Proverbs*. Accepting this conclusion, it will probably not be denied that in grandeur of conception, fair symmetry of form, as well as bold grappling with the fundamental enigmas with which it deals, the Book of Job towers far above the highest levels to be found either in *Proverbs* or *Ecclesiastes*. Better to sweep aside all conventional categories and say at once that the Book of Job is a unique spiritual epic, a supreme drama of the human soul.

STRUCTURE AND STORY

In the Hebrew Bible (and A.J. which follows its order of the various Books comprising the Sacred Library we call the Bible), Job occupies the third place in the third division. This third section is known in Hebrew as *Kethubim*; in Greek it bears the name *Hagiographa*, meaning 'written by inspiration,' or more simply, 'to write holy.' The English name is 'The Writings.'

Job comprises forty-two chapters. It stands after *Proverbs* and before the *Song of Songs*, the first of the Five Megilloth.

The structure of the Book has been variously analysed. Scientific students who may have stumbled on this introduction, and seek to be informed on the latest clinical dissections and hypotheses concerning the editorial redaction and

transmission of Job, are directed to Professor Robert H. Pfeiffer's painstaking chapter on *Job* in his *Introduction to the Old Testament*, pp. 660-707.
The learned Harvard Professor has diligently ransacked the immense literature on *Job* and set it forth in methodical digest. Discussing the integrity of
the literary composition of *Job* and the question as to whether the folk-
tale of the pious Job, forming the prose Prologue and Epilogue, was once a
separate ancient book that the poet borrowed as a frame in which to set his
own work, or his own work, or part his own and part later editorial redaction,
Pfeiffer remarks, 'The critics have suggested every possibility.' This observation holds not only at this point but throughout the difficult yet gripping
pages of *Job*.

For our own purposes, we must try to cleave to the principle laid down
by the General Editor of these Soncino Bible Commentaries, 'that the exposition is designed primarily for the ordinary reader of the Bible rather than
for the student.' We therefore content ourselves with having directed the
more painstaking reader on his way to richer pastures in which to browse.
Here we deal with the broad design of the Book, blithely ignoring the varied
patterns of reconstruction that the long caravan of *Job* scholars have each in
turn elaborated.

I. THE PROSE PROLOGUE (I-II)

The Book opens with a vigorous prose narration, a Prologue in scenes that
alternate between earth and heaven, that introduce us to all the *dramatis
personæ* in the drama save one, the youthful, loquacious Elihu who does
not appear until chapter xxxii, when he holds forth at length until chapter
xxxvii, and then abruptly drops from view.

The Prologue may be outlined thus:

The Opening Scene—in the land of Uz. We discover Job, a man of exemplary
virtue and piety, blessed by God with lavish material possessions and with
an ideal family, seven sons and three daughters.

The Second Scene—in Heaven. The celestial retinue, the *sons of God* in-
cluding the Satan, who has not yet become a Prince of Darkness usurping
the authority of the Lord, but here plays the rôle of an investigator, present
themselves before Him. God proudly shows off His servant Job. The
Satan seizes the opportunity to cast the suspicion of doubt upon Job's disinterested virtue. God, confident of the outcome of this test of faith, accepts
the Satan's challenge, imposing, however, the restriction that the Satan is
not to lay hand upon Job's person.

The Third Scene—the land of Uz. Now falls, like sudden hammer-blows
of crushing calamity, ruin, which sweeps away Job's wealth and his children.
Job bows submissive to disaster, his spiritual integrity finding expression in
words that enshrine the faith of Israel through the ages:

> ' The Lord gave, and the Lord hath taken away;
> Blessed be the name of the Lord.'

The Fourth Scene—in Heaven. Again the celestial court is convened.

Again the Lord confronts the Satan with the piety of Job, this time with a taunt that he had successfully met the Satan's test, although the Lord had been moved to destroy Job without cause. But the Satan, resourceful, again intrudes his doubt whether Job will persevere in his devotion to God. This time the Satan foretells that Job will blaspheme the Lord when his very bone and flesh are touched. Confident of His servant Job, God hands him over to the Satan, interposing only one last barrier—'spare his life.'

The Fifth Scene—in the land of Uz. Now the Satan smites Job with loathsome sore boils, a plague that the victim might construe in a peculiar sense as the stroke of God. When his wife, losing faith, urges him euphemistically to 'bless' God and die, Job, unlike the reader, ignorant of what has transpired in Heaven and unaware of the true cause of his calamities, rebukes her, saying: 'What? Shall we receive good at the hand of God, and shall we not receive evil?'

Now enter Job's three friends, Eliphaz, Bildad, and Zophar, who come to bemoan him and to comfort him. Dismayed at his misery and the catastrophe that has befallen him, they rend their mantles, throw dust upon their heads towards heaven, and sit beside him in silence for seven days and nights.

Thus ends the Prologue.

II. THE POETIC DIALOGUES BETWEEN JOB AND HIS THREE FRIENDS (III-XXXI)

The Prologue provides the background for the poetic colloquies which now ensue between the suffering Job and his three friends. Job breaks his silence with a passionate imprecation upon the day of his birth, picturing wistfully the dead where 'the wicked cease from troubling' and 'the weary are at rest.' Eliphaz, the eldest of the friends, replies to Job's outburst. So the body of the poem takes symmetrical shape. The drama is no longer external but moves within the thoughts and emotions of the speakers. There may be discerned three cycles of discourses. In each round of debate, Job speaks. Eliphaz, Bildad, and Zophar in turn reply, save in the last cycle of poems where Zophar does not again appear.

The chapter divisions of the cycles may thus be indicated:

1. First Cycle: chapters iv-xiv.
2. Second Cycle: chapters xv-xxi.
3. Third Cycle: chapters xxii-xxvi.

The dramatic conflict then reaches the point of exhaustion. Job, sure of his innocence, searching his heart, can find no adequate reason for a good and just God thus to destroy him. In the course of his quest for an answer and explanation of his wretchedness, he has moved from bewilderment to rebellion, even to blind accusations of the indiscriminate visitations of God, as when he explodes in this outburst:

'I am innocent—I regard not myself,
I despise my life.
It is all one—therefore I say:
He destroyeth the innocent and the wicked . . .

> The earth is given into the hand of the wicked;
> He covereth the faces of the judges thereof;
> If it be not He, who then is it?' (ix. 21-24).

But if, in his agony, Job has bitterly questioned the just government of God, in the desolate questing of his soul he has also caught momentary glimpses of the God of his righteousness. From his friends, with their limited theology that construed affliction as the certain proof of sin—a view that Job himself must once have shared—he turns increasingly to the God Who supports him in his struggle. The friends more openly deride Job as a sinner whose hypocrisies and pretences of goodness are now exposed. But Job, forsaken of family and friends, turns his streaming eyes towards God:

> 'Though He slay me, yet will I trust in Him . . .
> This also shall be my salvation,
> That a hypocrite cannot come before Him' (xiii. 15-16).

> 'Mine inward thoughts are my intercessors,
> Mine eye poureth out tears unto God' (xvi. 20).

> 'But as for me, I know that my Redeemer liveth,
> And that He will witness at the last upon the dust' (xix. 25).

Rebellion has turned to faith and a calmer perspective of the limitations of man's comprehension of the vast mysteries of the universe as Job rises to the lofty insight that:

> 'Lo, these are but the outskirts of His ways;
> And how small a whisper is heard of Him!
> But the thunder of His mighty deeds who can understand?' (xxvi. 14).

Perhaps the friends feel that it is useless to prolong the discussion further. Zophar, whose turn it is to reply, if we are to complete the third cycle of the dialogues, fails to appear.

Job now soliloquizes, affirming his resolve to hold fast to his righteousness as long as breath is in him. These chapters (xxvii-xxxi), which include the superb eulogy of Divine Wisdom (xxviii) and the exalted oath of clearance (xxxi), bring the three rounds of debate to an end.

III. THE INTRUSION AND ARGUMENT OF ELIHU
(XXXII-XXXVII)

Now enters a hitherto unknown disputant, Elihu, a young man full of words and full of wrath. A short prose preface explains that Elihu finds himself compelled to intrude into the argument in order to rebuke Job for having justified himself rather than God, and the three friends for having condemned Job although they could not refute his arguments. We wait in suspense for the wisdom of Elihu, and although he delivers himself of four speeches in succession, they seem to throw little further light upon the mystery of suffering, save perhaps to place more sharply into relief the idea that affliction comes as warning and moral discipline to the afflicted. The reader is

apt to recoil from the boastful fanfare and flourish that prefaces Elihu's intrusion, who now drops into the silence from which he had emerged without Job or the friends deigning to reply.

IV. THE ANSWERS OF THE LORD OUT OF THE WHIRLWIND AND JOB'S REPLIES (XXXVIII-XLII. 6)

Throughout the three cycles of the earlier dialogues, Job had variously entreated or challenged God to appear, so that, as in a court of law, he might demand of Him the reason for having thus smitten and ruined a righteous man. Now, dramatically, the Lord appears out of the whirlwind. In splendid array, there pass before Job the wonders of the world and the creatures that find their home upon the earth. Twice the Lord speaks, and twice Job replies, in humble confession of his human ignorance and presumption in speaking of things too wonderful for him:

> 'I had heard of Thee,' says Job, 'by the hearing of the ear;
> But now mine eye seeth Thee;
> Wherefore I abhor my words, and repent,
> Seeing I am dust and ashes' (xlii. 5-6).

V. THE PROSE EPILOGUE (XLII. 7-17)

The poem is ended but God's final verdict remains to seal the Book. The friends are condemned. 'They have not spoken of Me the thing that is right,' says God, repeating the sentence, 'as My servant Job hath.' When Job generously intercedes for them in prayer, they are forgiven. The trial of Job is ended and, with poetic justice, God makes the prosperity of Job twice what it had been at the beginning.

THE MEANING OF THE BOOK

The clash between dogma and human experience is the battlefield where the protagonists of these opposing convictions fight for victory. If we remember that dogma may be only the frozen insight of one generation that cherishes its hard-won truth and will fight with fanatical devotion to maintain its authority, we can understand why the heresies arising from the flux of life will always meet with stormy resistance.

The meanings of the Book of Job emerge from the smoke of this neverending war for truth. Prophetic Judaism had achieved the faith in an Almighty God Who ruled His universe with absolute justice. Ezekiel had applied this teaching to the individual in his doctrine of individual retribution. The Sages of Israel, speaking in the Book of Proverbs, further stressed the necessary connection between prosperity and piety. The belief had become intrenched that God rewards with material blessings those who live virtuously and punishes the sinner with suffering.

Now experience could not always confirm this comfortable faith. The problem of theodicy thus arose, made more urgent since what befell the individual was regarded as the immediate act of God. Nor had the notion yet taken shape that the scene of retribution and reward could be transferred

to another world hereafter. Some such rumours, it is true, were in the air, but Job wistfully speaks of them only to reject them:

'If a man die, may he live again?
All the days of my service would I wait,
Till my relief should come—' (xiv. 14).

'Man that is born of a woman
Is of few days, and full of trouble.
He cometh forth like a flower, and withereth;
He fleeth also as a shadow, and continueth not' (xiv. 1-2).

'Where then is my hope?
And as for my hope, who shall see it?
They shall go down to the bars of the nether-world,
When we are at rest together in the dust' (xvii. 15-16).

Job, then, is convinced that the fight for meaning and the struggle to reconcile faith with reason must be fought in the only theatre of battle he knows—here on earth. He himself, like the three friends, had accepted the inherited belief of his generation. Bitter human experience now compels him to search for a more adequate ground for spiritual support.

What conclusions does Job reach? To the overarching theme, 'What is the moral government by which God orders His universe?' he is finally forced to acknowledge his ignorance. When the Almighty laid the foundations of the earth and the morning stars sang together, he was not present as spectator or partner. Encompassed by the grandeurs of sky and earth, hemmed in by the infinite mysteries of Nature, he bows his head in humble acknowledgment of his human insignificance set against the cosmic majesty. Men cannot attain the absolute wisdom of God. His confidence must be rooted in the perception that:

'The fear of the Lord, that is wisdom;
And to depart from evil is understanding' (xxviii. 28).

The other question, subordinate but more obvious, 'Is there retributive justice in the world?' finds positive answer from Job. His own tragic struggle confirmed the paradox that, in appealing from the apparent injustice of God, Job found strength and support in the righteous God Who would one day establish his innocence. Job denies the adequacy of material retribution. Suffering is no sure proof of sin. But there does exist retribution of a higher order: the righteous man is never completely cut off from the fellowship of God. It is to this invincible trust that Job gives immortal utterance when out of the long ordeal of his soul he cries:

'But as for me, I know that my Redeemer liveth,
And that He will witness at the last upon the dust' (xix. 25).

THE BOOK IN JEWISH TRADITION

The modern reader who approaches the Book of Job should remember that, as a literary work, it must have passed through many minds and hands

before its final redaction in the shape we know it in the Hebrew Bible. Even as the Book itself shows the mark of heresy wrestling with tradition, so too, in the centuries that followed its inclusion in the Sacred Library of the Bible, the ferment of opinion continued to agitate men's minds.

Echoes of disagreement are preserved in the Talmud. In Baba Bathra 14b Moses is named as the author of *Job*. But on the next page, 15a, later dates are assigned for *Job*, ranging from the time of the Judges, the Babylonian Exile, to the generation of Ahasuerus.

Not only is the date of *Job* disputed by the Rabbis. They differ about the interpretation of the Book and the character of its hero. The famous observation of a certain Rabbi sitting before R. Samuel ben Nachmani, 'Job never was and never existed, but is only a typical figure,' was met with a sharp rejoinder. R. Samuel ben Nachmani did not approve of calling *Job* a parable.

Equally moot was the question of the character of Job. Did he serve God from love or from fear? R. Joshua ben Hyrcanus maintained that Job served God purely out of love, proving it by Job xiii. 15 and xxvii. 5, 'Though He slay me, yet will I trust in Him. . . . Till I die I will not put away mine integrity from me,' to the great indignation of R. Joshua (ben Chananiah), who broke out: 'Who will clear away the dust from thine eyes, Rabban Jochanan ben Zakkai, who didst teach all thy days that Job served God only out of fear (Job i. 1), and here is Joshua (ben Hyrcanus), the pupil of thy pupil, teaching that he acted out of love!' (M. Sotah v. 5; cf. Tos. Sotah vi. 1, cited by Moore, *Judaism*, II. p. 99). R. Meir shows that the two expressions are not exclusive: 'God-fearing' is said of Abraham (Gen. xxii. 12) as well as of Job (Job. i. 1). As God-fearing in Abraham's case sprang from love, so also did Job's.

There is some slight indication that a more positive attitude than Rabban Jochanan ben Zakkai's to the Book of Job prevailed in the priestly circle at the end of the Second Commonwealth. As a matter of fact, Job is quoted in the Mishnah in the first place among the Books read to the High Priest on the night of Atonement to prevent him from falling asleep (Yoma i. 6). Its selection was ascribed by the Jewish commentators to the merit of its content in attracting the attention of the mind. It is interesting to note that the first and only fleeting mention of Job's name in Scripture comes from Ezekiel, himself a priest.

Even in the later periods of Jewish life there is a difference in approach to the Book of Job. The Sephardic Liturgy introduced the reading of *Job* for Tisha b'Ab (9th of Ab), the anniversary of the destruction of the Temple. No such provision is made in the Ashkenazic Rite (cf. Sephardic Machzor, vol. Taanioth).

Our generation is not likely to take sides in such arguments. We treasure this monument of literary and religious splendour as a precious legacy from the past, and will return again and again to its pages to be challenged and inspired by the beauty of its metaphor and the power of its thought.

VICTOR E. REICHERT

JOB

JOB

1. THERE was a man in the land of Uz, whose name was Job; and that man was whole-hearted and upright, and one that feared God, and shunned evil. 2. And there were born unto him seven sons and three daughters. 3. His possessions also were seven thousand sheep, and three thousand camels, and five hundred yoke of oxen, and five hundred she-asses, and a very great household; so that this man was the greatest of all the children of the east. 4. And his sons used to go and

1 אִישׁ הָיָה בְאֶרֶץ־עוּץ אִיּוֹב שְׁמוֹ
וְהָיָה ׀ הָאִישׁ הַהוּא תָּם וְיָשָׁר וִירֵא
2 אֱלֹהִים וְסָר מֵרָע: וַיִּוָּלְדוּ לוֹ שִׁבְעָה
3 בָנִים וְשָׁלוֹשׁ בָּנוֹת: וַיְהִי מִקְנֵהוּ
שִׁבְעַת אַלְפֵי־צֹאן וּשְׁלֹשֶׁת אַלְפֵי
גְמַלִּים וַחֲמֵשׁ מֵאוֹת צֶמֶד־בָּקָר
וַחֲמֵשׁ מֵאוֹת אֲתוֹנוֹת וַעֲבֻדָּה רַבָּה
מְאֹד וַיְהִי הָאִישׁ הַהוּא גָּדוֹל מִכָּל־
4 בְּנֵי־קֶדֶם: וְהָלְכוּ בָנָיו וְעָשׂוּ

PART I—THE PROLOGUE I—II.

CHAPTER I

1-5 INTRODUCTION TO JOB

WE are introduced to the hero of this spiritual drama, the man of exemplary piety and extraordinary good fortune. We witness the merry-making of his children, and his scrupulous precautions to atone for any impiety on their part.

1. there was a man. The choice of the word *man* is significant. The author at the very outset of his work suggests the universal dimension of his theme. The problems of why the righteous often suffer and of how God is related to His universe transcend the boundaries of space and time.

in the land of Uz. It is useless to speculate too much about the location of *the land of Uz.* Gen. xxii. 21 refers to Uz, the son of Nahor. The name appears to denote an individual, but it may be a tribe. The abode of Uz seems to have been east of the Holy Land and north of Edom (cf. Lam. iv. 21).

whose name was Job. There is mention in Ezek. xiv. 20 of Job. The author may well have used this ancient tradition of a righteous man for his own purposes. Beyond that, the attempts to establish

the historicity of the Book are misguided and futile. The scene in heaven, the figure of the Satan, and the Lord speaking out of the whirlwind should be sufficient evidence against it. Already the Talmud (B.B. 15a) appreciated the overarching purpose of the Book by remarking: 'Job never was and never existed, but is only a typical figure' (to teach men the virtue of resignation). Maimonides likewise held that Job is 'a parable meant to exhibit the views of mankind in regard to providence.'

and that man was whole-hearted. The word *tam* is rendered 'perfect' by A.V. and R.V. Such a designation the Jewish mind would only accord to God. What the word connotes is 'without moral blemish, blameless, innocent.' Job is presented to us as a man of complete human integrity.

2. seven sons and three daughters. The round numbers *seven, three, five* for Job's children and his flocks express perfection and complete sufficiency.

3. the children of the east. Apparently a familiar expression to describe the peoples dwelling east of Canaan (cf. Judg. vi. 3, 33; 1 Kings v. 10; Isa. xi. 14; Ezek. xxv. 4, 10).

hold a feast in the house of each one upon his day; and they would send and invite their three sisters to eat and to drink with them. 5. And it was so, when the days of their feasting were gone about, that Job sent and sanctified them, and rose up early in the morning, and offered burntofferings according to the number of them all; for Job said: ' It may be that my sons have sinned, and blasphemed God in their hearts.' Thus did Job continually.

6. Now it fell upon a day, that the sons of God came to present themselves before the LORD, and ªSatan came also among them. 7. And the LORD said unto Satan: ' Whence comest thou ? ' Then Satan answered the LORD, and said: ' From going to and fro in the earth, and

ªThat is, the Adversary.

מִשְׁתֶּה בֵּית אִישׁ יוֹמוֹ וְשָׁלְחוּ וְקָרְאוּ
לִשְׁלֹשֶׁת אַחְיֹתֵיהֶם לֶאֱכֹל וְלִשְׁתּוֹת
עִמָּהֶם׃ וַיְהִי כִּי הִקִּיפוּ יְמֵי הַמִּשְׁתֶּה
וַיִּשְׁלַח אִיּוֹב וַיְקַדְּשֵׁם וְהִשְׁכִּים בַּבֹּקֶר
וְהֶעֱלָה עֹלוֹת מִסְפַּר כֻּלָּם כִּי אָמַר
אִיּוֹב אוּלַי חָטְאוּ בָנַי וּבֵרֲכוּ אֱלֹהִים
בִּלְבָבָם כָּכָה יַעֲשֶׂה אִיּוֹב כָּל־
הַיָּמִים׃ וַיְהִי הַיּוֹם וַיָּבֹאוּ בְּנֵי
הָאֱלֹהִים לְהִתְיַצֵּב עַל־יְהוָה וַיָּבוֹא
גַם־הַשָּׂטָן בְּתוֹכָם׃ וַיֹּאמֶר יְהוָה
אֶל־הַשָּׂטָן מֵאַיִן תָּבֹא וַיַּעַן הַשָּׂטָן
אֶת־יְהוָה וַיֹּאמַר מִשּׁוּט בָּאָרֶץ

4. *upon his day.* The picture is one of an endless round of festivity: a feast for each day in the week. Some commentators, however, have conjectured that *his day* may refer to 'birthday.' 'We are not reading prosaic history. The life depicted is like that of princes in fairy tales, a never-ending round of mirth, disclosing at once the great prosperity of Job and the happiness of his family' (Peake).

5. *Job sent and sanctified them.* Observe the emphasis upon Job's scrupulous piety and the inwardness of his religion: his concern lest his children might have sinned even in their thoughts.

blasphemed God. The Hebrew root usually means 'to bless.' Ibn Ezra points out that this is an euphemism for its opposite 'to curse, blaspheme.' Rashi likewise suggests that out of motives of reverence the verb 'bless' was substituted for 'curse.'

6-12 THE HEAVENLY SCENE
God proudly shows off His servant Job

to the Satan who openly questions Job's disinterested piety. Note that the Satan is one of *the sons of God*. His rôle is that of a celestial Intelligence Officer who must report to God in the Heavenly Council. God permits the Satan to put Job to the test, but he is forbidden to touch his person.

6. *now it fell upon a day.* Both Ibn Ezra and Rashi suggest that this was Rosh Hashanah, the Jewish religious New Year, when all the children of the world pass before the Divine Presence like rebels after surrender brought before a tribunal (cf. R.H. 18a). The rôle of the Satan, says Rashi, was to report on the merit and guilt of all God's creatures.

the sons of God. viz. the angels (cf. xxxviii. 7; Gen. vi. 2). For another illustration of the scene, cf. 1 Kings xxii. 19ff.

Satan. The Satan appears in the Hebrew Bible as 'the Adversary,' 'the Opposer.' His part is to oppose men in their pretensions to a right standing with God, and to test their sincerity (Job i-ii),

from walking up and down in it.'
8. And the LORD said unto Satan:
' Hast thou considered My servant
Job, that there is none like him in
the earth, a whole-hearted and an
upright man, one that feareth God,
and shunneth evil?' 9. Then Satan
answered the LORD, and said: 'Doth
Job fear God for nought? 10. Hast
not Thou made a hedge about him,
and about his house, and about all
that he hath, on every side? Thou
hast blessed the work of his hands,
and his possessions are increased in
the land. 11. But put forth Thy
hand now, and touch all that he
hath, surely he will blaspheme Thee
to Thy face.' 12. And the LORD
said unto Satan: 'Behold, all that
he hath is in thy power; only upon
himself put not forth thy hand.' So
Satan went forth from the presence
of the LORD.

13. And it fell on a day when his
sons and his daughters were eating
and drinking wine in their eldest
brother's house, 14. that there came

8 וּמֵהִתְהַלֵּךְ בָּהּ׃ וַיֹּאמֶר יְהֹוָה אֶל־
הַשָּׂטָן הֲשַׂמְתָּ לִבְּךָ עַל־עַבְדִּי אִיּוֹב
כִּי אֵין כָּמֹהוּ בָּאָרֶץ אִישׁ תָּם וְיָשָׁר
9 יְרֵא אֱלֹהִים וְסָר מֵרָע׃ וַיַּעַן הַשָּׂטָן
אֶת־יְהֹוָה וַיֹּאמַר הַחִנָּם יָרֵא אִיּוֹב
10 אֱלֹהִים׃ הֲלֹא־אַתְּ שַׂכְתָּ בַעֲדוֹ
וּבְעַד־בֵּיתוֹ וּבְעַד כָּל־אֲשֶׁר־לוֹ
מִסָּבִיב מַעֲשֵׂה יָדָיו בֵּרַכְתָּ וּמִקְנֵהוּ
11 פָּרַץ בָּאָרֶץ׃ וְאוּלָם שְׁלַח־נָא יָדְךָ
וְגַע בְּכָל־אֲשֶׁר־לוֹ אִם־לֹא עַל־
12 פָּנֶיךָ יְבָרְכֶךָּ׃ וַיֹּאמֶר יְהֹוָה אֶל־
הַשָּׂטָן הִנֵּה כָל־אֲשֶׁר־לוֹ בְּיָדֶךָ רַק
אֵלָיו אַל־תִּשְׁלַח יָדֶךָ וַיֵּצֵא הַשָּׂטָן
13 מֵעִם פְּנֵי יְהֹוָה׃ וַיְהִי הַיּוֹם וּבָנָיו
וּבְנֹתָיו אֹכְלִים וְשֹׁתִים יַיִן בְּבֵית
14 אֲחִיהֶם הַבְּכוֹר׃ וּמַלְאָךְ בָּא אֶל־

v. 10. אתה ק׳

to remind God, in no friendly spirit, of
their sins (Zech. iii. 1f.), and to prompt
them to do acts which will bring them
into disfavour with God (1 Chron. xxi. 1)
where *Satan* is substituted by the later
writer for *the Lord* of the original
passage (2 Sam. xxiv. 1). Not until
1 Chron. xxi. 1 does the Satan appear as
a true proper name. Elsewhere it
always has the article, *ha-Satan*, and
was felt therefore distinctly to mean 'the
Opposer' (Driver).

8. *hast thou considered My servant Job?*
Note that it is God, not the Satan, Who
calls attention to the exemplary life of
Job. Like a proud parent, God shows
off Job to the Satan, as though to challenge his cynical estimate of the best in
human nature.

9. *doth Job fear God for nought?* The

Satan, unable to deny Job's piety, casts
the shadow of doubt upon his motives.

10. *hast not Thou made a hedge about him?*
The image is that of a thorn-hedge about
a vineyard; he is under God's protection
so that no harm may touch him (Ibn
Ezra).

11. *surely he will blaspheme Thee.* The
force of this phrase is one of strong
assertion, as if the Satan had said, 'I
wager he will blaspheme Thee.' Note
again the euphemism of 'bless' for 'curse'
in the Hebrew.

13-22 THE EARTHLY SCENE

The first test of Job's disinterested service of God. Job is stripped of all his
worldly possessions—his cattle, servants
and children. While the latter were
feasting in the eldest brother's house,

3

a messenger unto Job, and said: 'The oxen were plowing, and the asses feeding beside them; 15. and the Sabeans made a raid, and took them away; yea, they have slain the servants with the edge of the sword; and I only am escaped alone to tell thee.' 16. While he was yet speaking, there came also another, and said: 'A fire of God is fallen from heaven, and hath burned up the sheep, and the servants, and consumed them; and I only am escaped alone to tell thee.' 17. While he was yet speaking, there came also another, and said: 'The Chaldeans set themselves in three bands, and fell upon the camels, and have taken them away, yea, and slain the servants with the edge of the sword; and I only am escaped alone to tell thee.' 18. While he was yet speaking, there came also another, and said: 'Thy sons and thy daughters were eating and drinking wine in their eldest brother's house; 19. and, behold, there came a great wind from across the wilderness, and smote the four corners of the house, and it fell upon the young people, and they are dead; and I only am escaped alone to tell thee.'

אִיּוֹב וַיֹּאמַר הַבָּקָר הָיוּ חֹרְשׁוֹת
וְהָאֲתֹנוֹת רֹעוֹת עַל־יְדֵיהֶם: וַתִּפֹּל
שְׁבָא וַתִּקָּחֵם וְאֶת־הַנְּעָרִים הִכּוּ
לְפִי־חָרֶב וָאִמָּלְטָה רַק־אֲנִי
לְבַדִּי לְהַגִּיד לָךְ: עוֹד | זֶה מְדַבֵּר
וְזֶה בָּא וַיֹּאמַר אֵשׁ אֱלֹהִים נָפְלָה
מִן־הַשָּׁמַיִם וַתִּבְעַר בַּצֹּאן וּבַנְּעָרִים
וַתֹּאכְלֵם וָאִמָּלְטָה רַק־אֲנִי לְבַדִּי
לְהַגִּיד לָךְ: עוֹד | זֶה מְדַבֵּר וְזֶה בָּא
וַיֹּאמַר כַּשְׂדִּים שָׂמוּ | שְׁלֹשָׁה רָאשִׁים
וַיִּפְשְׁטוּ עַל־הַגְּמַלִּים וַיִּקָּחוּם וְאֶת־
הַנְּעָרִים הִכּוּ לְפִי־חָרֶב וָאִמָּלְטָה
רַק־אֲנִי לְבַדִּי לְהַגִּיד לָךְ: עַד זֶה
מְדַבֵּר וְזֶה בָּא וַיֹּאמַר בָּנֶיךָ וּבְנוֹתֶיךָ
אֹכְלִים וְשֹׁתִים יַיִן בְּבֵית אֲחִיהֶם
הַבְּכוֹר: וְהִנֵּה רוּחַ גְּדוֹלָה בָּאָה |
מֵעֵבֶר הַמִּדְבָּר וַיִּגַּע בְּאַרְבַּע פִּנּוֹת
הַבַּיִת וַיִּפֹּל עַל־הַנְּעָרִים וַיָּמוּתוּ
וָאִמָּלְטָה רַק־אֲנִי לְבַדִּי לְהַגִּיד לָךְ:

---

four successive messengers announce to Job the loss of his wealth and children. Utterly desolate, he still blesses God, Who has given and taken away. He emerges unscathed spiritually from the first trial.

15. *the Sabeans.* The Sabeans (cf. Gen. x. 7, 28) were a powerful and wealthy people of S. Arabia, with a settlement in the neighbourhood of Edom. Their caravans, laden with gold, frankincense, and other treasures, are frequently mentioned in the Bible (cf. vi. 19; Jer. vi. 20; Ezek. xxvii. 22; Ps. lxxii. 10, etc.). This is the only mention of them in the Bible as a tribe of bandits.

16. *a fire of God.* i.e. lightning (cf. 2 Kings i. 12).

17. *the Chaldeans set themselves in three bands.* Here the picture of *the Chaldeans* is of marauding bands and not the great conquering people who founded the Babylonian Empire. (Perhaps it is a general term for 'plunderers' as *Canaan-ite* is for 'merchant.') The attack was made on three sides to prevent the camels from escaping (Metsudath David; cf. Judg. vii. 16, ix. 43; 1 Sam. xi. 11).

19. *the young people.* The term implies the daughters (it is literally 'the young men'), and it was not necessary expressly to mention them (Rashi). Note the pro-

20. Then Job arose, and rent his mantle, and shaved his head, and fell down upon the ground, and worshipped; 21. and he said:

Naked came I out of my mother's womb,
And naked shall I return thither;
The LORD gave, and the LORD hath taken away;
Blessed be the name of the LORD.

22. For all this Job sinned not, nor ascribed aught unseemly to God.

20 וַיָּ֣קָם אִיּ֗וֹב וַיִּקְרַ֤ע אֶת־מְעִלוֹ֙ וַיָּ֣גׇז אֶת־רֹאשׁ֑וֹ וַיִּפֹּ֥ל אַ֖רְצָה וַיִּשְׁתָּֽחוּ׃

21 וַיֹּאמֶר֩ עָרֹ֨ם יָצָ֜תִי מִבֶּ֣טֶן אִמִּ֗י וְעָרֹם֙ אָשׁ֣וּב שָׁ֔מָּה יְהֹוָ֣ה נָתַ֔ן וַיהֹוָ֖ה לָקָ֑ח

22 יְהִ֛י שֵׁ֥ם יְהֹוָ֖ה מְבֹרָֽךְ׃ בְּכׇל־זֹ֛את לֹא־חָטָ֥א אִיּ֖וֹב וְלֹא־נָתַ֥ן תִּפְלָ֖ה לֵאלֹהִֽים׃

2   CHAPTER II   ב

1. Again it fell upon a day, that the sons of God came to present themselves before the LORD, and Satan came also among them to present himself before the LORD. 2. And the LORD said unto Satan: 'From whence comest thou'; And Satan answered the LORD, and said: 'From going to and fro in the earth, and from walking up and down in it.' 3. And the LORD said unto Satan: 'Hast thou considered My servant Job, that

1 וַיְהִ֣י הַיּ֔וֹם וַיָּבֹ֙אוּ֙ בְּנֵ֣י הָֽאֱלֹהִ֔ים לְהִתְיַצֵּ֖ב עַל־יְהֹוָ֑ה וַיָּב֧וֹא גַם־הַשָּׂטָ֛ן

2 בְּתֹכָ֖ם לְהִתְיַצֵּ֥ב עַל־יְהֹוָֽה׃ וַיֹּ֤אמֶר יְהֹוָה֙ אֶל־הַשָּׂטָ֔ן אֵ֥י מִזֶּ֖ה תָּבֹ֑א וַיַּ֨עַן הַשָּׂטָ֤ן אֶת־יְהֹוָה֙ וַיֹּאמַ֔ר מִשֻּׁ֣ט

3 בָּאָ֔רֶץ וּמֵֽהִתְהַלֵּ֖ךְ בָּֽהּ׃ וַיֹּ֤אמֶר יְהֹוָה֙ אֶל־הַשָּׂטָ֔ן הֲשַׂ֥מְתָּ לִבְּךָ֖ עַל־עַבְדִּ֣י

v. 21. חסר א׳

gressive magnitude of the catastrophes, and the rapid hammer-blow succession in which the only messenger who escaped brings the tidings of each increasing disaster. What about Job's wife? She 'by a touch of quiet humour is spared; she seems to be recognized by Satan as an unconscious ally' (Cheyne).

20. *then Job arose.* We have in the verse a vivid description of ancient mourning practices.

and rent his mantle. The *meïl* was the exterior garment, worn over the inner tunic. It seems to have been the attire of men of rank (cf. 1 Sam. xviii. 4; xxiv. 4). Tearing off the upper garment, i.e. stripping oneself to the waist, is still a mourning custom among the Jews of Persia. Job then prostrated himself on the ground in the act of agonizing prayer.

21. *the LORD gave ... blessed be the name of the LORD.* This has been adopted as the accepted expression of Jewish faith, and is recited at a funeral service.

22. *nor ascribed aught unseemly.* In the midst of Job's grief, there was not the slightest element of murmuring or rebellion against God. His submission to the Divine will was unquestioning.

CHAPTER II

JOB is tested a second time in the challenge to God made by the Satan. He is smitten with a dreadful disease. His wife counsels him to curse God and die. Job, steadfast in his integrity, rebukes her. Once again the Satan's cynical prediction proves false.

1. *again it fell upon a day.* Note the heightened dramatic effect produced by the repetition of the words as in i. 6-8.

there is none like him in the earth, a whole-hearted and an upright man, one that feareth God, and shunneth evil? and he still holdeth fast his integrity, although thou didst move Me against him, to destroy him without cause.' 4. And Satan answered the LORD, and said: 'Skin for skin, yea, all that a man hath will he give for his life. 5. But put forth Thy hand now, and touch his bone and his flesh, surely he will blaspheme Thee to Thy face.' 6. And the LORD said unto Satan: 'Behold he is in thy hand; only spare his life.'

7. So Satan went forth from the presence of the LORD, and smote Job with sore boils from the sole of his foot even unto his crown. 8. And he took him a potsherd to scrape himself therewith; and he sat among the ashes. 9. Then said his wife unto

אִיּוֹב כִּי אֵין כָּמֹהוּ בָּאָרֶץ אִישׁ תָּם
וְיָשָׁר יְרֵא אֱלֹהִים וְסָר מֵרָע וְעֹדֶנּוּ
מַחֲזִיק בְּתֻמָּתוֹ וַתְּסִיתֵנִי בוֹ לְבַלְּעוֹ
חִנָּם: וַיַּעַן הַשָּׂטָן אֶת־יְהֹוָה וַיֹּאמַר
עוֹר בְּעַד־עוֹר וְכֹל אֲשֶׁר לָאִישׁ יִתֵּן
בְּעַד נַפְשׁוֹ: אוּלָם שְׁלַח־נָא יָדְךָ
וְגַע אֶל־עַצְמוֹ וְאֶל־בְּשָׂרוֹ אִם־
לֹא אֶל־פָּנֶיךָ יְבָרֲכֶךָּ: וַיֹּאמֶר יְהֹוָה
אֶל־הַשָּׂטָן הִנּוֹ בְיָדֶךָ אַךְ אֶת־נַפְשׁוֹ
שְׁמֹר: וַיֵּצֵא הַשָּׂטָן מֵאֵת פְּנֵי יְהֹוָה
וַיַּךְ אֶת־אִיּוֹב בִּשְׁחִין רָע מִכַּף רַגְלוֹ
עַד קָדְקֳדוֹ: וַיִּקַּח־לוֹ חֶרֶשׂ
לְהִתְגָּרֵד בּוֹ וְהוּא יֹשֵׁב בְּתוֹךְ־
הָאֵפֶר: וַתֹּאמֶר לוֹ אִשְׁתּוֹ עֹדְךָ

v. 7. וְעֹד ק׳

3. *although thou didst move Me against him.* Scripture here speaks in the language of man (Ibn Ezra).

to destroy him. The verb *bala*, lit. 'to swallow up,' is often used metaphorically for 'to ruin' (cf. viii. 18, x. 8 where the word is translated, following A.V. and R.V., *destroy*).

4. *skin for skin.* A difficult proverbial expression. It may mean, as Rashi and Ibn Ezra suggest, that a man will lose an arm to save his head against a threatening sword, or a hand to save an eye. How much more will one give all his possessions to save his life! Perhaps it originated as a trade expression. Everything has its set price; a skin can be traded only for another skin or for its monetary value. Life, on the other hand, the Satan implies is beyond price. A man will give up all else if he can keep his life. Jastrow ingeniously translates: 'There is a skin beneath the skin,' i.e. only the surface has been scratched. Scratch deeper and you will see what God will do. So far

Job has not been afflicted in person. The implication of Satan is clear: Job's resignation (i. 21) is not disinterested. It is still not proved that he serves God *for nought* (i. 9) (Driver).

5. *surely he will blaspheme Thee to Thy face.* The challenge of i. 11 is repeated.

6. *only spare his life.* Do not go beyond this. The Rabbis remarked: 'The pain of the Satan was worse than Job's. It was as if one said to his fellow, "Break this jug but do not spill its wine!"'

7. *and smote Job with sore boils.* Most modern commentators hold that Job was smitten with elephantiasis, black leprosy, so called 'because the swollen limbs and the black and corrugated skin of those afflicted by it resembled those of the elephant' (Davidson). Other symptoms are alluded to in vii. 4f., 14, xix. 17, 20, xxx. 17, 30 (Driver).

8. *and he sat among the ashes.* In the manner of mourners. He put on ashes

him: 'Dost thou still hold fast thine
integrity? blaspheme God, and die.'
10. But he said unto her: 'Thou
speakest as one of the impious
women speaketh. What? shall we
receive good at the hand of God, and
shall we not receive evil?' For all
this did not Job sin with his lips.

11. Now when Job's three friends
heard of all this evil that was come
upon him, they came every one from
his own place, Eliphaz the Temanite,
and Bildad the Shuhite, and Zophar
the Naamathite; and they made an
appointment together to come to
bemoan him and to comfort him.

מַחֲזִיק בְּתֻמָּתֶ֑ךָ בָּרֵ֥ךְ אֱלֹהִ֖ים וָמֻֽת׃

10 וַיֹּ֣אמֶר אֵלֶ֗יהָ כְּדַבֵּ֞ר אַחַ֤ת הַנְּבָלוֹת֙
תְּדַבֵּ֔רִי גַּ֣ם אֶת־הַטּ֗וֹב נְקַבֵּל֙ מֵאֵ֣ת
הָאֱלֹהִ֔ים וְאֶת־הָרָ֖ע לֹ֣א נְקַבֵּ֑ל
בְּכָל־זֹ֛את לֹא־חָטָ֥א אִיּ֖וֹב בִּשְׂפָתָֽיו׃

11 וַֽיִּשְׁמְע֞וּ שְׁלֹ֣שֶׁת ׀ רֵעֵ֣י אִיּ֗וֹב אֵ֣ת כָּל־־
הָרָעָ֤ה הַזֹּאת֙ הַבָּ֣אָה עָלָ֔יו וַיָּבֹ֙אוּ֙
אִ֣ישׁ מִמְּקֹמ֔וֹ אֱלִיפַ֤ז הַתֵּֽימָנִי֙ וּבִלְדַּ֣ד
הַשּׁוּחִ֔י וְצֹפַ֖ר הַנַּֽעֲמָתִ֑י וַיִּוָּעֲד֣וּ יַחְדָּ֗ו

and sat among the ashes (Ibn Ezra).
Some modern commentators say that
Job, afflicted with leprosy, had to sit
outside the city on the ash-heap of burned
animal dung (the *mazbala*). They interpret this as an indirect way of inform-
ing the reader that Job was stricken with
the terrible disease of leprosy (Buttenweiser).

9. *then said his wife unto him.* Scripture
does not name his wife. The Targum
supplies the omission and gives her the
name Dinah.

dost thou still hold fast thine integrity?
The meaning is: Are you still steadfast
in your piety? Job's wife implies that
death would be better than life with such
intolerable suffering. By cursing God,
the end will come at once, since the
blasphemer is smitten with death (Metsudath David). The word for *blaspheme*
is again 'bless.'

10. *one of the impious women.* Nabal
denotes not one weak intellectually, but
one deficient morally and spiritually who
has no perception of moral and religious
claims (cf. Isa. xxxii. 6 where *nabal* is
translated *vile person*, the description of
one irreligious and churlish) (Driver).

for all this did not Job sin with his lips.
With his lips, comments Rashi, but in his
heart he did sin. More probably the

verse indicates that he uttered no complaint (cf. *that I sin not with my tongue*,
Ps. xxxix. 2, for a similar use of the
phrase). Ibn Ezra detects in the phrase
an indication that he would yet sin with
his lips and bring forth from his mouth
words of reproach in his great affliction.

11-13 THREE FRIENDS COME TO COMFORT JOB

11. *Eliphaz the Temanite.* Eliphaz is
mentioned in Gen. xxxvi. 4, 10 as the
firstborn of Edom (Esau). Teman is the
name of an Edomite clan (Gen. xxxvi. 11)
possibly in N. Arabia, the district inhabited by the Temanites (Jer. xlix. 7;
Amos i. 12). Ibn Ezra remarks that the
Rabbis maintained that Moses wrote the
Book of Job (B.B. 15a), 'and it seems likely
to me that it is a translation. Therefore,
it is difficult to interpret, as is every
translation.'

Bildad the Shuhite. The home of Bildad
and Zophar must also be sought in the
region of N. Arabia. Shuhite, connected
with Shuah (cf. Gen. xxv. 2; 1 Chron.
i. 32), a brother tribe to Midian, also
related to the Hebrews, settled apparently
somewhere to the east of Canaan (Driver).

Zophar the Naamathite. We do not
know whether this refers to a place or a
family (Ibn Ezra). Zophar's nationality
is not known, since no tribe called

12. And when they lifted up their eyes afar off, and knew him not, they lifted up their voice, and wept; and they rent every one his mantle, and threw dust upon their heads toward heaven. 13. So they sat down with him upon the ground seven days and seven nights, and none spoke a word unto him; for they saw that his grief was very great.

לְבוֹא לָנוּד־לוֹ וּלְנַחֲמוֹ: וַיִּשְׂאוּ אֶת־
עֵינֵיהֶם מֵרָחוֹק וְלֹא הִכִּירֻהוּ וַיִּשְׂאוּ
קוֹלָם וַיִּבְכּוּ וַיִּקְרְעוּ אִישׁ מְעִלוֹ
וַיִּזְרְקוּ עָפָר עַל־רָאשֵׁיהֶם
הַשָּׁמָיְמָה: וַיֵּשְׁבוּ אִתּוֹ לָאָרֶץ שִׁבְעַת
יָמִים וְשִׁבְעַת לֵילוֹת וְאֵין־דֹּבֵר אֵלָיו
דָּבָר כִּי רָאוּ כִּי־גָדַל הַכְּאֵב מְאֹד:

3   CHAPTER III   ג

1. After this opened Job his mouth, and cursed his day. 2. And Job spoke and said:

אַחֲרֵי־כֵן פָּתַח אִיּוֹב אֶת־פִּיהוּ
יְקַלֵּל אֶת־יוֹמוֹ: וַיַּעַן אִיּוֹב וַיֹּאמַר:

Naamah is elsewhere mentioned. In view of the fact that the homes of Job and his other two friends are all outside the Holy Land, it is improbable that the town Naamah, in the west of Judah (Josh. xv. 41), is intended (Driver).

12. *and knew him not.* Because his face was disfigured from the intensity of his afflictions (Rashi).

they rent every one his mantle. Apparently as a sign of mourning.

and threw dust upon their heads toward heaven. In token of grief or deep trouble. Throwing dust upward above their heads was for them a sign of mourning (Rashi). A modern commentator points out that by these rites the friends meant to express not grief on Job's account, but rather solicitude on their own. They sought to ward off the danger of becoming affected themselves by the curse that had been visited upon Job (Buttenweiser).

13. *they saw that his grief was very great.* Or, 'the affliction was very great' (Buttenweiser). *Grief* was often used in Old English of bodily pain. Shakespeare

speaks of the 'grief of a wound,' and another writer of 'grief of the joints' (Driver). In xvi. 6 the same Hebrew word is translated *pain.*

PART II—THE DIALOGUE, III—XLII. 6

CHAPTER III

1-10 JOB CURSES HIS BIRTHDAY

JOB reviles the day of his birth and the night of his conception, and wishes that he had never been born. 'In the great conflict, in which faith and doubt wrestle strenuously for his soul, the rooted piety of a life-time and the happy memory of God's goodness retreat, though stubbornly, before the agonizing present. He knows himself to be in danger of losing the fear of the Almighty. All the more eagerly does he clutch at his friends to keep him from sinking, only to find that he has clutched at a straw. He is at last in the presence of his peers, holy men, deeply sympathetic, bound to him by ties of long affection. At last the iron frost of his reserve can thaw in the genial sunshine of their compassion' (Peake).

3 Let the day perish wherein I was
   born,
   And the night wherein it was said:
   'A man-child is brought forth.'

4 Let that day be darkness;
   Let not God inquire after it from
   above,
   Neither let the light shine upon it.

5 Let darkness and the shadow of
   death claim it for their own;

יָאבַד יוֹם אִוָּלֶד בּוֹ 3
וְהַלַּיְלָה אָמַר הֹרָה גָבֶר:
הַיּוֹם הַהוּא יְהִי־חֹשֶׁךְ 4
אַל־יִדְרְשֵׁהוּ אֱלוֹהַּ מִמָּעַל
וְאַל־תּוֹפַע עָלָיו נְהָרָה:
יִגְאָלֻהוּ חֹשֶׁךְ וְצַלְמָוֶת 5

v. 4. פתח באתנח

1. *after this opened Job his mouth.* Jonathan Swift used to read this chapter on his birthday (Cheyne). Kimchi, on Jer. xx. 14, calls attention to the similarity between Job's outcry and Jeremiah's. On the basis of this verse, a Talmudic Rabbi asserted: 'Comforters are not permitted to say a word until the mourner opens the conversation' (M. K. 28b).

and cursed his day. i.e. his fate to have been born on so baneful a day.

2. *and Job spoke.* The verb *anah* means literally 'to answer.' The sense is, ' and he cried out,' because all 'answering' that is mentioned in the Torah is only an expression of 'lifting up the voice.' The most instructive passage of all is Deut. xxvii. 14, *And the Levites shall speak* ('lit. answer') . . . *with a loud voice* (Rashi).

3. *let the day perish wherein I was born.* A day did not cease to be when it was succeeded by the following day. The same day would return in the following year. The days of the year had a kind of life of their own (cf. Ps. xix. 3) and paid annually recurring visits to mankind (Peake-Cheyne). The force of Job's imprecation is well expressed by Rashi: 'Would that the day had perished wherein I was destined to have been born, for then I would never have been born.'

and the night (layelah). Behind the day of birth lay the night of conception. The Rabbis remarked: 'The angel appointed over conception was named Layelah.' The old Ladino translation had the reading, *wehalayelah*, 'and the angel,

Layelah' (Isaiah Sonne, *Kiryath Sepher,* vol. xi, p. 500, quoted from *Cheshek Shelomoh*).

a man-child is brought forth. The LXX renders: 'behold a boy,' apparently reading M.T. *horah* as *harë.*

4. *let not God inquire after it from above.* One of the meanings of the root *darash* is 'to seek with care, care for' (cf. Deut. xi. 12; Ps. cxlii. 5). 'The days are summoned from their dwelling-place to play their part on earth and then return till their time comes again in the following year . . . Let God pass this day by when its turn arrives' (Peake).

neither let the light shine upon it. The Hebrew for *light* (*neharah*) occurs only here. Rashi gives as the synonym *orah,* 'light,' in the sense of *tsohar,* 'noon,' when the brilliance of the sun is at its maximum. Ibn Ezra likewise equates *neharah* with *or,* citing Dan. ii. 22, *the light* (*nehorah,* the Aramaic equivalent) *dwelleth with Him.*

5. *let darkness and the shadow of death.* The Masoretes vocalized *tsalmaweth,* 'the shadow of death,' i.e. 'darkness where there is never light' (Rashi). The meaning is, gloom comparable to the abode of death, viz. Sheol, the abode of thickest gloom (cf. *a land of the shadow of death,* x. 21). Modern scholars hold that the word should be vocalized not as a compound, but as an abstract form, meaning 'deep darkness.'

claim it. The verb *gaal* means 'to redeem, act as kinsman,' hence the signification is

Let a cloud dwell upon it;
Let all that maketh black the day
   terrify it.

6 As for that night, let thick dark-
   ness seize upon it;
   Let it not rejoice among the days
      of the year;
   Let it not come into the number
      of the months.

7 Lo, let that night be desolate;
   Let no joyful voice come therein.

8 Let them curse it that curse the
      day,
   Who are ready to rouse up levi-
      athan.

תִּשְׁכָּן־עָלָיו עֲנָנָה
יְבַעֲתֻהוּ כִּמְרִירֵי יוֹם:
הַלַּיְלָה הַהוּא יִקָּחֵהוּ אֹפֶל
אַל־יִחַדְּ בִּימֵי שָׁנָה
בְּמִסְפַּר יְרָחִים אַל־יָבֹא:
הִנֵּה הַלַּיְלָה הַהוּא יְהִי גַּלְמוּד
אַל־תָּבֹא רְנָנָה בוֹ:
יִקְּבֻהוּ אֹרְרֵי־יוֹם
הָעֲתִידִים עֹרֵר לִוְיָתָן:

'to claim (the right of a kinsman).' Ibn Ezra, however, thinks that this translation is far-fetched, and both he and Rashi connect the verb with *polluted bread* (*lechem megoal*, Mal. i. 7). Their rendering would be: 'let darkness . . . defile (or, desecrate) it.'

let a cloud dwell upon it. A cloud of darkness (Rashi).

let all that maketh black the day terrify it. The word *kimerirē* occurs nowhere else, but is derived from a root *kamar*, 'black, gloomy.' The 'blackness of the day' would be eclipses, or the alarming, abnormal darkness of tornadoes or sand-storms (Driver). Both Rashi and Ibn Ezra refer to Ps. xci. 6, *the destruction* (*keteb*) *that wasteth at noonday*, and *bitter destruction* (*keteb meriri*, Deut. xxxii. 24), and explain: 'like demons which rule at noon.'

6. *let it not rejoice among the days.* R.V. margin, following some ancient versions, translates 'be joined unto.' The difference is only in vocalization. Either yields good sense. Ibn Ezra gives both interpretations, agreeing with Rashi that 'let it not rejoice' is preferable.

7. *desolate.* *Galmud* is an adjective meaning 'hard, stony.' In Isa. xlix. 21 it is rendered *solitary*, descriptive of exiled Zion as a bereaved and barren woman. Ibn Ezra cites that verse to

define *galmud* as 'solitary.' Rashi defines it as 'alone,' forsaken of man and all creatures. Let that night, says Job, 'do to no others the wrong it did to him. Let it be cursed with sterility, so that no shout of joy may ring out upon it for the birth of a child' (Peake).

8. *let them curse it.* The root *kabab* has the more familiar synonym *kalal*, 'to utter a curse.' Enchanters were supposed in ancient times to have the power of making particular days unlucky (Driver).

ready to rouse up leviathan. Rashi and Ibn Ezra refer to a passage in the Palestinian Talmud which relates to wailing women at funerals: 'A woman should not stir up her funeral band (*liwyathah*) to wail during the intermediate days of the festivals' (M. K. 1. 3). They accordingly regard the final *nun* as the suffix 'their' and render: 'their mourning.' Ibn Ezra adds the comment: 'Some interpret the clause as an allusion to passengers on a vessel about to be shipwrecked. They curse the day they entered into it, for they are about to be devoured by leviathan, a sea-monster. More probably Job refers to the professional wailers in all tongues who pronounce a curse on days.' The modern view is that Job invokes the men who are able to rouse up the monster which,

9 Let the stars of the twilight thereof
    be dark;
  Let it look for light, but have none;
  Neither let it behold the eyelids
    of the morning;

10 Because it shut not up the doors
    of my [mother's] womb,
  Nor hid trouble from mine eyes.

11 Why died I not from the womb?
  Why did I not perish at birth?

12 Why did the knees receive me?
  And wherefore the breasts, that I
    should suck?

13 For now should I have lain still
    and been quiet;
  I should have slept; then had I
    been at rest—

9 יֶחְשְׁכוּ כּוֹכְבֵי נִשְׁפּוֹ
    יְקַו־לְאוֹר וָאַיִן
    וְאַל־יִרְאֶה בְּעַפְעַפֵּי־שָׁחַר׃

10 כִּי לֹא סָגַר דַּלְתֵי בִטְנִי
    וַיַּסְתֵּר עָמָל מֵעֵינָי׃

11 לָמָּה לֹא מֵרֶחֶם אָמוּת
    מִבֶּטֶן יָצָאתִי וְאֶגְוָע׃

12 מַדּוּעַ קִדְּמוּנִי בִרְכָּיִם
    וּמַה־שָּׁדַיִם כִּי אִינָק׃

13 כִּי־עַתָּה שָׁכַבְתִּי וְאֶשְׁקוֹט
    יָשַׁנְתִּי אָז ׀ יָנוּחַ לִי׃

v. 9. פתח באתנח

according to primitive ideas, was supposed to swallow the sun, or moon, at an
eclipse. A day on which an eclipse
occurred used to be considered most
inauspicious.

9. *let the stars of the twilight thereof
dark.* Let its morning stars never
appear! Let it ever remain a night, with
no day to follow it.

the eyelids of the morning. We have in
the phrase the relic of a Dawn myth, as
in Isa. xiv. 12, *O day-star, son of the
morning.* 'The Dawn is thought of as a
beautiful woman, and her eyelids are
"the long streaming rays of morning
light that come from the opening clouds
that reveal the sun; an exquisite image "
(Davidson). Let the day-spring from on
high never visit that night is Job's
prayer' (Peake).

10. *the doors of my [mother's] womb.* The
umbilius through which passes the food
to the embryo before birth (Ibn Ezra).

11-19 JOB WISHES HE HAD BEEN
STILLBORN
In his bitter suffering Job asks why did he
not die at birth. Then he might have
slept and been at rest with the mighty and

the wicked and the weary, who have been
delivered from all cares and are now at
peace in the democracy of death.

11. *why died I not from the womb?* If I
had to be born, he says in effect, why
could I not immediately have died?

12. *why did the knees receive me?* The
knees of the father, on whom the child
was laid, as a mark of acceptance and
legitimation (cf. Gen. l. 23) (Driver).

wherefore the breasts, that I should suck?
When born, why was he not left to perish,
abandoned by his father, unnourished by
his mother? (Peake).

13. *for now should I have lain still.* 'From
the tossing in agony which is his present
lot, he turns with a great longing to the
deep unruffled peace of Sheol that might
have been his. The conception of the
after-life was of a dreary monotony, a
bare existence without colour, or interest,
the dim shade, languid and strengthless
dwelling amid other shades, in whom the
flame of life flickered on but faintly, just
escaping extinction. For all its gloom
. . . Sheol has one attraction for him
which outweighs in his present mood all
the rich interest of life. There he would

14 With kings and counsellors of the earth,
  Who built up waste places for themselves;

15 Or with princes that had gold,
  Who filled their houses with silver;

16 Or as a hidden untimely birth I had not been;
  As infants that never saw light.

17 There the wicked cease from troubling;
  And there the weary are at rest.

18 There the prisoners are at ease together;
  They hear not the voice of the taskmaster.

19 The small and great are there alike;
  And the servant is free from his master.

20 Wherefore is light given to him that is in misery,
  And life unto the bitter in soul—

עִם־מְלָכִים וְיֹעֲצֵי אֶרֶץ
הַבֹּנִים חֳרָבוֹת לָמוֹ׃
אוֹ עִם־שָׂרִים זָהָב לָהֶם
הַמְמַלְאִים בָּתֵּיהֶם כָּסֶף׃
אוֹ כְנֵפֶל טָמוּן לֹא אֶהְיֶה
כְּעֹלְלִים לֹא־רָאוּ אוֹר׃
שָׁם רְשָׁעִים חָדְלוּ רֹגֶז
וְשָׁם יָנוּחוּ יְגִיעֵי כֹחַ׃
יַחַד אֲסִירִים שַׁאֲנָנוּ
לֹא שָׁמְעוּ קוֹל נֹגֵשׂ׃
קָטֹן וְגָדוֹל שָׁם הוּא
וְעֶבֶד חָפְשִׁי מֵאֲדֹנָיו׃
לָמָּה יִתֵּן לְעָמֵל אוֹר
וְחַיִּים לְמָרֵי נָפֶשׁ׃

at least be at rest. It is true that if the after-life has for Job no other attractions, it has also no extreme terrors; it is a pale, negative, cheerless existence, but without any element ot torture' (Peake).

14. *who built up waste places for themselves.* It is the way of kings and the great to rebuild ruined, desolate cities in order to leave a memorial for themselves (Metsudath David). Perhaps there is an allusion to the great pyramids, built as mausoleums by the kings of Egypt (Driver).

15. *with princes that had gold.* The allusion is to those wealthy and famous in this life with whom Job, had he died, would have been in company in death (Davidson).

17. *there the wicked cease from troubling.* The Hebrew word means 'rages' or 'raging.' Probably not from troubling others but from the unquiet of their own

evil. The two main ideas of verses 17-19 are that all, evil and good, great and small, are the same in the place of the dead. Second, that this common condition is one of profound rest. Even the wicked there are no more agitated by the turbulence of their passions (Davidson).

19. *the small and great are there alike.* The inequalities of earth vanish in the dead level of society in Sheol. The slave has won his freedom and his hard toil is for ever at an end (Peake). 'No slave is there nor master, no tyrant nor kings, no overweening lords' (Davidson).

20-26   WHY DOES GOD PROLONG LIFE FOR THE WRETCHED?

Job is confounded by the mystery of his suffering. He longs desperately to penetrate the eternal riddle of why a compassionate God should deny death to one whose life has become endless torment and misery.

20. *wherefore is light given to him that is*

21 Who long for death, but it
    cometh not;
  And dig for it more than for hid
    treasures;

22 Who rejoice unto exultation,
  And are glad, when they can find
    the grave?—

23 To a man whose way is hid,
  And whom God hath hedged in?

24 For my sighing cometh instead of
    my food,
  And my roarings are poured out
    like water.

25 For the thing which I did fear
    is come upon me,
  And that which I was afraid of
    hath overtaken me.

26 I was not at ease, neither was I
    quiet, neither had I rest;
  But trouble came.

21 הַמְחַכִּים לַמָּוֶת וְאֵינֶנּוּ
וַיַּחְפְּרֻהוּ מִמַּטְמוֹנִים׃

22 הַשְּׂמֵחִים אֱלֵי־גִיל
יָשִׂישׂוּ כִּי יִמְצְאוּ־קָבֶר׃

23 לְגֶבֶר אֲשֶׁר־דַּרְכּוֹ נִסְתָּרָה
וַיָּסֶךְ אֱלוֹהַּ בַּעֲדוֹ׃

24 כִּי־לִפְנֵי לַחְמִי אַנְחָתִי תָבֹא
וַיִּתְּכוּ כַמַּיִם שַׁאֲגֹתָי׃

25 כִּי פַחַד פָּחַדְתִּי וַיֶּאֱתָיֵנִי
וַאֲשֶׁר יָגֹרְתִּי יָבֹא לִי׃

26 לֹא שָׁלַוְתִּי ׀ וְלֹא־שָׁקַטְתִּי
וְלֹא־נָחְתִּי וַיָּבֹא רֹגֶז׃

---

4   CHAPTER IV   ד

1 Then answered Eliphaz the Temanite, and said:

1 וַיַּעַן אֱלִיפַז הַתֵּימָנִי וַיֹּאמַר׃

---

in misery? Why does the Holy One,
blessed be He, give light to him that is
in misery? (Rashi).

21. *and dig for it more than for hid treasures.* That is to say, they seek death
more than hid treasures (Ralbag). Peake
quotes Thomson, *The Land and the
Book*: 'There is not another comparison
within the whole compass of human
actions so vivid as this. I have heard of
diggers actually fainting when they have
come upon even a single coin. They
become positively frantic, dig all night
with desperate earnestness, and continue
to work till utterly exhausted.'

23. *to a man whose way is hid.* A.V. and
R.V. insert at the beginning of the verse:
Why is light given, repeated from verse
20.

25. *for the thing which I did fear.* Verses

25f. may be rendered more exactly and,
perhaps, more forcibly: 'For I fear a fear,
and it cometh upon me; and that which
I dread cometh unto me. I have no
ease, and no quiet, and no rest; and yet
turmoil cometh.'

CHAPTER IV

THE FIRST SPEECH OF ELIPHAZ

MANY commentators have dismissed
Job's friends with the quick judgment
that they were insincere and hypocritical.
The conciliatory opening tone of Eliphaz's first address is construed as a
mere cloak to conceal inner indignation at
what he regarded the blasphemous utterances of Job. It is possible, however,
that Eliphaz speaks as he does because he
so completely accepted the prevailing
theological dogmas of his day. He begins
his discourse with almost unconscious

2 If one venture a word unto thee,
   wilt thou be weary?
   But who can withhold himself
   from speaking?

3 Behold, thou hast instructed many,
   And thou hast strengthened the
   weak hands.

4 Thy words have upholden him
   that was falling,
   And thou hast strengthened the
   feeble knees.

5 But now it is come unto thee, and
   thou art weary;
   It toucheth thee, and thou art
   affrighted.

6 Is not thy fear of God thy confidence,
   And thy hope the integrity of thy
   ways?

הֲנִסָּ֬ה דָבָ֣ר אֵלֶ֣יךָ תִּלְאֶ֑ה
וַעְצֹ֥ר בְּמִלִּ֗ין מִ֣י יוּכָֽל׃

הִ֭נֵּה יִסַּ֣רְתָּ רַבִּ֑ים
וְיָדַ֖יִם רָפ֣וֹת תְּחַזֵּֽק׃

כּ֭וֹשֵׁל יְקִימ֣וּן מִלֶּ֑יךָ
וּבִרְכַּ֖יִם כֹּרְע֣וֹת תְּאַמֵּֽץ׃

כִּ֤י עַתָּ֨ה ׀ תָּב֣וֹא אֵלֶ֣יךָ וַתֵּ֑לֶא
תִּגַּ֥ע עָדֶ֗יךָ וַתִּבָּהֵֽל׃

הֲלֹ֣א יִ֭רְאָתְךָ כִּסְלָתֶ֑ךָ
תִּ֝קְוָתְךָ֗ וְתֹ֣ם דְּרָכֶֽיךָ׃

consideration for Job's feelings. One who offered advice to others should be willing to accept counsel in the moment of his own predicament. There is only the first faint hint of suggestion that since no innocent person has ever been punished, Job should confess openly his hidden sins and God will relent. While Eliphaz, in this address, gives expression to the conventional theology of his time, the belief in material retributive justice, we should not fail to appreciate the poetic magnificence in which he has clothed his limited spiritual penetration of the mystery of human suffering.

1-11 ONLY THE GUILTY ARE PUNISHED

1. *then answered Eliphaz.* He was a son of Esau (see on ii. 11) and since he was reared in the bosom of Isaac, he merited that the *Shechinah* should rest upon him (Rashi).

2. *wilt thou be weary?* i.e. wilt thou be vexed and irritated?

3. *thou hast instructed many.* The verb *yasar* is literally 'to discipline, admonish.' Behold, formerly, did you not admonish many who multiplied words against the Most High? (Metsudath David).

thou hast strengthened the weak hands. The hands that were weak in the faith of God you strengthened with words of instruction (Metsudath David). You were accustomed to strengthen them, saying, 'Fear not, for this is the Divine attribute of justice' (Rashi).

4. *thy words have upholden him that was falling.* Eliphaz is appealing to Job to apply to himself the counsel which formerly he had piously given to others. 'Your words were wont to support him that was falling' (Rashi).

5. *it toucheth thee, and thou art affrighted.* 'What Eliphaz fails to understand is that Job's disease needs not an irritant but an emollient' (Peake).

6. *is not thy fear of God thy confidence?* A.V. renders: 'Is not *this* thy fear, thy confidence?' A.J. correctly understands the Hebrew *yirathcha* as elliptical for *yirath shamayim*, 'thy fear of God.' Rashi wisely comments: 'Now thine end vindicates thy beginning, for thine awe with which thou didst revere God is thy confidence.'

7 Remember, I pray thee, who ever
perished, being innocent?
Or where were the upright cut off?

8 According as I have seen, they that
plow iniquity,
And sow mischief, reap the same.

9 By the breath of God they perish,
And by the blast of His anger are
they consumed.

10 The lion roareth, and the fierce
lion howleth—
Yet the teeth of the young lions
are broken.

11 The old lion perisheth for lack of
prey,
And the whelps of the lioness are
scattered abroad.

12 Now a word was secretly brought
to me,
And mine ear received a whisper
thereof.

7 זְכָר־נָא מִי הוּא נָקִי אָבָד
וְאֵיפֹה יְשָׁרִים נִכְחָדוּ׃

8 כַּאֲשֶׁר רָאִיתִי חֹרְשֵׁי אָוֶן
וְזֹרְעֵי עָמָל יִקְצְרֻהוּ׃

9 מִנִּשְׁמַת אֱלוֹהַּ יֹאבֵדוּ
וּמֵרוּחַ אַפּוֹ יִכְלוּ׃

10 שַׁאֲגַת אַרְיֵה וְקוֹל שָׁחַל
וְשִׁנֵּי כְפִירִים נִתָּעוּ׃

11 לַיִשׁ אֹבֵד מִבְּלִי־טָרֶף
וּבְנֵי לָבִיא יִתְפָּרָדוּ׃

12 וְאֵלַי דָּבָר יְגֻנָּב
וַתִּקַּח אָזְנִי שֵׁמֶץ מֶנְהוּ׃

---

7. *who ever perished, being innocent?* The
Talmud, citing this verse, declares: 'If
one is visited by suffering, afflicted with
disease, or has buried his children, one
must not speak to him as his companions
spoke to Job' (B.M. 58b). This is the
core of Eliphaz's argument: God is
absolutely just and will not suffer the
innocent to perish. It is the same argument that Abraham put forth in pleading
for Sodom and Gomorrah: *Shall not the
Judge of all the earth do justly?* (Gen.
xviii. 25).

or where were the upright cut off? The
verb *kachad* has the force of 'hide, be
effaced.' Ibn Ezra and Rashi suggest
that it is here used in the sense 'to be
cut off,' as in Exod. ix. 15, *and thou
hadst been cut off from the earth.*

8. *they that plow iniquity*, etc. It has
been suggested that Eliphaz may have
been quoting Prov. xxii. 8 (Jastrow).

10. *the lion roareth, and the fierce lion
howleth.* Some modern commentators
suggest that verses 10f. were familiar
proverbial sayings to illustrate the
belief that sooner or later the powerful

wicked are overthrown (Buttenwieser).
It is interesting to note in verses 10f. five
different words for lion. The *ari* is large
in size, the *shachal* medium, and the
kephir small. They typify kings, princes
and servants who all err (Rashi). Ibn
Ezra holds that the author compares the
rage of God to the roaring of the lion over
its prey. A modern view is that *the lion,
fierce lion*, etc., are here figures represent-
ing violent and wicked men (Driver). As
lions are made helpless after an attack,
so are the wicked.

12-21 THE MYSTIC AGITATION OF REVELA-
TION: NO MAN CAN BE PURE BEFORE GOD

This is one of the famous passages in the
Book, of singular poetic and mystic
beauty. Eliphaz asserts 'that no creature
can be spotless in God's sight, not even
the angels, who are pure spirit, far less
men, formed out of the dust and so frail
that they are crushed with ease. This
lesson he had learnt for himself in an
experience the horror of which is renewed as he relates it. The description
of it ranks with the most wonderful
triumphs of genius in the world's
literature' (Peake).

13 In thoughts from the visions of
   the night,
   When deep sleep falleth on men,

14 Fear came upon me, and trembling,
   And all my bones were made to
   shake.

15 Then a spirit passed before my
   face,
   That made the hair of my flesh
   to stand up.

16 It stood still, but I could not dis-
   cern the appearance thereof;
   A form was before mine eyes;
   I heard a still voice:

17 'Shall mortal man be just before
   God?
   Shall a man be pure before his
   Maker?

18 Behold, He putteth no trust in
   His servants,
   And His angels He chargeth with
   folly;

13 בִּשְׂעִפִּים מֵחֶזְיֹנֹות לָיְלָה
   בִּנְפֹל תַּרְדֵּמָה עַל־אֲנָשִׁים׃

14 פַּחַד קְרָאַנִי וּרְעָדָה
   וְרֹב עַצְמֹותַי הִפְחִיד׃

15 וְרוּחַ עַל־פָּנַי יַחֲלֹף
   תְּסַמֵּר שַׂעֲרַת בְּשָׂרִי׃

16 יַעֲמֹד ׀ וְלֹא־אַכִּיר מַרְאֵהוּ
   תְּמוּנָה לְנֶגֶד עֵינָי
   דְּמָמָה וָקֹול אֶשְׁמָע׃

17 הַאֱנֹושׁ מֵאֱלֹוהַּ יִצְדָּק
   אִם־מֵעֹשֵׂהוּ יִטְהַר־גָּבֶר׃

18 הֵן בַּעֲבָדָיו לֹא יַאֲמִין
   וּבְמַלְאָכָיו יָשִׂים תָּהֳלָה׃

12. *now a word was secretly brought to me.*
The verb implies 'snatched as in theft.'
Rashi comments homiletically that the
Holy Spirit is not revealed to heathen
prophets openly.

mine ear received a whisper thereof. Ibn
Ezra correctly states that *shemets (a
whisper*) has the same sense as in xxvi. 14,
How small a whisper is heard of Him! (so
too Ralbag).

13. *in thoughts from the visions of the night.*
The word rendered *thoughts* means 'dis-
quietings,' i.e. 'disquieting, or, excited
thoughts.' So too Rashi and Ibn Ezra.

14. *fear came upon me, and trembling.*
This resulted from the *spirit* (verse 15)
which came to him. *Spirit* is a Divine
messenger, as it is said, *Who makest
winds (ruchoth, plural of ruach, meaning
both 'wind' and 'spirit') Thy messengers*
(Ps. civ. 4) (Rashi).

15. *that made the hair of my flesh to stand
up.* lit. 'to bristle up' (cf. *my flesh shud-
dereth*, Ps. cxix. 120). Ibn Ezra quotes
Rabbenu Hai who connected the word

with *masmer,* 'nail,' for the pain is as a
fastened nail.

16. *it stood still.* This is in the dream
(Ibn Ezra).

I heard a still voice. Both Ibn Ezra and
Rashi compare 1 Kings xix. 12, the *still
small voice* that came to Elijah.

17. *shall mortal man be just before God?*
The revelation that comes to Eliphaz is
that man is imperfect and dare not
vindicate himself before God. It is a
presumption for him to imagine that
he can be pure before his Maker.

18. *behold, He putteth no trust in His
servants.* viz. the heavenly ministers,
as is seen from the parallel expression
His angels. The idea of the angels not
conforming to the Divine standard is in
striking accord with the Prologue, where
the Satan appears as a member of the
heavenly entourage, and shows himself
subject to error and human foible
(Buttenwieser).

and His angels He chargeth with folly. The

19 How much more them that dwell
in houses of clay,
Whose foundation is in the dust,
Who are crushed before the
moth!

20 Betwixt morning and evening
they are shattered;
They perish for ever without any
regarding it.

21 Is not their tent-cord plucked up
within them?
They die, and that without
wisdom.'

5   CHAPTER V

1 Call now; is there any that will
answer thee?
And to which of the holy ones wilt
thou turn?

אַף | שֹׁכְנֵי בָתֵּי־חֹמֶר 19
אֲשֶׁר־בֶּעָפָר יְסוֹדָם
יְדַכְּאוּם לִפְנֵי־עָשׁ׃
מִבֹּקֶר לָעֶרֶב יֻכַּתּוּ 20
מִבְּלִי מֵשִׂים לָנֶצַח יֹאבֵדוּ׃
הֲלֹא־נִסַּע יִתְרָם בָּם 21
יָמוּתוּ וְלֹא בְחָכְמָה׃

ה
קְרָא־נָא הֲיֵשׁ עוֹנֶךָּ 1
וְאֶל־מִי מִקְּדֹשִׁים תִּפְנֶה׃

v. 20. פתח באתנח

---

word for *folly* occurs only here. Its
meaning is established by the cognate
Ethiopic, meaning 'fault, error.'

19. *dwell in houses of clay . . . in the dust.*
If the angelic beings are not free from
fault, how much more so man with his
body and material nature! Man's frail
body is built upon a foundation of dust
(cf. xxxiii. 6).

20. *betwixt morning and evening they are
shattered.* 'The body is compared to a
tent (cf. Isa. xxxviii. 12) and the vital
force to the cord which holds the tent in
its place: as soon as that gives way, the
whole structure collapses' (Driver). Buttenweiser challenges this interpretation
and translates: 'when their life-thread
is broken off.' He maintains that though
the myth of the Parcae, who spin and
sever the thread of life, was unknown
among the Semitic peoples, the comparison of life to a thread or a web, and of
death to the severing of the thread or
web, occurs both in Hebrew and Arabic
literature. In Isa. xxxviii. 12 the comparison is carried out fully: *I have rolled
up like a weaver my life, He will cut me off
from the thrum.*

21. *they die, and that without wisdom.*

They died without having discovered
the time limitations and imperfections
of their nature (Driver). 'They thought
that they would accumulate wealth; but
this verse shows that man was only
created so that he might learn wisdom
(Ibn Ezra).

CHAPTER V

1-7   THE FOOLISH INCUR DISASTER

ELIPHAZ urges that since no man can be
just before God, it is only the foolish
who resents His dealings with him, and
in consequence incurs suffering.

1. *call now; is there any that will answer
thee?* Eliphaz now turns from the
revelation that man cannot be just or
pure in the sight of God to point out
how useless it is for Job to call for help
against the injustice which he contends
he is suffering. It would only be a
display of impotent rage.

*and to which of the holy ones wilt thou
turn?* The word *kedoshim, holy ones,* is
usually interpreted 'angels.' Buttenweiser contends that the belief in the
intercession of *welis* or 'saints' is meant
here. He cites, among other illustrations,

2 For anger killeth the foolish man,
  And envy slayeth the silly one.

3 I have seen the foolish taking root;
  But suddenly I beheld his habitation cursed.

4 His children are far from safety,
  And are crushed in the gate, with none to deliver them.

5 Whose harvest the hungry eateth up,
  And taketh it even out of the thorns,
  And the snare gapeth for their substance.

6 For affliction cometh not forth from the dust,
  Neither doth trouble spring out of the ground;

כִּי לֶאֱוִיל יַהֲרָג־כָּעַשׂ ²
וּפֹתֶה תָּמִית קִנְאָה:

אֲנִי רָאִיתִי אֱוִיל מַשְׁרִישׁ ³
וָאֶקּוֹב נָוֵהוּ פִּתְאֹם:

יִרְחֲקוּ בָנָיו מִיֶּשַׁע ⁴
וְיִדַּכְּאוּ בַשַּׁעַר וְאֵין מַצִּיל:

אֲשֶׁר קְצִירוֹ ׀ רָעֵב יֹאכֵל ⁵
וְאֶל־מִצִּנִּים יִקָּחֵהוּ
וְשָׁאַף צַמִּים חֵילָם:

כִּי ׀ לֹא־יֵצֵא מֵעָפָר אָוֶן ⁶
וּמֵאֲדָמָה לֹא־יִצְמַח עָמָל:

the story in the Midrash (Echah Rabbathi, Pethichta, sect. 55f.) where Jeremiah goes to the graves of the patriarchs and Moses and appeals to them to intercede with God in behalf of exiled Israel.

2. *for anger killeth the foolish man.* The display of temper will only lead to death. 'As for a fool like yourself, his anger will kill him; for if you will be silent, perhaps the attribute of mercy will turn upon you' (Rashi).

and envy slayeth the silly one. Anger and *envy*, in the sense of 'rage' and 'passion,' slay the fool, by causing him to murmur at his lot, and so bringing upon himself further calamities.

3. *but suddenly I beheld his habitation cursed.* The text is literally 'but suddenly I cursed his habitation' (A.V., R.V.). For the thought, cf. Ps. xxxvii. 35f. The meaning is: I never envied the prosperity of the foolish, because before I was tempted to do so I suddenly cursed his habitation, in the sense that the conviction entered my mind that ultimately disaster would overtake him (Metsudath David). Szold suggests that the root is *nakab* (and not *kabab*) and explains, 'I at once *marked out* his habitation' as doomed to destruction, in accord with the teaching, *The curse of the LORD is in the house of the wicked* (Prov. iii. 33).

4. *and are crushed in the gate.* His children do not obtain their rights in a court of judgment. The *gate* (or rather 'gate-way') of an Eastern city was the place where justice was usually administered (cf. xxxi. 21; Deut. xvi. 18, xxv.7). For the use of *crush* with the meaning of 'to deprive of one's rights,' cf. Prov. xxii. 22.

5. *whose harvest the hungry eateth up.* Verses 3-5 depict the scene of desolation that befalls the home and family of the foolish who harden themselves against God. The hungry plunder their grain, leaving nothing behind, not even that which grew among thorns.

and the snare gapeth for their substance. In xviii. 9 the word *tsammim* occurs again as parallel to *pach*, the common word for 'snare,' but it hardly yields a good sense. The Targum paraphrases 'robbers will make spoil of their wealth,' for which there is a striking parallel in Ps. cix. 11. R.V. margin has the note: 'according to many ancient versions, *the thirsty swallow up*,' identifying *tsammim* with *tsemeïm*, which gives the natural parallel to *the hungry*. This interpretation is adopted by Metsudath David.

6. *for affliction cometh not forth from the dust.* The meaning of verses 6f. is that affliction and misfortune are not some-

7 But man is born unto trouble,
  As the sparks fly upward.

8 But as for me, I would seek unto
  God,
  And unto God would I commit
  my cause;

9 Who doeth great things and unsearchable,
  Marvellous things without number;

10 Who giveth rain upon the earth,
   And sendeth waters upon the
   fields;

11 So that He setteth up on high
   those that are low,
   And those that mourn are exalted
   to safety.

7 כִּי אָדָם לְעָמָל יוּלָּד
  וּבְנֵי רֶשֶׁף יַגְבִּיהוּ עוּף׃

8 אוּלָם אֲנִי אֶדְרֹשׁ אֶל־אֵל
  וְאֶל־אֱלֹהִים אָשִׂים דִּבְרָתִי׃

9 עֹשֶׂה גְדֹלוֹת וְאֵין חֵקֶר
  נִפְלָאוֹת עַד־אֵין מִסְפָּר׃

10 הַנֹּתֵן מָטָר עַל־פְּנֵי אָרֶץ
   וְשֹׁלֵחַ מַיִם עַל־פְּנֵי חוּצוֹת׃

11 לָשׂוּם שְׁפָלִים לְמָרוֹם
   וְקֹדְרִים שָׂגְבוּ יֶשַׁע׃

v. 7. דגש אחר שורק

thing external to man, but result from causes inherent in his nature. Job, therefore, ought not to be surprised if he has to experience them. Ibn Ezra calls attention to Gen. viii. 21, *For the imagination of man's heart is evil from his youth.*

7. *but man is born unto trouble.* The verse is difficult and has perplexed the commentators. The intention appears to be that man, through his propensity to sin, begets trouble as naturally and inevitably as the sparks fly upward.

as the sparks fly upward. lit. 'and the sons of flame,' usually interpreted as *sparks* which, by their nature, *fly upward,* and so figurative of what is inevitable. The Targum understood the phrase as 'demons,' but some commentators explain it as referring to 'angels.' In verse 1 the futility of calling upon the *holy ones* was mentioned. Here, perhaps, the reason is given, viz. they fly upwards out of reach of man's cry for help in trouble. The translation would then be: 'and the sons of flame (angelic beings) fly upward,' and have no knowledge of, or ignore, human vicissitudes.

8-27 THE BENEFITS OF CHASTISEMENT

8-16. Eliphaz, in Job's place, would seek God Whose marvellous purpose of righteousness runs through all His universe.

8. *but as for me, I would seek unto God.* Eliphaz confesses, 'If these afflictions had come unto me, I would seek the Holy One, blessed be He, in prayer and in supplication' (Rashi). He would not rage as Job is doing. Alternatively, following on the suggested interpretation of the previous verse, he would not call on angels for help.

unto God would I commit my cause. State my case before Him.

9. *Who doeth great things and unsearchable.* Since man's knowledge is limited and finite, he may well entrust his cause to the infinite might of God. 'A touch of humanity seems here almost to get the better of the moral and religious severity of Eliphaz' (Davidson).

10. *Who giveth rain upon the earth.* The universal goodness of God is manifest in the rain He sends upon the parched earth. This thought is common in the Psalms (cf. lxv. 10, lxviii. 10, civ. 13).

11. *so that He setteth up on high those that are low.* He gives rain and thus defeats the design of the crafty who plan to create a panic and buy up the fields of the poor with a little grain (Rashi).

and those that mourn. They whose faces are pinched because of hunger (Rashi).

12 He frustrateth the devices of the
   crafty,
   So that their hands can perform
   nothing substantial.

13 He taketh the wise in their own
   craftiness;
   And the counsel of the wily is
   carried headlong.

14 They meet with darkness in the
   day-time,
   And grope at noonday as in the
   night.

15 But He saveth from the sword
   of their mouth,
   Even the needy from the hand of
   the mighty.

16 So the poor hath hope,
   And iniquity stoppeth her mouth.

17 Behold, happy is the man whom
   God correcteth;
   Therefore despise not thou the
   chastening of the Almighty.

מֵפֵר מַחְשְׁבוֹת עֲרוּמִים

וְלֹא־תַעֲשֶׂינָה יְדֵיהֶם תּוּשִׁיָּה׃

לֹכֵד חֲכָמִים בְּעָרְמָם

וַעֲצַת נִפְתָּלִים נִמְהָרָה׃

יוֹמָם יְפַגְּשׁוּ־חֹשֶׁךְ

וְכַלַּיְלָה יְמַשְׁשׁוּ בַצָּהֳרָיִם׃

וַיֹּשַׁע מֵחֶרֶב מִפִּיהֶם

וּמִיַּד חָזָק אֶבְיוֹן׃

וַתְּהִי לַדַּל תִּקְוָה

וְעֹלָתָה קָפְצָה פִּיהָ׃

הִנֵּה אַשְׁרֵי אֱנוֹשׁ יוֹכִיחֶנּוּ אֱלוֹהַּ

וּמוּסַר שַׁדַּי אַל־תִּמְאָס׃

12. *so that their hands can perform nothing substantial.* The word *tushiyyah*, *substantial*, belongs to the vocabulary of the Wisdom Literature, and is derived from *yesh*, 'substance.' 'They cannot execute the scheme they planned' (Rashi).

13. *is carried headlong.* lit. 'is hurried.' Rashi comments that any plan which is formulated in a hurry is folly.

14. *they meet with darkness in the day-time.* A picture of the utter confusion that overtakes the crafty (cf. Deut. xxviii. 29).

15. *from the sword of their mouth.* lit. 'from a sword, from their mouth.' Rashi has grasped the real meaning of this phrase, viz. 'from the sword into which they have converted their mouths.' His comment is: God saves those who have fallen from the sword. From which sword? From their mouths, for they thought to swallow them and planned to destroy them.

16. *so the poor hath hope.* With this verse, cf. Ps. cvii. 41f. 'The wicked are dumb with confusion when they see the

ignominious failure of their schemes, and the exaltation of the despised' (Peake).

17-27. In an eloquent peroration, Eliphaz describes the happiness of him who is chastened by God, and paints a lovely picture of the blessedness that awaits Job if he receives God's correction in the right spirit. Budde calls this 'the most beautiful and comforting passage in all the speeches of the friends.' 'Yet for all its sweet and soothing eloquence and promise of idyllic peace, the noble rhetoric rings hollow to Job's ear. For its fundamental assumption is that Job's suffering is punishment for sin, and his restoration conditional on meek submission to God's discipline. Thus the words which were meant to be healing, make his wounds smart the more. For how could he believe such comforting assurances, when his experience taught him only too plainly how God could torture the blameless?' (Peake).

17. *behold, happy is the man whom God correcteth.* Cf. Prov. iii. 11f. and Cohen's comment in the Soncino edition, p. 15. Eliphaz here applies the maxim cited from the Book of Proverbs.

18 For He maketh sore, and bindeth
    up;
    He woundeth, and His hands
    make whole.

19 He will deliver thee in six
    troubles;
    Yea, in seven there shall no evil
    touch thee.

20 In famine He will redeem thee
    from death;
    And in war from the power of the
    sword.

21 Thou shalt be hid from the
    scourge of the tongue;
    Neither shalt thou be afraid of
    destruction when it cometh.

22 At destruction and famine thou
    shalt laugh;
    Neither shalt thou be afraid of
    the beasts of the earth.

23 For thou shalt be in league with
    the stones of the field;
    And the beasts of the field shall
    be at peace with thee.

18 כִּי הוּא יַכְאִיב וְיֶחְבָּשׁ
  יִמְחַץ וְיָדָו תִּרְפֶּֽינָה׃

19 בְּשֵׁשׁ צָרוֹת יַצִּילֶךָ
  וּבְשֶׁבַע ׀ לֹא־יִגַּע בְּךָ רָֽע׃

20 בְּרָעָב פָּֽדְךָ מִמָּוֶת
  וּבְמִלְחָמָה מִֽידֵי חָֽרֶב׃

21 בְּשׁוֹט לָשׁוֹן תֵּחָבֵא
  וְלֹא־תִירָא מִשֹּׁד כִּי יָבֽוֹא׃

22 לְשֹׁד וּלְכָפָן תִּשְׂחָק
  וּמֵחַיַּת הָאָרֶץ אַל־תִּירָֽא׃

23 כִּי עִם־אַבְנֵי הַשָּׂדֶה בְרִיתֶךָ
  וְחַיַּת הַשָּׂדֶה הָשְׁלְמָה־לָּֽךְ׃

v. 18. וידיו ק׳

18. *He maketh sore, and bindeth up.*
Cf. Deut. xxxii. 39; Hosea vi. 1. God's
apparent harsh treatment is for the
sufferer's ultimate good, and the Hand
that deals the blow is also the Hand that
heals.

19. *in six troubles; yea, in seven.* 'The
real number meant is seven—not taken
literally, but to characterize the evils (as
enumerated in verses 20-23) as cardinal
evils. The use of the number seven to
denote the consummate character of
things is quite frequent in the Bible, as
in fact throughout ancient literature;
it has its origin in the ancient conception
of the universe as made up of seven
planets or spheres, and in the seven
planetary deities of the Assyrian-Baby-
lonian pantheon that developed out of
this conception' (Buttenweiser). Peake
remarks that the description which
follows reminds one of the exquisite
Ps. xci. 'The thrilling language is that
of a truly pious man who feels deeply
the truths he is expounding, and would
fain uplift Job with the confidence
that inspires him as he speaks. Once

more God's hedge will be about him so
that no evil can touch him.'

21. *scourge of the tongue.* i.e. slander
which is like a whip (Ibn Ezra). 'It
refers to the malicious tongue of the
Satan,' asserts Rashi.

22. *the beasts of the earth.* This phrase
may be understood literally, or metaphorically of robbers (Rashi).

23. *for thou shalt be in league,* etc. Poetic
figures implying that stones will not
accumulate to mar his fields, nor wild
beasts attack his folds or range his crops
(cf. Hos. ii. 20 where *covenant* is the same
Hebrew word as *league* here) (Driver).
It is as though a covenant were made
with the stones that they should not
cause damage and that thou hast made
peace with the beasts (Ibn Ezra).
Buttenweiser has an interesting note to
the effect that *abnë* may have been
originally *adonë*, 'even with the earth-
demons thou wilt be in league.' He
quotes K. Kohler who found the word

24 And thou shalt know that thy tent
    is in peace;
    And thou shalt visit thy habita-
    tion, and shalt miss nothing.
25 Thou shalt know also that thy
    seed shall be great,
    And thine offspring as the grass
    of the earth.
26 Thou shalt come to thy grave in
    ripe age,
    Like as a shock of corn cometh in
    in its season.
27 Lo this, we have searched it, so
    it is;
    Hear it, and know thou it for thy
    good.

וְיָדַעְתָּ כִּי־שָׁלוֹם אָהֳלֶךָ

וּפָקַדְתָּ נָוְךָ וְלֹא תֶחֱטָא:

וְיָדַעְתָּ כִּי־רַב זַרְעֶךָ

וְצֶאֱצָאֶיךָ כְּעֵשֶׂב הָאָרֶץ:

תָּבוֹא בְכֶלַח אֱלֵי־קָבֶר

כַּעֲלוֹת גָּדִישׁ בְּעִתּוֹ:

הִנֵּה־זֹאת חֲקַרְנוּהָ כֶּן־הִיא

שְׁמָעֶנָּה וְאַתָּה דַע־לָךְ:

6   **CHAPTER VI**   ו

1 Then Job answered and said:
2 Oh that my vexation were but
    weighed,
    And my calamity laid in the
    balances altogether!

וַיַּעַן אִיּוֹב וַיֹּאמַר:

לוּ שָׁקוֹל יִשָּׁקֵל כַּעְשִׂי

וְהַיָּתִי בְּמֹאזְנַיִם יִשְׂאוּ־יָחַד:

וְהַוָּתִי ק׳ v. 2.

---

as a variant in an Oxford fragment of
the Midrash Tanchuma. It is also mentioned as a variant by Rashi from Sifra to
Lev. xi. 27. The conjecture is that
adonë hassadeh are ground demons with
which the pious man will be in league.
The satyrs of the fields will not do him
harm.

24. *thy habitation.* The Hebrew is a
pastoral term, 'thy homestead.'

25. *thy seed shall be great.* In the fervour
of his pleading, Eliphaz appears to have
forgotten that Job's children had all
perished.

26. *in ripe age.* The word is found again
only in xxx. 2 and means 'firm strength,'
i.e. with the faculties unimpaired. 'He
will die in the full number of his days,
in old age' (Ibn Ezra). Eliphaz can
hold out no hope beyond the grave;
but promises all that is possible: a long
life, and death without the failure of
powers that usually attends old age. In
the Epilogue we are told that, after his
restoration, Job lived twice the three-

score years and ten that are assigned in
Ps. xc as the normal limit of a man's
whole life (Peake).

*like as a shock of corn cometh in in its
season.* A beautiful comparison borrowed
from agricultural life.

27. *lo this, we have searched it, so it is.*
Eliphaz sums up his entire speech by
affirming that it embodies the investiga-
tions into truth of himself and his friends.
He bids Job lay it to his heart. 'The
speech of Eliphaz is one of the master-
pieces of the Book. The surprising
literary skill of the author is hardly
anywhere so conspicuous' (Davidson).

CHAPTERS VI—VII JOB'S FIRST REPLY
—TO ELIPHAZ

CHAPTER VI

1-7 JOB JUSTIFIES HIS COMPLAINTS
Job defends the bitterness of his complaints, challenging his impatience to be
weighed against his calamity. He openly
accuses God of having shot poisoned
arrows into him. His friends should

3 For now it would be heavier than
   the sand of the seas;
   Therefore are my words broken.

4 For the arrows of the Almighty
   are within me,
   The poison whereof my spirit
   drinketh up;
   The terrors of God do set themselves in array against me.

5 Doth the wild ass bray when he
   hath grass?
   Or loweth the ox over his fodder?

6 Can that which hath no savour be
   eaten without salt?

3 כִּי־עַתָּה מֵחוֹל יַמִּים יִכְבָּד
   עַל־כֵּן דְּבָרַי לָעוּ׃

4 כִּי חִצֵּי שַׁדַּי עִמָּדִי
   אֲשֶׁר חֲמָתָם שֹׁתָה רוּחִי
   בִּעוּתֵי אֱלוֹהַּ יַעַרְכוּנִי׃

5 הֲיִנְהַק־פֶּרֶא עֲלֵי־דֶשֶׁא
   אִם־יִגְעֶה־שּׁוֹר עַל־בְּלִילוֹ׃

6 הֲיֵאָכֵל תָּפֵל מִבְּלִי־מֶלַח

have understood from the violence of
his outcry how intense was the terror of
his torture. His misery is so overpowering that he gives vent to a passionate cry
for death.

2. *oh that my vexation were but weighed.*
At least one Talmudic sage was shocked
at this outburst. Rab said: 'Dust should
be put in the mouth of Job, because he
makes himself the colleague of Heaven
(by desiring to weigh his pleas in the
balance with those of God)' (B.B. 16a).
Job seems to be replying to the criticism
of his impatience (cf. iv. 5, v. 2).

3. *heavier than the sand of the seas.* He
contends that his vexation and calamity
weighed together would outbalance the
sand of the seas (Rashi); cf. Prov.
xxvii. 3.

therefore are my words broken (la'u). Both
Rashi and Ibn Ezra refer to Obad. 16,
they shall drink, and swallow down (la'u).
Job's words are said by him to be
'stammering' (incoherent) like those of a
person who has swallowed too much
drink. But the verb here seems to have
the same meaning as in, *It is a snare to
a man rashly to say* (yala'): '*Holy*' (Prov.
xx. 25). The sense is: therefore are my
words (as you allege) rashly spoken.

4. *for the arrows of the Almighty are
within me.* Job now openly accuses God.
'The arrows of suffering that come from

the Almighty lodge with me constantly'
(Metsudath David). Not the afflictions
themselves terrify him. It is the moral
and spiritual problem that weighs him
down, the awful thought that God has
become his adversary. Davidson calls to
mind the line in Hamlet's soliloquy: 'The
slings and arrows of outrageous fortune.'

the poison whereof my spirit drinketh up.
'It is the custom of the Persians to put
the poison of a snake upon their arrows'
(Rashi).

the terrors of God . . . against me. The
metaphor changes to that of a hostile
army. 'They are arrayed in war against
me' (Ibn Ezra).

5. *doth the wild ass bray when he hath
grass?* 'Job compares his friends to the
ox and the ass that are content amidst
plentiful pasture, implying that their
own prosperity has made them incapable
of sympathy and the larger understanding' (Buttenweiser). 'They who dwell in
quietness will not cry out nor be in
dread. "Like these are ye," says Job
to his companions; "ye speak words that
have in them no reality." Such is the
force of the question, *Can that which hath
no savour be eaten without salt?*' (Ibn
Ezra).

6. *can that which hath no savour . . . salt?*
The commentators disagree over the
meaning of this and the next verse.
Some maintain that Job is comparing

Or is there any taste in the juice
of mallows?

7 My soul refuseth to touch them;
They are as the sickness of my
flesh.

8 Oh that I might have my request,
And that God would grant me the
thing that I long for!

9 Even that it would please God to
crush me;
That He would let loose His hand,
and cut me off!

10 Then should I yet have comfort;
Yea, I would exult in pain,
though He spare not;
For I have not denied the words
of the Holy One.

11 What is my strength, that I
should wait?

אִם־יֶשׁ־טַעַם בְּרִיר חַלָּמוּת׃
מֵאֲנָה לִנְגּוֹעַ נַפְשִׁי
הֵמָּה כִּדְוֵי לַחְמִי׃
מִי־יִתֵּן תָּבוֹא שֶׁאֱלָתִי
וְתִקְוָתִי יִתֵּן אֱלוֹהַּ׃
וְיֹאֵל אֱלוֹהַּ וִידַכְּאֵנִי
יַתֵּר יָדוֹ וִיבַצְּעֵנִי׃
וּתְהִי־עוֹד ׀ נֶחָמָתִי
וַאֲסַלְּדָה בְחִילָה לֹא יַחְמוֹל
כִּי־לֹא כִחַדְתִּי אִמְרֵי קָדוֹשׁ׃
מַה־כֹּחִי כִּי־אֲיַחֵל

his sufferings to insipid and repulsive
food. Others, like Ibn Ezra, to the
empty words of the friends. 'Eliphaz's
commonplaces are as repugnant to Job
as his own loathsome disease—repugnant
because they are shallow and unjust'
(Buttenweiser). 'Should I accept from
you empty words without wisdom?'
(Metsudath David).

the juice of mallows. lit. 'the slime of
hallamuth.' The latter word is said by
the Rabbis to mean 'the yolk of an egg,'
and the 'slime' of the yolk would accordingly be equivalent to the 'white' of an
egg (so A.V., R.V.). The corresponding
word in Syriac suggests that the true
meaning is 'the slime of purslain' (cf.
R.V. margin), a plant the flower of which,
as it fades away, resolves itself into an
insipid mucilaginous jelly (Driver).

7. *my soul refuseth to touch them.* Nephesh,
soul, is here as often the 'appetite' (cf.
Prov. x. 3, xiii. 25, xxvii. 7). Ibn
Ezra understands it literally: my soul
is sick and I shall die.

8-10 JOB WISHES HE COULD DIE

9. *even that it would please God to crush
me.* 'Job's deepest longing is that God

would put him out of his misery. Hitherto God has struck him with a fettered
hand, so to speak; now he would have
God release His hand and strike with
full force, so that he should not linger in
torture but be slain outright' (Peake).

10. *I would exult in pain.* If God would
only put an end to his misery, Job would
welcome the pain, dying in the comfort
that he had not denied the words of the
Holy One. He would at least know that
he had not merited the torture he was
called upon to endure. 'No accusing
conscience would impair his comfort in
death' (Driver).

11-13 HIS STRENGTH AND PATIENCE ARE EXHAUSTED

Eliphaz had urged upon Job hope (iv. 6)
and patience (v. 22-26); but Job can
endure his agony no longer. We must
imagine him, consumed by the ravages
of his disease, brought to the verge of
death.

11. *what is my strength, that I should
wait?* 'Were he strong like stones or
brass he might bear pain with fortitude
and patience, but he is so frail that he

And what is mine end, that I
should be patient?

וּמַה־קִּצִּי כִּי־אַאֲרִיךְ נַפְשִׁי׃

12 Is my strength the strength of
stones?
Or is my flesh of brass?

אִם־כֹּחַ אֲבָנִים כֹּחִי 12
אִם־בְּשָׂרִי נָחוּשׁ׃

13 Is it that I have no help in me,
And that sound wisdom is driven
quite from me?

הַאִם אֵין עֶזְרָתִי בִי 13
וְתֻשִׁיָּה נִדְּחָה מִמֶּנִּי׃

14 To him that is ready to faint
kindness is due from his friend,
Even to him that forsaketh the
fear of the Almighty.

לַמָּס מֵרֵעֵהוּ חָסֶד 14
וְיִרְאַת שַׁדַּי יַעֲזוֹב׃

15 My brethren have dealt deceitfully as a brook,

אַחַי בָּגְדוּ כְמוֹ־נָחַל 15

---

cannot repress his cry under torture. If
his suffering led to renewed health, he
might endure it in patience; but since it
can lead only to death, how can he be
other than impatient when death comes
so tardily to release him?' (Peake).

*and what is mine end, that I should be
patient?* 'Are not the days of man few,
and what good can come to me later in
those few days?' (Metsudath David).

be patient. lit. 'prolong my soul,' the
noun meaning, as frequently, the inclina-
tion of man's desire.

12. *is my strength the strength of stones?*
'Is my strength as stones and my flesh
strong as brass, that I should be able to
bear pains like these and return to my
former state?' (Metsudath David).

13. *is it that I have no help in me,* etc. In
the general context of verses 11-13, Job
seems to complain that he knows no way
of rescuing himself from his calamities.
Ha'im is an emphatic interrogative
particle as in Num. xvii. 28, and the
question form is employed to express a
strong avowal; so the meaning is: it is
a fact that it is not in me to help myself
(objective suffix), and that *tushiyyah* (see
on v. 12, here 'a substantial, or effective,
way' of gaining relief) is banished from
me.

14-23 HIS DISAPPOINTMENT OVER HIS
FRIENDS

In the hour of his need, Job's friends
have failed him. He compares his dis-

appointment, in metaphor of unforget-
table vividness and poetic strength, to the
disappointment of the Arabian traders
who, homeward bound in the summer,
find the rushing streams they had left
behind in the winter, now dried-up
river-beds. So, too, the sympathy and
understanding for which he longed have
evaporated into suspicion and rebuke.

14. *to him that is ready to faint.* lit. 'to
him who melteth,' i.e. whose spirit
despairs. 'A man who, in his despair,
is tempted to cast off his faith in God,
should be treated with kindness by his
friends, not with groundless insinuations
of his guilt' (Driver). The noun *chesed*,
translated *kindness*, occurs in Lev. xx. 17
and Prov. xiv. 34 with the meaning
shameful thing, reproach. Metsudath
David adopts that signification here and
explains: Is it right that a man whose
flesh melts from his suffering should
receive reproaches from his friend? Has
he not the fear of the Almighty before
him, to say, 'Is not his pain enough, why
should I vex him further?'

15. *my brethren have dealt deceitfully.*
Note that Job still calls his friends
brethren, not yet foes. He has not yet
come to this accusation.

as a brook. The Hebrew *nachal* corresponds to the Arabic *wadi*, a stream which
becomes a rushing torrent during the
rainy season but dries up, often com-

As the channel of brooks that overflow,

כַּאֲפִיק נְחָלִים יַעֲבֹרוּ׃

16 Which are black by reason of the ice,
And wherein the snow hideth itself;

הַקֹּדְרִים מִנִּי־קָרַח
עָלֵימוֹ יִתְעַלֶּם־שָׁלֶג׃

17 What time they wax warm, they vanish,
When it is hot, they are consumed out of their place.

בְּעֵת יְזֹרְבוּ נִצְמָתוּ
בְּחֻמּוֹ נִדְעֲכוּ מִמְּקוֹמָם׃

18 The paths of their way do wind,
They go up into the waste, and are lost.

יִלָּפְתוּ אָרְחוֹת דַּרְכָּם
יַעֲלוּ בַתֹּהוּ וְיֹאבֵדוּ׃

19 The caravans of Tema looked,
The companies of Sheba waited for them—

הִבִּיטוּ אָרְחוֹת תֵּמָא
הֲלִיכֹת שְׁבָא קִוּוּ־לָמוֹ׃

20 They were ashamed because they had hoped;
They came thither, and were confounded.

בֹּשׁוּ כִּי־בָטָח
בָּאוּ עָדֶיהָ וַיֶּחְפָּרוּ׃

---

pletely, in the summer. Such are his friends whose flow of sympathy has similarly dried up. The verse is reminiscent of Jer. xv. 18, where the prophet, in his pain, asks God, *Wilt Thou indeed be unto me as a deceitful brook, as waters that fail?*

as the channel of brooks that overflow. 'The brooks overflow in winter time when they are not needed, but fail in the heat of the summer; so Job's friends are full of kindness when none is needed, but when trouble comes they fail the sufferer' (Peake).

16. *which are black . . . the snow hideth itself.* The verse is descriptive of a thaw which breaks up the ice and sends the floes racing along in the strong current of the waters swollen with the melting snow. *Hideth itself* apparently means 'dissolves.'

17. *what time they wax warm.* The root *zarab* is found nowhere else in the Bible, but is a by-form of *tsarab* in Ezek. xxi. 3, *seared*. When the streams are scorched

by the summer sun, they disappear.

18. *the paths of their way do wind.* Ibn Ezra supports this translation. The meaning is that the paths of their way, i.e. of the streams, turn aside and go up into the waste and are lost. A.V. and R.V. render, as in the next verse, *the caravans*, and it is more probable that the noun has the same meaning in succeeding verses. With this translation the intention would be that travellers expect to find water in such wadis, but coming to them and finding none, they perish of thirst in the desert.

19. *the caravans of Tema . . . the companies of Sheba.* Tema lies in the northern highlands of Arabia, towards the Syrian desert, a trading Ishmaelite tribe (cf. Gen. xxv. 15; Isa. xxi. 14; Jer. xxv. 23). For Sheba, see on i. 15. These desert travellers *looked* for water, and *waited for them*, viz. the brooks.

20. *they were ashamed.* i.e. disappointed, put to shame because their expectation was not realized.

21 For now ye are become His;
   Ye see a terror, and are afraid.

22 Did I say: 'Give unto me'?
   Or: 'Offer a present for me of your
       substance'?

23 Or: 'Deliver me from the adver-
       sary's hand'?
   Or: 'Redeem me from the hand
       of the oppressors'?

24 Teach me, and I will hold my
       peace;
   And cause me to understand
       wherein I have erred.

25 How forcible are words of up-
       rightness!
   But what doth your arguing
       argue?

26 Do ye hold words to be an argu-
       ment,
   But the speeches of one that is
       desperate to be wind?

21 כִּֽי־עַ֭תָּה הֱיִ֣יתֶם ל֑וֹ
   תִּרְא֥וּ חֲ֝תַ֗ת וַתִּירָֽאוּ׃

22 הֲ‍ֽכִי־אָ֭מַרְתִּי הָ֣בוּ לִ֑י
   וּ֝מִכֹּחֲכֶ֗ם שִׁחֲד֥וּ בַעֲדִֽי׃

23 וּמַלְּט֥וּנִי מִיַּד־צָ֑ר
   וּמִיַּ֖ד עָרִיצִ֣ים תִּפְדּֽוּנִי׃

24 ה֭וֹרוּנִי וַאֲנִ֣י אַחֲרִ֑ישׁ
   וּמַה־שָּׁ֝גִ֗יתִי הָבִ֥ינוּ לִֽי׃

25 מַה־נִּמְרְצ֥וּ אִמְרֵי־יֹ֑שֶׁר
   וּמַה־יּוֹכִ֖יחַ הוֹכֵ֣חַ מִכֶּֽם׃

26 הַלְהוֹכַ֣ח מִלִּ֣ים תַּחְשֹׁ֑בוּ
   וּ֝לְר֗וּחַ אִמְרֵ֥י נֹאָֽשׁ׃

v. 21. בנ״א לא כתיב לו ק'

21. *for now ye are become His.* The *kethib*
reads 'not,' which A.V. and R.V. have
adopted in the impossible rendering, *for
now ye are nothing.* A.J. is based on the
kerë and follows Ibn Ezra's interpretation: 'Now ye are become His,' i.e. protagonists for God, since ye see the terror
that He hath brought upon me and are
afraid.' Rashi renders: 'Ye are become
like it (that brook). Ye see the fear and
dread that strike, so are afraid to say the
truth and flatter my Adversary.'

22. *did I say: 'Give unto me'?* 'Had he
presumed on their friendship to ask a
gift that would cost them anything, he
would not have been surprised at their
treatment. Such a test, he hints bitterly,
friendship could hardly be expected to
stand' (Peake).

offer a present for me. lit. 'give a bribe
on my behalf' to a captor who demanded
a ransom for my release.

your substance. lit. 'your strength.'
'Your wealth' (Rashi).

24-30 HE PLEADS FOR JUST CONSIDERATION
From bitter reproach that he had asked

nothing material from them, Job now
turns in plaintive appeal to be told explicitly the sins at which they had in-
directly hinted. He challenges them to
look upon him and say that he would lie
to their face.

24. *teach me, and I will hold my peace.*
'Teach me what is my sin, and I will
hold my peace to hearken unto your
speech; and cause me to understand what
is the thing in which I have erred, since
ye say that the afflictions have come upon
me to wipe away the sin' (Metsudath
David).

25. *how forcible are words of uprightness!* Rashi and Ibn Ezra define *forcible*
by *chazak*, 'strong, effective,' citing
1 Kings ii. 8, *a grievous curse.* 'If ye
spoke sincere words, they would be
received; but now what doth your
reasoning prove?' (Rashi).

26. *do ye hold words to be an argument,*
etc. Buttenwieser, on grammatical
grounds, renders the verse more con-
vincingly: 'Do you mean to juggle with
words? Or to account as wind the words

27 Yea, ye would cast lots upon the
    fatherless,
    And dig a pit for your friend.

28 Now therefore be pleased to look
    upon me;
    For surely I shall not lie to your
    face.

29 Return, I pray you, let there be
    no injustice;
    Yea, return again, my cause is
    righteous.

30 Is there injustice on my tongue?
    Cannot my taste discern crafty
    devices?

אַף עַל־יָתוֹם תַּפִּילוּ

וְתִכְרוּ עַל־רֵיעֲכֶם׃

וְעַתָּה הוֹאִילוּ פְנוּ־בִי

וְעַל־פְּנֵיכֶם אִם־אֲכַזֵּב׃

שֻׁבוּ נָא אַל־תְּהִי עַוְלָה

וְשֻׁבוּ עוֹד צִדְקִי־בָהּ׃

הֲיֵשׁ־בִּלְשׁוֹנִי עַוְלָה

אִם־חִכִּי לֹא־יָבִין הַוּוֹת׃

7   CHAPTER VII   ז

1 Is there not a time of service to
    man upon earth?
    And are not his days like the days
    of a hireling?

הֲלֹא־צָבָא לֶאֱנוֹשׁ עַל־אָרֶץ

וְכִימֵי שָׂכִיר יָמָיו׃

v. 29. עלי ק'   v. 1. ושבו ק'

of him who is in despair?' He contends
that *millim* is not the object of *hochach*,
but accusative of specification; the phrase
an idiom equivalent to our 'juggle with
words.' *Tachshobu*, from *chashab* 'to
think, reckon,' i.e. 'do ye hold,' is a case
of zeugma. Ibn Ezra points in the same
direction: 'Real words by which you
would be able to argue,' and the meaning
is: 'You have no evidence. You think
that your words are correct and hold the
words of him who is in anguish to be
vanity.'

27. *yea, ye would cast lots upon the
fatherless.* He charges his friends with
utter lack of pity. Like merciless
creditors they would cast lots for the
orphan child who had been their debtor,
in order to sell him into slavery (Driver).
Cast lots (tappilu) occurs again in 1 Sam.
xiv. 42. The A.V. rendering: *Yea, ye
overwhelm the fatherless*, follows Ibn
Ezra who comments: 'Even if a wall or
something similar fell upon an orphan,
ye would not care.'

dig a pit for your friend. This translation
would seem a natural parallel to the first
clause. But the verb may also mean 'get
by trade.' Buttenweiser construes it in
this sense, translating: 'Ye would even

cast (dice) over an orphan or barter your
friend.'

28. *be pleased to look upon me.* Conscious
of his inward integrity, he pleads with
his friends not to avert their gaze but
look him straight in the face. Only an
innocent man could propose such a
test.

29. *return, I pray you, let there be no
injustice.* Turn from your false judgment
of assuming that I am guilty of sin.

my cause is righteous. lit. 'my righteousness is in it,' i.e. in the plea I make.

30. *is there injustice on my tongue?* 'Job
uses metaphorical language. He asks
if any deadly poison were on his tongue,
would he not notice it? Even so, if he
had committed any grave sin, would his
conscience not be aware of it?' (Buttenweiser).

cannot my taste discern crafty devices? As
his palate has not lost the power to dis-
tinguish taste, so his moral sense has not
ceased to discern right from wrong.

CHAPTER VII

1-10 THE WEARISOMENESS AND BREVITY
OF LIFE

FOR a moment Job turns to bitter reflec-

2 As a servant that eagerly longeth
for the shadow,
And as a hireling that looketh for
his wages;

3 So am I made to possess—months
of vanity,
And wearisome nights are appointed to me.

4 When I lie down, I say: 'When
shall I arise?'
But the night is long, and I am full
of tossings to and fro unto the
dawning of the day.

2 כְּעֶבֶד יִשְׁאַף־צֵל
וּכְשָׂכִיר יְקַוֶּה פָעֳלוֹ:

3 כֵּן הָנְחַלְתִּי לִי יַרְחֵי־שָׁוְא
וְלֵילוֹת עָמָל מִנּוּ־לִי:

4 אִם־שָׁכַבְתִּי וְאָמַרְתִּי מָתַי אָקוּם
וּמִדַּד־עָרֶב
וְשָׂבַעְתִּי נְדֻדִים עֲדֵי־נָשֶׁף:

tion upon the endless drudgery and
hardships of human existence at best.
It is only a flash. Once more, beset by
his unabating misery, he describes the
horror of his own dread disease, and
laments that his breath-like life speeds,
swifter than a weaver's shuttle, hopelessly
to the grave.

1. *a time of service.* Again in xiv. 14.
The Hebrew word usually means 'warfare' (Num. i. 3; I Sam. xxviii. 1). Here
it is figurative for 'time of hard service,
the battle of life.' Ibn Ezra and Rashi
interpret as a 'determined' or 'limited'
time; Ralbag and Metsudath David as
'an end and an appointed time.'

like the days of a hireling. The image is
of a hired labourer, trapped in his un-
ceasing toil.

2. *as a servant that eagerly longeth for the
shadow.* 'When he can cease from his
labour' (Ibn Ezra). 'Like a servant who
toils through the long day and yearns for
the shades of evening; or like a hireling
who hopes for his wages at evening and
longs for the setting sun' (Rashi).

3. *months of vanity, and wearisome
nights.* Job now turns from contemplation of the universal misery to lament his
own wretched lot. *Months of vanity* and
wearisome nights are strikingly contrasted.

'I keep watch; when will the months
pass away? Perhaps my sickness will
lighten in the months to come. Each and
every night I watch, when will it pass
away? Lo, in vain I hope' (Metsudath
David). *Shaw* may mean not only
'vanity, emptiness,' but also 'moral evil'
as in xi. 11 (*base men*), xxxi. 5 (parallel to
deceit). Here it is employed in the sense
of physical wretchedness.

4. *but the night is long* (middad). To
explain the verb Rashi cites *my sleep
fled* (tiddad) (Gen. xxxi. 40). But there
the root is *nadad* from which *tossings to
and fro* (nedudim) is derived. *Middad*
is Piel of *madad*, 'to measure,' and signifies 'to be extended.'

unto the dawning (nesheph) *of the day.*
The Hebrew of this verse has a wondrous
beauty. *Nesheph* here means 'morning,
twilight' and is contrasted with *ereb*,
'sunset, evening.' The seemingly endless night is spent in acute discomfort,
the sufferer tossing from side to side in a
vain effort to sleep, and in the occasional
intervals of dozing haunted by nightmares
(verse 14). 'The full meaning can be
understood only by those who have
suffered through a night from violent
pain; time literally seems to stand still. . . .
The poet must have suffered so himself,
and known with how much greater
slowness time seems to move through a
night than through a day of pain' (Peake).

5 My flesh is clothed with worms
and clods of dust;
My skin closeth up and breaketh
out afresh.

6 My days are swifter than a
weaver's shuttle,
And are spent without hope.

7 Oh remember that my life is a
breath;
Mine eye shall no more see good.

8 The eye of him that seeth me shall
behold me no more;
While Thine eyes are upon me,
I am gone.

9 As the cloud is consumed and
vanisheth away,
So he that goeth down to the grave
shall come up no more.

5 לָבַשׁ בְּשָׂרִי רִמָּה וְגִישׁ עָפָר
עוֹרִי רָגַע וַיִּמָּאֵס׃

6 יָמַי קַלּוּ מִנִּי־אָרֶג
וַיִּכְלוּ בְּאֶפֶס תִּקְוָה׃

7 זְכֹר כִּי־רוּחַ חַיָּי
לֹא־תָשׁוּב עֵינִי לִרְאוֹת טוֹב׃

8 לֹא־תְשׁוּרֵנִי עֵין רֹאִי
עֵינֶיךָ בִּי וְאֵינֶנִּי׃

9 כָּלָה עָנָן וַיֵּלַךְ
כֵּן יוֹרֵד שְׁאוֹל לֹא יַעֲלֶה׃

v. 5. ג' זעירא וגוש ק' v. 9. פתח באתנח

5. my flesh is clothed with worms, etc. Job gives a graphic description of the horrible symptoms of his disease. The hard, earth-like crusts of his sores alternately gather and run again. In elephantiasis, the hardened boils make the skin look as if it were covered with dirty 'elephant skin' (Buttenweiser).

6. my days are swifter than a weaver's shuttle. This is one of the famous, oft-quoted lines of the poem. 'There is no radical inconsistency in the complaint that life passes swiftly and the complaint that it drags on interminably. It is simply a change in point of view. A swift death is preferable to life in agony, but if life could be passed without constant pain, its brevity is an evil, since none would willingly exchange its warm glow and thrilling interest for the cold and colourless monotony of Sheol' (Peake).

and are spent without hope. *Tikwah* means 'cord' as well as *hope*, and an alternative translation proposed is, 'they come to an end through want of thread.' Ibn Ezra suggests both possibilities: 'When the cord of thread is cut; or it may mean hope.'

7. Oh remember that my life is a breath. These lines are addressed not to Eliphaz but to God, as Ibn Ezra pointed out. They are deeply moving in their pathos and passionate appeal (cf. Ps. lxxviii. 39).

mine eye shall no more see good. The Hebrew word for *good* often has the meaning of 'prosperity' (cf. Ps. iv. 7, xxxiv. 13). 'Mine eye shall no more see good, after my death. So here Job denies the dogma of the Resurrection of the Dead,' comments Rashi.

8. while Thine eyes are upon me, I am gone. 'To the Holy One, blessed be He, Job speaks, "Why was it necessary to smite me and crush me with afflictions?"' (Rashi). 'When Thou settest Thine eyes on me to requite me, I shall no longer be in the world' (Metsudath David).

9. as the cloud is consumed and vanisheth away. Verses 9f. are an emphatic denial of the possibility of a return to earth after death. 'How subtly the poet by the very energy of Job's denial shows the fascination the thought had for him, and suggests to the reader a recoil from his hopeless outlook (cf. x. 21f., xiv. 7-22, xvi. 22). The Babylonians called the underworld "the land of no return." As

10 He shall return no more to his
   house,
   Neither shall his place know him
   any more.

11 Therefore I will not refrain my
   mouth;
   I will speak in the anguish of my
   spirit;
   I will complain in the bitterness
   of my soul.

12 Am I a sea, or a sea-monster,
   That Thou settest a watch over
   me?

13 When I say: 'My bed shall comfort me,
   My couch shall ease my complaint';

14 Then Thou scarest me with
   dreams,
   And terrifiest me through visions;

10 לֹא־יָשׁוּב עוֹד לְבֵיתוֹ
וְלֹא־יַכִּירֶנּוּ עוֹד מְקֹמוֹ׃

11 גַּם־אֲנִי לֹא אֶחֱשָׂךְ־פִּי
אֲדַבְּרָה בְּצַר רוּחִי
אָשִׂיחָה בְּמַר נַפְשִׁי׃

12 הֲיָם־אָנִי אִם־תַּנִּין
כִּי־תָשִׂים עָלַי מִשְׁמָר׃

13 כִּי־אָמַרְתִּי תְּנַחֲמֵנִי עַרְשִׂי
יִשָּׂא בְשִׂיחִי מִשְׁכָּבִי׃

14 וְחִתַּתַּנִי בַחֲלֹמוֹת
וּמֵחֶזְיֹנוֹת תְּבַעֲתַנִּי׃

v. 14. פתח בס"ף

an illustration of the thought, Lucretius,
Book III, lines 907-9 may be compared:

" Never shalt thou behold thy dear ones
         more,
   Never thy wife await thee at the door,
   Never again thy little climbing boy
   A father's kindness in thine eyes
         explore" '

(Mallock's paraphrase: *Lucretius On Life
and Death*, p. 26, quoted by Peake.)

the grave. Hebrew *Sheol*, signifying the
abode of the dead, corresponding to the
Greek Hades.

10. *neither shall his place know him any
more.* Note the wealth of imagery that
Job used to describe life's brevity: the
weaver's shuttle, a breath, a passing
cloud, and finally a residence which is
only temporary.

11-21 JOB'S BITTER REPROACH TO GOD

Before he dies, Job will pour out his
complaint in the bitterness of his soul.
Why does God set a watch over him as if
he were a sea-monster? Why does God
terrify him so that he loathes his life ?

Why does the majestic Watcher of men
think so much of an insignificant creature like man, to assail and oppress him
unremittingly?

12. *am I a sea.* God had set a limit to
the area occupied by the mighty ocean
(Gen. i. 10) and watches that it does not
transgress its boundary. Do I, a frail
mortal, need to be watched similarly by
Him!

or a sea-monster. 'The reference is to the
Babylonian-Assyrian creation myth, the
attack by Marduk and his hosts on
Tiamat, who held dominion over the
primeval sea' (Buttenweiser). The
dragon Tiamat was subdued by the
Creator in the hoary past, but it is still
closely guarded and confined lest once
more it break loose to destroy the world.
But I, a helpless creature, do not need
such watchfulness on God's part!

14. *terrifiest me through visions.* He
alludes to the nightmares which made the
night a terrifying experience for him.
'Alarming dreams are said to be one of
the symptoms of elephantiasis' (Driver).

31

15 So that my soul chooseth strangling,
   And death rather than these my
   bones.

16 I loathe it; I shall not live alway;
   Let me alone; for my days are
   vanity.

17 What is man, that Thou shouldest
   magnify him,
   And that Thou shouldest set Thy
   heart upon him,

18 And that Thou shouldest remember him every morning,
   And try him every moment?

19 How long wilt Thou not look
   away from me,
   Nor let me alone till I swallow
   down my spittle?

20 If I have sinned, what do I unto
   Thee, O Thou watcher of men?

וַתִּבְחַר מַחֲנָק נַפְשִׁי
מָוֶת מֵעַצְמוֹתָי׃
מָאַסְתִּי לֹא־לְעֹלָם אֶחְיֶה
חֲדַל מִמֶּנִּי כִּי־הֶבֶל יָמָי׃
מָה־אֱנוֹשׁ כִּי תְגַדְּלֶנּוּ
וְכִי־תָשִׁית אֵלָיו לִבֶּךָ׃
וַתִּפְקְדֶנּוּ לִבְקָרִים
לִרְגָעִים תִּבְחָנֶנּוּ׃
כַּמָּה לֹא־תִשְׁעֶה מִמֶּנִּי
לֹא־תַרְפֵּנִי עַד־בִּלְעִי רֻקִּי׃
חָטָאתִי מָה אֶפְעַל לָךְ נֹצֵר הָאָדָם

---

15. *so that my soul chooseth strangling.* 'Elephantiasis not infrequently ends in a fatal choking fit' (Driver). Death from suffocation is preferable to such an existence as mine.

and death rather than these my bones. 'My soul prefers death to dwelling in these my bones. For the body is to the soul as a house, and the root of the body are the bones like the foundation and columns' (Ibn Ezra). More probably he describes the wasting of his flesh until he is little more than a living skeleton.

16. *I loathe it.* *Ma'asti* is ellipsis for *ma'asti bechayyai*, 'I loathe my life.' The full phrase is found in ix. 21, *I despise my life.*
I shall not live alway. Or alternatively: 'I would not live alway' (A.V., R.V.). Were everlasting life offered to me, I should reject it.

let me alone. A characteristically bold phrase in Job's mouth.

for my days are vanity. lit. 'a breath' (cf. Eccles. i. 2, and often in this Book).

17. *what is man.* The verse is a reminiscence of Ps. viii. 5, but uttered in a mood of bitterness, not reverential wonder.

18. *every morning.* i.e. 'constantly' (cf. Lam. iii. 23, *new every morning*). Verses 17f. seem to be an ironical parody of Ps. viii. 4ff. where man is magnified as *little lower than the angels.* In the Psalm God remembers man with providential care. Here He tries his faith and tests his endurance with constant suffering.

19. *how long wilt Thou not look away from me.* Cf. xiv. 6; Ps. xxxix. 14. In his physical and mental distress, the Divine watchfulness over human beings is misinterpreted by Job as spying to discover an opportunity to inflict punishment.

till I swallow down my spittle. A proverbial phrase, not unusual among the Arabs, meaning, 'Give me a moment's respite or time.' In De Sacy's notes to Hariri, a person tells the following: 'I said to one of my sheikhs (teachers), "Let me swallow my spittle"; to which he replied, "I will let you swallow the two confluents (the Tigris and Euphrates)"' (Davidson).

20. *if I have sinned, what do I unto Thee.* If, for the sake of argument, he admits that he had sinned, how did his act so

Why hast Thou set me as a mark
for Thee,

So that I am a burden to myself?

21 And why dost Thou not pardon
my transgression,

And take away mine iniquity?

For now shall I lie down in the
dust;

And Thou wilt seek me, but I
shall not be.

לָמָה שַׂמְתַּנִי לְמִפְגָּע לָךְ

וָאֶהְיֶה עָלַי לְמַשָּׂא:

²¹ וּמֶה ׀ לֹא־תִשָּׂא פִשְׁעִי

וְתַעֲבִיר אֶת־עֲוֹנִי

כִּי־עַתָּה לֶעָפָר אֶשְׁכָּב

וְשִׁחֲרְתַּנִי וְאֵינֶנִּי:

v. 20. רפה ומלעיל

affect God that He retaliates with such fierceness? Davidson points out that the idea that God is too high to be affected by men's actions, whether sinful or righteous, is repeatedly expressed in the Book. He cites xxii. 2f., xxxv. 5f. It is significant to observe that in chapter xxii. Eliphaz has appropriated this argument, and in xxxv. 5 Elihu has borrowed it.

watcher of men. Here a bitter phrase used in reproach of God's hostile espionage and His relentless scrutiny of man's most innocent conduct.

as a mark. lit. 'a thing to strike against, an object of attack.' Job feels that he is continually in the way of God, a stumbling-block, an obstacle against which the Almighty is always of set purpose striking Himself. The thought is one of unprecedented boldness (cf. Davidson).

so that I am a burden to myself. According to Masoretic tradition, *to myself* is a correction of the Scribes out of piety for an original text that read 'a burden to Thee.' Ibn Ezra, however, remarked that 'its interpretation as it stands without alteration is correct.' Many, but not all, modern scholars, accept 'to Thee' as the original reading. Peake accepts the scribal tradition as correct and comments: 'The thought is one of amazing boldness, that Job is a burden on the Almighty, but not too bold for the poet.'

21. *why dost Thou not pardon my transgression.* 'What is this thing that I have done that Thou dost not forgive my transgression?' (Rashi). Job reproaches God for His seeming lack of magnanimity.

for now shall I lie down in the dust. Now has the force of 'soon.' *Dust* is an abbreviated form of 'dust of death,' i.e. the grave (cf. Ps. xxii. 16). Buttenweiser construes the verbs as subjunctive and renders: 'For then might I lie at rest in the grave, and if Thou wouldest search for me, I should be no more.'

Thou wilt seek me, but I shall not be. 'Thou wilt seek me but wilt not find me' (Rashi). Peake makes this admirable comment: 'With matchless pathos Job brings his speech to an end, he will die; but God will not remain in His present mood; He will think on His devoted servant once more in love, filled with remorse for His fit of anger. He will long to renew the old communion. But His vain regrets will come too late, Job will be gone beyond recall. It is strange how wonderfully the poet depicts the rising of this double conception of God in Job's mind. God as he feels Him to be in the present has not driven out God as he knew Him to be in the past. This thought of God's higher and lower self is prominent in some of Job's subsequent utterances.'

8　　　　CHAPTER VIII　　　　ח

1 Then answered Bildad the Shuhite, and said:

2 How long wilt thou speak these
things,
Seeing that the words of thy
mouth are as a mighty wind?

3 Doth God pervert judgment?
Or doth the Almighty pervert
justice ?

4 If thy children sinned against Him,
He delivered them into the hand
of their transgression.

וַיַּעַן בִּלְדַּד הַשּׁוּחִי וַיֹּאמַר׃

עַד־אָן תְּמַלֶּל־אֵלֶּה

וְרוּחַ כַּבִּיר אִמְרֵי־פִיךָ׃

הַאֵל יְעַוֵּת מִשְׁפָּט

וְאִם־שַׁדַּי יְעַוֵּת־צֶדֶק׃

אִם־בָּנֶיךָ חָטְאוּ־לוֹ

וַיְשַׁלְּחֵם בְּיַד־פִּשְׁעָם׃

CHAPTER VIII

THE FIRST SPEECH OF BILDAD

BILDAD, more outspoken than Eliphaz,
but with no new argument, condemns
Job's words as *mighty wind* and maintains firmly the traditional belief in
retributive justice. God is just. The
tragic fate of Job's children was punishment for their sins. God would make
Job's habitation prosperous if he were
righteous. The teaching of former generations—the inherited beliefs of the fathers
—attests that the godless perish even as
the reed-grass withers without water.
God does not forsake the innocent. If
Job deserves joy he will receive it.

1-7　GOD IS JUST

2. *how long wilt thou speak these things.*
Or, 'these words.' ' Are not the words
of thy mouth to be reckoned as strong
provocation?' (Metsudath David).

as a mighty wind. Rashi renders as: 'many,'
but Ibn Ezra defines it as 'great' and
quotes as a parallel *brought down as one
mighty* (Isa. x. 13, where *aleph* is added to
kabbir). Buttenwieser translates: 'bois-
terous wind' (cf. *windy knowledge* and
windy words, xv. 2, xvi. 3). Job's speech
had certainly been stormy, violent as a
wind, uprooting cherished notions.

3. *doth God pervert judgment?* To
Bildad, it is utterly incredible that God
should be unrighteous. 'Will God indeed pervert justice without giving
punishment to the wicked as he deserves?
Or will He pervert righteousness without giving the recompense of reward
to the righteous? And how can you say
that He hands all into the power of the
Order of Heaven? For if this were so,
the righteous becomes as the wicked!'
(Metsudath David).

4. *if thy children sinned against Him.*
'Nothing happens in this world by chance.
God's watchful care is according to the
deed.' So observes Metsudath David,
suggesting that Job's children had
sinned with their constant feasting that
brought them to frivolity. Then they
were driven from the world in the very
place of their transgressions, for they
died in the house of feasting. In the place
of wickedness, there was the judgment.

He delivered them. The verb *shallach* is
here ellipsis for *shallach me'al panaw*, 'to
cast out of His presence' (cf. Jer. xv. 1).
It connotes 'to deliver up to death.'
Buttenwieser translates: 'He cast them
out of His presence in penalty for their
transgression.' The sentence is conditional, the apodosis using the verb in the
imperfect tense with *waw* consecutive.

5 If thou wouldest seek earnestly
  unto God,
  And make thy supplication to the
  Almighty;

6 If thou wert pure and upright;
  Surely now He would awake for
  thee,
  And make the habitation of thy
  righteousness prosperous.

7 And though thy beginning was
  small,
  Yet thy end should greatly increase.

8 For inquire, I pray thee, of the
  former generation,
  And apply thyself to that which
  their fathers have searched
  out—

5 אִם־אַתָּה תְּשַׁחֵר אֶל־אֵל
וְאֶל־שַׁדַּי תִּתְחַנָּן:

6 אִם־זַךְ וְיָשָׁר אָתָּה
כִּי־עַתָּה יָעִיר עָלֶיךָ
וְשִׁלַּם נְוַת צִדְקֶךָ:

7 וְהָיָה רֵאשִׁיתְךָ מִצְעָר
וְאַחֲרִיתְךָ יִשְׂגֶּה מְאֹד:

8 כִּי־שְׁאַל־נָא לְדֹר רִישׁוֹן
וְכוֹנֵן לְחֵקֶר אֲבוֹתָם:

 v. 8. י' במקום א'

---

5. *if thou wouldest seek earnestly unto God.* The pronoun *thou* is emphatic, in contrast to *thy children* in the preceding verse. It is possible that Bildad is speaking here in rebuke of Job's bold declaration at the end of his speech in vii. 21 where he says to God, *Thou wilt seek me, but I shall not be.* 'Thou shouldest seek Him. He does not have to seek thee,' is the retort.

6. *if thou wert pure and upright.* Bildad here speaks with mental reservations. Job had maintained his innocence and integrity. But with the open testimony of all Job's misfortunes before them, neither Bildad nor the others really believe that he is speaking the truth in his heart.

surely now He would awake for thee. Cf. *Rouse Thee, and awake to my judgment* (Ps. xxxv. 23). God would bestir Himself on thy behalf with His unfailing mercies.

the habitation of thy righteousness. Cf. *The habitation of the righteous* (Prov. iii. 33), *habitation of righteousness* (Jer. xxxi. 23). Ibn Ezra holds that the phrase is figurative of 'soul': Job's soul would then be at peace and reconciled with God. Bildad, however, is thinking of a more material retribution for piety.

Tsidkecha is a descriptive genitive with the force, 'and would make thy house prosper again in proof of thy righteousness' (Buttenweiser).

7. *though thy beginning was small.* In view of the later statement, *So the Lord blessed the latter end of Job more than his beginning* (xlii. 12), the verse seems an unconscious and unintended prophecy on the part of Bildad. Only a happy ending would accord completely with Bildad's belief in material retribution.

8-10 THE EXPERIENCE OF FORMER
GENERATIONS

8. *for inquire . . . of the former generation.* Rashi cites, *For ask now of the days past* (Deut. iv. 32). Bildad appeals to historic experience. Or it may be that he calls on the authority of the wisdom of the ancients which he considers superior.

that which their fathers have searched out. 'By referring to a former age, and then to the fathers of that age or generation, Bildad intimates that his truth was recognized through all antiquity backwards till history loses itself in the beginnings of time' (Davidson).

9 For we are but of yesterday, and
  know nothing,
  Because our days upon earth are
  a shadow—

10 Shall not they teach thee, and tell
   thee,
   And utter words out of their
   heart?

11 Can the rush shoot up without
   mire?
   Can the reed-grass grow without
   water?

12 Whilst it is yet in its greenness,
   and not cut down,
   It withereth before any other
   herb.

13 So are the paths of all that forget
   God;
   And the hope of the godless man
   shall perish;

כִּי־תְמוֹל אֲנַחְנוּ וְלֹא נֵדָע

כִּי צֵל יָמֵינוּ עֲלֵי־אָרֶץ׃

הֲלֹא־הֵם יוֹרוּךָ יֹאמְרוּ לָךְ

וּמִלִּבָּם יוֹצִאוּ מִלִּים׃

הֲיִגְאֶה־גֹּמֶא בְּלֹא בִצָּה

יִשְׂגֶּה־אָחוּ בְלִי־מָיִם׃

עֹדֶנּוּ בְאִבּוֹ לֹא יִקָּטֵף

וְלִפְנֵי כָל־חָצִיר יִיבָשׁ׃

כֵּן אָרְחוֹת כָּל־שֹׁכְחֵי אֵל

וְתִקְוַת חָנֵף תֹּאבֵד׃

9. *for we are but of yesterday.* This statement is made parenthetically. There is half ironic modesty here. The ancients are commonly but illogically supposed to be wiser than their children who, as Bildad himself claims, inherit and can extend their experiences (Lofthouse). On the brevity of life, a constant theme of Scriptural writers, cf. xiv. 2; Ps. cii. 12, cxliv. 4; Eccles. vi. 12, viii. 13.

10. *shall not they teach thee.* The pronoun is emphatic and refers back to the wisdom *which their fathers have searched out.*

and utter words out of their heart. i.e. words of authority which came out of their hearts, but were scrutinized by the intellect and had stood the test of the ages. The contrast is to what Bildad conceives to be the hasty, ill-considered and tempestuous words of Job (cf. verse 2).

11-22   THE GODLESS PERISH

11. *the rush.* Hebrew *gomē* (cf. Exod. ii. 3; Isa. xviii. 2, xxxv. 7) is the papyrus, a reed with a stem ten feet or more in height, once common in Egypt and still found in the Jordan Valley. It was anciently used as writing material. Bildad means to say that just as the papyrus cannot grow unless there is moisture in the soil, so man cannot prosper who renounces God. Peake observes that the Egyptian imagery suggests that Bildad regarded the Egyptians as possessors of the most ancient wisdom. It also affords evidence, he claims, of the poet's acquaintance with Egypt.

the reed-grass. Hebrew *achu* is an Egyptian word and occurs again in Gen. xli. 2, 18 and perhaps in Hosea xiii. 15.

12. *it withereth before any other herb.* No one has to injure or cut its roots. The mere absence of moisture will quickly bring it to ruin of itself, although it be still in the full vigour of its greenness.

13. *so are the paths of all that forget God.* Paths has here the meaning of 'fate.' The wicked may grow like the grass (Ps. xxxvii. 2), but it is only for a moment. When God withdraws His favour, he quickly withers.

the hope of the godless man. i.e. 'his end'; finally the godless man shall perish.

14 Whose confidence is gossamer,
And whose trust is a spider's
web.

אֲשֶׁר־יָקוֹט כִּסְלוֹ 14
וּבֵית עַכָּבִישׁ מִבְטַחוֹ׃

15 He shall lean upon his house, but
it shall not stand;
He shall hold fast thereby, but it
shall not endure.

יִשָּׁעֵן עַל־בֵּיתוֹ וְלֹא יַעֲמֹד 15
יַחֲזִיק בּוֹ וְלֹא יָקוּם׃

16 He is green before the sun,
And his shoots go forth over his
garden.

רָטֹב הוּא לִפְנֵי־שָׁמֶשׁ 16
וְעַל־גַּנָּתוֹ יֹנַקְתּוֹ תֵצֵא׃

17 His roots are wrapped about the
heap,
He beholdeth the place of stones.

עַל־גַּל שָׁרָשָׁיו יְסֻבָּכוּ 17
בֵּית אֲבָנִים יֶחֱזֶה׃

18 If he be destroyed from his place,
Then it shall deny him: ' I have
not seen thee.'

אִם־יְבַלְּעֶנּוּ מִמְּקֹמוֹ 18
וְכִחֶשׁ בּוֹ לֹא רְאִיתִיךָ׃

19 Behold, this is the joy of his way,
And out of the earth shall others
spring.

הֶן־הוּא מְשׂוֹשׂ דַּרְכּוֹ 19
וּמֵעָפָר אַחֵר יִצְמָחוּ׃

14. *whose confidence is gossamer*. The Hebrew *yakot* is derived from *kot* and signifies something fragile. It is not a verb, but, on the authority of Saadia, a substantive. Their confidence rests on gossamer, and their estate is no stronger than a spider's web.

15. *he shall lean upon his house*. The godless will find his house as flimsy as a spider's house, unsafe to lean against (cf. xxvii. 18). The verse is a composite relative clause with the meaning: 'Which will not stand if one leaneth against it' (Buttenweiser).

16. *he is green before the sun*. Bildad introduces a new simile: the comparison with a plant, thriving and firmly rooted, but destroyed and forgotten by the very soil on which it had flourished.

17. *the heap*. viz. of stones.

he beholdeth the place of stones. The clause has troubled the commentators. The verb *chazah*, 'to behold,' is taken by some as a by-form of *chazaz*, 'to pierce.' Then the meaning will be: 'Though his roots wind round the rocks (and) penetrate the stones, yet when he is wiped out from his place, it will deny him (saying), "I have never seen thee".' Another suggestion is that of Szold, that *chazah* is a poetical equivalent of *achaz*, 'to seize hold of,' and this verb and the parallel *sabach*, *wrapped about*, were suggested by the phrase *ne'echaz ba-sebach*, *caught in the thicket* (Gen. xxii. 13). The line describes the firm hold that the plant has of the soil.

19. *this is the joy of his way*. Bildad speaks sardonically. This is all the joy the godless man has: the momentary *green before the sun*. Suddenly he is destroyed. He vanishes and is utterly forgotten.

out of the earth. lit. 'out of the dust,' sometimes used poetically for *earth* (cf. xxviii. 2, xxx. 6). Others take his place, unmindful that he had been there before them.

20 Behold, God will not cast away
   an innocent man,
   Neither will He uphold the evil-
   doers;

21 Till He fill thy mouth with laughter,
   And thy lips with shouting.

22 They that hate thee shall be
   clothed with shame;
   And the tent of the wicked shall
   be no more.

9   CHAPTER IX

1 Then Job answered and said:

2 Of a truth I know that it is so;
  And how can man be just with
  God?

הֶן־אֵל לֹא יִמְאַס־תָּם
וְלֹא־יַחֲזִיק בְּיַד־מְרֵעִים׃

עַד־יְמַלֶּה שְׂחוֹק פִּיךָ
וּשְׂפָתֶיךָ תְרוּעָה׃

שֹׂנְאֶיךָ יִלְבְּשׁוּ־בֹשֶׁת
וְאֹהֶל רְשָׁעִים אֵינֶנּוּ׃

ט

וַיַּעַן אִיּוֹב וַיֹּאמַר׃
אָמְנָם יָדַעְתִּי כִי־כֵן
וּמַה־יִּצְדַּק אֱנוֹשׁ עִם־אֵל׃

'v. 21. ה' במקום א

---

20. *God will not cast away an innocent man.* God does not forsake the truly pious. For *tam, innocent*, see on i. 1.

21. *till He fill thy mouth with laughter.* i.e. He will yet fill thy mouth with laughter, give Thee happiness (cf. Ps. cxxvi. 2).

22. *they that hate thee,* etc. Some see in this verse an intended sinister suggestion. But, possibly, Bildad wishes to put himself and his friends right with Job, just as he has tried to put Job right with God. By referring to Job's haters, he intimates that he and his friends are none of them. He lets Job know that he regards him as at heart one who belongs to quite a different class (Davidson).

CHAPTERS IX-X

IRONICALLY conceding Bildad's position that God doth not pervert justice, Job reverts to Eliphaz's claim and admits that man cannot be just in the sight of God. All nature attests to the immensity of God's power. Job perceives the vast mystery that enshrouds the omnipotence of God and the inherent fallacy that pursues the finite mind of man, seeking to encompass the Infinite God. In His unlimited might, God does not seem restrained by man's moral standards. Job, however innocent he feels himself to be, cannot hope successfully to plead before Him. God destroys the innocent and the wicked alike and gives the earth into the hand of the wicked. After this violent outburst (ix. 22-24), in a more subdued mood, Job laments the swift flight of his wretched life. He deplores the hopelessness of his attempt, whether he be innocent or guilty, to vindicate the justice of his cause before God, Whose terror makes him afraid. Weary of life, he asks in bitterness what inexplicable purpose can God have in afflicting him since he is the work of God's hands, the creature of His favour and providence. Why does God hunt him as men set a trap for a lion in the jungle? If this be His ultimate purpose for man, why has God given him life? Why does God not relent, seeing how few are his days, so that he may have some small comfort before he goes to the land of the shadow of death whence he will not return?

CHAPTER IX

1-13 JOB'S HELPLESSNESS BEFORE GOD'S INFINITE MIGHT

2. *how can man be just with God?* Job ironically replies that Bildad's question

3 If one should desire to contend
   with Him,
   He could not answer Him one of a
   thousand.

4 He is wise in heart, and mighty in
   strength;
   Who hath hardened himself against
   Him, and prospered?

5 Who removeth the mountains, and
   they know it not,
   When He overturneth them in His
   anger.

6 Who shaketh the earth out of her
   place,
   And the pillars thereof tremble.

‏אִם־יַחְפֹּץ לָרִב עִמּוֹ‎ 3
‏לֹא־יַעֲנֶנּוּ אַחַת מִנִּי־אָלֶף:‎

‏חֲכַם לֵבָב וְאַמִּיץ כֹּחַ‎ 4
‏מִי־הִקְשָׁה אֵלָיו וַיִּשְׁלָם:‎

‏הַמַּעְתִּיק הָרִים וְלֹא יָדָעוּ‎ 5
‏אֲשֶׁר הֲפָכָם בְּאַפּוֹ:‎

‏הַמַּרְגִּיז אֶרֶץ מִמְּקוֹמָהּ‎ 6
‏וְעַמּוּדֶיהָ יִתְפַלָּצוּן:‎

(viii. 3) is valid. God never acts unjustly. He refers back to Eliphaz's
claim (iv. 17) with slightly different
expression, that mortal man cannot be
just in the sight of God. *Just* is employed
here, as often in Scripture, to denote the
innocent party in a suit. Job means to
say, 'How can man ever be in the right in
a contest with God?'

3. *he could not answer Him one of a
thousand.* Man is in a hopeless position
with God as his Opponent. In His
wisdom He could pose a thousand questions beyond his power to answer. 'If
the righteous desired to dispute with the
Omnipresent concerning the outrage of
withholding His reward, he could not
even give Him one answer out of His
thousand questions' (Metsudath David).

4. *He is wise in heart, and mighty in
strength.* How hopeless, then, for man to
match his puny intellect or strength
against the overwhelming wisdom and
might of the Supreme God!

*who hath hardened himself against Him,
and prospered?* Rashi cites the example
of Pharaoh. 'Who hath hardened his
heart and walked unimpaired? Pharaoh
hardened his heart and was destroyed,
and so it is with all who act similarly.'
No one can defy God and succeed.

5. *Who removeth the mountains.* Verses
5-10 describe God's omnipotence in

Nature. This and the next verse refer to
earthquakes.

they know it not. On the assumption
that *they* relates to *the mountains*,
modern interpreters have commented on the
strangeness of the statement that the
mountains do not know that God over-
turns them, and following the Syriac
Version (Peshitta), they read 'He knows'
for *they know.* But the LXX supports
M.T. by rendering: 'Who wears out the
mountains, and (men) know it not.'
Similarly Metsudath David explains: 'Is
it not God Who removes the mountains
from their place, and the multitude of
men do not know Who it is that over-
turns them in His anger, because the
(Divine) cause of their overthrow is
hidden from all.'

6. *Who shaketh the earth out of her place.*
A poetical description of an earthquake. The earth was pictured by the
ancients as resting on massive pillars
erected in the sea. The classical location
of these 'pillars of Hercules' was between
Africa and Eurasis or the Straits of Gib-
raltar. References to these pillars are
found in xxxviii. 6; 1 Sam. ii. 8; Ps.
lxxv. 4, civ. 5; Prov. viii. 29. Buttenweiser argues that (He) *hangeth the earth
over nothing* (xxvi. 7) is proof that the
writer of Job had attained a more
advanced cosmological view. His use of
the popular expression *the pillars . . .
tremble* is for poetical effect.

7 Who commandeth the sun, and it
　　riseth not;
　　And sealeth up the stars.

8 Who alone stretcheth out the
　　heavens,
　　And treadeth upon the waves of
　　the sea.

9 Who maketh the Bear, Orion, and
　　the Pleiades,
　　And the chambers of the south.

10 Who doeth great things past
　　finding out;
　　Yea, marvellous things without
　　number.

הָאֹמֵר לַחֶרֶס וְלֹא יִזְרָח
וּבְעַד כּוֹכָבִים יַחְתֹּם׃
נֹטֶה שָׁמַיִם לְבַדּוֹ
וְדוֹרֵךְ עַל־בָּמֳתֵי־יָם׃
עֹשֶׂה עָשׁ כְּסִיל
וְכִימָה וְחַדְרֵי תֵמָן׃
עֹשֶׂה גְדֹלוֹת עַד־אֵין חֵקֶר
וְנִפְלָאוֹת עַד־אֵין מִסְפָּר׃

7. *Who commandeth the sun.* The allusion appears to be not only to astronomical phenomena, such as eclipses, but also to atmospheric disturbances such as sudden storms. The stars apparently had a special abode where they could be 'sealed.' They are brought forth at night to shine in the sky (cf. Isa. xl. 26).

8. *Who alone stretcheth out the heavens.* 'The angels were created on the second day lest you say that Michael stretched (the world) in the South and Gabriel in the North' (Midrash cited by Rashi). This is a comment on *alone*.

treadeth upon the waves. The waters of the ocean were believed to be higher than the earth, and their pride had to be humbled so that they would not overflow and cover the earth. Driver believes the reference to be to a tempest, when the sea swells into huge billows, and God was supposed to walk on their crest (cf. xxxvi. 30). Buttenweiser poetically translates: 'Who . . . hath dominion over the billows of the sea.'

9. With this verse, cf. Amos v. 8.

the Bear. Hebrew '*ash*, but in xxxviii. 32 it is '*ayish*'; a group of seven stars. In North Abyssinian folk-lore, the seven stars of Ursa Major are called the 'seven brothers.'

Orion. Hebrew *kesil*, lit. 'fool.' In xxxviii. 31 occurs the phrase *loose the bands of Orion*, which suggests a mythological allusion to a giant bound in the sky, probably in connection with some titanic revolt against God.

the Pleiades. Hebrew *kimah*, lit. 'an accumulation, heap.' Ibn Ezra identifies *kesil* and *kimah* (Orion and the Pleiades) as two great stars, the former at the left extremity of the sphere of the Zodiac as it inclines, the latter at the southern extremity, while *ash* (the Bear) is at the northern limit of the great sphere of the Zodiac.

the chambers of the south. i.e. the chambers of the southern sky from which the warm south wind comes that brings heat and storms (cf. xxxvii. 9) (Metsudath David). In later astrological and apocalyptic literature *the chambers of the south* are identified with the constellation 'Altar,' near the southern horizon, where Hades was believed to be located, and where the souls of the righteous were kept. Ibn Ezra believed *the chambers of the south* to be stars on the southern limit of the great sphere of the Zodiac. Driver agreed with this view and remarked, 'Probably constellations which, as the poet knew, appeared above the horizon as a traveller journeyed south'; or (Schiaperelli, *Astronomy in the Old Testament*, p. 66) which were actually above the horizon, in the latitude of Palestine, in the age in which the Book was written.

10. *Who doeth great things past finding out.* God's omnipotence in Nature is

11 Lo, He goeth by me, and I see
   Him not;
   He passeth on also, but I perceive
   Him not.

11 הֵן יַעֲבֹר עָלַי וְלֹא אֶרְאֶה
    וְיַחֲלֹף וְלֹא־אָבִין לוֹ׃

12 Behold, He snatcheth away, who
   can hinder Him?
   Who will say unto Him: 'What
   doest Thou?'

12 הֵן יַחְתֹּף מִי יְשִׁיבֶנּוּ
    מִי־יֹאמַר אֵלָיו מַה־תַּעֲשֶׂה׃

13 God will not withdraw His anger;
   The helpers of Rahab did stoop
   under Him.

13 אֱלוֹהַּ לֹא־יָשִׁיב אַפּוֹ
    תַּחְתָּו שָׁחֲחוּ עֹזְרֵי רָהַב׃

14 How much less shall I answer
   Him,
   And choose out my arguments
   with Him?

14 אַף כִּי־אָנֹכִי אֶעֱנֶנּוּ
    אֶבְחֲרָה דְבָרַי עִמּוֹ׃

v. 13. תחתיו ק׳

beyond all human comprehension. The verse is almost a verbatim repetition of v. 9 where Eliphaz argues that he would surrender himself unreservedly to Almighty God Whose power is evinced not only in the world of Nature, but likewise in the moral world. Job, on the other hand, speaks only of Divine omnipotence before which man is helpless.

11. *lo, He goeth by me, and I see Him not.* Buttenweiser construes *hen* (*lo*) as a conditional particle, translating: 'If He passed by me, I should not perceive Him. If He swept past, I should not be aware of Him.' From the description of God's infinite power in Nature described in verses 5-10, Job now turns to describe His invisible and often destructive might among men. It is His elusive, unseen working that fills him with dread.

12. *He snatcheth away, who can hinder Him?* The noun from the root *chataph*, *snatcheth away*, occurs in *lieth in wait as a robber* (Prov. xxiii. 28) which is cited by Rashi and Ibn Ezra. They define the verb as 'He smites suddenly.' *Hinder Him* is literally 'turn Him back' (cf. xi. 10, xxiii. 13).

who will say unto Him: 'What doest Thou?' 'Who will say unto Him: "Wherefore hast

Thou acted like this?"' (Metsudath David).

13. *God will not withdraw His anger.* 'Because of the fear (or, righteousness, according to another reading) of man' (Rashi).

the helpers of Rahab did stoop under Him. Rahab is the name in Hebrew folk-lore (corresponding to Tiamat in Babylonian mythology, see on vii. 12) for the ocean-monster which had to be overcome by God before chaos gave place to an ordered universe (cf. xxvi. 12; Isa. li. 9). *The helpers of Rahab* alludes to those who were allied to the monster in the contest; but they all succumbed before God's invincible might.

14-35   JOB DENIES DIVINE JUSTICE

14. *how much less shall I answer Him.* The pronoun is emphatic. The force of *aph* is that of *kol shechen*, 'so much the more' (Rashi).

my arguments. lit. 'my words.' How could Job hope to engage in debate with Him! Before the majesty and destructive fury of His might, how utterly futile to think that he could find the fit word to argue and defend himself!

41

15 Whom, though I were righteous,
    yet would I not answer;
    I would make supplication to
    Him that contendeth with me.

אֲשֶׁר אִם־צָדַקְתִּי לֹא אֶעֱנֶה
לִמְשֹׁפְטִי אֶתְחַנָּן׃

16 If I had called, and He had an-
    swered me;
    Yet would I not believe that He
    would hearken unto my voice—

אִם־קָרָאתִי וַיַּעֲנֵנִי
לֹא־אַאֲמִין כִּי־יַאֲזִין קוֹלִי׃

17 He that would break me with a
    tempest,
    And multiply my wounds with-
    out cause;

אֲשֶׁר־בִּשְׂעָרָה יְשׁוּפֵנִי
וְהִרְבָּה פְצָעַי חִנָּם׃

18 That would not suffer me to take
    my breath,
    But fill me with bitterness.

לֹא־יִתְּנֵנִי הָשֵׁב רוּחִי
כִּי יַשְׂבִּעַנִי מַמְּרֹרִים׃

19 If it be a matter of strength, lo,
    He is mighty!
    And if of justice, who will appoint
    me a time?

אִם־לְכֹחַ אַמִּיץ הִנֵּה
וְאִם־לְמִשְׁפָּט מִי יוֹעִידֵנִי׃

20 Though I be righteous, mine own
    mouth shall condemn me;
    Though I be innocent, He shall
    prove me perverse.

אִם־אֶצְדָּק פִּי יַרְשִׁיעֵנִי
תָּם אָנִי וַיַּעְקְשֵׁנִי׃

---

15. *righteous.* In the sense of 'innocent.'

would I not answer. I would be afraid to lift up my voice before Him (Rashi). Job affirms that even though his cause were just, he could not answer, but would be compelled to implore the mercy of his Opponent-at-law.

16. *if I had called, and He had answered me.* If Job had cited God to appear in judgment as in a court of law, he still could not believe that He had given ear to his pleadings. The verbs are apparently borrowed from legal terminology.

17. *He that would break me with a tempest.* Here and in verse 18, Job describes what God would do to him in the event that He appeared in summons to Job's citation. The pessimistic prospects of such a legal argument with the Almighty are provoked by the terrible afflictions he now endures. The verb *break* is found in Gen. iii. 15, *bruise thy head.*

18. *that would not suffer me to take my breath.* God would give him no pause to breathe, so constant would be his anguish (cf. Lam. iii. 15 for the phrase *fill . . . with bitterness*).

19. *if it be a matter of strength.* Better: 'If it is a question of power of the mighty, behold (Him)! If it is a question of right, who would summon me?' Job repeats the plea of verse 14 that it is futile to attempt to challenge God whether in a contest of strength or a suit of law. In the last clause, he asks who would dare to summon Him and adjudicate between him and God (cf. Jer. xlix. 19).

20. *though I be righteous, mine own mouth shall condemn me.* God's vast might, were He suddenly to appear, would be so terrifying that Job, though innocent, in his confusion would find his own mouth unable to establish his innocence.

He shall prove me perverse. lit. 'twisted, crooked,' here in the moral sense of 'guilty.' 'Lo, though I am righteous, my own mouth would condemn me, because my words would be shut out of fear, and my mouth would declare me crooked' (Rashi).

21 I am innocent—I regard not
   myself,
   I despise my life.

22 It is all one—therefore I say:
   He destroyeth the innocent and
   the wicked.

23 If the scourge slay suddenly,
   He will mock at the calamity of
   the guiltless.

24 The earth is given into the hand
   of the wicked;
   He covereth the faces of the
   judges thereof;
   If it be not He, who then is it?

25 Now my days are swifter than a
   runner;
   They flee away, they see no good.

כא תָּם אָנִי לֹא־אֵדַע נַפְשִׁי
   אֶמְאַס חַיָּי׃
כב אַחַת הִיא עַל־כֵּן אָמַרְתִּי
   תָּם וְרָשָׁע הוּא מְכַלֶּה׃
כג אִם־שׁוֹט יָמִית פִּתְאֹם
   לְמַסַּת נְקִיִּם יִלְעָג׃
כד אֶרֶץ ׀ נִתְּנָה בְיַד־רָשָׁע
   פְּנֵי־שֹׁפְטֶיהָ יְכַסֶּה
   אִם־לֹא אֵפוֹ מִי־הוּא׃
כה וְיָמַי קַלּוּ מִנִּי־רָץ
   בָּרְחוּ לֹא־רָאוּ טוֹבָה׃

v. 22. פתח באתנח

21. *I am innocent—I regard not myself, I despise my life.* We can hardly fail to feel the passionate eloquence of these flaming words. Though fully aware of his utter helplessness before the omnipotence of God, Job, in reckless defiance of the consequences which the friends warn will follow such bold talk, stoutly maintains his innocence. 'Let it cost me my life,' he says in effect, 'I do not care for it.' To the merit of his piety, Job now adds the higher virtue of courage and complete intellectual honesty.

22. *it is all one.* 'It is all one and the same,' cries Job passionately, 'God shows no moral discrimination and annihilates the innocent and the wicked alike.' 'Here Job explicitly denies that there is a moral order of the universe' (Peake), and he defiantly rejects Bildad's faith in Divine justice as asserted in viii. 20.

23. *if the scourge slay suddenly.* By *scourge* is meant a calamity like an epidemic, or famine or war which does not discriminate in the selection of its victims, sparing the good. Rashi, piously reluctant to ascribe such a charge to God, comments that 'it is an expression

of Satan.' But Job explicitly holds God, not the Satan, answerable.

24. *the earth is given into the hand of the wicked.* A sweeping indictment that injustice rules universally; and that God, blinding the faces of the judges so that they cannot see right from wrong, is directly responsible. 'In this passage Job's spirit reaches the lowest abyss of its alienation from God. From this time onward his mind is calmer and the moral idea of God begins to reassert its place in his thoughts. Here God appears to him as a mere omnipotent power, with a bias, if He have one, to evil and cruelty, and he speaks of Him distantly as *He* (Davidson).

if it be not He. Rashi says of the question approvingly, 'A true word is this statement; who is it that destroys the innocent?'

who then. Will make me a liar? i.e. prove me to be so (cf. xxiv. 25) (Ibn Ezra).

25. *now my days are swifter than a runner.* Having fearlessly expressed his opinion of the absence of moral order in the

43

26 They are passed away as the
    swift ships;
    As the vulture that swoopeth on
    the prey.

27 If I say: 'I will forget my com-
    plaint,
    I will put off my sad counten-
    ance, and be of good cheer,'

28 I am afraid of all my pains,
    I know that Thou wilt not hold
    me guiltless.

29 I shall be condemned;
    Why then do I labour in vain?

30 If I wash myself with snow water,
    And make my hands never so
    clean;

חָלְפוּ עִם־אֳנִיּוֹת אֵבֶה
כְּנֶשֶׁר יָטוּשׂ עֲלֵי־אֹכֶל׃
אִם־אָמְרִי אֶשְׁכְּחָה שִׂיחִי
אֶעֶזְבָה פָנַי וְאַבְלִיגָה׃
יָגֹרְתִּי כָל־עַצְּבֹתָי
יָדַעְתִּי כִּי־לֹא תְנַקֵּנִי׃
אָנֹכִי אֶרְשָׁע
לָמָּה־זֶּה הֶבֶל אִיגָע׃
אִם־הִתְרָחַצְתִּי בְמוֹ־שָׁלֶג
וַהֲזִכּוֹתִי בְּבֹר כַּפָּי׃

v. 30. ‏במ״י ק׳‎   v. 30. ‏בנ״א בבור‎

world, he turns again to his own wretched
plight. His life is ebbing faster than the
speed of a swift messenger.

no good. i.e. no good fortune or happiness
is experienced in the present, nor is there
any such prospect in his remaining days
until death makes an end of him.

26. *as the swift ships.* 'Skiffs of papyrus
were anciently a common sight upon the
Nile. Something much lighter than
what we should call a "ship" is intended'
(Driver). Rashi and Metsudath David
think *ebeh* the name of a certain rushing
(overflowing) river. 'Some say,' remarks
Ibn Ezra, 'that *ebeh* is a place name or
the name of a rushing river and others
say that it is fruit, as in *the fruit* (inbeh)
thereof much (Dan. iv. 9); but the first is
correct.'

as the vulture that swoopeth. The swift-
ness of the vulture's flight is often mentioned in the Bible (cf. Deut. xxviii. 49;
2 Sam. i. 23; Lam. iv. 19). Note the
wealth of poetic imagery Job employs
to describe life's brevity: a runner, a
skiff of reed, an eagle swooping on its
prey.

27. *and be of good cheer.* The root-

meaning is 'to gleam, smile.' Here it
signifies more than merely to flash a smile,
but, as the mediæval Jewish commentators
suggest, 'to take courage.'

28. *I am afraid of all my pains.* The
happier mood of the preceding verse was
only fleeting. It is quickly followed by
awareness of his wretched and painful
state, and his condemnation by God.
Nevertheless it has an aftermath in the
more intimate converse with God suggested subtly by the use of the second, as
against the third, person: Thou *wilt not
hold me guiltless.*

29. *I shall be condemned.* This meaning
is clearer if we render: 'I needs must
stand condemned; why make vain
efforts?' (Buttenweiser). God has determined to count me as guilty whether I am
really innocent. Why strive in vain to
clear myself?

30. *if I wash myself with snow water.*
This rendering follows the *kerë*; the
R.V. margin, 'with snow,' agrees with
the *kethib.*

make my hands never so clean. More
literally and forcibly: 'cleanse my hands

31 Yet wilt Thou plunge me in the
    ditch,
    And mine own clothes shall abhor
    me.

32 For He is not a man, as I am, that
    I should answer Him,
    That we should come together
    in judgment.

33 There is no arbiter betwixt us,
    That might lay his hand upon us
    both.

34 Let Him take His rod away from
    me,
    And let not His terror make me
    afraid;

35 Then would I speak, and not fear
    Him;
    For I am not so with myself.

31 אָז בַּשַּׁחַת תִּטְבְּלֵנִי
וְתִעֲבוּנִי שַׂלְמוֹתָי:

32 כִּי־לֹא־אִישׁ כָּמֹנִי אֶעֱנֶנּוּ
נָבוֹא יַחְדָּו בַּמִּשְׁפָּט:

33 לֹא יֵשׁ־בֵּינֵינוּ מוֹכִיחַ
יָשֵׁת יָדוֹ עַל־שְׁנֵינוּ:

34 יָסֵר מֵעָלַי שִׁבְטוֹ
וְאֵמָתוֹ אַל־תְּבַעֲתַנִּי:

35 אֲדַבְּרָה וְלֹא אִירָאֶנּוּ
כִּי־לֹא־כֵן אָנֹכִי עִמָּדִי:

v. 34. ט׳ רבתי.   v. 34. פתח בס'ף

with lye,' *bor* being regarded as the
equivalent of *borith* in Jer. ii. 22, translated
soap. It was in fact a mixture of plant-
ash containing alkali and water.

31. *mine own clothes shall abhor me.* Rejecting a slight emendation which would
read 'my friends' instead of *mine own
clothes*, Peake remarks: 'But the text gives
a striking metaphor. Though Job washes
himself with snow and cleanses his hands
with alkali, God plunges him in the ditch,
and thus makes him so foul that his
clothes loathe to cover him.' Job does
not admit that God is justified in regarding him as vile. On the contrary, he
stoutly defends his innocence, and
openly accuses God of making him seem
guilty and a loathsome spectacle of
moral foulness.

32. *in judgment.* Rashi defines three
ways in which the word *mishpat*, 'judgment,' is used in Scripture, viz. verbal
argument, judicial decision, and execu-
tion of chastisement or exaction of guilt.
Here the meaning that fits the context
seems to be 'that we could go together to
the tribunal.' Rashi, however, is of the
opinion that not the place is intended so
much as the thought that 'we could come
together *in words of argument of justice*.'

Job's complaint is that he and God
cannot meet as plaintiff and defendant in
an equitable court of law.

33. *there is no arbiter betwixt us.* The
duty of the arbiter would be to lay his
hand upon both parties to the dispute
and make them submit to his decision.
But that is impossible when one of them
is God.

34. *let Him take His rod away from me.*
Cf. xiii. 21, and Elihu refers to this plea
in xxxiii. 7. *Rod* is figurative for the
afflictions (cf. Lam. iii. 1) which were
unquestionably accepted as evidence of
Job's guilt. Were these removed from
him, he would have an opportunity of
vindicating himself.

35. *for I am not so with myself.* The
clause is obscure. Ibn Ezra interprets:
'In my own soul, I am not as you
think,' i.e. in my own conscience. According to Szold the meaning is, 'but not so
do I (now think) with myself,' to contend
with One stronger than myself. Buttenweiser construes *ken* as a verbal adjective
from the root *kun* which, combined with
the negative *lo* and *immadi*, denotes
'mental confusion.' He renders: '(as it
is) my mind is thrown into confusion,'
literally 'I am not right with myself.'

10   CHAPTER X   י

1 My soul is weary of my life;
 I will give free course to my complaint;
 I will speak in the bitterness of my soul.

2 I will say unto God: Do not condemn me;
 Make me know wherefore Thou contendest with me.

3 Is it good unto Thee that Thou shouldest oppress,
 That Thou shouldest despise the work of Thy hands,
 And shine upon the counsel of the wicked?

4 Hast Thou eyes of flesh,
 Or seest Thou as man seeth?

5 Are Thy days as the days of man,
 Or Thy years as a man's days,

נָקְטָה נַפְשִׁי בְּחַיָּי
אֶעֶזְבָה עָלַי שִׂיחִי
אֲדַבְּרָה בְּמַר נַפְשִׁי:
אֹמַר אֶל־אֱלוֹהַּ אַל־תַּרְשִׁיעֵנִי
הוֹדִיעֵנִי עַל מַה־תְּרִיבֵנִי:
הֲטוֹב לְךָ ׀ כִּי־תַעֲשֹׁק
כִּי־תִמְאַס יְגִיעַ כַּפֶּיךָ
וְעַל־עֲצַת רְשָׁעִים הוֹפָעְתָּ:
הַעֵינֵי בָשָׂר לָךְ
אִם־כִּרְאוֹת אֱנוֹשׁ תִּרְאֶה:
הֲכִימֵי אֱנוֹשׁ יָמֶיךָ
אִם־שְׁנוֹתֶיךָ כִּימֵי גָבֶר:

CHAPTER X

1-7 WHAT SECRET PURPOSE CAN GOD HAVE IN AFFLICTING HIM?

1. *my soul is weary of my life.* Cf. vii. 11 where the thought is similar. We may well imagine Job, horribly stricken as he was, finding life increasingly burdensome and bitter.

2. *do not condemn me.* The evils that had come upon him were considered as incontrovertible proof of his inner wickedness. 'Let me know why Thou contendest with me to judge me according to the judgment of the wicked. What is my transgression?' (Metsudath David).

3. Verses 3-7 describe Job seeking to fathom the mysterious conceivable cause to account for God's cruel treatment of him.

is it good. The commentators wonder about the intention of this phrase. It might mean, 'is it a pleasure?' or (cf. Lam. iii. 27) 'is it an advantage?' The Jewish commentators seem to give the

question the meaning, 'is it fair, right or just?' Thus Rashi: 'Is it fair that Thou shouldest oppress and steal from the righteous his righteousness, but upon the counsel of the wicked and their vexations that Thou shouldest shine Thy splendour to show them a smiling countenance?'

the work of Thy hands. Although all human beings, whether good or bad, were the work of God's hands, the righteous were such in a special degree.

4. *or seest Thou as man seeth?* The poignant probing question that Job directs to God recalls 1 Sam. xvi. 7 where He said to Samuel, *For it is not as man seeth: for man looketh on the outward appearance, but the LORD looketh on the heart.* Does God afflict Job because He can see no deeper into the human heart than man?

5. *are Thy days as the days of man.* 'Are Thy days as the days of man to attack and pursue him?' (Rashi). Metsudath

6 That Thou inquirest after mine
  iniquity,
  And searchest after my sin,

7 Although Thou knowest that I
  shall not be condemned;
  And there is none that can deliver
  out of Thy hand?

8 Thy hands have framed me and
  fashioned me
  Together round about; yet Thou
  dost destroy me!

9 Remember, I beseech Thee, that
  Thou hast fashioned me as clay;
  And wilt Thou bring me into dust
  again?

10 Hast Thou not poured me out as
  milk,
  And curdled me like cheese?

11 Thou hast clothed me with skin
  and flesh,
  And knit me together with bones
  and sinews.

כִּי־תְבַקֵּשׁ לַעֲוֹנִי 6
וּלְחַטָּאתִי תִדְרוֹשׁ׃

עַל־דַּעְתְּךָ כִּי־לֹא אֶרְשָׁע 7
וְאֵין מִיָּדְךָ מַצִּיל׃

יָדֶיךָ עִצְּבוּנִי וַיַּעֲשׂוּנִי 8
יַחַד סָבִיב וַתְּבַלְּעֵנִי׃

זְכָר־נָא כִּי־כַחֹמֶר עֲשִׂיתָנִי 9
וְאֶל־עָפָר תְּשִׁיבֵנִי׃

הֲלֹא כֶחָלָב תַּתִּיכֵנִי 10
וְכַגְּבִנָּה תַּקְפִּיאֵנִי׃

עוֹר וּבָשָׂר תַּלְבִּישֵׁנִי 11
וּבַעֲצָמוֹת וְגִידִים תְּשֹׂכְכֵנִי׃

David suggests that the question implies:
'Are God's days as fleeting as man's
that He must hasten to exact punishment
in this world? Does God not live for
ever and am I not in His hands for all
time?'

6. inquirest after mine iniquity. Seeking
to uncover my guilt by inflicting suffering
relentlessly upon me.

**7. Thou knowest that I shall not be con-
demned.** Job insists that God alone must
know that he is innocent.

there is none that can deliver. Moreover,
'were I wicked,' says Job, 'I could not
escape from Thy power for Thou art
the Creator' (Ibn Ezra).

8-12 GOD'S WONDROUS CARE IN THE PAST

8. Thy hands have framed me. lit.
'shaped me.' God moulded the embryo
which grew into the child he had been
born (cf. Ps. cxxxix. 15).

yet Thou dost destroy me. The afflictions
sent by God were destroying His work.

Rashi, by commenting 'they are the
worms,' makes the phrase refer to the
fate of the body in the grave.

9. Thou hast fashioned me as clay. The
comparison of God to the potter and man
as clay has parallels in Scripture (cf. Isa.
xlv. 9; especially Jer. xviii. 4ff.).

wilt Thou bring me into dust again?
Rashi interprets 'at the end,' meaning
in the normal course of nature. But
Job must intend here the sudden and
seemingly wanton ruin of a man after
God had lavished such painstaking
care in first fashioning him and now
destroying him so fearfully.

**10. poured me out as milk, and curdled me
like cheese.** The Hebrew is particularly
vivid and powerful. The allusions are
to the formation of the embryo in the
womb.

11. clothed me with skin and flesh. The
mysterious processes of human formation are further elaborated.

12 Thou hast granted me life and
    favour,
    And Thy providence hath pre-
       served my spirit.

13 Yet these things Thou didst hide
    in Thy heart;
    I know that this is with Thee;

14 If I sin, then Thou markest me,
    And Thou wilt not acquit me
       from mine iniquity.

15 If I be wicked, woe unto me;
    And if I be righteous, yet shall I
       not lift up my head—
    Being filled with ignominy
    And looking upon mine affliction.

16 And if it exalt itself, Thou hunt-
    est me as a lion;
    And again Thou showest Thyself
       marvellous upon me.

חַיִּים וָחֶסֶד עָשִׂיתָ עִמָּדִי
וּפְקֻדָּתְךָ שָׁמְרָה רוּחִי׃
וְאֵלֶּה צָפַנְתָּ בִלְבָבֶךָ
יָדַעְתִּי כִּי־זֹאת עִמָּךְ׃
אִם־חָטָאתִי וּשְׁמַרְתָּנִי
וּמֵעֲוֹנִי לֹא תְנַקֵּנִי׃
אִם־רָשַׁעְתִּי אַלְלַי לִי
וְצָדַקְתִּי לֹא־אֶשָּׂא רֹאשִׁי
שְׂבַע קָלוֹן וּרְאֵה עָנְיִי׃
וְיִגְאֶה כַּשַּׁחַל תְּצוּדֵנִי
וְתָשֹׁב תִּתְפַּלָּא בִי׃

12. *Thy providence hath preserved my spirit.* Cf. Ps. viii. 5 where the same Hebrew root, here translated *Thy providence*, occurs in *thinkest of him.* God's providential care of the human being is evidenced both at birth and during the whole of his existence on earth. 'The view expressed in the verse is of extreme importance for the interpretation of chapters ix-x. It shows that, although Job wrestles with God, he is conscious of his absolute dependence upon Him' (Buttenweiser).

13-17 WAS GOD'S CARE ONLY THAT HE MIGHT AFFLICT HIM?

13. *Thou didst hide in Thy heart.* Job charges God with having intentionally concealed His true design upon him, caring for him with love but planning from the beginning suddenly to overwhelm him with terror.

14. *if I sin, then Thou markest me.* Verses 14-17, describing what, as Job imagines, God had planned to do in particular cases, would be clearer if rendered hypothetically: 'If I sinned, then Thou wouldest mark me, and wouldest not . . .

If I were wicked, etc.' *If I sin* and *if I be wicked* (verse 15) seem to contrast minor and major offences. Whatever Job might do, God had from the outset determined upon punishing him.

15. *and looking upon mine affliction.* The verb has either to be construed as an unusual form of infinitive, 'and experiencing mine affliction' (cf. Lam. iii. 1), or as imperative, 'and look upon' (as R.V. margin), a cry to God to end his misery. The former is the more probable interpretation.

16. *and if it exalt itself.* The pronoun *it* is taken by R.V. to refer back to *my head* in the preceding verse: 'and if *my head* exalt itself' and present the alternative. Were I to raise my head, either in the experiencing of relief from my calamities, or as evidence of my sense of guiltlessness, then God would again hunt me down. Szold construes as a question: 'and is it a matter for pride that Thou huntest me?' God had worked marvellously in his formation as a human being, and in that He may take pride; but is there any cause for pride that He

17 Thou renewest Thy witnesses
against me,
And increasest Thine indignation
upon me;
Host succeeding host against me.

18 Wherefore then hast Thou brought
me forth out of the womb?
Would that I had perished, and
no eye had seen me!

19 I should have been as though I
had not been;
I should have been carried from
the womb to the grave.

20 Are not my days few? cease then,
And let me alone, that I may take
comfort a little,

21 Before I go whence I shall not
return,
Even to the land of darkness and
of the shadow of death;

17 תְּחַדֵּשׁ עֵדֶיךָ ׀ נֶגְדִּי
וְתֶרֶב כַּעַשְׂךָ עִמָּדִי
חֲלִיפוֹת וְצָבָא עִמִּי׃

18 וְלָמָּה מֵרֶחֶם הֹצֵאתָנִי
אֶגְוַע וְעַיִן לֹא־תִרְאֵנִי׃

19 כַּאֲשֶׁר לֹא־הָיִיתִי אֶהְיֶה
מִבֶּטֶן לַקֶּבֶר אוּבָל׃

20 הֲלֹא־מְעַט יָמַי יַחְדָּל
יָשִׁית מִמֶּנִּי וְאַבְלִיגָה מְּעָט׃

21 בְּטֶרֶם אֵלֵךְ וְלֹא אָשׁוּב
אֶל־אֶרֶץ חֹשֶׁךְ וְצַלְמָוֶת׃

v. 20. וַחְדָּל ק׳   v. 20. וְשִׁית ק׳   v. 20. נ״א מְעָט

hunts me down, as the hunter of a lion
glories in his exploit?

as a lion. Doubt has been expressed as
to whether God or Job is intended by the
lion. Rashi takes it to mean Job: 'Thou
spreadest a trap for me as if I were
strong as a lion.'

and again Thou showest, etc. He speaks
in bitter irony. God displays His
marvellous power by bringing upon him
overwhelming anguish and pain.

17. *Thou renewest Thy witnesses against
me.* The *witnesses* are the visible proofs
of Job's guilt.

host succeeding host against me. R.V.
more literally 'changes and warfare are
against me.' The figure seems to be
that of an attacking army where fresh
relays of troops are constantly sent to
attack the enemy (cf. xvi. 14, xix. 12).

18-22 JOB PLEADS FOR A BRIEF RESPITE
BEFORE DEATH

18. *wherefore then hast Thou brought me
forth.* Once more, as in iii. 11, he asks

why God had been so ruthless as to have
brought him to birth. Why did he not
perish at birth? He is perplexed to
despair at the inscrutable purpose of the
Almighty.

19. *I should have been carried from the
womb to the grave.* 'Would that I had
been carried from the womb to the
grave!' (Rashi). 'Then it would have
been as though I had never been created
at all' (Metsudath David).

20. *are not my days few?* God having
decreed at his birth that he should live,
the least He should do is to allow him to
pass the brief span of life in peace and
without incessant affliction.

that I may take comfort. The same verb
translated *be of good cheer* in ix. 27. Ibn
Ezra takes it in the sense 'to strengthen
himself, renew his courage.'

21. *before I go whence I shall not return.*
Cf. iii. 5, vii. 9f., xiv. 7-22. Only the
nether-world with its utter darkness
awaits him after his weary days of pain
on earth are ended.

49

22 A land of thick darkness, as darkness itself;
A land of the shadow of death,
without any order,
And where the light is as darkness.

אֶרֶץ עֵפָתָה ׀ כְּמוֹ־אֹפֶל
צַלְמָוֶת וְלֹא־סְדָרִים
וַתֹּפַע כְּמוֹ־אֹפֶל׃

---

11   **CHAPTER XI**   **יא**

1 Then answered Zophar the Naamathite, and said:

2 Should not the multitude of words
be answered?
And should a man full of talk be
accounted right?

וַיַּעַן צֹפַר הַנַּעֲמָתִי וַיֹּאמַר׃
הֲרֹב דְּבָרִים לֹא יֵעָנֶה
וְאִם־אִישׁ שְׂפָתַיִם יִצְדָּק׃

---

22. *a land of thick darkness.* Note the
heaped emphasis of Stygian darkness.

without any order. Ibn Ezra, followed
by Metsudath David, takes this to mean
the panoplied order of the stars. The
quintessence of chaos is complete confusion and disorder. With this chilling
description of Sheol enveloped in impenetrable blackness is to be contrasted
the beneficent effect of light upon the
earth in xxxviii. 12-14.

the light is as darkness. Cf. Milton's
beautiful paraphrase in *Paradise Lost:*
'The light in that region is no light, but
rather darkness visible.' Summing-up
the position so far, Peake well remarks:
'The reader cannot fail to be struck with
the poet's skill in depicting the tumult in
Job's soul. He oscillates between the
sense of God's ruthless injustice to him
now and the memory of blessed fellowship with Him in the past. . . . He closes
with an appeal to God, an indication
that the old temper of soul towards
Him had not been killed out. Much of
the interest of this drama of the soul lies
in the growth of a consciousness in
Job that God's present anger does not
represent His inmost self. It is a mood
that will pass, a dark cloud eclipsing His
truest character. This thought does not,
however, emerge as yet.'

CHAPTER XI
ZOPHAR'S FIRST SPEECH

IN language of outspoken cruelty, devoid
of all pity for the physical torments
which had prompted Job's volcanic
words, Zophar rebukes him for what he
charges are his boasts of innocence. In
reality such assertion is to mock at
religion. Zophar can only repeat the
arguments of Eliphaz and Bildad (cf.
xi. 18-20 with viii. 20-22), without
advancing any new idea. He insists that
God, omniscient and unfathomable, can
detect sin when man is unconsciously
blind or wilfully stubborn. By the
allusions to an *empty man* and a *wild
ass's colt,* he implies Job's own folly and
unrepentant obstinacy. Let him set his
heart aright, put the evil from him and
return to God; then will his darkness
turn to morning and he will be secure.

2-6 ZOPHAR REBUKES JOB'S BOASTS OF INNOCENCE

2. *should not the multitude of words be
answered?* Zophar, less sensitive than
the dignified Eliphaz and the gentle
Bildad, appears annoyed by the long
second speech of Job. He brushes it
aside as mere verbal sophistry.

a man full of talk. lit. 'a man of lips,'
insinuating that, like a ventriloquist,
Job's words rise from his throat and

3 Thy boastings have made men hold
   their peace,
   And thou hast mocked, with none
   to make thee ashamed;

4 And thou hast said: 'My doctrine
   is pure,
   And I am clean in Thine eyes.'

5 But oh that God would speak,
   And open His lips against thee;

6 And that He would tell thee the
   secrets of wisdom,
   That sound wisdom is manifold!
   Know therefore that God exacteth
   of thee less than thine iniquity
   deserveth.

3 בַּדֶּיךָ מְתִים יַחֲרִישׁוּ
  וַתִּלְעַג וְאֵין מַכְלִם:

4 וַתֹּאמֶר זַךְ לִקְחִי
  וּבַר הָיִיתִי בְעֵינֶיךָ:

5 וְאוּלָם מִי־יִתֵּן אֱלוֹהַּ דַּבֵּר
  וְיִפְתַּח שְׂפָתָיו עִמָּךְ:

6 וְיַגֶּד־לְךָ ׀ תַּעֲלֻמוֹת חָכְמָה
  כִּי־כִפְלַיִם לְתוּשִׁיָּה
  וְדַע ׀ כִּי־יַשֶּׁה לְךָ אֱלוֹהַּ מֵעֲוֺנֶךָ:

mouth but not from his heart (cf. Isa.
xxix. 13).

3. *thy boastings.* i.e. hollow protestations. 'Lies which he invents out of his
heart' (Ibn Ezra).

thou hast mocked. Zophar accuses Job
of scoffing at religion. He is thinking
of the assertions in vi. 28, 30, ix. 21, x. 15.
Job denied the doctrine of retributive
justice. In Zophar's theology, that was
mocking at religion.

4. *my doctrine is pure.* viz. that God
punishes as guilty one whom He knows
to be innocent (ix. 30f., x. 6f.). At first
Job had not asserted his innocence but
only lamented his fate. Later he had
denied his guilt with such vehemence
that the friends had to reckon with it.
To them, with their theology, his afflictions are irrefutable proof that God regards him as guilty. Job's setting up
of his knowledge of himself against God's
knowledge of him as demonstrated by
his chastisements is sheer blasphemy.

I am clean in Thine eyes. 'Zophar quite
justly discovers here a novel doctrine to
which he certainly had not been accustomed ... Zophar begins to surmise ...
that Job's principles, instead of being
identical with theirs, cut clean athwart
them. This discovery accounts for the

rather unworthy tone of his language.
His irritation was natural. He had
never met a man with such ideas as those
of Job before, and he is driven out of
patience and decorum by his new
theories. Elihu (later) is even more
shocked, and thinks that such another as
Job does not exist' (xxxiv. 7) (Davidson).

5. *oh that God would speak.* If God
were to appear and speak, He would soon
show Job that he was being punished
more lightly than he deserved.

6. *the secrets of wisdom.* i.e. the things
hidden from wisdom. The translators
failed to recognize that *chochmah, wisdom,* is objective genitive (Buttenweiser).

that sound wisdom is manifold. Too deep
for human comprehension. 'Men may
not fathom it' (Ibn Ezra). *Manifold* is
literally 'double.'

know therefore that God exacteth of thee.
'Then wouldest thou know that God
reckoneth not many of thy sins.' The
verb means, 'He casts into oblivion' or
'obliterates from memory.' The use of
the imperfect tense implies that not only
in the present case, but over and over
again in the past, God has been similarly
lenient to Job.

7 Canst thou find out the deep
   things of God?
  Canst thou attain unto the purpose
   of the Almighty?

8 It is high as heaven; what canst
   thou do?
  Deeper than the nether-world;
   what canst thou know?

9 The measure thereof is longer than
   the earth,
  And broader than the sea.

10 If He pass by, and shut up,
  Or gather in, then who can hinder
   Him?

11 For He knoweth base men;
  And when He seeth iniquity, will
   He not then consider it?

12 But an empty man will get understanding,
  When a wild ass's colt is born a
   man.

הַחֵקֶר אֱלוֹהַּ תִּמְצָא ⁷

אִם עַד־תַּכְלִית שַׁדַּי תִּמְצָא׃

גׇּבְהֵי שָׁמַיִם מַה־תִּפְעָל ⁸

עֲמֻקָּה מִשְּׁאוֹל מַה־תֵּדָע׃

אֲרֻכָּה מֵאֶרֶץ מִדָּהּ ⁹

וּרְחָבָה מִנִּי־יָם׃

אִם־יַחֲלֹף וְיַסְגִּיר ¹⁰

וְיַקְהִיל וּמִי יְשִׁיבֶנּוּ׃

כִּי־הוּא יָדַע מְתֵי־שָׁוְא ¹¹

וַיַּרְא־אָוֶן וְלֹא יִתְבּוֹנָן׃

וְאִישׁ נָבוּב יִלָּבֵב ¹²

וְעַיִר פֶּרֶא אָדָם יִוָּלֵד׃

7–12 GOD SEES SIN WHERE MAN IS BLIND

7. *canst thou find out the deep things of God?* Wilt thou seek to fathom the inscrutable God or to plumb the depths of the Almighty? A.V. and R.V.: 'Canst thou by searching find out God? Canst thou find out the Almighty unto perfection?' Driver claims that 'by searching' is grammatically impossible. He gives a powerful rendering: 'Canst thou find out the immensity of God? Canst thou attain unto the limits of the Almighty?' *Cheker*, rendered *the deep things*, means properly 'something to be searched out, or, explored.' In xxxviii. 16 it is translated *recesses*; here it denotes the entire range of the Divine nature.

8. *deeper than the nether-world; what canst thou know?* For *nether-world* (Sheol), see on vii. 9. How immeasurable and unfathomable is the Divine wisdom! The extreme dimensions of the universe cannot be used as a standard by which to measure it. Cf. Eccles. vii. 24 on the 'wisdom' pursued by man, which is described as *far off, and exceeding deep; who can find it out?*

9. *longer than the earth, and broader*

than the sea. The ultimate *secrets of wisdom* (verse 6) lie beyond all human boundaries.

10. In this verse Zophar appears to take up Job's own words (ix. 11f.).

and shut up. 'With afflictions whomever He desires' (Rashi); 'arrest and put into prison' (Ralbag).

or gather in. R.V. 'call unto judgment.' 'Or assemble all His Divine ministers to justify His act in having shut up' (Rashi).

then who can hinder Him? Who can turn Him back from His decision? Who can reply to Him in words to say that He has acted unjustly?

11. *for He knoweth base men.* God sees the iniquity of base men which they do through the days and years. It may appear to them that He does not consider it, because He is slow to anger.

12. The verse has troubled the commentators. Davidson comments that the verse 'seems to be in the shape of a proverb, and is full of alliterations which

13 If thou set thy heart aright,
And stretch out thy hands toward
Him—

14 If iniquity be in thy hand, put it
far away,
And let not unrighteousness
dwell in thy tents—

15 Surely then shalt thou lift up
thy face without spot;
Yea, thou shalt be stedfast, and
shalt not fear;

16 For thou shalt forget thy misery;
Thou shalt remember it as waters
that are passed away;

17 And thy life shall be clearer than
the noonday;
Though there be darkness, it
shall be as the morning.

13 אִם־אַתָּה הֲכִינוֹתָ לִבֶּ֑ךָ
וּפָרַשְׂתָּ אֵלָיו כַּפֶּֽךָ׃

14 אִם־אָ֣וֶן בְּֽיָדְךָ הַרְחִיקֵ֑הוּ
וְאַל־תַּשְׁכֵּ֖ן בְּאֹהָלֶ֣יךָ עַוְלָֽה׃

15 כִּי־אָ֤ז ׀ תִּשָּׂ֣א פָנֶ֣יךָ מִמּ֑וּם
וְהָיִ֥יתָ מֻ֝צָ֗ק וְלֹ֣א תִירָֽא׃

16 כִּי־אַ֭תָּה עָמָ֣ל תִּשְׁכָּ֑ח
כְּמַ֖יִם עָבְר֣וּ תִזְכֹּֽר׃

17 וּֽמִצָּהֳרַ֗יִם יָק֥וּם חָ֑לֶד
תָּ֝עֻ֗פָה כַּבֹּ֥קֶר תִּהְיֶֽה׃

cannot be reproduced in translation.'
Buttenwieser translates: 'So the empty-
headed man gaineth understanding, and
the wild-ass colt is reborn as man.'
The verse brings out for what purpose
God pays close attention to sinners. By
inflicting punishment upon them He
seeks to break their obstinacy and to
effect a change of heart, so that they may
humble themselves before Him, as
Zophar admonishes Job to do in the
following verses.

an empty man. 'Hollow, without a heart,
who does not understand his way will
acquire for himself a heart to return to
his Creator and scrutinize his deeds'
(Rashi).

a wild ass's colt. The wild ass was an
untamable, obstinate creature (cf. xxxix.
5-8). Zophar implies that as a result of
the judgments of the Almighty (verses
10f.), conceit and ignorance are removed
and a wilful, defiant nature like Job's is
softened (Davidson).

13-20   AMENDMENT WILL BRING SECURITY

13. *if thou set thy heart aright.* The
pronoun *thou* is emphatic. The meaning
of *set thy heart aright* is to allow God's
visitations to have the effect of directing
his heart towards Him.

stretch out thy hands. In supplication
to God for pardon.

14. *if iniquity be in thy hand.* Zophar
is here openly accusing Job of sin, and
suggests that he set himself and his house
in order.

15. *surely then shalt thou lift up thy face.*
Cf. Job's words in x. 15, *and if I be righteous, yet shall I not lift up my head.*

without spot. i.e. without blemish. The
expression is figurative for a mark of a
guilty conscience.

and shalt not fear. 'Henceforth thou
shalt be strong and not fear the terror,
for it shall not come nigh unto thee'
(Metsudath David).

16. *for thou shalt forget thy misery. Thou*
is emphatic. 'Thou shalt forget all
misery; and as waters that pass and are
gone, so shall be all remembrance of
misery unto thee' (Rashi).

17. *thy life* (cheled) *shall be clearer than
the noonday. Cheled* means 'duration'
(of life) with reference to its brevity.
Cf. *O remember how short my time is*
(Ps. lxxxix. 48). Job had said, *I go to
the land of darkness and of the shadow of
death* (x. 21). The antithesis that Zophar

18 And thou shalt be secure, because there is hope;
Yea, thou shalt look about thee,
and shalt take thy rest in safety.

19 Also thou shalt lie down, and
none shall make thee afraid;
Yea, many shall make suit unto
thee.

20 But the eyes of the wicked shall
fail,
And they shall have no way to
flee,
And their hope shall be the
drooping of the soul.

וּבָטַחְתָּ כִּי־יֵשׁ תִּקְוָה
וְחָפַרְתָּ לָבֶטַח תִּשְׁכָּב׃
וְרָבַצְתָּ וְאֵין מַחֲרִיד
וְחִלּוּ פָנֶיךָ רַבִּים׃
וְעֵינֵי רְשָׁעִים תִּכְלֶינָה
וּמָנוֹס אָבַד מִנְהֶם
וְתִקְוָתָם מַפַּח־נָפֶשׁ׃

now presents is striking. Life will
become full of light for a repentant Job.

though there be darkness (ta'uphah). 'If
thou doest repentance, then shall thy life
stand as the noon-day sun; and when it
groweth dark, it shall return as the
morning. The meaning is the same as
he returneth to the days of his youth
(xxxiii. 25), and *so that thy youth is
renewed like the eagle* (Ps. ciii. 5).' (Ibn
Ezra). Rashi gives this interpretation,
but suggests as an alternative that
ta'uphah has the meaning of *the eyelids*
('aphappë) *of the morning* (iii. 9) on the
ground that the word should be pointed
te'uphah if the signification were 'darkness.'

18. *thou shalt be secure, because there is
hope.* Zophar rebukes Job's gloomy talk
of despair (vi. 11, ix. 25, x. 20), making
it of course conditional upon his removing
the guilt which he has surely committed.

thou shalt look about thee. The meaning
is perhaps 'to search' as in Deut. i. 22,
that they may search the land. Ibn Ezra
defines the verb 'to dig': 'as if thou didst
dig round about thee as men dig round
about the walls of a city.'

19. *many shall make suit unto thee.* 'The
court favourite has many flatterers;
when Job is once more God's favourite
he will not lack this testimony to his
dignity. In his prosperity he had received deep respect even from the
princes and the aged (xxix. 7-10, 21-25).
Now, as he bitterly complains, the lowest
ranks of society, and those younger than
himself, have him in derision (xxx. 1-10),
the very children despise and mock at
him (xix. 18)' (Peake). When Job is
absolved and restored, distinguished
persons will entreat his favour to fulfil
their requests, since power is again in
his hands.

20. *but the eyes of the wicked shall fail.* A
hidden warning is implied for Job if he
remains impenitent. *The eyes fail*
signifies that they look in vain for safety
or deliverance.

and they shall have no way to flee. More
literally 'and refuge is perished from
them.' The wicked shall have no place
of refuge.

the drooping of the soul. lit. 'breathing
out,' an expression of grief (cf. *her spirit
droopeth,* Jer. xv. 9).

12	CHAPTER XII	יב

1 Then Job answered and said:

2 No doubt but ye are the people,
And wisdom shall die with you.

3 But I have understanding as well
 as you;
I am not inferior to you;
Yea, who knoweth not such things
 as these?

4 I am as one that is a laughing-stock
 to his neighbour,

וַיַּעַן אִיּוֹב וַיֹּאמַר: 1

אָמְנָם כִּי אַתֶּם־עָם 2
וְעִמָּכֶם תָּמוּת חָכְמָה:

גַּם־לִי לֵבָב ׀ כְּמוֹכֶם 3
לֹא־נֹפֵל אָנֹכִי מִכֶּם
וְאֶת־מִי־אֵין כְּמוֹ־אֵלֶּה:

שְׂחֹק לְרֵעֵהוּ ׀ אֶהְיֶה 4

CHAPTERS XII-XIV

JOB'S THIRD REPLY—TO ZOPHAR

JOB sarcastically replies to Zophar that their pretensions of superior wisdom to his do not impress him. He knows as much as they. He scorns their efforts to convict, on the basis of their wisdom, an innocent man and make him a laughing-stock. Nature and human experience attest to the truth that God, the Creator, endowed with wisdom and might, rules the world. But this rule is arbitrary. No moral purpose can be discovered in it. He frustrates all human endeavour and overthrows all human institutions. Nevertheless, Job still desires to maintain his moral integrity and reason with God. Job rebukes his friends for seeking to condemn him and daring to believe that by distorting the truth they can glorify God (xiii. 7). He would willingly present his case before God, provided only He would not crush him with His might. His inner consciousness of rectitude gives him courage to speak out as he bids his friends attend in silence while he pleads his case with God.

He then pleads with God. He asks what are his sins (xiii. 23). Why does God persecute so frail and shattered a creature as he? Do the sadness and brevity of human life, its inescapable pain and the hopelessness of its close, awaken in Him no pity? A tree, severed, sprouts again; but man perishes, and where is he (xiv. 10)? Would, indeed, that there were another life! If the Almighty would only hide him in the nether-world and revive him after the Divine wrath be past! But death is the end. *Thou destroyest the hope of man* (xiv. 19). Thus, in a sigh of misery over the wretched fate of man, ends Job's speech.

CHAPTER XII

1-6 JOB'S IRONIC REBUKE OF HIS FRIENDS' WISDOM

2. *no doubt but ye are the people.* Cf. Zophar's exhortation to Job in xi. 6. To this Job replies with biting sarcasm: 'Of course you are everybody, and when you die, all wisdom will perish with you!'

3. *but I have understanding.* lit. 'also to me there is a heart,' that organ being considered the seat of intelligence. Job evidently makes a retort to Zophar's cruel imputation that he, *an empty man, will get understanding when a wild ass's colt is born a man* (xi. 12).

who knoweth not such things as these? viz. what Zophar had spoken about the Divine power (xi. 7-12).

4. *a laughing-stock to his neighbour.* Job rightly expected sympathy from his friends, but they only deride and mock his piety.

55

A man that called upon God, and
  He answered him;
The just, the innocent man is a
  laughing-stock,

5 A contemptible brand in the
  thought of him that is at ease,
A thing ready for them whose foot
  slippeth.

6 The tents of robbers prosper,
And they that provoke God are
  secure,
In whatsoever God bringeth into
  their hand.

7 But ask now the beasts, and they
  shall teach thee;
And the fowls of the air, and they
  shall tell thee;

קֹרֵא לֶאֱלוֹהַּ וַיַּעֲנֵהוּ

שְׂחוֹק צַדִּיק תָּמִים׃

לַפִּיד בּוּז לְעַשְׁתּוּת שַׁאֲנָן

נָכוֹן לְמוֹעֲדֵי רָגֶל׃

יִשְׁלָיוּ אֹהָלִים ׀ לְשֹׁדְדִים

וּבַטֻּחוֹת לְמַרְגִּיזֵי אֵל

לַאֲשֶׁר הֵבִיא אֱלוֹהַּ בְּיָדוֹ׃

וְאוּלָם שְׁאַל־נָא בְהֵמוֹת וְתֹרֶךָּ

וְעוֹף הַשָּׁמַיִם וְיַגֶּד־לָךְ׃

*a man that called upon God, and He
answered him.* That happened in the
past, in the days of his prosperity. Cf.
xxix. 2-5 where he enlarges upon his
converse with God and how He watched
over him.

5. *a contemptible brand in the thought of
him that is at ease.* This may have been
a familiar adage expressing the attitude
of his fellow-men toward one who has
fallen into adversity. 'Contempt should
be dealt out to him who suffers misfortune, a kick be given to them that have
lost their footing' (Buttenweiser). The
Hebrew *lappid, brand,* presents difficulties. A.J. has translated it as though
it were one word *lappid* which means
'torch' or 'brand.' Rashi understood it
so and comments: 'The fire of Gehinnom stands against him who is at ease
in his thoughts, saying, "I shall have
peace".' A.V. renders: 'He that is ready
to slip with his feet is as a lamp despised
in the thought of him that is at ease.'
Ibn Ezra, however, regards the *lamed* as
a preposition added to *pid*, 'ruin, disaster.' This is accepted by R.V.: 'In the
thought of him that is at ease there is
contempt for misfortune.' 'A bitter
exclamation, referring to himself! Job is
the man overtaken by misfortune; and

his more prosperous friends have nothing for him but contempt' (Davidson).

whose foot slippeth. When they fall into
adversity, they are kicked and trampled
upon.

6. *the tents of robbers prosper.* Job now
presents the other side of the anomalies
of the Divine Government: the prosperity
of robber bands. They that provoke
God by their wickedness are secure although they recognize no God but their
own strong arm.

in whatsoever God bringeth into their hand.
The text is difficult and Buttenweiser
suggests the translation:'They whose god
is their fist.' The meaning seems to be
'whose only god is their physical strength.'

7-25 GOD IS OMNIPOTENT, BUT WHAT OF
HIS JUSTICE?

7. *but ask now the beasts.* Why was it
necessary for the friends to dilate on
God's might and control of the universe?
Even the beasts and birds know it! On
another interpretation, Job is referring to
the sad experience of brute and predatory
force which seems to prevail in Nature
as well as in society (cf. Buttenweiser
quoted on verse 9).

8 Or speak to the earth, and it shall
teach thee;

And the fishes of the sea shall declare unto thee;

9 Who knoweth not among all these,

That the hand of the LORD hath
wrought this?

10 In whose hand is the soul of every
living thing,

And the breath of all mankind.—

11 Doth not the ear try words,

Even as the palate tasteth its
food?

12 Is wisdom with aged men,

And understanding in length of
days?—

8 אוֹ שִׂיחַ לָאָרֶץ וְתֹרֶךָּ

וִיסַפְּרוּ לְךָ דְּגֵי הַיָּם:

9 מִי לֹא־יָדַע בְּכָל־אֵלֶּה

כִּי יַד־יְהֹוָה עָשְׂתָה זֹּאת:

10 אֲשֶׁר בְּיָדוֹ נֶפֶשׁ כָּל־חָי

וְרוּחַ כָּל־בְּשַׂר־אִישׁ:

11 הֲלֹא־אֹזֶן מִלִּין תִּבְחָן

וְחֵךְ אֹכֶל יִטְעַם־לוֹ:

12 בִּישִׁישִׁים חָכְמָה

וְאֹרֶךְ יָמִים תְּבוּנָה:

8. *speak to the earth.* The phrase, it
has been suggested, may be an abbreviation of *zochalē arets*, 'the reptiles of the
earth.' The difficulty arises because we
do not expect, in an enumeration of the
various living creatures, to have the earth
specially mentioned. Metsudath David
sees an allusion to the four fundamental
elements (earth, air, fire and water).

9. *who knoweth not among all these.* Cf.
Isa. xli. 20 where the clause *that the
hand of the LORD hath wrought this*
occurs verbatim. Buttenwieser asserts,
'The widely prevailing interpretation . . .
who among the animals does not know
that God is the Creator and Ruler of the
universe, cannot be entertained. The
thought is not of the creation and dominion of the universe, but of the unjust
system which is permitted by God to
prevail in it. It is far-fetched to make
this refer to the visible world. The
emphasis is altogether on the fact—
irreconcilable to the author—that the
wicked enjoy prosperity, while the innocent are allowed to suffer.' Who does
not know, Job here contends on this
interpretation, that God allows tyranny
and brute force—the law of the jungle—
to hold sway in the world? The more

usual explanation is expressed in the
comment of Metsudath David: Who is
such a fool as not to know such a com-
monplace as that behind the visible
phenomena of Nature is the deep unfathomable wisdom of God's rule?

10. *in whose hand is the soul of every living
thing.* No one beside God is responsible
for good and evil. All that happens
occurs through Him.

11. *doth not the ear try words.* As the
palate can tell whether food be sweet or
sour, so the ear can test the words it
hears. It can accept those which, like the
wisdom of the aged (verse 12), embody
sound knowledge. But there is the
possibility that Job is sarcastic and means
that the ear can refuse to be intimidated
by the prestige and authority of the aged,
merely because it is venerable with age,
and can exercise its own independent,
discriminating judgment based upon
observation and experience. A.J. apparently understands it so.

12. *is wisdom with aged men.* A.V.
translates: 'with the ancient is wisdom.'
This translation follows Rashi and Ibn
Ezra. They interpret the letter *beth* as
serving both phrases in the verse: 'with

13 With Him is wisdom and might;
    He hath counsel and understanding.

עִמּוֹ חָכְמָה וּגְבוּרָה
לוֹ עֵצָה וּתְבוּנָה:

14 Behold, He breaketh down, and
    it cannot be built again;
    He shutteth up a man, and there
    can be no opening.

הֵן יַהֲרוֹס וְלֹא יִבָּנֶה
יִסְגֹּר עַל־אִישׁ וְלֹא יִפָּתֵחַ:

15 Behold, He withholdeth the
    waters, and they dry up;
    Also He sendeth them out, and
    they overturn the earth.

הֵן יַעְצֹר בַּמַּיִם וְיִבָשׁוּ
וִישַׁלְּחֵם וְיַהַפְכוּ־אָרֶץ:

16 With Him is strength and sound
    wisdom;
    The deceived and the deceiver
    are His.

עִמּוֹ עֹז וְתוּשִׁיָּה
לוֹ שֹׁגֵג וּמַשְׁגֶּה:

17 He leadeth counsellors away
    stripped
    And judges maketh He fools.

מוֹלִיךְ יוֹעֲצִים שׁוֹלָל
וְשֹׁפְטִים יְהוֹלֵל:

the ancient is wisdom and with length of days is understanding, viz. to know that wisdom is His (to do good or evil as He wills)' (Rashi). 'Since Zophar was younger than he, he said: "How dare you lord it over me in wisdom, since I am older and wiser than you!"' (Metsudath David). Berechiah, an otherwise unknown mediæval French Rabbi, who has left a commentary on *Job*, comments on this verse: 'I heard the following explanation. Job says: I thought that "with aged men is wisdom" and that you had "understanding," since you have "length of days"—referring to the beginning of his speech, *wisdom shall die with you*—but it is not as I thought; there is no wisdom with you' (W. Aldis Wright and S. A. Hirsch, from a Hebrew MS. in the University Library, Cambridge).

13. *with Him is wisdom and might.* 'Because of my many years, I know without you that to God belongs the perfection of wisdom and might' (Metsudath David) 'With Him—God alone—is wisdom, and also might, for one can be wise without being mighty' (Berechiah).

14. *behold, He breaketh down.* 'Job now describes the working of God, in which His might and wisdom are displayed. He begins with God's destruction of cities,

and then passes to His imprisonment of men in dungeons from which there is no escape. Probably some definite historical events are in the poet's mind' (Peake).

15. *He withholdeth the waters.* The reference is generally to calamities of drought and flood. Rashi understands the verse as an allusion to the incident of the Red Sea.

16. *sound wisdom.* See on v. 12. 'The word *tushiyyah* must be explained according to the context, the word denoting either counsel or wisdom or might' (Berechiah).

the deceived and the deceiver are His. Better: 'he who is led astray and who leads astray.' God is the cause of both happening. Rashi identifies *the deceiver* with the Satan.

17. *He leadeth counsellors away stripped.* The last word probably means 'barefooted' (cf. Micah i. 8). The Jewish commentators interpret it metaphorically of reason: 'Each one of them He leads away stripped of his knowledge' (Ibn Ezra). Rashi defines *sholal* as *shtuth*, 'folly': 'He leadeth them away with folly when He desires to confuse and swallow up their wisdom.'

18 He looseth the bond of kings,
   And bindeth their loins with a
   girdle.

19 He leadeth priests away stripped,
   And overthroweth the mighty.

20 He removeth the speech of men
   of trust,
   And taketh away the sense of the
   elders.

21 He poureth contempt upon
   princes,
   And looseth the belt of the strong.

18 מוּסַר מְלָכִים פִּתֵּחַ
וַיֶּאְסֹר אֵזוֹר בְּמָתְנֵיהֶם׃

19 מוֹלִיךְ כֹּהֲנִים שׁוֹלָל
וְאֵיתָנִים יְסַלֵּף׃

20 מֵסִיר שָׂפָה לְנֶאֱמָנִים
וְטַעַם זְקֵנִים יִקָּח׃

21 שׁוֹפֵךְ בּוּז עַל־נְדִיבִים
וּמְזִיחַ אֲפִיקִים רִפָּה׃

---

judges maketh He fools. The *judges* were
normally men of superior attainments
who acted as governors as well as magis-
trates.

18. *He looseth the bond of kings.* The
word for *bond*, *musar*, properly denotes
'discipline, control.' In those days kings
were autocrats; but it is in the power of
God to put an end to their despotic rule.

and bindeth their loins with a girdle.
Metsudath David takes this, as does
Rashi, to mean that He strengthens their
might. Driver renders the line: 'And
bindeth a waistcloth on their loins,' the
waistcloth being the badge of a captive,
and this is the more probable meaning.
God can turn rulers into humbled prisoners.

19. *He leadeth priests away stripped.*
Rashi interprets as 'princes.' This emphasis on priests as princes and honoured
men is strikingly illustrated in 2 Sam.
viii. 18 which A.J. translates, *And
David's sons were chief ministers*, where
the Hebrew has the usual word for
'priests.' The priests in antiquity were
an influential, hereditary caste.

the mighty. lit. 'the perpetual,' i.e. men
of influential status, inherited from their
fathers, which they had regarded as
unshakable.

20. *He removeth the speech of men of trust.*
The allusion is to ministers of State who

were the trusted advisers of the king. An
alternative explanation is proposed by
Saadia who regards *ne'emanim* as derived from *na'am* (like *rachamanim* from
racham), i.e. the prophets. Szold suggests the same derivation and explains
the word as meaning 'orators.'

the sense of the elders. In Prov. xi. 22
the first noun is translated *discretion*.
The *elders* were the counsellors of the
nation.

21. *He poureth contempt upon princes,
and looseth the belt of the strong.* Cf.
Ps. cvii. 40 which is identical with the
first line of this verse and the second line
of verse 24. Dr. A. Cohen holds the
verse in *Psalms* to be a quotation from
Job (see *Psalms*, Soncino ed., *ad loc.*).

princes. The word is rendered *nobles*
in xxxiv. 18 and has that wider meaning.

the belt. The Hebrew is an Egyptian
loan-word. 'To loose the belt' is an
idiom for incapacitating. The Oriental,
with his flowing robes, had to gird them
up for active exertion. Loosening them
hampered freedom of movement and
action.

the strong. The word *aphik* normally
denotes 'water-channels.' 'Streams are
called *aphikim* for the reason that they
flow strongly' (Berechiah). The root
means 'to be strong,' and 'channel' is a
derived sense from the idea of holding
and confining the water.

22 He uncovereth deep things out of
    darkness,
    And bringeth out to light the
    shadow of death.

23 He increaseth the nations, and
    destroyeth them;
    He enlargeth the nations, and
    leadeth them away.

24 He taketh away the heart of the
    chiefs of the people of the land,
    And causeth them to wander in a
    wilderness where there is no
    way.

25 They grope in the dark without
    light,
    And He maketh them to stagger
    like a drunken man.

מְגַלֶּה עֲמֻקוֹת מִנִּי־חֹשֶׁךְ

וַיֹּצֵא לָאוֹר צַלְמָוֶת׃

מַשְׂגִּיא לַגּוֹיִם וַיְאַבְּדֵם

שֹׁטֵחַ לַגּוֹיִם וַיַּנְחֵם׃

מֵסִיר לֵב רָאשֵׁי עַם־הָאָרֶץ

וַיַּתְעֵם בְּתֹהוּ לֹא־דָרֶךְ׃

יְמַשְׁשׁוּ־חֹשֶׁךְ וְלֹא־אוֹר

וַיַּתְעֵם כַּשִּׁכּוֹר׃

13   CHAPTER XIII   יג

1 Lo, mine eye hath seen all this,
    Mine ear hath heard and under-
    stood it.

הֶן כֹּל רָאֲתָה עֵינִי
שָׁמְעָה אָזְנִי וַתָּבֶן לָהּ׃

v. 22. בנ׳׳א הק׳ דגושה

22. *He uncovereth deep things out of darkness.* God brings to light hidden plots
and conspiracies, planned in the deepest
darkness, dark as the shadow of death.
Nothing is concealed from Him, as He
exposes well-guarded secrets and carefully concealed schemes.

23. *He increaseth the nations, and destroyeth them.* 'He maketh nations great and
destroyeth them; He causeth nations to
spread and layeth them low' (Buttenweiser who cites Isa. xxviii. 2, *casteth
down to the earth*). God makes nations
great only afterwards to destroy them.
and leadeth them away. Into exile.
Although the verb usually means 'to
lead' in a helpful sense, the meaning here
is paralleled in 2 Kings xviii. 11.

24. *He taketh away the heart.* i.e. their
intelligence. God may suddenly deprive
the leaders of a people of their understanding and throw them into bewilderment.
in a wilderness. The word is rendered
waste (an element of chaos) in Gen. i. 2,

and in Deut. xxxii. 10 is descriptive of
the desert. Another translation of the
last clause might be, 'in pathless confusion.'

25. *He maketh them to stagger like a
drunken man.* As a drunken person does
not walk in a straight line and lurches
from side to side, so the people's leaders,
deprived of their reason, are unable to
pursue a definite policy (cf. Ps. cvii. 27).
The same image is used of Egypt in
Isa. xix. 14. Thus far Job spoke of rulers
and leaders generally and not his own
counsellors. He dwelt on these hidden
things because Zophar had expressed the
wish for Job, *that He would tell thee the
secrets of wisdom* (xi. 6). He now addresses himself to his friends.

CHAPTER XIII

1-12 JOB CRITICIZES HIS FRIENDS AS
             GOD'S ADVOCATES

1. *lo, mine eye hath seen all this.* Job now
stresses that what he has described of
God's might has come to him out of his

2 What ye know, do I know also;
  I am not inferior unto you.

3 Notwithstanding I would speak to
  the Almighty,
  And I desire to reason with God.

4 But ye are plasterers of lies,
  Ye are all physicians of no value.

5 Oh that ye would altogether hold
  your peace!
  And it would be your wisdom.

6 Hear now my reasoning,
  And hearken to the pleadings of
  my lips.

7 Will ye speak unrighteously for
  God,

² כְּדַעְתְּכֶם יָדַעְתִּי גַם־אָנִי
לֹא־נֹפֵל אָנֹכִי מִכֶּם:

³ אוּלָם אֲנִי אֶל־שַׁדַּי אֲדַבֵּר
וְהוֹכֵחַ אֶל־אֵל אֶחְפָּץ:

⁴ וְאוּלָם אַתֶּם טֹפְלֵי־שָׁקֶר
רֹפְאֵי אֱלִל כֻּלְּכֶם:

⁵ מִי־יִתֵּן הַחֲרֵשׁ תַּחֲרִישׁוּן
וּתְהִי לָכֶם לְחָכְמָה:

⁶ שִׁמְעוּ־נָא תוֹכַחְתִּי
וְרִבוֹת שְׂפָתַי הַקְשִׁיבוּ:

⁷ הַלְאֵל תְּדַבְּרוּ עַוְלָה

own observation. Both eye and ear have been his teachers in making vivid for him the incalculable might of God.

2. *I am not inferior unto you.* Repeated from xii. 3. Job scorns their pretensions of superior knowledge of God's inscrutable ways. Zophar had said (as though the Almighty had admitted him to His mysteries and kept Job out), *But oh that God would speak . . . and that He would tell thee the secrets of wisdom* (xi. 5f.).

3. *notwithstanding I would speak to the Almighty.* The two introductory words are strongly emphatic. Despite his penetrating more profoundly than his friends the principles upon which God rules His universe, he will not, on the strength of it, acknowledge guilt. He still maintains his spiritual integrity, and would much rather debate the matter with God than with them. As Rashi comments: 'I only seek to speak with Him, and I desire to argue it out with Him.'

4. *but ye are plasterers of lies.* The verb means 'to besmear' (cf. *forged a lie*, Ps.

cxix. 69). Their purpose is to conceal what is wrong in God's control of the world by covering it over with a layer of lies. Rashi and Metsudath David interpret the phrase in the sense of adding one lie to another.

physicians of no value. All of you are 'physicians of vanity'; for how do you comfort me by saying that I should return to God and He will make great my latter end? The word for *no value* (*elil*) may be connected with *al*, 'not,' hence 'worthless.'

5. *it would be your wisdom.* Cf. *Even a fool, when he holdeth his peace, is counted wise* (Prov. xvii. 28). *Si tacuisses, philosophus mansisses.*

6. *hear now my reasoning.* Rather 'my reproof' (cf. Prov. i. 23, 25). The impeachment follows in verses 7-9.

7. *will ye speak unrighteously for God.* For God stands at the beginning of the Hebrew sentence and is thereby emphasized. Is it on behalf of God, thinking to flatter Him, that ye speak iniquity against me?

And talk deceitfully for Him?

8 Will ye show Him favour?
Will ye contend for God?

9 Would it be good that He should
search you out?
Or as one mocketh a man, will ye
mock Him?

10 He will surely reprove you,
If ye do secretly show favour.

11 Shall not His majesty terrify you,
And His dread fall upon you?

12 Your memorials shall be like unto
ashes,

וְלוֹ תְּדַבְּרוּ רְמִיָּה:

8 הֲפָנָיו תִּשָּׂאוּן
אִם־לָאֵל תְּרִיבוּן:

9 הֲטוֹב כִּי־יַחְקֹר אֶתְכֶם
אִם־כְּהָתֵל בֶּאֱנוֹשׁ תְּהָתֵלּוּ בוֹ:

10 הוֹכֵחַ יוֹכִיחַ אֶתְכֶם
אִם־בַּסֵּתֶר פָּנִים תִּשָּׂאוּן:

11 הֲלֹא שְׂאֵתוֹ תְּבַעֵת אֶתְכֶם
וּפַחְדּוֹ יִפֹּל עֲלֵיכֶם:

12 זִכְרֹנֵיכֶם מִשְׁלֵי־אֵפֶר

v. 9. דגש אחר ת״ג

talk deceitfully for Him. The order of
the Hebrew is, 'for His sake will ye talk
deceitfully?' Will you defend Him by
making false accusations against me?

8. *will ye show Him favour?* lit. 'lift up
His face.' The idiom is used both in a
good and bad sense; here the latter, the
signification being, 'will ye be partisans
for Him?' Commenting on verses 7f.,
Kraeling (*The Book of the Ways of God*)
pointedly says: 'It would not be to their
benefit should He suddenly decide to
investigate their advocacy of his cause.
God, the foe of all unfairness, will discern the secret partiality of these self-
constituted judges. His cause must be
an honourable one—a cause of truth.'

will ye contend for God? Seeking to
flatter Him by playing the part of His
advocate.

9. *would it be good that He should search
you out?* 'Would it be good that He
should search you out and find lies?'
(Rashi). 'God is too great to be flattered,
too keen of perception to be beguiled.
It will not be a pleasant experience for
them when God strips bare their paltry
souls and shows that which masqueraded
as pious reverence to be cowardly sycoph-
ancy' (Peake).

10. *He will surely reprove you.* It is
dramatically significant that Job's unconscious prediction is later fulfilled (cf.
xlii. 7f.). Note also the paradox of Job's
spiritual torment. He can deny God's
justice and yet affirm His moral perfection and righteous indignation against
those who by flattery offer false testimony on His behalf.

11. *shall not His majesty terrify you.*
A.V. and R.V. translate *se'etho, His
majesty*, by 'His excellency,' an archaism,
as Driver shows, from the Latin *excel-
lentia* (derived from *excello*, 'to rise up
out of'). Buttenweiser renders: 'when
He appeareth,' i.e. when He appears to
take you to task for your unfairness.
Rashi comments: 'His loftiness and His
terror shall they not terrify you? But
some explain, the burning of His fire.'
Ibn Ezra likewise understands *se'etho* as
'His fire,' citing Judg. xx. 40, *but when
the beacon began to arise.*

12. *your memorials shall be like unto ashes.*
A.V. translates: 'Your remembrances
are like unto ashes, your bodies to bodies
of clay'; R.V.: 'Your memorable sayings
are proverbs of ashes, your defences are
defences of clay.' Buttenweiser's rendering is: 'Your time-honoured notions are

Your eminences to eminences of
clay.

13 Hold your peace, let me alone,
that I may speak,
And let come on me what will.

14 Wherefore? I will take my flesh
in my teeth,
And put my life in my hand.

15 Though He slay me, yet will I
trust in Him;
But I will argue my ways before
Him.

לְנַבֵּי־חֹמֶר גַּבֵּיכֶם׃

13 הַחֲרִישׁוּ מִמֶּנִּי וַאֲדַבְּרָה־אָנִי
וְיַעֲבֹר עָלַי מָה׃

14 עַל־מָה ׀ אֶשָּׂא בְשָׂרִי בְשִׁנָּי
וְנַפְשִׁי אָשִׂים בְּכַפִּי׃

15 הֵן יִקְטְלֵנִי לֹא אֲיַחֵל
אַךְ־דְּרָכַי אֶל־פָּנָיו אוֹכִיחַ׃

v. 15. לוֹ ק׳

---

rubbish, your arguments are as breastworks of clay.' Eliphaz had urged,
*Remember, I pray thee, who ever perished,
being innocent?* (iv. 7). Modern commentators take this verse to be an ironic
reference to the traditional maxims
which had supported the friends in their
contention with Job. These shall burn
to ashes.

eminences of clay. The Hebrew word *gab*
may mean 'back,' but also as here 'bul-
warks, breastworks,' a figure for arguments. In the *American Journal for
Semitic Languages and Literatures* (xl p.
165), Dr. A. Cohen contends that this
derivation gives the reverse sense to that
required, since Job clearly intends that
the arguments adduced against him are
trivial and unsound, whereas 'a breast-
work of clay' is a symbol of strength and
endurance. With Ehrlich he connects
gab with the root *gabab* used in Rabbinical literature with the meaning 'rake
together' (leaves and straw). In Yoma
76a the phrase occurs, 'How long wilt
thou rake trifles (*megabbeb*) and bring
them against me?' in connection with a
controversy. He renders the line:
'Like useless bits of clay is your array of
arguments.'

13-19 JOB AGAIN CHALLENGES GOD

13. *that I may speak*. In the Hebrew
the pronoun *I* is stressed. Happen what
may, without fear of the dread punishment, he must speak out to God.

14. *wherefore? I will take my flesh in
my teeth*. A.V. renders: 'Wherefore do
I (R.V., should I) take my flesh in my
teeth.' Rashi, who apparently understood the verse in that sense, comments:
'To afflict myself and force myself to
silence.' Buttenweiser quotes an Arabic
parallel: 'Salim escaped with his life
between his jaws,' i.e. his life or ghost was
about to pass out from his mouth. The
expression is based on the primitive
notion that when a man dies, his soul
passes out of his body through his mouth
or nostrils. Similarly, the expression,
'I hold my life between my teeth,'
means I am at the point of death. Job
says he need not hesitate to risk his life,
since he may pass away any moment.
Many commentators have read in the
line the metaphor of a wild beast that
takes its prey in its teeth and carries it
away to safety.

and put my life in my hand. Equivalent
to the proverbial expression, 'to take
one's life in one's hand' (cf. Judg. xii. 3;
1 Sam. xix. 5, xxviii. 21). Although the
verse presents difficulties, the general
sense is clear: In defiant jeopardy of his
life, Job will speak out his innocence.

15. *though He slay me, yet will I trust in
Him*. This is one of the deservedly
imperishable lines in the Book, and one
of the most widely quoted and familiar
translations of A.V. William James, in
his *Varieties of Religious Experience*,
speaks of this tremendous utterance as

16 This also shall be my salvation,
That a hypocrite cannot come before Him.

נַּם־הוּא־לִי לִישׁוּעָה
כִּי־לֹא לְפָנָיו חָנֵף יָבוֹא:

17 Hear diligently my speech,
And let my declaration be in your ears.

שִׁמְעוּ שָׁמוֹעַ מִלָּתִי
וְאַחֲוָתִי בְּאָזְנֵיכֶם:

18 Behold now, I have ordered my cause;
I know that I shall be justified.

הִנֵּה־נָא עָרַכְתִּי מִשְׁפָּט
יָדַעְתִּי כִּי־אֲנִי אֶצְדָּק:

19 Who is he that will contend with me?
For then would I hold my peace and die.

מִי־הוּא יָרִיב עִמָּדִי
כִּי־עַתָּה אַחֲרִישׁ וְאֶגְוָע:

---

the quintessence of the Hebraic spirit of magnificent faith as contrasted with the sullen acquiescence in Fate of the stoic, pagan philosophy. It seems a pity to have to part with this line, particularly because such a declaration of absolute trust in God is in complete harmony with Job's character. Modern scholars maintain that the statement is premature in its present context, and with the frame of mind in which Job is here speaking. Accordingly Buttenweiser translates: 'If He killeth me—well and good! I have nothing to hope for. Only my conduct I desire to justify to His face.' This follows the *kethib*, *lo* (with *aleph*), 'not'; the reading of the Masoretes is *lo* (with *vaw*) 'in Him.' Rashi explains the *kerē*: 'Even though He slay me, I will not be separated from Him, but I will constantly hope for Him. Therefore, there is no running away or rebellion in my words.' Another interpretation of the *kerē* is, 'for it (His slaying) do I hope (or, wait)'; I would welcome death at His hands, since life has become distasteful to me.

I will argue my ways. He means that he will defend his uprightness and innocence.

16. *this also shall be my salvation.* The fuller implication of this statement, rightly described as an exquisite and heart-searching verse, is in the fact that Job finds courage and strength in the inner consciousness of his probity to speak openly and honestly before God. The godless man (*a hypocrite*), tormented by his sense of guilt, would have to keep silent before his fate. It is the knowledge of his clear conscience that becomes for Job the firm ground of assurance that at last his struggles will be crowned with deliverance and salvation.

17. *my declaration.* The word is an Aramaism, found only here in Scripture. Ibn Ezra calls attention to the unique form.

18. *I have ordered my cause.* This is an archaism, meaning 'arranged, set in order'; 'I have stated my case.' There is a new note of confidence in Job's speech, the growing inner conviction that his innocence will at last be vindicated and that God will justify his integrity.

19. *who is he that will contend with me?* Note the similar phrase in Isa. l. 8. He speaks with the boldness of one whose life has been an open, spotless book. He knows that none can bring proof of any real stain on his soul.

would I hold my peace and die. Were anyone to challenge his innocence and prove a charge against him, he would remain silent and be content to die.

20 Only do not two things unto me,
   Then will I not hide myself from
   Thee:

21 Withdraw Thy hand far from
   me;
   And let not Thy terror make me
   afraid.

22 Then call Thou, and I will
   answer;
   Or let me speak, and answer
   Thou me.

23 How many are mine iniquities
   and sins?
   Make me to know my transgression and my sin.

24 Wherefore hidest Thou Thy face,
   And holdest me for Thine enemy?

20 אַךְ־שְׁתַּיִם אַל־תַּעַשׂ עִמָּדִי
   אָז מִפָּנֶיךָ לֹא אֶסָּתֵר:

21 כַּפְּךָ מֵעָלַי הַרְחַק
   וְאֵמָתְךָ אַל־תְּבַעֲתַנִּי:

22 וּקְרָא וְאָנֹכִי אֶעֱנֶה
   אוֹ־אֲדַבֵּר וַהֲשִׁיבֵנִי:

23 כַּמָּה לִי עֲוֺנוֹת וְחַטָּאוֹת
   פִּשְׁעִי וְחַטָּאתִי הֹדִיעֵנִי:

24 לָמָּה־פָנֶיךָ תַסְתִּיר
   וְתַחְשְׁבֵנִי לְאוֹיֵב לָךְ:

v. 21. פתח באתנח   v. 21. פתח בס״פ

20-28 JOB PLEADS WITH GOD

20. only do not two things unto me. Cf.
his former plea, ix. 34f. The *two things*,
actually one and the same thing—that
God may remove His afflicting hand and
not terrify him with His omnipotence—
are stated in verse 21. Other examples
of this stylistic peculiarity are found in
Isa. li. 19; Jer. ii. 13. Job pleads that
God may grant his request so that he
may have a fair trial.

21. withdraw Thy hand. Ibn Ezra takes
this to mean 'Thy stroke,' because it is
known that the stroke proceeds from man
with the *palm* (so lit.) of the hand. So
too Ralbag. Rashi interprets as 'Thy
force' and cites Elihu's words, *Neither
shall my pressure* (achpi) *be heavy upon
thee* (xxxiii. 7). He finds it difficult to
accept the explanation of *kapecha* as *Thy
hand* (yadecha), since we do not find the
word *kaph* used in a bad but in a beneficent sense (to shield), as in (I) *will
cover thee with My hand* (Exod. xxxiii.
22).

22. then call Thou, and I will answer.
The imagery is that of a legal trial where
Job offers to appear either as respondent
or appellant. Peake calls attention to
the similar expression in xiv. 15, but

with how different a sense! Here a call
to a lawsuit, there a call to fellowship
and love.

23. how many are mine iniquities and sins?
Confident of his innocence, Job begins
his plea by demanding to know the
number and the nature of his sins.
Confessing that he may have been guilty
of minor sins in his youth (verse 26), he
asks to know what sins of magnitude he
has committed to account for his great
calamities. 'Job and his friends both
agree in the theory that great afflictions
are evidence that God holds those whom
He afflicts guilty of great offences. The
friends believe that Job is guilty of such
offences; he knows he is not, and he
here demands to know what the sins are
of which God holds him guilty' (Davidson).

24. wherefore hidest Thou Thy face. The
suggestion has been made that there is a
dramatic pause after verse 23 while Job
waits to hear the accusation made against
him. The silence remains unbroken,
and he indignantly demands, *Wherefore
hidest Thou Thy face?* The more probable interpretation is that Job complains
at the hiding of God's face in that He
fails to bring him respite from his trials.

25 Wilt Thou harass a driven leaf?
And wilt Thou pursue the dry
stubble?

26 That Thou shouldest write bitter
things against me,
And make me to inherit the iniquities of my youth.

27 Thou puttest my feet also in the
stocks,
And lookest narrowly unto all my
paths;
Thou drawest Thee a line about
the soles of my feet;

28 Though I am like a wine-skin
that consumeth,
Like a garment that is moth-
eaten.

הַעֲלֶה נִדָּף תַּעֲרוֹץ
וְאֶת־קַשׁ יָבֵשׁ תִּרְדֹּף׃

כִּי־תִכְתֹּב עָלַי מְרֹרוֹת
וְתוֹרִישֵׁנִי עֲוֹנוֹת נְעוּרָי׃

וְתָשֵׂם בַּסַּד רַגְלַי
וְתִשְׁמוֹר כָּל־אָרְחֹתָי
עַל־שָׁרְשֵׁי רַגְלַי תִּתְחַקֶּה׃

וְהוּא כְּרָקָב יִבְלֶה
כְּבֶגֶד אֲכָלוֹ עָשׁ׃

14   CHAPTER XIV   יד

1 Man that is born of a woman
Is of few days, and full of trouble.

אָדָם יְלוּד אִשָּׁה
קְצַר יָמִים וּשְׂבַע־רֹגֶז׃

---

25. *a driven leaf.* The phrase is elliptical for 'a leaf driven by the wind.'
The driven leaf is the sport of the
winds, helpless and utterly at their mercy.
Why should God, in His infinite might,
assail one so insignificant as he?

the dry stubble. Dispersed by a gust of
wind (cf. Ps. i. 4).

26. *make me to inherit the iniquities of my
youth.* The meaning is, that God
should decree bitter punishment and
make him now to suffer for some un-
remembered venial sin committed in his
youth (cf. Ps. xxv. 7).

27. *Thou puttest my feet also in the stocks.*
The three figures in the verse evoke
images of arrest and impossibility of
escape. The comparison of feet in the
stocks is that of the malefactor held fast
to a block of wood. The Hebrew, *sad,*
is an Aramaic loan-word (cf. xxxiii. 11
for another occurrence).

lookest narrowly unto all my paths. God
carefully and closely watches every step
he takes.

Thou drawest Thee a line. Beyond which
his feet may not pass.

28. *though I am like a wine-skin that
consumeth.* An impossible rendering.
Though I am is 'and he' in the Hebrew,
and there appears to be no authority for
the meaning *wine-skin* given to *rakab.*
This word and *ash, moth,* both occur in
Hosea v. 12, *Therefore am I unto Ephraim
as a moth, and to the house of Judah as
rottenness.* The most probable translation is: 'And he (the person upon whom
Thou hast directed all this attention) is
like rottenness that decayeth, like a
moth-eaten garment.' The use of the
third person, 'and he,' intensifies the
sense of insignificance which possesses
the speaker. He is too unworthy an
object to receive such notice from the
Almighty God.

CHAPTER XIV

1-6 PLAINT OVER MAN'S FRAILTY AND
BREVITY

1. *man that is born of a woman.* Man's
frailty is the natural condition of his

2 He cometh forth like a flower, and
    withereth;
  He fleeth also as a shadow, and
    continueth not.

3 And dost Thou open Thine eyes
    upon such a one,
  And bringest me into judgment
    with Thee?

4 Who can bring a clean thing out of
    an unclean? not one.

5 Seeing his days are determined,
  The number of his months is with
    Thee,
  And Thou hast appointed his
    bounds that he cannot pass;

2 כְּצִיץ יָצָא וַיִּמָּל
וַיִּבְרַח כַּצֵּל וְלֹא יַעֲמוֹד:

3 אַף־עַל־זֶה פָּקַחְתָּ עֵינֶךָ
וְאֹתִי תָבִיא בְמִשְׁפָּט עִמָּךְ:

4 מִי־יִתֵּן טָהוֹר מִטָּמֵא
לֹא אֶחָד:

5 אִם־חֲרוּצִים ׀ יָמָיו
מִסְפַּר־חֳדָשָׁיו אִתָּךְ
חֻקּוֹ עָשִׂיתָ וְלֹא יַעֲבֹר:

v. 5. חֻקָּיו ק'

---

birth. 'Akabya, the son of Mahalalel,
said: Reflect upon three things, and
thou wilt not come within the power of
sin: know whence thou camest, and
whither thou art going, and before Whom
thou wilt in future have to give account
and reckoning. Whence thou camest:
from a putrefying drop, etc.' (Aboth
iii. 1).

2. *he cometh forth like a flower, and
withereth.* The short-lived beauty of the
flower and the quick flight of the shadow
are the melancholy metaphors of man's
pilgrimage on earth (cf. Isa. xl. 6ff.;
Ps. xc. 5f.; Eccles. vi. 12). *Withereth* is
from a root *malal*, 'to languish, fade,
hang down.' R.V. 'Is cut down.'

he fleeth also as a shadow. 'Man fleeth
speedily from the world like the shadow
which does not remain for a long time
in one place; as the sun sets so the shadow
declines from its place' (Metsudath
David).

3. *and dost Thou open Thine eyes upon
such a one.* He expresses wonder at
God's severity in judging his life so
minutely, and punishing such a fleeting
creature so severely. *Open Thine eyes*
means to scrutinize in order to punish;

'to examine carefully for his sins' (Rashi).

4. *who can bring a clean thing . . . one.*
The brevity of the Hebrew line and its
seeming rhythmic abruptness, as well as
the use of the phrase *who can bring* (*mi
yitten*, literally 'who will give') make its
interpretation doubtful. Buttenweiser
maintains that it must be rendered: 'Oh,
if there might be found but one pure
man among the impure—but not even
one.' The reference would accordingly
be to the faulty state which is inevitable
in the human being (cf. Ps. li. 7; Prov.
xx. 9; Eccles. vii. 20). Ibn Ezra compares
the verse to Ps. li. 7, *Behold, I was
brought forth in iniquity*, which 'is the
Oriental way of expressing the idea that
the human being is naturally prone to
err,' and the plea is made 'as urging the
essential need for God's clemency'
(Cohen, in Soncino ed., *ad loc.*). Like the
Psalmist, Job contends that God should
exercise clemency towards a creature
born with the tendency to err.

5. *seeing his days are determined.* Since
God has determined precisely the limits
of man's life and the human boundaries
beyond which he cannot go in the world,
let these indemnities suffice Him.

6 Look away from him, that he may
  rest,
    Till he shall accomplish, as a hire-
    ling, his day.

7 For there is hope of a tree,
    If it be cut down, that it will
    sprout again,
    And that the tender branch there-
    of will not cease.

8 Though the root thereof wax old
  in the earth,
    And the stock thereof die in the
    ground;

9 Yet through the scent of water it
  will bud,
    And put forth boughs like a plant.

6 שְׁעֵה מֵעָלָיו וְיֶחְדָּל
עַד־יִרְצֶה כְּשָׂכִיר יוֹמוֹ:

7 כִּי יֵשׁ לָעֵץ תִּקְוָה
אִם־יִכָּרֵת וְעוֹד יַחֲלִיף
וְיֹנַקְתּוֹ לֹא תֶחְדָּל:

8 אִם־יַזְקִין בָּאָרֶץ שָׁרְשׁוֹ
וּבֶעָפָר יָמוּת גִּזְעוֹ:

9 מֵרֵיחַ מַיִם יַפְרִחַ
וְעָשָׂה קָצִיר כְּמוֹ־נָטַע:

6. look away from him, that he may rest.
Verse 5 appears to be the protasis of this
verse and has been so rendered by
Buttenweiser: 'If man's days are limited,
the number of his moons determined by
Thee; if Thou hast fixed the bounds
beyond which he cannot pass, turn
Thou away from him, that he may rest,
that at least he may enjoy his day like
the hired labourer.' This thought is
paralleled by Ps. xxxix. 14, *Look away
from me, that I may take comfort, before
I go hence, and be no more,* upon which
Cohen remarks: 'Usually the petition is
for God to look towards the suppliant
and show favour to him. But here He
is the One whose eyes behold the
thoughts and deeds of man, the Critic
of his way of living.' So it is here: let
God relent from His cruel watchfulness
that he may enjoy, as a day-labourer
finds satisfaction in the evening when
his day's task is over, the evening of his
earthly existence.

7-22 IS THERE LIFE AFTER DEATH?

7. for there is hope of a tree. Job now
turns to the bitter destiny of man's
extinction in death. Out of the stump of
a tree, grown old and lopped off, there
may come new growth. But man's

sleep in death knows no awakening. It is
poignantly significant, none the less, that
the possibility, with which he fondly toys
in his mind only to reject, passes before his
tormented imagination. Davidson cites
a striking passage contrasting man's
final extinction in death with the rebirth
of trees and flowers: 'Alas! the mallows
when they die in the garden, and the
green parsley and the vigorous woolly
dill, live once more and spring up for
another year. But we the great and
mighty, the wise men, whensoever we
die, sleep unheard in the bosom of the
earth, the long, unending, unwaking
sleep' (Moschus, iii. 106f.).

**8. though the root thereof wax old in the
earth.** 'Yea, even if the root thereof wax
old in the earth so that there remain no
sap in it' (Metsudath David). Verses
7-9 refer to the custom in Palestine of
cutting off the tops, or even the trunks
of trees that have become old and decayed, in order to produce a new growth
(cf. Isa. vi. 13).

9. yet through the scent of water it will bud.
Buttenweiser, regarding *nata, plant*, as a
verbal noun (cf. Isa. xvii. 11), translates:
'As soon as it scenteth water, it will bud
again, and send forth sprouts as if newly
planted.'

10 But man dieth, and lieth low;
   Yea, man perisheth, and where is
   he?

11 As the waters fail from the sea,
   And the river is drained dry;

12 So man lieth down and riseth not;
   Till the heavens be no more, they
   shall not awake,
   Nor be roused out of their sleep.

13 Oh that Thou wouldest hide me
   in the nether-world,
   That Thou wouldest keep me
   secret, until Thy wrath be past,
   That Thou wouldest appoint me
   a set time, and remember
   me!—

14 If a man die, may he live again ?

וְגֶ֣בֶר יָ֭מוּת וַֽיֶּחֱלָ֑שׁ 10
וַיִּגְוַ֖ע אָדָ֣ם וְאַיּֽוֹ׃

אָֽזְלוּ־מַ֭יִם מִנִּי־יָ֑ם 11
וְ֝נָהָ֗ר יֶחֱרַ֥ב וְיָבֵֽשׁ׃

וְאִ֥ישׁ שָׁכַ֗ב וְֽלֹא־יָ֫ק֥וּם 12
עַד־בִּלְתִּ֣י שָׁ֭מַיִם לֹ֣א יָקִ֑יצוּ
וְלֹֽא־יֵ֝עֹ֗רוּ מִשְּׁנָתָֽם׃

מִ֤י יִתֵּ֨ן ׀ בִּשְׁא֬וֹל תַּצְפִּנֵ֗נִי 13
תַּ֭סְתִּירֵנִי עַד־שׁ֣וּב אַפֶּ֑ךָ
תָּ֤שִׁ֥ית לִ֖י חֹ֣ק וְתִזְכְּרֵֽנִי׃

אִם־יָמ֥וּת גֶּ֝֗בֶר הֲיִחְיֶ֥ה 14

---

10. *but man dieth, and lieth low.* The
latter verb is literally 'becometh weak, prostrate.' Peake well expresses the contrast
thus: 'While the tree hewn down to its
stump, and its roots all decayed, still
holds on so tenaciously to life that at the
slightest stimulus, the mere scent of water,
it bursts into new shoots and foliage
like a tender plant in the lusty vigour
of its early growth, man dies and lies
prostrate, his old haunts know him no
more, he never rises out of death's everlasting sleep.'

11. *as the waters fail from the sea.* The
verse is a reminiscence, with slight varia-
tion, of Isa. xix. 5 where the reference is
to the Nile. *The sea* here means inland
water, a lake; and the word for *river*
(*nahar*) denotes a normally permanent
flow as against that of the *nachal*, the
wadi (see on vi. 15). The figure is
graphic in its comparison of man's utter
extinction in death.

12. *so man lieth down and riseth not.*
'When man dieth, he shall never rise
again, till the heavens fade away and are
destroyed, i.e. never shall the dead awake

or be roused from sleep' (Metsudath
David). According to Buttenweiser, the
clause is hypothetical: 'Even should the
heavens be no more' altogether, and not
indicative of any eschatological notion,
such as we meet with in later literature.
Wishing to be most emphatic, Job says
that he can sooner conceive of the dis-
appearance of the heavens (which in
both the older and contemporary literature are spoken of as established for
ever; cf. Ps. lxxxix. 30) than of the
resurrection of man.

13. *oh that Thou wouldest hide me in the
nether-world.* There appears in this
impassioned appeal some groping toward the hope of a life beyond. The
thought strikes him that there is a possibility of another fate than that of eternally
abiding in Sheol. Perhaps he would
remain there for *a set time*, and then be
remembered by God.

14. *if a man die, may he live again?* The
all-important question forces itself to his
mind, despite his doubts. He does not
answer it, but reflects wistfully upon it.
How gladly would he wait, if there were

All the days of my service would
  I wait,
Till my relief should come—

15 Thou wouldest call, and I would
     answer Thee;
Thou wouldest have a desire to
  the work of Thy hands.

16 But now Thou numberest my
     steps,
Thou dost not even wait for my
  sin;

17 My transgression is sealed up in
     a bag,
And Thou heapest up mine
  iniquity.

18 And surely the mountain falling
     crumbleth away,
And the rock is removed out of
  its place;

כָּל־יְמֵי צְבָאִי אֲיַחֵל
עַד־בּוֹא חֲלִיפָתִי׃
תִּקְרָא וְאָנֹכִי אֶעֱנֶךָּ
לְמַעֲשֵׂה יָדֶיךָ תִכְסֹף׃
כִּי־עַתָּה צְעָדַי תִּסְפּוֹר
לֹא־תִשְׁמֹר עַל־חַטָּאתִי׃
חָתֻם בִּצְרוֹר פִּשְׁעִי
וַתִּטְפֹּל עַל־עֲוֹנִי׃
וְאוּלָם הַר־נוֹפֵל יִבּוֹל
וְצוּר יֶעְתַּק מִמְּקֹמוֹ׃

but a chance of another life, both through
his period of trouble upon earth, and
the weary darkness of the grave, till his
'change' or 'release' (A.J. *relief*)—viz.
from the darkness of Sheol (x. 21f.) to a
new life—came, and he heard (verse 15)
the voice of his Creator calling him back
to Himself, and no longer estranged from
the work of His hands! (cf. Davidson).

15. *Thou wouldest call, and I would
answer Thee*. The verse echoes the
thought of vii. 21. When God relented,
how eagerly would Job, languishing in
Sheol, respond to His friendly approach!
The meaning becomes clearer if we
construe the sentence conditionally, as
does Buttenweiser who gives this force-
ful translation of verses 15-17: 'If Thou
didst call me, I would answer Thee, if
Thou didst long for the work of Thy
hands; for then wouldest Thou take full
account of my steps, not merely watch
for my sin. My transgressions would
be sealed up, as in a bag, Thou wouldest
whitewash my sin.'

16. *but now Thou numberest my steps*.
As A.J. translates the verse, the vision
of revival after death, which had flashed
through Job's mind for a moment, is now
followed with a description of God's

jealous watchfulness of his every step, as
if he had committed some great wrong
(cf. xiii. 27). Rashi and Ibn Ezra support this interpretation: 'Thou dost not
watch *except* for my sins.'

17. *my transgression is sealed up in a bag*.
My transgression is sealed up and
guarded in a purse, like silver or pearls,
that it be not lost (Rashi).

Thou heapest up mine iniquity. The root
meaning of the verb is 'to smear,' and in
xiii. 4 it occurs in the phrase *plasterers of
lies*. Some authorities find in this line
the signification 'to glue,' God glued the
iniquity up 'for safe keeping against the
day of reckoning' (BDB) (cf. for the idea,
his sin is laid up in store, Hos. xiii. 12).
Others assign to it the meaning of 'smear
over, whitewash, palliate' (cf. Buttenweiser above).

18. *and surely the mountain falling
crumbleth away*. Even as the mighty
mountains perish and the great rock is
worn away by the ravages of time or by
the violence of an earthquake, so too man
is destroyed, not to return and flourish
again (cf. Metsudath David). For the
perishability of mountains, cf. Isa. liv. 10.

19 The waters wear the stones;
   The overflowings thereof wash
      away the dust of the earth;
   So Thou destroyest the hope of
      man.

20 Thou prevailest for ever against
      him, and he passeth;
   Thou changest his countenance,
      and sendest him away.

21 His sons come to honour, and he
      knoweth it not;
   And they are brought low, but he
      regardeth them not.

22 But his flesh grieveth for him,
   And his soul mourneth over him.

19 אֲבָנִים ׀ שָׁחֲקוּ מַיִם
תִּשְׁטֹף־סְפִיחֶיהָ עֲפַר־אָרֶץ
וְתִקְוַת אֱנוֹשׁ הֶאֱבַדְתָּ:

20 תִּתְקְפֵהוּ לָנֶצַח וַיַּהֲלֹךְ
מְשַׁנֶּה פָנָיו וַתְּשַׁלְּחֵהוּ:

21 יִכְבְּדוּ בָנָיו וְלֹא יֵדָע
וְיִצְעֲרוּ וְלֹא־יָבִין לָמוֹ:

22 אַךְ בְּשָׂרוֹ עָלָיו יִכְאָב
וְנַפְשׁוֹ עָלָיו תֶּאֱבָל:

19. *the waters wear the stones.* 'The waters rub away the stones after a long time; the waves of the flowing stream wash away the dust; so Thou destroyest the hope of man in his death' (Ibn Ezra). Job has dismissed the possibility of life beyond the grave. He apparently means, as Ibn Ezra interprets, that man's hope of existence is completely destroyed in death.

20. *Thou prevailest . . . Thou changest his countenance.* Ibn Ezra explains the verse as referring to the physical change which sets in with rigor mortis. It may describe the decay of the body after death. The verb *takeph*, 'prevail, overpower,' is an Aramaism whose sound and sense combine in tremendous force. *Yahaloch, he passeth,* lit. 'goeth,' is used as a poetical synonym (or as Buttenwieser suggests, a euphemism) for *yamuth*, 'he dieth.'

21. *his sons come to honour, and he knoweth it not.* This thought, that knowledge ceases at death, is impressively formulated in Eccles. ix. 5f. The verb *kabed* means 'heavy, weighty' as well as *honour*. Ibn Ezra comments: 'They become heavy (i.e. wealthy) in silver and gold, but he knoweth it not; and they are brought low (impoverished), but he regardeth it not.'

22. *but his flesh grieveth for him.* The customary explanation of verses 21f. is that the self of the dead man, though it has no other knowledge of what transpires on earth, does have a dim awareness of the pain of the decaying body in the grave and of the dreary and mournful existence of the soul in the nether-world. A radically different interpretation has been suggested by Buttenwieser, which lifts these verses into another and far more advanced conception. He translates: 'If his children are wealthy, he doth not know it, neither is he concerned about them if they are poor. Only his kin grieve after him, and his servants mourn for him.' He claims that *basar, flesh*, here means 'kin' as in Gen. xxxvii. 27; Isa. lviii. 7; and *nephesh, soul*, signifies 'serfs, servants' as in Gen. xii. 5, xiv. 21, xxxvi. 6; Ezek. xxvii. 13. In these two verses, as later in xxi. 21, the author expresses a view far in advance of his age. The prevailing belief of the time was that the shades in Sheol not only retain memory of their own life on earth, but have knowledge of the fortunes of their kin after their death; and they were thought to be able to exert influence on the affairs of the living. In contrast to this, the writer denies that there is such a thing as a shadowy continuance of one's existence after death; for him when a man dies, he ceases to be. He has no longer any knowledge of the life and happenings on earth, and he is altogether unconcerned about those he leaves behind; whether they are prosperous or poor does not affect him.

JOB

1 Then answered Eliphaz the Temanite, and said:

2 Should a wise man make answer
with windy knowledge,
And fill his belly with the east
wind?

3 Should he reason with unprofitable talk,
Or with speeches wherewith he
can do no good?

4 Yea, thou doest away with fear,
And impairest devotion before
God.

וַיַּעַן אֱלִיפַז הַתֵּימָנִי וַיֹּאמַר:

הֶחָכָם יַעֲנֶה דַעַת־רוּחַ
וִימַלֵּא קָדִים בִּטְנוֹ:

הוֹכֵחַ בְּדָבָר לֹא יִסְכּוֹן
וּמִלִּים לֹא־יוֹעִיל בָּם:

אַף־אַתָּה תָּפֵר יִרְאָה
וְתִגְרַע שִׂיחָה לִפְנֵי־אֵל:

CHAPTERS XV-XXI

THE SECOND CYCLE OF SPEECHES

THE second cycle of colloquies carries forward the spiritual drama that rages in the soul of Job. They are significant in deepening the contrast between the character of Job and his three friends. We see Eliphaz, Bildad and Zophar clinging stubbornly and with increasing fanaticism to their inherited beliefs, repeating with growing irritation their stale arguments about the dreadful fate that overtakes the wicked. Whereas the friends only become more intolerant and less understanding of Job's inward struggle until they finally lay open though unfounded charges against his piety and integrity, Job moves painfully forward toward inner light and peace. A large part of the spiritual splendour of this masterpiece is to be found in the skilful psychological artistry that portrays the progress in thought of the stricken righteous man as he turns from blind, fanatical men and a seeming cruel God to the God of justice and mercy Who shall be his Witness and Vindicator, his Champion in the struggle for truth.

CHAPTER XV

THE SECOND SPEECH OF ELIPHAZ

IN sonorous rhetoric and the dignified tones of one advanced in years, Eliphaz repeats his platitudes about the speedy and terrible destruction that comes upon the wicked. He rails at Job for his blasphemies, the fruit of an evil conscience. Eliphaz, for all the flow of his speech, remains static in his arguments and incapable of probing the heart of Job, or of comprehending his daring spiritual contest with God.

1-6 JOB REPROVED AS IRRELIGIOUS

2. *should a wise man make answer with windy knowledge.* The mention of *a wise man* alludes to Job's claims in xii. 3, xiii. 2. Eliphaz makes the retort that Job's answer consisted of nothing else than windy words, empty of substantial reasoning.

the east wind. The scorching sirocco which blows from the deserts on the east and south-east and brings no refreshing coolness. It therefore typifies what is useless and harmful (cf. Hos. xii. 2).

3. *should he reason with unprofitable talk.* lit. 'reasoning with a word (i.e. argument) which has no use' (cf. *it profiteth a man nothing,* xxxiv. 9).

or with speeches. He implies that Job had talked at great length but without producing conviction in his listeners.

4. *yea, thou doest away with fear.* i.e. the fear of God, the equivalent of our word

5 For thine iniquity teacheth thy
mouth,
And thou choosest the tongue of
the crafty.

6 Thine own mouth condemneth
thee, and not I;
Yea, thine own lips testify against
thee.

7 Art thou the first man that was
born?
Or wast thou brought forth before
the hills?

8 Dost thou hearken in the council
of God?
And dost thou restrain wisdom to
thyself?

5 כִּי־יְאַלֵּף עֲוֹנְךָ פִּיךָ
וְתִבְחַר לְשׁוֹן עֲרוּמִים׃

6 יַרְשִׁיעֲךָ פִיךָ וְלֹא־אָנִי
וּשְׂפָתֶיךָ יַעֲנוּ־בָךְ׃

7 הֲרִאישׁוֹן אָדָם תִּוָּלֵד
וְלִפְנֵי גְבָעוֹת חוֹלָלְתָּ׃

8 הַבְסוֹד אֱלוֹהַ תִּשְׁמָע
וְתִגְרַע אֵלֶיךָ חָכְמָה׃

v. 7. י יתיר י.   v. 8. בב״א הב״א בדגש

'religion' (cf. iv. 6). Eliphaz makes the
charge that Job's words are calculated
to destroy religion.

impairest devotion before God. lit. 'dimin-
ishest meditation before God.' Job's
words, blasphemous in tone, have the
effect of undermining religious faith in
others.

5. *for thine iniquity teacheth thy mouth.*
Job's utterances, it is alleged, are the
result and proof of his guilt. *Iniquity*
here signifies 'consciousness of sin.' In
vain has Job chosen *the tongue of the
crafty* to conceal his guilt. 'Thy very
mouth instructeth man and maketh him
to know thine iniquity' (Ibn Ezra).

6. *thine own mouth condemneth thee, and
not I.* 'The words of thy mouth declare
thy wickedness, and it is not necessary
for me to say it; and the words of thy
lips witness against thee for the iniquity
which is in thy hand' (Metsudath David).
Job is convicted out of his own mouth.

7-16 JOB ACCUSED OF
PRESUMPTUOUS IRREVERENCE

7. *art thou the first man that was born?*
Eliphaz ironically asks him if he thinks
the wisdom of the ages is embodied in
him. From what superior source does
Job derive his boasted wisdom? 'Wast

thou created before Adam?' interprets
Rashi, 'wast thou first created, before
Adam was formed from the ground, that
thou knowest to ascertain all the wisdom
commanded of the Creator?' 'Wast
thou born before Adam, and has extreme
longevity made thee so exceedingly wise?'
(Berechiah). The commentators quote
a Hindu proverb: 'Yes, indeed, he is the
first man; no wonder that he is so wise!'

wast thou brought forth before the hills?
The line is usually taken to mean: 'Is
Job like the primæval man?—who, coming fresh from his Creator's hand, was
supposed to be endowed with super-
human wisdom (cf. 7b with Prov. viii.
25b referring to the Divine wisdom)'
(Davidson). Opposing this view, Buttenweiser argues on grammatical grounds
that verses 7f. contain no reference to the
Demiurgic Wisdom or the notion of
Primæval Man brought into being before
the creation of the universe and endowed
with the creative wisdom of God.
Rishon adam can only mean 'the first
of men.' The expression for Primæval
Man in the later Jewish literature dealing
with this concept is *adam ha-kadmon*, or
more frequently the Aramaic *adam
kadma'a*.

8. *dost thou hearken in the council of God?*
Has Job's wisdom come to him through
revelation? he asks sarcastically. The
council of God means the company of
angels in attendance upon Him (cf.

9 What knowest thou, that we know
  not?
  What understandest thou, which
  is not in us?

מַה־יָּדַעְתָּ וְלֹא נֵדָע

תָּבִין וְלֹא־עִמָּנוּ הוּא:

10 With us are both the gray-headed
   and the very aged men,
   Much older than thy father.

גַּם־שָׂב גַּם־יָשִׁישׁ בָּנוּ

כַּבִּיר מֵאָבִיךָ יָמִים:

11 Are the consolations of God too
   small for thee,
   And the word that dealeth gently
   with thee?

הַמְעַט מִמְּךָ תַּנְחֻמוֹת אֵל

וְדָבָר לָאַט עִמָּךְ:

12 Why doth thy heart carry thee
   away?
   And why do thine eyes wink?

מַה־יִּקָּחֲךָ לִבֶּךָ

וּמַה־יִּרְזְמוּן עֵינֶיךָ:

---

1 Kings xxii. 19f.; cf. also Jer. xxiii. 18, 22; Ps. lxxxix. 8).

dost thou restrain wisdom to thyself? lit. 'draw away, reserve.' The question implies, Hast thou monopolized wisdom?

9. *what knowest thou, that we know not?* The sarcasm of Eliphaz's string of questions is unwarranted. Job never claimed to be wiser than his friends. He had only criticized their pretensions to know God's thoughts, and asserted, *I have understanding as well as you; I am not inferior to you* (xii. 3).

10. *with us are . . . the very aged men.* Buttenweiser understands *with us* as the editorial 'we,' a case of brachyology where the pronominal suffix of *with us* in the first clause is to be construed as nominative of the second clause. He translates vividly: 'I am an old, gray-haired man, more advanced in years than thy father.' Eliphaz seems to argue that because he is older than Job's father, he is necessarily more experienced in life and wiser than Job. Such a contention accords with Hebraic usage, whereby the 'elders' were appointed the national councillors on the assumption that with old age comes wisdom.

11. *are the consolations of God too small for thee.* The verse has presented difficulties to scholars and there have been conflicting interpretations. The first line appears to mean the consoling doctrine of God's providence and care for the righteous, and the persuasive admonitions, addressed to Job by Eliphaz in his first speech (v. 17-27). In the second line, *that dealeth gently* (*la'at*) appears to denote Eliphaz's description of the seeming conciliatory tone of his former address. Ibn Ezra explains *la'at* as 'spoken in a whisper with thee, as though in secret.' Buttenweiser, apparently following this clue, renders the line: 'Have the consolations of God expressed to thee, and the word revealed in whispers, have they no weight with thee?' The translation 'revealed in whispers' finds support in the Hebrew word *itti* (which BDB relate to *la'at*) meaning 'mutterer, soothsayer' (cf. Isa. xix. 3). The expression would then allude to Eliphaz's belief that he had received a revelation from God and regarded himself as the Divine instrument for expounding to Job the meaning of his suffering. Job may be making a retort to the use of the word *consolations* when he says to his friends, *sorry comforters are ye all* (xvi. 2).

12. *why doth thy heart carry thee away?* Having challenged Job's claims to superior wisdom, Eliphaz now proceeds to censure Job's violent and irreverent outbursts against God.

why do thine eyes wink? More properly 'flash' in rage. The word occurs only

13 That thou turnest thy spirit
   against God,
   And lettest such words go out of
   thy mouth.

14 What is man, that he should be
   clean?
   And he that is born of a woman,
   that he should be righteous?

15 Behold, He putteth no trust in
   His holy ones;
   Yea, the heavens are not clean in
   His sight.

16 How much less one that is abominable and impure,
   Man who drinketh iniquity like
   water!

17 I will tell thee, hear thou me;
   And that which I have seen I will
   declare—

13 כִּי־תָשִׁיב אֶל־אֵל רוּחֶךָ
   וְהֹצֵאתָ מִפִּיךָ מִלִּין׃

14 מָה־אֱנוֹשׁ כִּי־יִזְכֶּה
   וְכִי־יִצְדַּק יְלוּד אִשָּׁה׃

15 הֵן בִּקְדֹשָׁו לֹא יַאֲמִין
   וְשָׁמַיִם לֹא־זַכּוּ בְעֵינָיו׃

16 אַף כִּי־נִתְעָב וְנֶאֱלָח
   אִישׁ־שֹׁתֶה כַמַּיִם עַוְלָה׃

17 אֲחַוְךָ שְׁמַע־לִי
   וְזֶה־חָזִיתִי וַאֲסַפֵּרָה׃

v. 15. v. 17. בקדשיו ק׳ בנ״א הו׳ בדגש

---

here. Rashi suggests that the verb is
identical with *ramaz*, an Aramaic root,
'to flash' in anger.

13. *that thou turnest thy spirit against
God*. *Spirit* here means 'anger' (temper),
as in Prov. xvi. 32, xxv. 28, xxix. 11.

such words. lit. 'words.' Buttenwieser
contends that this is an instance of
emphatic indetermination and translates
'unheard-of words.'

14. *what is man, that he should be clean?*
Eliphaz reverts to his former argument
(iv. 12-21), and the revelation that had
come to him.   With this verse, cf. especially iv. 17. 'Who is the man who is so
pure in his deeds as to say that God
perverts His justice by exacting punishment from him for no reason' (Metsudath
David).

15. *He putteth no trust in His holy ones*.
Cf. iv. 18. By *holy ones* the angels are
intended.

the heavens are not clean in His sight. Two
interpretations have been attached to
the heavens.   Some moderns, as did
Rashi, explain it as ellipsis for 'the host
of heaven' and quote in support *the
stars are not pure in His sight* (xxv. 5).
As Peake points out, 'The stars were

regarded as animate beings,' and so are
a designation of the angels.   Less probable is the alternative that, although the
sky is described as pure (Exod. xxiv. 10;
Ezek. i. 22), it is not always so, as when
it is clouded.

16. *how much less one that is abominable
and impure*. Cf. Ps. xiv. 3. The root
alach, translated *impure*, means 'to be
corrupt,' originally of milk that has
turned sour.   It occurs again only in Ps.
xiv. 3, liii. 4 where it is translated 'become tainted' by Cohen.   Eliphaz speaks
of men in general, although the implication is to Job that if the shoe fits, he
may wear it.

drinketh iniquity like water. 'To drink
like water is, as Duhm takes it, to drink
in full gulps, stronger liquids being drunk
cautiously; others take it, as eagerly as a
thirsty man drinks water, or that it is as
natural for man to do evil as for him to
drink water' (Peake).

17-35 EVIL CONSCIENCE AND DISASTER
         OVERTAKE THE WICKED

17. *I will tell thee*. Having completed
his reproof of Job, Eliphaz now dwells
upon the theme of the destruction and
disaster that overtake the wicked.   He

75

18 Which wise men have told
    From their fathers, and have not
    hid it;

19 Unto whom alone the land was
    given,
    And no stranger passed among
    them.

20 The wicked man travaileth with
    pain all his days,
    Even the number of years that are
    laid up for the oppressor.

21 A sound of terrors is in his ears:
    In prosperity the destroyer shall
    come upon him.

22 He believeth not that he shall
    return out of darkness,
    And he is waited for of the sword.

אֲשֶׁר־חֲכָמִים יַגִּידוּ
וְלֹא כִחֲדוּ מֵאֲבוֹתָם׃
לָהֶם לְבַדָּם נִתְּנָה הָאָרֶץ
וְלֹא־עָבַר זָר בְּתוֹכָם׃
כָּל־יְמֵי רָשָׁע הוּא מִתְחוֹלֵל
וּמִסְפַּר שָׁנִים נִצְפְּנוּ לֶעָרִיץ׃
קוֹל־פְּחָדִים בְּאָזְנָיו
בַּשָּׁלוֹם שׁוֹדֵד יְבוֹאֶנּוּ׃
לֹא־יַאֲמִין שׁוּב מִנִּי־חֹשֶׁךְ
וְצָפוּ הוּא אֱלֵי־חָרֶב׃

v. 22. וצפוי ק׳

introduces this part of his speech by claiming it to be ancient, unspoiled wisdom. This verse is spoken in a tone of condescension: the knowledge he will impart is certified by his own observation. The verb for *tell* (*chiwwah*) is a poetical word. Buttenweiser explains it here as ellipsis for *chiwwah de'a* or *da'ath*, 'impart knowledge, or wisdom.' The full phrase occurs in xxxii. 6, 10, 17; Ps. xix. 3.

18. *which wise men have told from their fathers.* Verses 18f. seem a parenthetical remark. The doctrine Eliphaz is about to expound has been treasured by the wise men out of the lore of their forefathers.

19. *unto whom alone the land was given.* Eliphaz claims that the tradition he represents is pure and unadulterated, and has not been contaminated by contact with foreign elements. He hints that the foreigners in their midst are responsible for Job's heretical opinions.

20. *the wicked man travaileth with pain.* This is the teaching which the wise have handed down from of yore: the wicked may appear to live in outward prosperity, but they are constantly tormented by forebodings of disaster. Eliphaz's state-

ment may be his retort to Job's assertion that *the tents of robbers prosper* (xii. 6). Driver declares that 'the picture of the evil conscience is drawn here with great force and is without parallel in the Old Testament.'

21. *a sound of terrors is in his ears.* This passage describes not what the wicked man actually experiences but the forebodings which haunt his mind. It vividly depicts the workings of a guilty conscience.

in prosperity the destroyer shall come upon him. His constant dread is that his ill-gotten gains will be lost to him by the act of another unscrupulous person.

22. *he believeth not that he shall return out of darkness.* The darkness of misfortune haunts his thoughts, from which he fears that he may never escape to find his way back to the light of prosperity. *Darkness* is often used figuratively of misfortune (cf. verses 23, 30, xix. 8).

he is waited for of the sword. The wicked man feels that he is marked out as the victim of violence. Others explain *the sword* as symbolic of Divine retribution (cf. Isa. xxxi. 8).

23 He wandereth abroad for bread:
  'Where is it?'
  He knoweth that the day of darkness is ready at his hand.
24 Distress and anguish overwhelm
  him;
  They prevail against him, as a
  king ready to the battle.
25 Because he hath stretched out his
  hand against God,
  And behaveth himself proudly
  against the Almighty;
26 He runneth upon him with a stiff
  neck,
  With the thick bosses of his bucklers.
27 Because he hath covered his face
  with his fatness,
  And made collops of fat on his
  loins;
28 And he hath dwelt in desolate
  cities,

נֹדֵד הוּא לַלֶּחֶם אַיֵּה 23
יָדַע כִּי־נָכוֹן בְּיָדוֹ יוֹם־חֹשֶׁךְ׃
יְבַעֲתֻהוּ צַר וּמְצוּקָה 24
תִּתְקְפֵהוּ כְּמֶלֶךְ עָתִיד לַכִּידוֹר׃
כִּי־נָטָה אֶל־אֵל יָדוֹ 25
וְאֶל־שַׁדַּי יִתְגַּבָּר׃
יָרוּץ אֵלָיו בְּצַוָּאר 26
בַּעֲבִי גַּבֵּי מָגִנָּיו׃
כִּי־כִסָּה פָנָיו בְּחֶלְבּוֹ 27
וַיַּעַשׂ פִּימָה עֲלֵי־כָסֶל׃
וַיִּשְׁכּוֹן עָרִים נִכְחָדוֹת 28

23. *he wandereth ... for bread.* His troubled
conscience makes his fears so realistic
that he actually thinks of himself as
impoverished and going about in search
for bread.

he knoweth ... at his hand. His fears are
not imaginary. *He knoweth*, has the
awareness, that the day of reckoning
cannot be escaped by him.

24. *distress and anguish overwhelm him.*
Some scholars, following the LXX,
attach the last two words of verse 23
with this verse and translate: 'The day of
darkness makes him afraid; distress and
anguish prevail against him, as a king
ready to the battle.' The noun *kidor*,
battle, occurs nowhere else and is connected with an Arabic root meaning the
onrush of an attacking army. Distress
and anguish will overwhelm the wicked
man as the flames of destruction lay waste
the city attacked by the king's armies.

25. *because he hath stretched out his hand
against God.* He stretches his hand in
scorn against God, and proudly imagines
that his power and the might of his hand
secured his wealth for him (cf. Deut.
viii. 17). Such arrogance brings about
his undoing.

26. *he runneth upon him with a stiff neck.*
lit. 'a neck,' an abbreviation of *a haughty
neck* (Ps. lxxv. 6). The figure in verses
25-7 is that of a warrior making an assault.

with the thick bosses of his bucklers. The
bosses are the convex sides of the shields,
the sides turned to the foe, who is here
God. Ibn Ezra interprets *thick* as referring to the thickness of his neck; *his
bucklers* to the bones; the *bosses* are the
muscles that strengthen the body. 'He
runneth against the Creator with his
body and his haughty neck, provoking
Him to anger' (Rashi).

27. *because he hath covered his face with
his fatness.* The picture is one of glut-
tonous fatness, the mark of spiritual
insensibility (cf. Deut. xxxii. 15; Jer.
v. 28), or the way the evil-doer battened
on his victims.

collops of fat. The Hebrew *pimah* is
derived from a root which in Arabic
signifies 'to fill'; hence 'superabundance.'

28. *and he hath dwelt in desolate cities.*
Inhabited places which had fallen into a
state of desolation were considered in

In houses which no man would
inhabit,
Which were ready to become
heaps.

29 He shall not be rich, neither shall
his substance continue,
Neither shall their produce bend
to the earth.

30 He shall not depart out of darkness;
The flame shall dry up his
branches,
And by the breath of His mouth
shall he go away.

31 Let him not trust in vanity, de-
ceiving himself;
For vanity shall be his recompense.

32 It shall be accomplished before
his time,

בָּתִּים לֹא־יֵשְׁבוּ לָמוֹ
אֲשֶׁר הִתְעַתְּדוּ לְגַלִּים׃
לֹא־יֶעְשַׁר וְלֹא־יָקוּם חֵילוֹ
וְלֹא־יִטֶּה לָאָרֶץ מִנְלָם׃
לֹא־יָסוּר ׀ מִנִּי־חֹשֶׁךְ
יֹנַקְתּוֹ תְּיַבֵּשׁ שַׁלְהָבֶת
וְיָסוּר בְּרוּחַ פִּיו׃
אַל־יַאֲמֵן בַּשָּׁו נִתְעָה
כִּי־שָׁוְא תִּהְיֶה תְמוּרָתוֹ׃
בְּלֹא־יוֹמוֹ תִּמָּלֵא

v. 31. חסר א׳

ancient times to have incurred God's
curse and believed to be haunted by evil
spirits. They were held in superstitious
dread and carefully avoided, especially
at night-time (cf. Isa. xiii. 20ff., xxxiv.
10ff.). Furthermore it was regarded as
an affront to God to rebuild them;
nevertheless that is what the wicked
person has done, thereby displaying
defiance of Him.

which were ready to become heaps. Better:
'which were destined to be heaps', and
remain in their ruined state.

29. *neither shall their produce bend to the
earth.* The word *minlam, their produce,*
is unique and has given the commentators, ancient and modern, great difficulty. BDB place the word under the
root *nalah,* 'what one obtains,' and
render 'gain, acquisition,' but confess
that it is dubious. Buttenweiser contends that it is a composite word meaning
'possessions' of whatever form, and translates 'his harvest will not bend to the
ground.' The general sense is, their
stacks of corn will not be heavy with
grain so as to bend under its weight.

30. *he shall not depart out of darkness.*
The verse describes the fate which over-

takes the evil-doer. *Darkness,* as in
verses 22f., is figurative for calamity.

his branches. The comparison is of the
wicked man to a tree (cf. 32f., viii. 16f.).

by the breath of His mouth. His end is not
accidental but determined by a Divine
act (cf. *by the breath of God they perish,*
iv. 9). 'He departs like chaff that
cannot stand against the wind. All this
is said metaphorically, as in Ps. xcii. 8,
when the wicked spring up as the grass'
(Berechiah).

31. *let him not trust in vanity.* By *vanity*
is meant wickedness. He will be unable
to save himself by resorting to tortuous
methods.

his recompense. lit. 'what is received in
exchange.' Evil will only produce a
harvest of evil for him. The thought is
the same as in iv. 8.

32. *it shall be accomplished before his time.*
The subject *it* refers to *his recompense*
which will be demanded of him *before his
time,* i.e. before the normal number of
his years is completed. He will meet
with a premature end. Ibn Ezra remarks that the verb *malë (be accomplished)*
is explained by most commentators as

And his branch shall not be
leafy.

33 He shall shake off his unripe
grape as the vine,
And shall cast off his flower as the
olive.

34 For the company of the godless
shall be desolate,
And fire shall consume the tents
of bribery.

35 They conceive mischief, and
bring forth iniquity,
And their belly prepareth deceit.

וְכִפָּתוֹ לֹא רַעֲנָנָה:

33 יַחְמֹס כַּגֶּפֶן בִּסְרוֹ
וְיַשְׁלֵךְ כַּזַּיִת נִצָּתוֹ:

34 כִּי־עֲדַת חָנֵף גַּלְמוּד
וְאֵשׁ אָכְלָה אָהֳלֵי־שֹׁחַד:

35 הָרֹה עָמָל וְיָלֹד אָוֶן
וּבִטְנָם תָּכִין מִרְמָה:

being here the equivalent of *malal*, 'be
withered.' The first line would then
continue the image of the tree.

his branch. The word denotes the frond
of the palm-tree. It will become
withered and dry (cf. Isa. ix. 13). The
metaphor gains power and vividness
when it is remembered that the palm-
tree was long-lived, the symbol of
longevity.

33. *he shall shake off his unripe grape as the
vine.* The verb translated *shake off* really
means 'to treat violently, to wrong';
here used figuratively of the vine that
fails to nourish. It has been pointed
out that the vine does not shake off its
unripe grapes. The wicked man is
likened to a vine that never brings its
fruit to maturity. *His unripe grape*,
says Buttenwieser, 'is an interesting case
of zeugma, being used to denote, in
addition to its usual meaning, "immature young".' He renders the line: 'he
will wrong his immature young, as a
vine its unripe grapes.'

as the olive. This tree is most prodigal
in the blossom that it shakes off in
thousands. 'The olive is the most prodigal of all fruit-bearing trees in flowers.
It literally bends under the load of them.
But then, not one in a hundred comes to
maturity. The tree casts them off by
millions, as if they were of no more

value than flakes of snow, which they
closely resemble' (Thomson).

34. *and fire shall consume the tents of
bribery.* 'He compares the wrath of
God to fire, because they conceive evil'
(Ibn Ezra). Bribery is frequently condemned in Scripture; it is here perhaps
used as a general term for injustice.

35. *they conceive mischief, and bring forth
iniquity.* Cf. Isa. lix. 4; Ps. vii. 15 almost
verbatim. It seems to have been a proverbial phrase.

their belly. The Hebrew word also denotes 'the womb.' Ibn Ezra says that
its meaning hints at their *secret* designs.
The wicked conceive mischief for others,
but its fruit is only *deceit*, i.e. calamity
and disappointment for themselves.
'Eliphaz adopts here a tone strikingly
different from that of his first speech.
He had become convinced that Job's
utterances about God were not mere
surface froth, but represented his settled
mind. With such a blasphemer strong
measures must be taken, hence his picture of the fate of the godless, while intended as an answer to Job's assertion
that it was well with the wicked, also
served the purpose of holding up a warning to Job. As yet Eliphaz does not take
the step of directly applying this to Job;
it is a general description that he gives,
but the application is all that remains to
be made' (Peake).

JOB

1 Then Job answered and said:

2 I have heard many such things;
Sorry comforters are ye all.

3 Shall windy words have an end?
Or what provoketh thee that thou
answerest?

4 I also could speak as ye do;

וַיַּעַן אִיּוֹב וַיֹּאמַר׃

שָׁמַעְתִּי כְאֵלֶּה רַבּוֹת

מְנַחֲמֵי עָמָל כֻּלְּכֶם׃

הֲקֵץ לְדִבְרֵי־רוּחַ

אוֹ מַה־יַּמְרִיצְךָ כִּי תַעֲנֶה׃

גַּם ׀ אָנֹכִי כָּכֶם אֲדַבֵּרָה

CHAPTERS XVI-XVII

JOB'S FOURTH REPLY—TO ELIPHAZ

JOB scornfully dismisses the consolations
of God that Eliphaz had offered in his
address as the windy words of sorry
comforters. They bring empty solace
to the stricken, baffled, righteous man.
Were the positions reversed, Job could
shake his head too and offer them the
same hollow rhetoric. Turning abruptly
from the shallow uncomprehension of his
friends, he paints a pitiable picture of
the dread misery to which he has been
reduced. Despite his innocence and the
purity of his prayer, God has broken him
with breach upon breach until his face
is reddened with weeping and on his
eyelids is the shadow of death. Convinced that he must die an unjust death,
Job suddenly and passionately cries out
for justice. Now his clear conscience
becomes his support. Though his
friends deride him, his streaming eyes
turn towards God in the conviction that
all appearances to the contrary notwithstanding, He in the end will vindicate
his innocence. He can expect nothing
from his friends. His afflictions have
made him a derision and a byword. From
unsympathetic man he directs himself to
God, appealing that He be his surety
and vouch for his integrity. Once more,
in derision of the prospects of hope which
the friends have held out, Job, knowing
them to be illusory, ends his address in
the bitter reflection that his only hope is

the nether-world where he must spread
his couch in the darkness of the dust.

CHAPTER XVI

1-5 JOB SCORNS THE SOLACE OF HIS FRIENDS

2. *sorry comforters are ye all*. Job gives
vent to his impatience with the monoto-
nous sameness of his friends' talk. They
have urged him to repent and thus to be
restored. He knows of nothing for which
to repent. The consolations they proffer
are vain. *Sorry comforters* is literally
'comforters of trouble,' whose attempts at
bringing solace only add salt to the
wound.

3. *shall windy words have an end?* Job
reacts to Eliphaz's opening remarks in
xv. 2. Will not the friends stop their
hollow and useless talk which has the
only effect of provoking him to still more
vehement reply?

what provoketh thee. The point of the
question is well brought out in the comment: 'What evil that thou hast found in
me is too strong for thee, and overcomes
thee as an inducement to speak wickedly
against me? For thy speech is only
appropriate against a man whom an
ordinary misfortune and accident have
befallen, but not such have befallen me'
(Berechiah).

4. *I also could speak as ye do*. Were the
positions reversed, Job could also have

If your soul were in my soul's
  stead,
I could join words together against
  you,
And shake my head at you.
5 I would strengthen you with my
  mouth,
And the moving of my lips would
  assuage your grief.
6 Though I speak, my pain is not
  assuaged;
And though I forbear, what am I
  eased?
7 But now He hath made me weary;
Thou hast made desolate all my
  company.
8 And Thou hast shrivelled me up,
  which is a witness against me;
And my leanness riseth up against
  me, it testifieth to my face.

לוּ יֵשׁ נַפְשְׁכֶם תַּחַת נַפְשִׁי
אַחְבִּירָה עֲלֵיכֶם בְּמִלִּים
וְאָנִיעָה עֲלֵיכֶם בְּמוֹ רֹאשִׁי׃
5 אֲאַמִּצְכֶם בְּמוֹ־פִי
וְנִיד שְׂפָתַי יַחְשֹׂךְ׃
6 אִם־אֲדַבְּרָה לֹא־יֵחָשֵׂךְ כְּאֵבִי
וְאַחְדְּלָה מַה־מִּנִּי יַהֲלֹךְ׃
7 אַךְ־עַתָּה הֶלְאָנִי
הֲשִׁמּוֹתָ כָּל־עֲדָתִי׃
8 וַתִּקְמְטֵנִי לְעֵד הָיָה
וַיָּקָם בִּי כַחֲשִׁי בְּפָנַי יַעֲנֶה׃

no difficulty in playing the part of the
unctuous moralist, shaking his head in
scandalized self-righteousness over one
generally reputed to be a pious person
now clearly proved by his calamities to
have been in truth a terrible sinner. How
Job had actually conducted himself in the
past in such circumstances is casually
portrayed by Eliphaz in iv. 3f.

I could join words together against you. By
this statement Job intends stringing
words and phrases together as Eliphaz
had done in xv. 20ff.

shake my head at you. An insulting
gesture (cf. Isa. xxxvii. 22; Ps. xxii. 8).

5. *I would strengthen you with my mouth.*
Better: 'I could strengthen . . . could
assuage.' The sarcasm of the remark lies
in *with my mouth* and *the moving of my
lips.* It is so easy to offer lip-comfort to
a person in trouble.

6-17 JOB'S PITIABLE STATE

6. *though I speak . . . and though I forbear.*
The alternatives forcibly depict his
dilemma. Neither the vehement protestations to which he was driven by their
accusations nor silence in face of them
would bring him relief.

my pain. i.e. both his physical suffering
and his mental anguish.

what am I eased? lit. 'what departeth from
me?' 'My pain does not go away' (Ibn
Ezra).

7. *He hath made . . . Thou hast made.*
Note the sudden transition from the
third person in the first line to the second
person in the second, which is not un-
common in Hebrew style (cf. verses 8f.).
Ibn Ezra with less probability renders:
'(the pain) hath exhausted me.' The
affliction God has visited upon him has
left him physically weak.

Thou hast made desolate. The further
effect has been to deprive him of the
companionship of his family and friends
(cf. xix. 13f.).

8. *Thou hast shrivelled me up.* R.V.
renders: 'Thou hast laid fast hold
on me.' The Hebrew *kamat* means 'to
seize, grasp.' Ibn Ezra defines it as 'to
bind'; but in Rabbinic Hebrew it means
'to wrinkle.' Job contends that his
shrivelled body and emaciation are a
witness against him in the sight of his
friends, testifying to the verdict that he
is a sinner.

9 He hath torn me in His wrath, and
    hated me;
  He hath gnashed upon me with
    His teeth;
  Mine adversary sharpeneth his
    eyes upon me.

10 They have gaped upon me with
    their mouth;
  They have smitten me upon the
    cheek scornfully;
  They gather themselves together
    against me.

11 God delivereth me to the un-
    godly,
  And casteth me into the hands of
    the wicked.

12 I was at ease, and He broke me
    asunder;
  Yea, He hath taken me by the
    neck, and dashed me to pieces;
  He hath also set me up for His
    mark.

אַפּוֹ טָרַף ׀ וַיִּשְׂטְמֵנִי
חָרַק עָלַי בְּשִׁנָּיו
צָרִי ׀ יִלְטוֹשׁ עֵינָיו לִי׃
פָּעֲרוּ עָלַי ׀ בְּפִיהֶם
בְּחֶרְפָּה הִכּוּ לְחָיָי
יַחַד עָלַי יִתְמַלָּאוּן׃
יַסְגִּירֵנִי אֵל אֶל עֲוִיל
וְעַל־יְדֵי רְשָׁעִים יִרְטֵנִי׃
שָׁלֵו הָיִיתִי ׀ וַיְפַרְפְּרֵנִי
וְאָחַז בְּעָרְפִּי וַיְפַצְפְּצֵנִי
וַיְקִימֵנִי לוֹ לְמַטָּרָה׃

9. *He hath torn me in His wrath.* Job pictures God's hostility to him in the figure of a ferocious beast, tearing in its fury and gnashing its teeth.

and hated me. The verb *satam* means 'to bear a grudge, cherish animosity against.'

mine adversary. Rashi piously comments: 'The Satan is the adversary,' but Job, of course, means God.

sharpeneth his eyes. The verb is used of the 'flashing' sword, here of the pitiless glint in the eye of a beast of prey. The figure of God inflicting punishment as an attacking wild animal occurs also in Hos. xiii. 7f.

10. *they have gaped upon me with their mouth.* His treatment at the hand of God has resulted in a corresponding attitude towards him from his fellow-men. To 'gape at with the mouth' may mean 'to devour' as in Ps. xxii. 14, but more probably 'to deride' as in Isa. lvii. 4.

smitten me upon the cheek. An insulting action (cf. Lam. iii. 30).

they gather themselves together. This either denotes that they combine against him, or is to be explained from Jer. xii. 6, *they have cried aloud after thee*, where *aloud* is literally 'full' (the same word as here), i.e. 'with their mouths full'; they talk openly behind his back.

11. *God delivereth me to the ungodly.* The word for *ungodly* means 'young boys, urchins' (cf. xix. 18, xxi. 11). It may also denote 'unjust ones, unrighteous.' Their behaviour towards him is graphically described in xxx. 9ff.

casteth me. The verb *ratah* may mean 'wring out'; 'upon the hands of wicked men He wrings me out' (BDB). Ibn Ezra, however, compares *thy way is contrary unto me* (Num. xxii. 32), and understands the phrase apparently: 'the way is precipitate (headlong) before me.' We should accordingly render the line: 'into the hands of wicked men He precipitates me.'

12. *I was at ease, and He broke me asunder. I was at ease* refers to the happy and prosperous life as related in i. 2ff. God's attack is described under two different metaphors. The first two lines of the verse convey the figure of a fierce wrestler who suddenly pounces upon his unsuspecting victim and dashes him to the

13 His archers compass me round
   about,
   He cleaveth my reins asunder,
   and doth not spare;
   He poureth out my gall upon the
   ground.

14 He breaketh me with breach
   upon breach;
   He runneth upon me like a giant.

15 I have sewed sackcloth upon my
   skin,
   And have laid my horn in the
   dust.

16 My face is reddened with weeping,
   And on my eyelids is the shadow
   of death;

13 יָסֹבּוּ עָלַי ׀ רַבָּיו
יְפַלַּח כִּלְיוֹתַי וְלֹא יַחְמֹל
יִשְׁפֹּךְ לָאָרֶץ מְרֵרָתִי׃
14 יִפְרְצֵנִי פֶרֶץ עַל־פְּנֵי־פָרֶץ
יָרֻץ עָלַי כְּגִבּוֹר׃
15 שַׂק תָּפַרְתִּי עֲלֵי גִלְדִּי
וְעֹלַלְתִּי בֶעָפָר קַרְנִי׃
16 פָּנַי חֲמַרְמְרָה מִנִּי־בֶכִי
וְעַל עַפְעַפַּי צַלְמָוֶת׃

v. 14. ק׳ זעירא   v. 16. חמרמרו ק׳

ground. The third line abruptly introduces a new metaphor: God now becomes
the archer shooting his arrows at a defenceless target (cf. vii. 20; Lam. iii. 12).

13. *His archers compass me round about.*
The Hebrew word for *archers* (rabbim) is
found again in Jer. l. 29. Many scholars,
to avoid mixing the metaphor, render
'arrows.' 'Having set Job up as a target,
God shoots at him, first letting His
arrows whistle all about him, thus keeping
him in suspense, dreading that every
shaft would strike its mark, then sporting
with him no longer, but sending every
arrow home into his vitals, till he has
strewed the ground with them. The
realism of the description is powerful
(cf. vi. 4) (Peake).

my reins. Cf. Lam. iii. 13 for a similar
hyperbolical reference to the *reins* (i.e.
kidneys); here the meaning is metaphorical of the most sensitive and vital
part of the body.

my gall. Ibn Ezra remarks that this
corresponds to the *kabed*, 'liver.' It was
regarded as the 'heavy' (kabed) organ
par excellence, the seat of the emotions.
Job says that he is mortally stricken,
God having dealt him a death blow.

14. *He breaketh me with breach upon
breach.* Job likens his body to a fortress
which is assailed again and again by the
enemy until breaches are made in its

walls. The simile is repeated in xxx. 14.

He runneth. 'Suddenly, swiftly He
bringeth afflictions upon me like a warrior who hasteneth to run forth to battle'
(Metsudath David).

like a giant. More lit. 'like a warrior.'

15. *I have sewed sackcloth upon my skin.*
The first half of the verse may mean that
he has tied sackcloth—the ancient sign
of mourning, worn next to the skin—
about his body. But the verb *sewed* may
indicate that 'it is his habitual garment,
which he never puts off; though the
word may also suggest the closeness with
which it adheres to his shrunk and
emaciated frame' (Davidson).

my horn. The symbol of pride and
strength. Job speaks figuratively; he
has abandoned hope because of the deep
humiliation which he feels.

16. *my face is reddened with weeping.*
For the verb (chamar), cf. *mine inwards
burn* (Lam. ii. 11). Ibn Ezra remarks
that in Arabic it means 'to become red
because of excessive heat (inflammation),
or it may be compared with *the waters
thereof roar and foam* (Ps. xlvi. 4)'. Rashi
renders: 'wrinkled, shrivelled.'

the shadow of death. He feels the approach of death to be so close that it casts
a shadow over his eyes. How poignant
is the phrase!

17 Although there is no violence in
    my hands,
  And my prayer is pure.

18 O earth, cover not thou my blood,
  And let my cry have no resting-
    place.

19 Even now, behold, my Witness
    is in heaven,
  And He that testifieth of me is on
    high.

עַל לֹא־חָמָס בְּכַפָּי

וּתְפִלָּתִי זַכָּה:

אֶרֶץ אַל־תְּכַסִּי דָמִי

וְאַל־יְהִי מָקוֹם לְזַעֲקָתִי:

גַּם־עַתָּה הִנֵּה־בַשָּׁמַיִם עֵדִי

וְשָׂהֲדִי בַּמְּרוֹמִים:

17. *although there is no violence in my hands.* Despite his upright life, this cruel fate has come upon him. Job categorically denies that he had ever been guilty of any wicked deed. On the contrary, he affirms that he had lived a pious, religious life. The language is reminiscent of Isa. liii. 9.

my prayer is pure. 'I have not cursed my companion nor have I prayed that evil should befall him' (Rashi). More probably he intends to convey that whenever he addressed himself to God, he did so with a pure heart and clear conscience.

xvi. 18-xvii. 5 LET GOD TESTIFY TO HIS INTEGRITY

18. *O earth, cover not thou my blood.* The customary interpretation of this passionate outburst is: May my blood lie exposed that it may call for vengeance. Blood not covered by the earth was understood to have been violently shed, and was regarded as calling for revenge on the murderer (Gen. iv. 10; Ezek. xxiv. 7f.). Buttenweiser in a learned article, 'Revenge and Burial Rites in Ancient Israel' (Journal of American Oriental Society, 1919, pp. 303-321), excerpts of which are quoted in his commentary on *Job*, disputes the correctness of this interpretation. He believes the verse is a momentary prayer—the simplest, the most natural, that can be imagined. Job cries, 'Let me not sink into the earth, let me not die.' He begs that he be saved from the grave, so that there may be no place any more for his complaint (*cry*) that, notwithstanding his blameless life, he has been stricken with death.

19. *even now, behold, my Witness is in heaven.* 'My Creator,' comments Rashi, 'Who knoweth my ways.' 'Very fine is the transition from earth to heaven. Let earth not burke his case, for heaven will soon speak! . . . For even before Job dies, nay, even now as he speaks, his Witness Who will vindicate him is in heaven' (Peake). There is the implication that though his friends now despise him—they who formerly held him to be a righteous man, but seeing how the hand of God has struck him, now attribute great iniquity to him—nevertheless, exclaims Job, 'even now I have found a Witness on my behalf for the uprightness of my heart and He is the Lord Who knoweth all' (Metsudath David).

He that testifieth of me. Sahed, 'witness,' is an Aramaic loan-word (cf. Gen. xxxi. 47). 'It is difficult to find a corresponding noun (for *sahed*) in English; perhaps advocate or sponsor comes pretty near, as there was no difference between advocate and witness in the Hebrew courts, the part of a witness being to testify on behalf of one and see justice done to him, as verse 21 describes what part Job desires his witness to play for him. "Witness" does not mean merely one who *knows* Job's innocence, but one who will testify to it and see it recognized, just as in xvii. 3 *surety* is one who undertakes to see right maintained' (Davidson).

20 Mine inward thoughts are my
   intercessors,
   Mine eye poureth out tears unto
   God;

21 That He would set aright a man
   contending with God,
   As a son of man setteth aright his
   neighbour!

22 For the years that are few are
   coming on,
   And I shall go the way whence I
   shall not return.

20 מְלִיצַי רֵעָי
אֶל־אֱלוֹהַ דָּלְפָה עֵינִי׃

21 וְיוֹכַח לְגֶבֶר עִם־אֱלוֹהַ
וּבֶן־אָדָם לְרֵעֵהוּ׃

22 כִּי־שְׁנוֹת מִסְפָּר יֶאֱתָיוּ
וְאֹרַח לֹא־אָשׁוּב אֶהֱלֹךְ׃

20. *mine inward thoughts are my intercessors.* A.V. renders the verse: 'my friends scorn me,' retained by R.V. Buttenweiser beautifully translates: 'and since my friends deride me, my streaming eyes are turned to God.' A.J.: *mine inward thoughts are my intercessors* understood *re'ai, mine inward thoughts*, in the way this Aramaic loan-word is used in Ps. cxxxix. 2, 17. (The Hebrew word *re'a* means 'friend.') *Melitsai, my intercessors*, may be derived from the root *lits*, 'to scorn'; but it also admits of the translation 'interpreter, ambassador, intercessor' (cf. xxxiii. 23). The Targum here translates with *peraklitai*, 'advocate, intercessor.' In either case, whether following A.V. or A.J. a good sense is obtained. Job may mean that his inner consciousness of rectitude becomes his advocate to God as he turns his tearful face towards Him. Or, though his friends have now become alienated from him, indeed, though they deride him, his streaming eyes are turned to God. The verse is profoundly moving.

21. This verse is one of the amazing peaks of spiritual faith and human paradox that make this Book immortal. Job here appeals from the God Who had cruelly smitten him to the God of his faith, the God of justice and loving mercy. 'The defendant implores the plaintiff to be his judge. He has already lamented that there is no daysman (arbiter) between them (ix. 33). Now he utters the striking thought, "Let God Himself be his daysman." There is no one who is God's equal, who can confront God and force Him to do justice—no one but God Himself . . . Just now God is Job's settled enemy, by and by He

will be his friend. But Job feels that this future mood may modify God's present action, He being conscious even now that His temper towards Job will change, and suffering this knowledge to protect Him from going too far. The religious feeling that comes here to such strange expression may be illustrated by the beautiful saying from the Qur'an, "There is no refuge from God but unto Him" (Sur. ix. 119)' (Peake). Similarly exclaimed the Jewish poet, Solomon Ibn Gabirol (*The Royal Crown*, xxxviii), 'I will flee from Thee to Thyself.'

that He would set aright. 'Would that He would do this for me, that He would give me a place to argue as a man with God to place side by side the two contentions: the contention of a man with his Maker, and the contention of a man with his friend' (Rashi).

as a son of man. A Hebrew idiom for 'man.' Buttenweiser points out that five Hebrew MSS. have the vocalization *ubēn*, 'and between' instead of *ubēn* (*and a son of*). Accordingly he translates: 'That He may plead for a man with God, and take sides in the conflict between a man and his fellow-man.'

22. *for the years that are few are coming on.* The few years allotted to me draw quickly to completion. The meaning appears to be that Job calls upon God for the vindication of his innocence, before the fatal nature of his affliction overtakes him and deprives him of the satisfaction of knowing that God Himself has sustained his honour. Peake, however, states that 'it is Job's settled conviction that God will not vindicate him during his lifetime.' While Job certainly gives

CHAPTER XVII

17   CHAPTER XVII   יז

1 My spirit is consumed, my days
  are extinct,
  The grave is ready for me.

2 Surely there are mockers with me,
  And mine eye abideth in their
  provocation.

3 Give now a pledge, be surety for
  me with Thyself;
  Who else is there that will strike
  hands with me?

4 For Thou hast hid their heart from
  understanding;
  Therefore shalt Thou not exalt
  them.

רוּחִי חֻבָּלָה יָמַי נִזְעָכוּ
קְבָרִים לִי׃
אִם־לֹא הֲתֻלִים עִמָּדִי
וּבְהַמְּרוֹתָם תָּלַן עֵינִי׃
שִׂימָה־נָּא עָרְבֵנִי עִמָּךְ
מִי־הוּא לְיָדִי יִתָּקֵעַ׃
כִּי־לִבָּם צָפַנְתָּ מִשָּׂכֶל
עַל־כֵּן לֹא תְרֹמֵם׃

v. 2. בנ"א הל' דגושה   2. v. המ' דגושה

way again and again to dark despair, his momentary flashes of faith never absolutely rule out the hope that God will somehow appear to justify him. The fact that God's appearance out of the storm is the great dramatic climax of the Book supports the interpretation that Job never totally abandons the belief that before he dies God will manifest Himself as his Champion.

CHAPTER XVII

1. my spirit is consumed. The word *ruach* has a variety of meanings. Here it signifies the vital principle (cf. Ps. cxlvi. 4 where it is translated *breath*).

my days are extinct. The verb *za'ach* is apparently a variant of the more usual *da'ach*, 'be extinguished.' Ibn Ezra defines it in the sense 'my days are shattered,' and points out that the verb occurs only here in Scripture.

the grave is ready for me. lit. 'graves are mine.' Death is very near to me. 'I am marked for the grave' (Rashi).

2. surely there are mockers with me. lit. 'mockery'; 'truly mockery surrounded me' (BDB). Eliphaz had held out to Job illusory promises of restoration (v. 17-26) and these he decries as 'mockeries.'

mine eye abideth in their provocation. The

text is difficult. Job appears to be referring to the friends' provocative insistence upon his guilt. The word for *provocation* comes from a root 'to be rebellious (*marah*).' Ibn Ezra comments: 'I cannot sleep because they embitter (from *marar*) my life, or it may mean "stubborn, rebellious" '; and Rashi: 'ye have been rebellious in your provocations.' Job declares that his *eye abideth*, i.e. he cannot shut his eyes to their accusations.

3. *give now a pledge, be surety for me with Thyself.* Job turns to God with the appeal that He stand surety for him.

that will strike hands. An idiom frequently used in *Proverbs* to ratify an agreement. The image is that of a business transaction. Davidson correctly maintains that 'a suretyship necessarily refers to the future; though undertaken in the present it is to be fulfilled later. Job beseeches God to undertake now that He will cause his innocence to be yet acknowledged with God. The same division of God into two parties, God Who persecutes Job and wrongs him, and God Who becomes surety for Job and undertakes to see his cause righted with God, appears here as before in xvi. 21.'

4. *Thou hast hid their heart from understanding.* The verse answers the question in the second line of the preceding.

5 He that denounceth his friends for
the sake of flattering,
Even the eyes of his children shall
fail.

6 He hath made me also a byword of
the people;
And I am become one in whose
face they spit.

7 Mine eye also is dimmed by reason
of vexation,
And all my members are as a
shadow.

8 Upright men are astonished at this,
And the innocent stirreth up himself against the godless.

5 לְחֵלֶק יַגִּיד רֵעִים
וְעֵינֵי בָנָיו תִּכְלֶנָה׃

6 וְהִצִּגַנִי לִמְשֹׁל עַמִּים
וְתֹפֶת לְפָנִים אֶהְיֶה׃

7 וַתֵּכַהּ מִכַּעַשׂ עֵינִי
וִיצֻרַי כַּצֵּל כֻּלָּם׃

8 יָשֹׁמּוּ יְשָׁרִים עַל־זֹאת
וְנָקִי עַל־חָנֵף יִתְעֹרָר׃

The answer is, nobody but God Himself.
Since He blinded the friends from per-
ceiving the truth of his innocence, therefore Job feels that in the end He will not
permit them to triumph over him.

5. *he that denounceth his friends.* The
verse is difficult and has evoked a
variety of translations. A.V. has: 'He
that speaketh flattery to his friends,' and
R.V.: 'He that denounceth his friends
for a prey.' *Chelek* (from *chalak*, 'to be
smooth') was understood by the older
Jewish commentators as 'flattery.' The
verse would then mean that Job warns
his friends that if they denounce him,
seeking to flatter God, even their children would be punished. A hypocrite
cannot stand before God. The alternative is to translate *chelek* as 'portion'
(from *chalak*, 'to divide') and *yaggid*
(lit. 'tell') as 'invite' and not 'denounce.'
We then get a meaning accepted by Peake,
Buttenweiser and many others: 'One
invites friends to partake, while his
children's eyes fail'; i.e. he keeps open
house and lets his own children starve.
Job is possibly quoting a popular proverb. 'The friends have no understanding, but they invite Job to partake of
their wisdom, while they have not enough
wisdom to supply their own needs at
home' (Peake). Job is mocking the
presumption of his friends who, despite
their mental darkness, think to enlighten
him.

6-16 JOB IS CONSCIOUS OF HIS HUMILIATION

6. *He hath made me also a byword of the
people.* Ibn Ezra interprets: 'The pain
hath set me as a byword; but some
explain that Eliphaz has made him a byword.' *People* is literally 'peoples.' Neigh-
bouring peoples hear of Job and mock
him as one now exposed to be a sinner.
one in whose face they spit. Such an
action was regarded as a bitter insult
(cf. xxx. 10; Isa. l. 6, although the
Hebrew is different). The translation
of A.V. 'as a tabret' follows Rashi who
mistakenly identified *topheth* with *toph*.

7. *mine eye also is dimmed by reason of
vexation.* Cf. Ps. vi. 8. Job's vexation,
induced by what he considers God's
undeserved treatment of him, has made
him weep until he is practically blind.
all my members are as a shadow. Rashi
and Ibn Ezra understand the word,
which only occurs here, as 'limbs.' His
body is reduced to the shadow of its
former self. Another interpretation,
offered by Szold, Peake and others is,
'and as for my visions they are all as a
shadow;' the effect of his weeping is that
his sight has become blurred.

8. *upright men are astonished at this.* The
minds of the righteous are perplexed
when they see a good man like himself
so afflicted, and the consequence is that
their indignation is aroused at seeing
the prosperity of the wicked.

9 Yet the righteous holdeth on his
    way,
  And he that hath clean hands wax-
    eth stronger and stronger.

10 But as for you all, do ye return,
    and come now;
  And I shall not find a wise man
    among you.

11 My days are past, my purposes
    are broken off,
  Even the thoughts of my heart.

12 They change the night into day;
  The light is short because of
    darkness.

וְיֹאחֵז צַדִּיק דַּרְכּוֹ
וּטְהָר־יָדַיִם יֹסִיף אֹמֶץ׃
וְאוּלָם כֻּלָּם תָּשֻׁבוּ וּבֹאוּ נָא
וְלֹא־אֶמְצָא בָכֶם חָכָם׃
יָמַי עָבְרוּ זִמֹּתַי נִתְּקוּ
מוֹרָשֵׁי לְבָבִי׃
לַיְלָה לְיוֹם יָשִׂימוּ
אוֹר קָרוֹב מִפְּנֵי־חֹשֶׁךְ׃

v. 9. בנ״א הט׳ בשוא

9. *yet the righteous holdeth on his way.*
Job here directly contradicts Eliphaz
who had said, *Thou doest away with fear,
and impairest devotion with God* (xv. 4).
Despite his bewilderment at what appears the moral anomaly of the universe,
the righteous man will cleave ever more
to the right.   Davidson remarks that
'the passage is perhaps the most surprising and lofty in the Book . . . No mysteries
or wrongs shall make him falter in the
way of righteousness.   And the human
spirit rises to the height of moral grandeur, when it proclaims its resolution
to hold on the way of righteousness inde-
pendently both of men and God.'   The
verse is compared by Delitzsch to 'a
rocket which shoots above the tragic
darkness of the Book, lighting it up
suddenly, although only for a short time.'

10. *but as for you all, do ye return, and
come now.*   Renew your attack on me,
Job challenges his friends, take up your
stale arguments, if you like, deriding
me for what has come upon me.   You
will only expose the more your unfeeling
folly.   By *return* he does not imply that
the friends were going away.   He means,
'repeat your arguments and your accusations of my guilt.'

I shall not find a wise man among you.
The repetition of their arguments will
not convince Job that they have wisdom.

11. *my days are past, my purposes are
broken off.*   In sharp contrast to the false

hopes advanced by the friends, Job confesses that his former happy days are
for ever vanished, the purposes he had
that he might live out his life in prosperity
and peace are destroyed, and the dearest
thoughts of his heart have been utterly
broken.

the thoughts of my heart. lit. 'possessions.'
Ibn Ezra understands it as 'thoughts'
although referring to Moses Ibn Chiquitilla who interprets 'possessions,' which
seemed far-fetched to Ibn Ezra. 'The
thoughts which my heart made me to
possess, for my heart said that I would
inherit good because of my (righteous)
way' (Rashi).

12. *they change the night into day.*   The
verse is difficult.   'These mockeries (of
the friends) change the night into day for
me.   Because of the distress at the mockeries, I cannot sleep at night' (Rashi).
The first line probably means that the
friends endeavour to renew his hope by
assuring him that with repentance there
will be a change for the better in his
fortunes (cf. xi. 17).

the light is short because of the darkness.
'The light' (say they), 'is near unto the
darkness,' so R.V. renders.   In this
translation, the thought would be similar
to our phrase, 'It is always darkest before
dawn.'   The friends try to persuade me,
says Job, that the light of prosperity will
soon succeed my present dark misery.
They declare light near in the face of
darkness.

13 If I look for the nether-world as
my house;
If I have spread my couch in the
darkness;

14 If I have said to corruption:
'Thou art my father',
To the worm: 'Thou art my
mother, and my sister';

15 Where then is my hope?
And as for my hope, who shall
see it?

16 They shall go down to the bars of
the nether-world,
When we are at rest together in
the dust.

13 אִם־אֲקַוֶּה שְׁאוֹל בֵּיתִי
בַּחֹשֶׁךְ רִפַּדְתִּי יְצוּעָי׃

14 לַשַּׁחַת קָרָאתִי אָבִי אָתָּה
אִמִּי וַאֲחֹתִי לָרִמָּה׃

15 וְאַיֵּה אֵפוֹ תִקְוָתִי
וְתִקְוָתִי מִי יְשׁוּרֶנָּה׃

16 בַּדֵּי שְׁאֹל תֵּרַדְנָה
אִם־יַחַד עַל־עָפָר נָחַת׃

18   CHAPTER XVIII   יח

1 Then answered Bildad the Shuhite, and said:

1 וַיַּעַן בִּלְדַּד הַשֻּׁחִי וַיֹּאמַר׃

v. 16. פתח באתנח

13. *if I look for the nether-world as my house.* Job knows how vain is any other hope than the darkness of the grave which soon must overtake him. Buttenweiser understands *im*, 'if', as the emphatic particle 'verily.'

if I have spread my couch. Cf. *If I make my bed in the nether-world* (Ps. cxxxix. 8).

14. *if I have said to corruption.* The word *shachath* here means 'the pit of the nether-world' (cf. Ps. xvi. 10). 'The words *father*, *mother*, *sister*, expressing the nearest relationship, indicate how closely Job now feels himself connected with the grave; he wholly belongs to it, and he greets it as taking the place of all related to him on earth' (Davidson).

the worm. Which covers the body in the grave (xxi. 26).

15. *where then is my hope?* Since Job knows of a certainty that death is near, where is the hope of future prosperity and well-being that his friends have held out?

16. *the bars of the nether-world.* The phrase does not appear elsewhere; but

in Isa. xxxviii. 10 we read of *the gates of the nether-world.* This was conceived as a great subterranean dungeon with gates. It might naturally have *bars* too. But what is the subject of *they shall go down?* Szold explains that this verse answers the question, *who shall see it?* Job pessimistically declares that the only ones to witness his *hope* will be they who shall go down to Sheol with him, because only there has he a future (the fem. plural of the verb refers to the 'souls' of the dead). He construes the second line: 'When we who are upon the earth (lit. dust) descend together.' For the verb in this sense, cf. *they go down to the grave* (xxi. 13).

CHAPTER XVIII

THE SECOND SPEECH OF BILDAD

BILDAD, indignant, rejects for himself and his friends the charge of being dumb as beasts. Job's rage will not change the order of the world. Job is mistaken when he argues that the sinner prospers (cf. xii. 6). On the contrary, calamity

2 How long will ye lay snares for
　　words?
　Consider, and afterwards we will
　　speak.
3 Wherefore are we counted as
　　beasts,
　And reputed dull in your sight?
4 Thou that tearest thyself in thine
　　anger,
　Shall the earth be forsaken for
　　thee?
　Or shall the rock be removed out
　　of its place?
5 Yea, the light of the wicked shall
　　be put out,
　And the spark of his fire shall not
　　shine.

עַד־אָנָה ׀ תְּשִׂימוּן קִנְצֵי לְמִלִּין
תָּבִינוּ וְאַחַר נְדַבֵּר :
מַדּוּעַ נֶחְשַׁבְנוּ כַבְּהֵמָה
נִטְמִינוּ בְּעֵינֵיכֶם :
טֹרֵף נַפְשׁוֹ בְּאַפּוֹ
הַלְמַעַנְךָ תֵּעָזַב אָרֶץ
וְיֶעְתַּק צוּר מִמְּקֹמוֹ :
גַּם אוֹר רְשָׁעִים יִדְעָךְ
וְלֹא־יִגַּהּ שְׁבִיב אִשּׁוֹ :

seizes and overwhelms him on every side,
brimstone shall be scattered upon his
habitation, and his remembrance perish
from the earth. In the lurid description
of the consequences of sin that come
upon the sinner, it is transparent that
Bildad has Job in mind.

1-4 'WHEREFORE ARE WE COUNTED AS
BEASTS?'

2. *how long will ye lay snares for words?*
The plural, *ye lay*, is strange. According
to Metsudath David, Bildad begins by
reproving his two co-visitors. Szold
suggests that in verses 2f. Bildad summarizes the attitude which Job had
assumed towards his would-be comforters, and then addresses him in verse 4.
In the view of Davidson, *ye* is due to
Job identifying himself with the class of
righteous sufferers persecuted by the
wicked. The word for *snares* (*kintsë*)
occurs nowhere else. Rashi understood
it as equal to *kets*, 'end': 'how long will
you make an end of words?' The meaning appears to be: 'How long will you
hunt after words?' The inference is
that Job is hunting after words to make
a rhetorical effect; or on Szold's interpretation: that, says Bildad, is the charge
brought by Job against him and his two
friends.

consider, and afterwards we will speak.
Better: 'understand,' Job having in fact
accused them of a lack of understanding

(xvii. 4). If Bildad is addressing Job
as typical of a complaining class, he
flings back the charge and says that it is
useless to continue the discussion unless
they comprehend more truly God's
government of the world.

3. *wherefore are we counted as beasts.*
Bildad resents Job's utterances about the
friends as if they were as unfeeling and
unintelligent as dumb beasts (cf. Ps.
lxxiii. 22).

reputed dull. From a root *tamah*, 'stop
up' (BDB), here intellectually.

4. *tearest thyself.* He alludes to Job's
allegation against God, *He hath torn me
in His wrath* (xvi. 9), and retorts that it is
not God's fury but his own rage that is
consuming him.

shall the earth be forsaken for thee? Bildad
implies: Does Job imagine that the established order of the world, where suffering
is a consequence and proof of sin, is to
be interrupted in order that he may continue to be reputed righteous? Is the
physical universe (*the rock*) to be over-
turned to gratify his personal wishes?

5-21 CALAMITY AND DISHONOUR OVER-
TAKE THE WICKED

5. *the light of the wicked shall be put out.*
The Hebrew tenses in the verse convey
the meaning of something that takes place

6 The light shall be dark in his tent,
And his lamp over him shall be
put out.

7 The steps of his strength shall be
straitened,
And his own counsel shall cast
him down.

8 For he is cast into a net by his own
feet,
And he walketh upon the toils.

9 A gin shall take him by the heel,
And a snare shall lay hold on him.

10 A noose is hid for him in the
ground,
And a trap for him in the way.

11 Terrors shall overwhelm him on
every side,
And shall entrap him at his feet.

6 אוֹר חָשַׁךְ בְּאָהֳלוֹ
וְנֵרוֹ עָלָיו יִדְעָךְ׃

7 יֵצְרוּ צַעֲדֵי אוֹנוֹ
וְתַשְׁלִיכֵהוּ עֲצָתוֹ׃

8 כִּי־שֻׁלַּח בְּרֶשֶׁת בְּרַגְלָיו
וְעַל־שְׂבָכָה יִתְהַלָּךְ׃

9 יֹאחֵז בְּעָקֵב פָּח
יַחֲזֵק עָלָיו צַמִּים׃

10 טָמוּן בָּאָרֶץ חַבְלוֹ
וּמַלְכֻּדְתּוֹ עֲלֵי נָתִיב׃

11 סָבִיב בִּעֲתֻהוּ בַלָּהוֹת
וֶהֱפִיצֻהוּ לְרַגְלָיו׃

constantly, not merely in the future.
The *light* is that burning in a house,
symbolizing the owner's continued prosperity (cf. verse 6, xxi. 17; 1 Kings xi. 36;
Prov. xiii. 9, xxiv. 20).

6. *the light shall be dark in his tent.* **Cf.**
xxix. 3. Bildad's speech is studded with
sententious and proverbial sayings, as in
chapter viii. The history of the wicked
man's downfall is followed through all
its stages: 5-7, the principle—the sinner's
light goes out; 8-11, the progress of his
downfall; 12-14, the final scenes; 15-17,
the extinction of his race and name; 18-21
men's horror of his fate and memory
(Davidson).

his lamp over him. His home is engulfed
in darkness as the lamp that hangs from
the roof of his tent goes out.

7. *the steps of his strength shall be straitened.* The metaphor changes. In
prosperity and security, he walked with
firm, wide steps (cf. Prov. iv. 12). Now
in adversity they are narrowed and
constricted. His evil designs bring him
down to calamity and ruin.

8. *he is cast into a net by his own feet.*
The *net* and *toils* are figurative expressions, signifying the means by which he
is brought to disaster. His own evil
principles land him in calamity (cf.
Prov. xix. 9).

the toils. lit. 'network'; 'like the *coiffe*
(filet) that is on the head of women'
(Rashi). The reference is to the lattice-
work placed over a pit to conceal it upon
which the hunted animal steps and is
caught. The sinner falls suddenly and
unawares into it like a trapped beast.

9. *a gin . . . a snare.* 'It is remarkable
how many words for "trap" Bildad
contrives to heap together, as if to
suggest that the world is full of traps to
catch the feet that stray from the right
path' (Peake).

10. *a noose is hid for him in the ground.*
The cord lies hidden in the ground
under his feet and he is trapped as one
traps birds.

11. *terrors shall overwhelm him on every
side.* 'And now he is harried by terrors,
which close in upon him on every side.

12 His trouble shall be ravenous,
   And calamity shall be ready for
   his fall.

13 It shall devour the members of
   his body,
   Yea, the first-born of death shall
   devour his members.

14 That wherein he trusteth shall be
   plucked out of his tent;
   And he shall be brought to the
   king of terrors.

15 There shall dwell in his tent that
   which is none of his;
   Brimstone shall be scattered
   upon his habitation.

16 His roots shall dry up beneath,
   And above shall his branch
   wither.

17 His remembrance shall perish
   from the earth,
   And he shall have no name
   abroad.

יְהִי־רָעֵב אֹנוֹ
וְאֵיד נָכוֹן לְצַלְעוֹ:
יֹאכַל בַּדֵּי עוֹרוֹ
יֹאכַל בַּדָּיו בְּכוֹר מָוֶת:
יִנָּתֵק מֵאָהֳלוֹ מִבְטַחוֹ
וְתַצְעִדֵהוּ לְמֶלֶךְ בַּלָּהוֹת:
תִּשְׁכּוֹן בְּאָהֳלוֹ מִבְּלִי־לוֹ
יְזֹרֶה עַל־נָוֵהוּ גָפְרִית:
מִתַּחַת שָׁרָשָׁיו יִבָשׁוּ
וּמִמַּעַל יִמַּל קְצִירוֹ:
זִכְרוֹ־אָבַד מִנִּי־אָרֶץ
וְלֹא־שֵׁם לוֹ עַל־פְּנֵי־חוּץ:

The hell-hounds are hard at his heels, yet as he seeks in mad distraction to escape from these it can only be by rushing to meet others as ghastly, while all about him his way is thickly sown with snares' (Peake).

12. *his trouble shall be ravenous*. As the verse is translated by A.J. it conveys the meaning that the trouble and calamity about to seize him are hungry for their prey.

and calamity shall be ready for his fall. R.V. renders this line more literally: 'and calamity shall be ready for his halting.' Should he slip or limp, calamity is at hand to pounce upon him and bring him to the ground.

13. *it shall devour . . . the first-born of death*. The verse is a cryptic allusion to the deadly disease that consumes Job. *It* is defined by *the first-born of death*, the strongest child of death, a figurative phrase for the deadly disease of elephantiasis.

14. *that wherein he trusteth*. Rashi and Metsudath David understand the first line to mean that he will be torn away from his wife, his trust. More probably Bildad repeats the thought he expressed in viii. 15, *he shall lean upon his house, but it shall not stand.*

the king of terrors. i.e. death. 'He sought to flee from terrors, he is brought at last to the king of them' (Davidson).

15. *there shall dwell . . . none of his*. Strange animals and noxious weeds will roam and grow where formerly he dwelt (Ibn Ezra). Cf. the picture of desolation in Isa. xxxiv. 11ff.

brimstone shall be scattered. The mark of the curse of heaven will be on his former home (cf. Gen. xix. 24; Deut. xxix. 22).

16. *his roots shall dry up . . . his branch wither*. *Roots* and *branch* in the figure of a tree are metaphorical expressions meaning that the entire family of the wicked will perish with him (cf. Amos ii. 9).

17. *his remembrance shall perish from the earth*. His children having been destroyed, there will not remain even his name and he will be utterly forgotten.

18 He shall be driven from light into darkness,
And chased out of the world.

19 He shall have neither son nor son's son among his people,
Nor any remaining in his dwellings.

20 They that come after shall be astonished at his day,
As they that went before are affrighted.

21 Surely such are the dwellings of the wicked,
And this is the place of him that knoweth not God.

18 יֶהְדְּפֻהוּ מֵאוֹר אֶל־חֹשֶׁךְ
וּמִתֵּבֵל יְנִדֻּהוּ׃

19 לֹא נִין לוֹ וְלֹא־נֶכֶד בְּעַמּוֹ
וְאֵין שָׂרִיד בִּמְגוּרָיו׃

20 עַל־יוֹמוֹ נָשַׁמּוּ אַחֲרֹנִים
וְקַדְמֹנִים אָחֲזוּ שָׂעַר׃

21 אַךְ־אֵלֶּה מִשְׁכְּנוֹת עַוָּל
וְזֶה מְקוֹם לֹא־יָדַע אֵל׃

19   CHAPTER XIX   יט

1 Then Job answered and said:

1 וַיַּעַן אִיּוֹב וַיֹּאמַר׃

---

18. *he shall be driven from light to darkness.* lit. 'they shall drive him . . . they shall chase.' 'The troubles that will come upon him will drive him from the light of the world into the darkness of the grave' (Metsudath David). It is a common idiom in Hebrew to express the passive by means of the active verb with an indeterminate subject.

19. *neither son nor son's son.* Hebrew *nin, neched.* Again in Isa. xiv. 22 where the translation is *offshoot and offspring.* The phrase appears to have been one of those alliterative proverbial expressions, similar to our 'kith and kin.' Rashi takes *neched* to mean 'son's son.'

20. *they that come after shall be astonished at his day.* The verse is obscure and has elicited various interpretations. As rendered in A.J. it means that later as well as earlier generations will retain for ever the horror of his dreadful end. *At his day* has the meaning of our phrase 'his hour has come.' *They that went before* is explained by Ibn Ezra as his contemporaries. There is a logical difficulty in the interpretation that later generations will remember his end, because verse 17 had expressed the

thought that his remembrance would perish from the earth. Consequently some scholars explain the contrast to be 'those of the West . . . those of the East' will think of him with horror. Buttenweiser translates: 'Over his end coming generations will be appalled, and his contemporaries will be seized with shuddering.'

21. *surely such are the dwellings of the wicked.* 'Such is their end' (Rashi); more literally, such is the fate that befalls the homes of the wicked and all who reside there.

CHAPTER XIX

JOB'S FIFTH REPLY—TO BILDAD

JOB, touched to the quick by Bildad's venomous words, reproaches his friends for cruel insinuations. He denies again that it is his own sin that has brought calamity upon him. 'I cry aloud,' he exclaims, 'but I am not heard. There is no justice.' In vain does he seek for hope. God has plucked him up like a tree. Beaten down by the relentless Adversary, Job feels his terrible loneliness and the universal contempt in

2 How long will ye vex my soul,
And crush me with words ?

עַד־אָנָה תּוֹגְיוּן נַפְשִׁי
וּתְדַכְּאוּנַנִי בְמִלִּים׃

3 These ten times have ye reproached me;
Ye are not ashamed that ye deal
harshly with me.

זֶה | עֶשֶׂר פְּעָמִים תַּכְלִימוּנִי
לֹא־תֵבֹשׁוּ תַּהְכְּרוּ־לִי׃

4 And be it indeed that I have erred,
Mine error remaineth with myself.

וְאַף־אָמְנָם שָׁגִיתִי
אִתִּי תָּלִין מְשׁוּגָתִי׃

which he is held. He has become an
object of horror to kith and kin, even his
wife loathes his breath. Yet the awful
suffering has but served to bring out his
essential nobility of soul and uncon-
querable faith. Pathetically, though in
vain, he turns to his friends, asking them
for the pity that the Almighty seems to
withhold. Abruptly, perhaps because
he realizes how futile it is to appeal to
their limited spiritual understanding,
Job invokes posterity to pass fair judgment on his undeserved suffering. 'Would
that my words,' he cries, 'with an iron
pen and lead were graven in the rock
for ever.'

Now his clear conscience rises majestic-
ally over the fate that must soon crush
his plague-ridden body. Boldly Job
turns to God and in words that still
retain the fire of magnificent faith through
all the centuries, he speaks the firm
conviction, 'I know that my Redeemer
liveth, and that He will witness at the
last upon the dust.' God, revealed to
Job through the integrity of his life,
will appear in the end to champion his
innocence. This momentous speech,
which contains one of the highest sum-
mits on the mountainous road to the
vast mystery of God, ends with a warning from Job to his friends to beware of
fastening false charges upon him lest
the sword of the Divine Avenger come
finally upon them.

1-20 JOB'S REMONSTRANCE WITH
FRIENDS AND GOD

2. *how long will ye vex my soul.* The

verb expresses 'grief, sorrow' according
to Rashi and Ibn Ezra. Much more than
impatience is implied. Job has been
grievously hurt by Zophar's dreadful
insinuations of his concealed wickedness.
He is weighed down by the sorrow of
realizing how little they can ever, or will
ever, understand his innocence.

3. *these ten times have ye reproached me.*
Ten times is an idiom for 'often' (cf. Gen.
xxxi. 7, 41; Num. xiv. 22). Rashi offers
a literal interpretation: 'There are ten
speeches up to here' (Job having made
five and the friends a total of five). Ibn
Ezra credits this literal interpretation
to Saadia, but prefers to regard the
phrase as a round number.

ye deal harshly with me. The conjectured root *hachar* is of uncertain
meaning. It has been taken for 'ye cause
me to wonder; ye deal hardly with, wrong
me' (BDB). Rashi understands it in the
sense, 'Ye act like strangers unto me,'
as though related to the root *nachar*
(Gen. xlii. 7).

4. *and be it indeed that I have erred.*
Note that Job does not admit that he
has erred. He merely grants his friend's
view for the sake of argument. On the
assumption that he had sinned, his
error remains with himself.

mine error remaineth with myself. The
meaning of this line is uncertain. Rashi
interprets: 'I am the one who receives
blows for his error.' Thus understood,
Job would be saying, 'I am certainly

5 If indeed ye will magnify yourselves against me,
  And plead against me my reproach;

6 Know now that God hath subverted my cause,
  And hath compassed me with His
  net.

7 Behold, I cry out: 'Violence!' but
  I am not heard;
  I cry aloud, but there is no justice.

8 He hath fenced up my way that
  I cannot pass,
  And hath set darkness in my paths.

9 He hath stripped me of my glory,
  And taken the crown from my
  head.

5 אִם־אָמְנָם עָלַי תַּגְדִּילוּ
וְתוֹכִיחוּ עָלַי חֶרְפָּתִי׃

6 דְּעוּ־אֵפוֹ כִּי־אֱלוֹהַּ עִוְּתָנִי
וּמְצוּדוֹ עָלַי הִקִּיף׃

7 הֵן אֶצְעַק חָמָס וְלֹא אֵעָנֶה
אֲשַׁוַּע וְאֵין מִשְׁפָּט׃

8 אָרְחִי גָדַר וְלֹא אֶעֱבוֹר
וְעַל־נְתִיבוֹתַי חֹשֶׁךְ יָשִׂים׃

9 כְּבוֹדִי מֵעָלַי הִפְשִׁיט
וַיָּסַר עֲטֶרֶת רֹאשִׁי׃

being punished enough and not you.'
The sentence may, however, bear the
meaning: 'My sin injures no one but
myself; it has no repercussions which
affect you.' In that sense he applies to
his friends what he had previously said
to God (cf. vii. 20).

**5. if indeed ye will magnify yourselves
against me.** He chides them for assuming
superior airs of self-righteousness and
maintaining against him the reproach
that the calamities crushing him are the
result of his sins. Some scholars prefer
R.V. margin which construes the verse
as a question: 'Will ye indeed magnify
yourselves against me, and plead against
me my reproach?'

**6. know now that God hath subverted my
cause.** Cf. *To subvert a man in his cause,
the LORD approveth not* (Lam. iii. 36).
'Subvert' means to pervert justice, to
treat one unfairly. The emphatic word
is *God.* It is He, Job insists, Who has
handled him unjustly. It is God's injustice, not his own sins, which must
explain the cruel vicissitudes he is
compelled to suffer. God's net that
snares him and drags him down is the
consequence of His miscarriage of justice and not for any misdeed on his part.
Here Job emphatically repudiates the
statements of Bildad in xviii. 8ff.

7. *I cry aloud, but there is no justice.* His
helpless cries for a fair judgment go
unheeded (cf. Jer. xx. 8; Hab. i. 2).

8. *He hath fenced up my way.* Job speaks
metaphorically. God has built a wall
to block his path. All ways of escape are
cut off (cf. Hos. ii. 8; Lam. iii. 7, 9).

hath set darkness in my paths. The
metaphor is changed. God has enveloped him in darkness so that he can
only grope his way uncertainly. Berechiah makes the comparison to one who
cries before a king who pretends not to
hear him, and orders his imprisonment so
that he should not come before him any
more, as if he had hated him from the
first. He does not allow him to arrange
his defence, and orders to strip him of
his garments.

9. *taken the crown from my head.* By
crown he means the 'crown of his righteousness.' This had been his pride and
glory (xxix. 14) until his afflictions
stamped him in the eyes of the world as
a sinner. Metsudath David understands
crown as rulership. Job had been honoured as a wealthy and powerful prince
(i. 3).

10 He hath broken me down on
   every side, and I am gone;
   And my hope hath He plucked
   up like a tree.

11 He hath also kindled His wrath
   against me,
   And He counteth me unto Him
   as one of His adversaries.

12 His troops come on together,
   And cast up their way against me,
   And encamp round about my
   tent.

13 He hath put my brethren far from
   me,
   And mine acquaintance are
   wholly estranged from me.

14 My kinsfolk have failed,
   And my familiar friends have forgotten me.

15 They that dwell in my house,
   and my maids, count me for a
   stranger;
   I am become an alien in their
   sight.

יִתְּצֵנִי סָבִיב וָאֵלַךְ

וַיַּסַּע כָּעֵץ תִּקְוָתִי׃

וַיַּחַר עָלַי אַפּוֹ

וַיַּחְשְׁבֵנִי לוֹ כְצָרָיו׃

יַחַד ׀ יָבֹאוּ גְדוּדָיו

וַיָּסֹלּוּ עָלַי דַּרְכָּם

וַיַּחֲנוּ סָבִיב לְאָהֳלִי׃

אַחַי מֵעָלַי הִרְחִיק

וְיֹדְעַי אַךְ־זָרוּ מִמֶּנִּי׃

חָדְלוּ קְרוֹבָי

וּמְיֻדָּעַי שְׁכֵחוּנִי׃

גָּרֵי בֵיתִי וְאַמְהֹתַי לְזָר תַּחְשְׁבֻנִי

נָכְרִי הָיִיתִי בְעֵינֵיהֶם׃

v. 10. פתח באתנח

10. *He hath broken me down on every side.*
God pulls him down as one wrecks a
building. By *I am gone* Job intends the
hopelessness of his disease. Death is at
hand and he has no hope of recovery.

plucked up like a tree. The figure changes
to that of a tree uprooted from its place.

11. *counteth me unto Him as one of His
adversaries.* The metaphor again changes
and is taken from warfare. God directs
one assault after another against him
(cf. x. 17, xvi. 12ff.). Job uses this
figure to describe the ravages of his
sickness.

12. *His troops come on together.* The
military metaphor continues. The picture is one of throwing up a rampart as
though to make heavy siege against a
fortress or a beleaguered city. Davidson
sees pathos in the thought of God's
armies used to besiege not a mighty
fortress, but a *tent.* The *troops* are
troubles (Ralbag).

13. *He hath put my brethren far from me.*
'The bands of affliction have placed far

from me my relatives, since because of
these afflictions they impute to me great
transgression' (Metsudath David). Even
more touching than Job's complaint that
God has assailed him like an army is the
charge that He has estranged him from
his friends, his relatives and his immediate family. The bonds of human
sympathy and association have been
severed. 'There is something more
breaking to the heart in the turning
away of men from us than in the severest
sufferings. It crushes us quite. We steel
ourselves against it for a time, and rise
to it in bitterness and resentment, but
gradually it breaks us and we are crushed
at last. And this seems the way whether
men frown on us with justice or no'
(Davidson).

14. *my familiar friends have forgotten me.*
Cf. Ps. lxxxviii. 19. Job had a right to
expect that those who, by close association with him, knew the kind of man he
really was would stand by him in his
dark hours of desperate need.

15. *they that dwell in my house.* This
probably means Job's dependants, not

16 I call unto my servant, and he
   giveth me no answer,
   Though I entreat him with my
   mouth.

17 My breath is abhorred of my wife,
   And I am loathsome to the children of my tribe.

18 Even urchins despise me;
   If I arise, they speak against me.

19 All my intimate friends abhor
   me;
   And they whom I loved are
   turned against me.

16 לְעַבְדִּי קָרָאתִי וְלֹא יַעֲנֶה
   בְּמוֹ־פִי אֶתְחַנֶּן־לוֹ׃

17 רוּחִי זָרָה לְאִשְׁתִּי
   וְחַנֹּתִי לִבְנֵי בִטְנִי׃

18 גַּם־עֲוִילִים מָאֲסוּ בִי
   אָקוּמָה וַיְדַבְּרוּ־בִי׃

19 תִּעֲבוּנִי כָּל־מְתֵי סוֹדִי
   וְזֶה־אָהַבְתִּי נֶהְפְּכוּ־בִי׃

of his own household, but settled more or less temporarily under his roof and protection. They were sojourning guests. Others understand it as the servants of his household.

16. *I call unto my servant.* He may mean his personal attendant or one of his many servants. To be ignored in this way is the bitterest of humiliation and a proof of the incredible depth into which he had sunk.

though I entreat him. Once obsequious, he now does not even respond to the humble entreaties of his master. 'Even though I entreat him with my mouth and address him softly, yet he does not answer' (Metsudath David).

17. *my breath is abhorred of my wife.* This is preferable to A.V., R.V.: 'my breath is strange to my wife,' the verb, although spelt like *zar*, 'to be strange,' being connected with a different Arabic root meaning 'to be abhorrent.' What he intends is probably that his wife loathes his intimate embrace (Metsudath David).

I am loathsome. A.V. 'I am entreated' and R.V. 'my supplication' connect *channothi* with *chanan*, 'be gracious.' It is, however, derived from a root *chanan* which in the cognate Arabic signifies 'to be loathsome.'

the children of my tribe. lit. 'of my womb' *Womb* is used of man in the sense of

'body' in Mic. vi. 7; Ps. cxxxii. 11. The phrase would ordinarily mean 'his children,' but they are all dead (i. 19). Various explanations have been offered: 'those that I reared in my house as if they were my children' (Rashi); the children of his concubines (but there is no mention of them in the Book); his grandchildren (it is not stated that any of his children was married); 'sons of my (mother's) womb,' i.e. his brothers (cf. iii. 10). The most probable explanation connects it with an Arabic noun meaning 'clan.'

18. *even urchins despise me.* Cf. in contrast the honour formerly paid to him, xxix. 8ff., 21ff. Even children hold him in contempt.

if I arise, they speak against me. Some scholars understand by *arise* his feeble and faltering efforts to stand on his feet. For *speak against* in the sense of 'insult,' cf. Ps. l. 20. The force of the allusion becomes more pitiful when it is remembered how great is the emphasis in Scripture on the honour and respect that children must accord their elders. Eitan contends that the verb *dibber* here signifies 'to recede, turn the back, flee' and renders: 'When I arise (to come near to them), they turn away from me (turn their back on me)'.

19. *all my intimate friends.* lit. 'all the men of my council,' i.e. his closest friends,

20 My bone cleaveth to my skin and
   to my flesh,
   And I am escaped with the skin
   of my teeth.

בְּעוֹרִי וּבִבְשָׂרִי דָּבְקָה עַצְמִי
וָאֶתְמַלְּטָה בְּעוֹר שִׁנָּי׃

21 Have pity upon me, have pity
   upon me, O ye my friends;
   For the hand of God hath
   touched me.

חָנֻּנִי חָנֻּנִי אַתֶּם רֵעָי
כִּי יַד־אֱלוֹהַּ נָגְעָה בִּי׃

22 Why do ye persecute me as God,
   And are not satisfied with my
   flesh?

לָמָּה תִּרְדְּפֻנִי כְמוֹ־אֵל
וּמִבְּשָׂרִי לֹא תִשְׂבָּעוּ׃

with whom he shared intimate confid-
ences, now abhor him and are turned
against him (cf. Ps. lv. 15). 'The reference is to such as his three friends, men
whose high converse and fellowship
seemed to Job, as a thoughtful godly
man, something almost better than
relationship' (Davidson).

20. *my bone cleaveth to my skin*. Cf. *my
bones cleave to my flesh* (Ps. cii. 6). The
disease has wasted his body until he is a
mere bag of bones, terribly emaciated.

the skin of my teeth. The phrase has
become proverbial and is perhaps quoted
here as a proverb, meaning 'barely escaped with next to nothing.' 'All my
flesh has been smitten with leprosy and
with worms except the gums of my teeth,'
comments Rashi. BDB also understand
the skin of the teeth to mean the gums;
only these are left unattacked by the
leprosy. Ibn Ezra comments: 'I escape
only as teeth through the skin.' The
probable interpretation is that his entire
body is ravaged with disease, even his
teeth have fallen out and he is left with
the bare gums.

21-29 JOB'S APPEAL FOR SYMPATHY AND TO POSTERITY

21. *have pity upon me*. Peake comments
with deep perception and beauty on the
verse: 'Utterly broken by the sad recital
of his woes, and feeling that God is his
relentless enemy, the cause of all his

misery, he turns to the friends to implore
their compassion. It is with great art
that the poet has introduced this fine
transition. In itself the appeal is moving,
but still more when we see the proud man
who has lashed his friends with scorn and
anger, reduced to become a suppliant
for their pity. An appeal all the more
hopeless that the reason he urges is the
very reason why the friends will not
respond. How should God's sycophants
succour him whom God has smitten? But
the supreme art of the poet in placing it
here lies in this, that it greatly heightens
the effect of the wonderful passage that
is to follow. From God he turns to man
in his desperation, but man fails him,
and in a burst of sublime confidence he
returns from man to God.'

the hand of God hath touched me. Cf.
Isa. liii. 4-9. This supports the view
that Job was smitten with elephantiasis,
since leprosy was regarded in a special
sense as a stroke of God.

22. *why do ye persecute me as God*. Why
do you add to my physical torments with
words reviling my character? Because
God has seen fit to afflict me, why do
you follow His example?

are not satisfied with my flesh. An Oriental idiom for 'are ever slandering me.'
In Dan. iii. 8 *brought accusation against*
is literally 'ate fragments of.' Buttenwieser translates: 'Why can ye not get
enough of feasting on my body?'

23 Oh that my words were now
    written!
  Oh that they were inscribed in a
    book!

24 That with an iron pen and lead
  They were graven in the rock for
    ever!

25 But as for me, I know that my
    Redeemer liveth,
  And that He will witness at the
    last upon the dust;

23 מִי־יִתֵּן אֵפוֹ וְיִכָּתְבוּן מִלָּי
מִי־יִתֵּן בַּסֵּפֶר וְיֻחָקוּ׃

24 בְּעֵט־בַּרְזֶל וְעֹפָרֶת
לָעַד בַּצּוּר יֵחָצְבוּן׃

25 וַאֲנִי יָדַעְתִּי גֹּאֲלִי חָי
וְאַחֲרוֹן עַל־עָפָר יָקוּם׃

23. *oh that my words were now written!*
The Hebrew *mi yitten*, *oh that*, expresses
a wish, but not a wish past realization
(cf. Deut. v. 26; Ps. xiv. 7). Buttenweiser accordingly renders: 'Oh, let my
words be written down, let them be
inscribed in a book.' The phrase does
not mean *book* literally but 'committed
to writing.' By *words* Job intends his
repeated assertions of his innocence.
Convinced that he will not receive justice from his contemporaries, Job seeks
refuge in the future unbiased verdict of
posterity, and so longs for a record of his
case to be preserved for that purpose.

24. *that with an iron pen and lead.*
Buttenweiser's rendering is: 'Oh let
them be written with an iron pen in lead,
or be cut in the rock to be preserved for
ever.' Job wishes that his words may be
cut into the rock so that they would
stand indelible for all time. He expresses the desire that they might be
engraved in rock with an iron pen, and
afterwards that lead (which is dark) might
be passed over them to make the letters
legible and durable.

25. *I know that my Redeemer liveth.* We
have come to one of the peak passages
in the Book. Dogmatic preconceptions
have, however, made of verses 25-27 a
battlefield of theological controversy,
since they were given a Christological
interpretation by the Church. What
Job expresses in these momentous verses
is the exultant confidence to which he
has won his way through the torment of
unbearable affliction and the harsh condemnation of his erstwhile friends that
God is really on his side, and that He
will ultimately champion his cause before
the world.

Buttenweiser renders verses 25-27
with beautiful clarity:

> But I know that my Redeemer liveth,
> And that at last He will appear on
>   earth.
> Even after my skin hath been torn
>   from my flesh,
> Still will I cherish the hope that I
>   shall see God.
> The heart in my bosom pineth
> That I may see Him, a champion in
>   my behalf,
> That my eyes may see Him, and not
>   as an enemy.'

His note on the passage is significant:
'Into this classic passage the Occidental
Church, following Origines, has read a
belief in immortality and resurrection,
an interpretation which not only has
no basis in the passage itself, but which
is, in fact, contradicted by the rest of the
dramatic poem—by Job's emphatic
denial of a life after death (xiv. 11f., 14)
and by the fact that no cognizance of
such a hope is taken in the dénouement.
It is for vindication in his lifetime, not
after his death, that Job hopes. Not that
he expects to be restored to health and
prosperity—this he knows cannot be.
He expresses the hope that God may
reveal Himself to justify him and to
attest to his innocence before all the
world—a hope which is fulfilled in the
dénouement.'

my Redeemer. Or, 'my Vindicator,' to
establish my innocence and free me from
unjust imputations of guilt.

He will witness. lit. 'rise up' (as witness);
cf. Deut. xix. 15; Isa. ii. 19 (as judge).

upon the dust. i.e. the earth (cf. xli. 25
where it is so translated).

26 And when after my skin this is
    destroyed,
    Then without my flesh shall I see
    God;

27 Whom I, even I, shall see for my-
    self,
    And mine eyes shall behold, and
    not another's.
    My reins are consumed within
    me.

וְאַחַר עוֹרִי נִקְּפוּ־זֹאת

וּמִבְּשָׂרִי אֶחֱזֶה אֱלוֹהַּ׃

אֲשֶׁר אֲנִי ׀ אֶחֱזֶה־לִּי

וְעֵינַי רָאוּ וְלֹא־זָר

כָּלוּ כִלְיֹתַי בְּחֵקִי׃

26. *and when after my skin this is destroyed.* The meaning is: 'Even after my
skin hath been torn from my flesh,'
i.e. when his illness has reached the very
last stage. So Buttenweiser, who comments on *this* that it is a case of the
interjectional use of the demonstrative,
which the grammarians and exegetes
have here as well as in a number of other
cases failed to recognize (e.g. Cant. vii.
8). And as to the joining of *mibbesari*
(*my flesh*) by *u* ('and') to the rest of the
clause, he compares the similar instances
in 2 Sam. xiii. 20; Isa. lvii. 11; Amos
iv. 10. The function of the conjunctive
particle in all these cases is to add emphasis to the prepositional phrase.

shall I see God. To 'see God' is the
privilege of the righteous, whom God
regards with His favour (xxxiii. 26;
Ps. xi. 7 on which Cohen comments:
'The godly are, so to speak, admitted
into His Presence and enjoy His radiance,
whereas evil-doers are banished into
darkness'). When Job says that he will
see God, it is implied that he will see
Him reconciled to himself, acknowledging his innocence.

27. *whom I, even I, shall see for myself.*
Buttenweiser maintains that the clauses
beginning *whom I* are not relative sen-
tences but objective, dependent on *kalu*
(*are consumed*, but rendered by him
'pineth,' see on verse 25). They are put
in dominant position, at the head of the
sentence, for the sake of emphasis, and
also for the reason that the object of
eloah (*God*) of the preceding verse is to
be construed also with them—a case of
brachyology of which we have had
examples.

for myself. This signifies 'on my side'

(cf. Ps. cxviii. 7). God will appear as a
Champion on my behalf.

and not another's. This translation makes
the words an emphatic qualification of
mine eyes. R.V. margin renders: 'and
not as a stranger', i.e. Job asserts that
he will behold God, not in His aspect of
stranger or enemy, but a friend.

my reins. The seat of emotion, as in
xvi. 13.

are consumed. Better: 'yearn.' The verb
occurs in Ps. cxix. 81f., *my soul pineth*
and *mine eyes fail* (i.e. 'his sight is
strained by looking out for relief,'
Cohen).

The summary which Buttenweiser
gives of his interpretation of this con-
tested passage deserves to be noted: 'It
will be seen that the accurate grammatical
analysis of verses 25-27 leaves room for
one interpretation only, that as in the
parallel passages xvi. 19-22, xvii. 3 and
xxxi. 35-37, Job gives expression to his
ever-growing conviction that in the end
God Himself will appear as his Vindicator, and as the parallel passages state
explicitly, vouch for his innocence. It
should be added that the view that the
verses express the hope in immortality
or resurrection has been refuted again
and again in modern times as incompatible with the text, the first to do so being
Eichorn in 1787, also that it has no basis
either in the Greek version or in the
Syriac and Targum. The first to carry
this mistaken interpretation into the
verses was Origines, whose interpretation, though refuted at the time by
Chrysostomus (who pointed to xiv. 12ff.
as precluding it), was later adopted by
Augustine and Jerome. The latter made

28 If ye say: 'How we will persecute
him!'
Seeing that the root of the matter
is found in me;

29 Be ye afraid of the sword;
For wrath bringeth the punishments of the sword,
That ye may know there is a
judgment.

כִּי תֹאמְרוּ מַה־נִּרְדָּף־לֹו 28
וְשֹׁרֶשׁ דָּבָר נִמְצָא־בִי׃
גּוּרוּ לָכֶם | מִפְּנֵי־חֶרֶב 29
כִּי־חֵמָה עֲוֹנוֹת חָרֶב
לְמַעַן תֵּדְעוּן שַׁדִּין׃

---

20   CHAPTER XX   ב

1 Then answered Zophar the Naamathite, and said:

וַיַּעַן צֹפַר הַנַּעֲמָתִי וַיֹּאמַר׃ 1

 v. 29. שׁדון ק'

---

it the basis for his translation of the
verse in the Vulgate, whence it found its
way into the Lutheran and into the
English Bible.'

28. *if ye say: 'How we will persecute him!'*
Job warns his friends against keeping
up their slanderous charges. *The root
of the matter* is the subject under discussion, viz. the real cause of Job's afflictions. Many Hebrew MSS. and the
Targum read 'in him' for *in me*, thus
carrying on the direct narration of the
friends who are presumed to be speaking
against Job in the first line.

29. *be ye afraid of the sword.* The Divine
avenging sword (cf. Isa. xxxi. 8, xxxiv.
5f.) will overtake the friends. In Babylonian literature the sword is a frequent
ideograph of Nergal, the god of war and
pestilence. The word is used in the verse
without the definite article and suggests
this original character as a proper noun
(Buttenweiser).

wrath. i.e. the Divine wrath. The
Targum has, 'For when God is wroth
because of sinfulness He incites wars.'

that ye may know there is a judgment.
The Targum translates: 'Wherefore ye
will know that the supreme Judge is a
righteous Judge.' You will know the

secret of retribution that comes to the
wicked. The rendering of A.J. corresponds to the *kethib, shaddin*; the *kerĕ,
shaddun,* is probably intended to signify
'One Who judges.' The use of the relative *sha* is paralleled in Judg. v. 7;
Cant. i. 7.

CHAPTER XX

THE SECOND SPEECH OF ZOPHAR

ZOPHAR begins his address by showing
openly his exasperation and impatience
at Job, thus revealing the widening gulf of
misunderstanding between them. With
growing insinuation that it is Job himself
he has in mind, Zophar almost mali-
ciously describes the sudden downfall of
the wicked man. His ill-gotten gains
soon turn to gall, his prosperity does
not endure. God's fierce wrath overtakes him and he perishes terror-haunted,
heaven and earth witnessing to his guilt.
Such is the portion of a wicked man from
God!

2-3 ZOPHAR'S AGITATION

2. *therefore do my thoughts give answer to
me.* Zophar has waited long enough in
exasperating silence, listening to words

2 Therefore do my thoughts give
answer to me,
Even by reason of mine agitation
that is in me.

3 I have heard the reproof which
putteth me to shame,
But out of my understanding my
spirit answereth me.

4 Knowest thou not this of old time,
Since man was placed upon earth,

5 That the triumphing of the wicked
is short,
And the joy of the godless but for
a moment?

6 Though his excellency mount up
to the heavens,
And his head reach unto the
clouds;

7 Yet he shall perish for ever like his
own dung;
They that have seen him shall say:
'Where is he?'

לָכֵן שְׂעִפַּי יְשִׁיבוּנִי
וּבַעֲבוּר חוּשִׁי בִי׃
מוּסַר כְּלִמָּתִי אֶשְׁמָע
וְרוּחַ מִבִּינָתִי יַעֲנֵנִי׃
הֲזֹאת יָדַעְתָּ מִנִּי־עַד
מִנִּי שִׂים אָדָם עֲלֵי־אָרֶץ׃
כִּי רִנְנַת רְשָׁעִים מִקָּרוֹב
וְשִׂמְחַת חָנֵף עֲדֵי־רָגַע׃
אִם־יַעֲלֶה לַשָּׁמַיִם שִׂיאוֹ
וְרֹאשׁוֹ לָעָב יַגִּיעַ׃
כְּגֶלְלוֹ לָנֶצַח יֹאבֵד
רֹאָיו יֹאמְרוּ אַיּוֹ׃

that have given him offence and deeply
touched his emotions (cf. xix. 2f., 29).

mine agitation that is in me. A.V.: 'for
this I make haste,' and R.V.: 'my haste
that is in me,' follow Ibn Ezra's explanation, 'I make haste to answer thee.' The
phrase, which is literally 'my haste in
me,'denotes'my inner excitement' (BDB).

3. *the reproof which putteth me to shame.*
lit. 'the chastisement of my reproach.'
Zophar may be thinking especially of
xix. 29, *be ye afraid of the sword*, the dire
warning that Job had sounded against his
friends.

out of my understanding my spirit. The
preposition *min* is expletive: the spirit
which is the source of one's intuition or
experience (Buttenweiser). Zophar asserts that he does not utter empty words
like Job (xi. 2). He claims to speak
out of his understanding.

4-29 THE MOMENTARY TRIUMPH AND
CATASTROPHIC FALL OF THE WICKED

4. *knowest thou not this of old time.* The
negative *not* does not occur in the text,

but is expressed in the LXX and some
Hebrew MSS. insert it. If we render,
'knowest thou this of old time,' the
question is sarcastic as in xv. 7f. Zophar
is leading up to his argument that the
wicked only enjoy a brief moment of
triumph.

5. *the triumphing of the wicked is short.*
That is the solution of the problem that
the wicked prosper in Ps. xxxvii. 2.

6. *though his excellency mount up to the
heavens.* For *his excellency*, cf. xiii. 11,
i.e. his loftiness. Zophar contends that
the wicked may reach eminence of
influence and position momentarily.
But how ignominious will be their fall!

7. *yet he shall perish for ever like his own
dung.* Observe the brutal inelegance of
Zophar's comparison, which is found
again in 2 Kings ix. 37. 'It is unnecessary
to eliminate by mistranslation or emendation the vigorous coarseness, so charac-
teristic of the speaker' (Peake). The
force of the tenses is not in the future
but in the present. This continues
throughout the speech.

8 He shall fly away as a dream, and
    shall not be found;
  Yea, he shall be chased away as a
    vision of the night.

9 The eye which saw him shall see
    him no more;
  Neither shall his place any more
    behold him.

10 His children shall appease the
    poor,
  And his hands shall restore his
    wealth.

11 His bones are full of his youth,
  But it shall lie down with him in
    the dust.

12 Though wickedness be sweet in
    his mouth,
  Though he hide it under his
    tongue;

8 כַּחֲלוֹם יָעוּף וְלֹא יִמְצָאֻהוּ
  וְיֻדַּד כְּחֶזְיוֹן לָיְלָה׃

9 עַיִן שְׁזָפַתּוּ וְלֹא תוֹסִף
  וְלֹא־עוֹד תְּשׁוּרֶנּוּ מְקוֹמוֹ׃

10 בָּנָיו יְרַצּוּ דַלִּים
  וְיָדָיו תָּשֵׁבְנָה אוֹנוֹ׃

11 עַצְמוֹתָיו מָלְאוּ עֲלוּמָו
  וְעִמּוֹ עַל־עָפָר תִּשְׁכָּב׃

12 אִם־תַּמְתִּיק בְּפִיו רָעָה
  יַכְחִידֶנָּה תַּחַת לְשׁוֹנוֹ׃

v. 11. עלומיו ק׳

8. he shall fly away as a dream. He is like a dream which flies away when one awakes; so shall he fly away from the world, and he who pursues after him will not find him (Metsudath David); cf. Isa. xxix. 8; Ps. lxxiii. 20.

9. the eye which saw him shall see him no more. For the phraseology of the verse, cf. vii. 8, 10, viii. 18; Ps. ciii. 16. The verb translated *saw* means 'catch sight of, look on.'

10. his children shall appease the poor. The wicked man's children will be forced to seek the favour of the poor, placating them for the robberies and extortions of their father. Less probable is R.V. margin: 'the poor shall oppress his children.'

his hands shall restore his wealth. This line seems to return to the wicked man himself during his lifetime. That which he had extorted with his own hands, he will have to restore.

11. his bones are full of his youth. The meaning of the verse has been well expressed in these words: 'Though youthful vigour filleth his bones, it will be buried with him in the dust.' He will die suddenly at the height of his power.

'Whom the gods love die young,' it has been said, is an alien thought to the Hebrew mind. A.V. follows Ibn Ezra's interpretation: 'His bones are full (of the sin) of his youth, which shall lie down with him in the dust.' Metsudath David accepts this explanation, adding that the wicked man will die and be buried unrepentant of the sins of his youth. Rashi understands the verse as referring to 'the strength of his youth,' i.e. he dies suddenly in his strength. Berechiah comments that *alumaw (his youth)* is from the root *alam*, 'hidden': 'That which was hitherto hidden and concealed from men, who thought him to be righteous; while he secretly stole and murdered, and concealed his deeds. Now God reveals by chastisements, so that men understand that all this is the consequence of his sin, and that he was not righteous, as the world considered him. Thus they do also in regard to thee.'

12. though wickedness be sweet in his mouth. It is the way of the wicked, though evil be sweet in his mouth and he does not see now the moment for it to take effect, he hides it under his tongue until the time comes when it will prosper (Rashi); cf. Ps. x. 7. 'Sin is described as a dainty tit-bit, which the

13 Though he spare it, and will not
let it go,
But keep it still within his mouth;
14 Yet his food in his bowels is
turned,
It is the gall of asps within him.
15 He hath swallowed down riches,
and he shall vomit them up
again;
God shall cast them out of his
belly.
16 He shall suck the poison of asps;
The viper's tongue shall slay him.
17 He shall not look upon the rivers,
The flowing streams of honey
and curd.
18 That which he laboured for shall
he give back, and shall not
swallow it down;
According to the substance that
he hath gotten, he shall not
rejoice.

יַחְמֹל עָלֶיהָ וְלֹא יַעַזְבֶנָּה
וְיִמְנָעֶנָּה בְּתוֹךְ חִכּוֹ׃
לַחְמוֹ בְּמֵעָיו נֶהְפָּךְ
מְרוֹרַת פְּתָנִים בְּקִרְבּוֹ׃
חַיִל בָּלַע וַיְקִאֶנּוּ
מִבִּטְנוֹ יוֹרִשֶׁנּוּ אֵל׃
רֹאשׁ־פְּתָנִים יִינָק
תַּהַרְגֵהוּ לְשׁוֹן אֶפְעֶה׃
אַל־יֵרֶא בִפְלַגּוֹת
נַהֲרֵי נַחֲלֵי דְּבַשׁ וְחֶמְאָה׃
מֵשִׁיב יָגָע וְלֹא יִבְלָע
כְּחֵיל תְּמוּרָתוֹ וְלֹא יַעֲלֹס׃

sinner will not swallow, but keeps turning round and round in his mouth to let
the whole expanse of his organ of taste
enjoy its delicious sweetness' (Peake).

13. *though he spare it, and will not let it
go.* The verb translated *spare* means also
'have compassion on.' Accordingly,
Metsudath David comments: 'It is as
if out of his great love for it (i.e. wickedness) he has compassion on it and will
not let it go.'

keep it still within his mouth. This is the
concealment of his hidden sins.

14. *it is the gall of asps within him.* Zophar
compares sin to a delicious morsel when
savoured, but when swallowed it soon
turns to bitter and deadly poison. The
phrase *gall of asps* may reflect the ancient
belief, mentioned by Pliny, that 'it is the
gall which constitutes the poison of asps.'

15. *he shall vomit them up again.* The
wicked man must soon disgorge the
wealth he had amassed. The figure, in
keeping with Zophar's tone, is coarse.
'The LXX, shocked at Zophar's language, substituted "an angel" for *God*'

(Peake). He has swallowed down his
ill-gotten wealth in secret; God compels
him to vomit it up in public (Berechiah).

16. *he shall suck the poison of asps.* Ibn
Ezra points out that *the poison of asps*
(cf. Deut. xxxii. 33) is contrasted with *the
flowing streams of honey and curd* (verse
17), and both expressions are by way of
metaphor. The line has been given two
interpretations: the food he sucks will
destroy and not nourish him; or his
body will absorb the poison from the
bite of the asp. The latter is supported
by the second line.

17. *he shall not look upon the rivers.* The
word for *rivers* occurs in Judg. v. 15
where it is rendered *divisions*; hence
'canals' cut through the land. The pre-
cise meaning here is in doubt. The LXX
has: 'let him not see the milking of the
flocks,' and Buttenwieser renders: 'He
will not look upon (the herds grazing) in
the valleys.'

honey and curd. Symbolic of plenty; as
in *a land flowing with milk and honey*
(Exod. iii. 8).

18. *that which he laboured for shall he
give back.* He will not be able to hold on

19 For he hath oppressed and forsaken the poor;
He hath violently taken away a
house, and he shall not build it
up.
20 Because he knew no quietness
within him,
In his greed he suffered nought
to escape,
21 There was nothing left that he
devoured not—
Therefore his prosperity shall not
endure.
22 In the fulness of his sufficiency
he shall be in straits;
The hand of every one that is in
misery shall come upon him.
23 It shall be for the filling of his
belly;
He shall cast the fierceness of His
wrath upon him,
And shall cause it to rain upon
him into his flesh.

כִּי־רִצַּץ עָזַב דַּלִּים 19
בַּיִת גָּזַל וְלֹא יִבְנֵהוּ:
כִּי ׀ לֹא־יָדַע שָׁלֵו בְּבִטְנוֹ 20
בַּחֲמוּדוֹ לֹא יְמַלֵּט:
אֵין־שָׂרִיד לְאָכְלוֹ 21
עַל־כֵּן לֹא־יָחִיל טוּבוֹ:
בִּמְלֹאות שִׂפְקוֹ יֵצֶר לוֹ 22
כָּל־יַד עָמֵל תְּבוֹאֶנּוּ:
יְהִי ׀ לְמַלֵּא בִטְנוֹ 23
יְשַׁלַּח־בּוֹ חֲרוֹן אַפּוֹ
וְיַמְטֵר עָלֵימוֹ בִּלְחוּמוֹ:

v. 22. י יתיר

to his ill-gotten gains, and so his unscrupulous actions do not benefit him.

that he hath gotten. lit. 'of his exchange.'
Driver calls this an oxymoron (a figure
of speech with pointed conjunction of
seeming contradictories, of which a
striking illustration is 'faith unfaithful
kept him falsely true'). Here the meaning appears to be: the wealth gained by
him from his bargains is a source of disappointment to him and not of joy.

19. *forsaken the poor.* After robbing the
poor, he callously left them in their
desolate state.

he hath violently taken away a house. The
house which he had stolen he will not
inhabit.

20. *he knew no quietness within him.* His
greed was insatiable.

in his greed he suffered nought to escape.
R.V. renders: 'He shall not save aught
of that wherein he delighted.' A.J.
follows Ibn Ezra.

21. *therefore his prosperity shall not endure.* Verses 20f. add up to mean that
utter destitution is the reward and retribution that overtake the wicked, greedy

and avaricious man. The retribution
corresponds to the sin: the insatiable
greediness is recompensed by utter loss
and want.

22. *he shall be in straits.* Destitution will
suddenly beset him in the midst of his
luxury. Rashi interprets, 'trouble will
come upon him.' The suddenness of the
wicked man's reversal of fortune is
compared by Ibn Ezra to that described
in Ps. xcii. 8.

the hand . . . come upon him. Those whom
he reduced to penury will turn against
him.

23. *it shall be for the filling of his belly.*
Better: 'Let it be for the filling of his
belly (or, when his belly is filled), that
He cast . . . and cause it to rain.' As the
person is addicted to greed, may God
send him abundance—but of His wrath.

into his flesh. The Hebrew word *lechum*
probably means 'intestines, bowels.' 'To
fill his belly, God sendeth into him His
burning anger, and raineth it upon him,
into his (very) flesh' (BDB). Ibn Ezra
understands *lechum* as 'into his flesh,'
but says that it may mean more lit. 'into
his belly.' R.V. margin has 'as his food.'

24 If he flee from the iron weapon,
　The bow of brass shall strike him
　　through.

25 He draweth it forth, and it com-
　eth out of his body;
　Yea, the glittering point cometh
　　out of his gall;
　Terrors are upon him.

26 All darkness is laid up for his
　　treasures;
　A fire not blown by man shall
　　consume him;
　It shall go ill with him that is left
　　in his tent.

27 The heavens shall reveal his
　　iniquity,
　And the earth shall rise up
　　against him.

28 The increase of his house shall
　　depart,
　His goods shall flow away in the
　　day of his wrath.

יִבְרַח מִנֵּשֶׁק בַּרְזֶל
תַּחְלְפֵהוּ קֶשֶׁת נְחוּשָׁה:
שָׁלַף וַיֵּצֵא מִגֵּוָה
וּבָרָק מִמְּרֹרָתוֹ
יַהֲלֹךְ עָלָיו אֵמִים:
כָּל־חֹשֶׁךְ טָמוּן לִצְפוּנָיו
תְּאָכְלֵהוּ אֵשׁ לֹא־נֻפָּח
יֵרַע שָׂרִיד בְּאָהֳלוֹ:
יְגַלּוּ שָׁמַיִם עֲוֺנוֹ
וְאֶרֶץ מִתְקוֹמָמָה לוֹ:
יִגֶל יְבוּל בֵּיתוֹ
נִגָּרוֹת בְּיוֹם אַפּוֹ:

v. 26. מלעיל

24. *if he flee from the iron weapon.* The
metaphor changes from the fiery rain
from heaven to that of heavily armed foes
surrounding him. While he may elude
one death-dealing weapon, he will fall by
another. His destruction is inescapable.
He flees from one manner of death only
to run into another (cf. Amos v. 19). 'If
he flees from the iron weapon, such as the
sword—which is possible—he cannot
flee from the bow; for the arrow overtakes him, and enters and sticks in his
belly' (Berechiah).

25. *he draweth it forth.* A description of
the wicked man, wounded, seeking to
draw out the arrow that has pierced
through his body.

the glittering point. lit. 'lightning,'
descriptive of the flashing sword (Deut.
xxxii. 41) or spear (Hab. iii. 11); here of
the metal tip of the arrow.

terrors are upon him. i.e. the terrors of
death. 'If the line connects with what
goes before, the description reaches a
powerful climax in the horrors that close
in on the death-stricken man' (Peake).

26. *all darkness is laid up for his treasures.*
Darkness is figurative for calamity (cf.

xv. 22f.). That which he had acquired
and hoarded will end in ruin.

a fire not blown by man. Either lightning
(cf. i. 16) or a blaze the origin of which is
unknown.

him that is left in his tent. i.e. his wife
and children (Metsudath David). It is
the same word as in verse 21, *there was
nothing left,* and so may mean here 'what
is left' of his treasures.

27. *the heavens shall reveal his iniquity.*
Job had asserted that his Witness was
in heaven, and appealed to the earth not
to cover his blood (xvi. 18f.). Zophar
may be hinting at this as he now sums
up how God's judgments overtake the
wicked man. Heaven and earth combine
to testify to his guilt. 'Heaven "reveals"
his iniquity in the chastisements, e.g. the
fire of heaven (i. 16), that fall on him;
and earth rises up against him in the
hostility of men (i. 15, 17, xvii. 6)'
(Davidson).

28. *the increase of his house shall depart.*
Shall depart is from a root meaning 'to go
into exile.' His property will be carried
from his possession into that of others.

29 This is the portion of a wicked
     man from God,
     And the heritage appointed unto
     him by God.

29 זֶה ׀ חֵלֶק־אָדָם רָשָׁע ׀ מֵאֱלֹהִים
וְנַחֲלַת אִמְרוֹ מֵאֵל׃

---

21   CHAPTER XXI   כא

1 Then Job answered and said:

1 וַיַּעַן אִיּוֹב וַיֹּאמַר׃

---

his goods shall flow away. The image is
that a raging flood that sweeps away his
possessions.

his wrath. Usually explained by ancient
and modern commentators as God's
wrath. By not printing *his* with a
capital, A.J. takes it as 'the day when
wrath comes upon him,' the objective
suffix.

29. *this is the portion of a wicked man
from God.* Zophar concludes his speech
with the warning sentence that such is
the recompense that overtakes a wicked
man from God. The implication to Job
is cutting: this is thy sin and such is the
fruit thereof.

heritage appointed unto him. lit. 'the
heritage of his saying (*imro*).' Eitan
questions this translation, and points
out that the verse closely resembles
xxvii. 13, but there the phrase is *the
inheritance of oppressors.* He contends
that *imro* is not connected with *amar*,
'to say,' but is derived from *mara* with
prosthetic *aleph*, like *ephroach, ezro'a.*
From the root comes *mar, marë* in Aramaic, 'master, lord, ruler,' and in Arabic
it signifies 'manhood, power, strength.'
He therefore claims that the signification here is 'oppressor, violent man.'

We have seen here no essential view
added to that already expounded by
Eliphaz and Bildad that the wicked are
doomed to destruction. Zophar speaks
with a certain coarseness and brutality—
at times, almost vulgarly. He had ended
his vigorous speech of the abrupt and
dismal end of the wicked man with the

words, *This is the portion of a wicked man
from God.* 'These words *from God* call
up before Job's soul the great mystery
with which he is struggling. According
to his own former faith as well as that of
his friends this should have been a true
account of God's rule in the world. But
Job's vision had been sharpened as well
as widened by his own history, and he
now observed much in the world which
had formerly escaped him. He saw that
this was no true statement of God's
dealing with wickedness. God dealt
with it quite otherwise; and the mystery
overwhelms him, and instead of chiding
his friends he can only appeal to them to
contemplate the awful riddle of Providence, at the thought of which he himself
trembles (xxi. 6). This riddle, the
prosperity of the wicked in God's hands
(xxi. 16), their peaceful death (xxi. 13),
and even the renown of their memory
(xxi. 33) he then proceeds to unfold'
(Davidson).

CHAPTER XXI

JOB'S SIXTH REPLY—TO ZOPHAR

JOB begins his argument, which is calculated to demolish the contention of the
friends that material retributive justice
prevails in the universe, by requesting
them to attend his words carefully. Let
them be astonished, even as he is, at the
evidence he is about to lay bare before
them. Contrary to the claims of the
friends, Job maintains that the wicked
prosper, grow old, die in peace. Some
scoundrels are never overwhelmed with
misfortune. 'How oft is it that the lamp

2 Hear diligently my speech;
And let this be your consolations.

3 Suffer me, that I may speak;
And after that I have spoken,
mock on.

4 As for me, is my complaint to
man?
Or why should I not be impatient?

5 Turn unto me, and be astonished,
And lay your hand upon your
mouth.

6 Even when I remember I am
affrighted,
And horror taketh hold on my
flesh.

שִׁמְעוּ שָׁמוֹעַ מִלָּתִי

וּתְהִי־זֹאת תַּנְחוּמֹתֵיכֶם׃

שָׂאוּנִי וְאָנֹכִי אֲדַבֵּר

וְאַחַר דַּבְּרִי תַלְעִיג׃

הֶאָנֹכִי לְאָדָם שִׂחִי

וְאִם־מַדּוּעַ לֹא־תִקְצַר רוּחִי׃

פְּנוּ־אֵלַי וְהָשַׁמּוּ

וְשִׂימוּ יָד עַל־פֶּה׃

וְאִם־זָכַרְתִּי וְנִבְהָלְתִּי

וְאָחַז בְּשָׂרִי פַּלָּצוּת׃

v. 5. פתח באתנח בב״א הה׳ בק״ח והש׳ דגושה או הה׳ בת״ק

of the wicked is put out?' he asks, controverting Bildad's contention in xviii. 5. It is no punishment to them if their sins are visited only upon their children. Will you presume to dictate to God His methods of government, as you do when you maintain that men's lots in life are always according to their deserts? I have seen otherwise: 'One dieth . . . at ease and quiet . . . and another in bitterness of soul . . . they lie down alike in the dust.' Far from ending his life in ruin, the evil man may end his days in honour, be buried in pomp and watch kept over his tomb. Many are his imitators. Job concludes his speech by rejecting as useless sophistry the argument of the misfortunes of the wicked which the friends have monotonously advanced.

2-6 'TURN UNTO ME, AND BE ASTONISHED'

2. *let this be your consolations.* Eliphaz had smugly presumed to describe his words as *the consolations of God* (xv. 11). Job turns the phrase about: If they will heed diligently what he has to say about the actual moral government of the world, that will be all the consolation he seeks from them.

3. *mock on.* The verbs in the chapter so far were all plural, but this is singular.

One Hebrew MS. has the plural. It may be that Job makes a point here of addressing Zophar, whose language describing the fate of the wicked, had been particularly offensive. 'After what I am about to say about the prosperity of the wicked,' Job says in effect, 'you will hardly dare to mock any more.'

4. *as for me, is my complaint to man?* Job is not complaining of, or concerning, man. His friends need not become heated. What he protests against are the moral anomalies that God allows in His world. It is this baffling moral mystery that accounts for his impatient tone of speech. 'And since He does not answer me, why should I not become impatient, and how not cry out in bitterness of soul?' (Metsudath David).

5. *lay your hand upon your mouth.* A gesture of awe-struck silence (cf. xl. 4; Mic. vii. 16). The mystery of God's moral government in allowing the wicked to prosper, with which Job is about to confront them, will leave them awe-stricken, unable to find an adequate reply.

6. *even when I remember I am affrighted.* Even to think of this anomaly—the prosperity of wicked persons—is to fill him with dismay and horror.

E

7 Wherefore do the wicked live, Become old, yea, wax mighty in power?	⁷ מַדּוּעַ רְשָׁעִים יִחְיוּ עָתְקוּ גַּם־גָּבְרוּ חָיִל:
8 Their seed is established in their sight with them, And their offspring before their eyes.	⁸ זַרְעָם ׀ נָכוֹן לִפְנֵיהֶם עִמָּם וְצֶאֱצָאֵיהֶם לְעֵינֵיהֶם:
9 Their houses are safe, without fear, Neither is the rod of God upon them.	⁹ בָּתֵּיהֶם שָׁלוֹם מִפָּחַד וְלֹא־שֵׁבֶט אֱלוֹהַּ עֲלֵיהֶם:
10 Their bull gendereth, and faileth not; Their cow calveth, and casteth not her calf.	¹⁰ שׁוֹרוֹ עִבַּר וְלֹא יַגְעִל תְּפַלֵּט פָּרָתוֹ וְלֹא תְשַׁכֵּל:
11 They send forth their little ones like a flock, And their children dance.	¹¹ יְשַׁלְּחוּ כַצֹּאן עֲוִילֵיהֶם וְיַלְדֵיהֶם יְרַקֵּדוּן:
12 They sing to the timbrel and harp, And rejoice at the sound of the pipe.	¹² יִשְׂאוּ כְּתֹף וְכִנּוֹר וְיִשְׂמְחוּ לְקוֹל עוּגָב:

7-16 THE WICKED LIVE IN PROSPERITY

7. *wherefore do the wicked live.* 'Job is not seeking a dialectical triumph over the friends, for the question he puts to them is, as verse 6 shows, one that overpowers him with horror. He propounds to them the problem that torments himself: Why do the wicked prosper?' (Peake). Why should a good God permit the wicked thus to flourish?

8. *their seed is established in their sight with them.* In this verse and those to follow, Job takes issue flatly with Bildad in xviii. 5-21 where he had painted a graphic picture of the calamities that overtake the wicked. Job begins, pathetically in the light of the disasters that had deprived him of his own, by maintaining that the wicked live to see their children grow to manhood.

9. *their houses are safe, without fear.* lit. 'peace, without fear'; their homes are secure and undisturbed.

neither is the rod of God upon them. The terrifying *rod* (ix. 34), which had fallen so devastatingly upon Job and his children, spares them. Note how he denies what each of his friends had said: Eliphaz in xv. 28, Zophar in xx. 28, Bildad in xviii. 14.

10. *their bull gendereth.* The wicked man's cattle increase and multiply without mishap.

11. *they send forth their little ones like a flock.* The children of the wicked are as numerous as a flock (cf. Ps. cvii. 41).

their children dance. 'It is curious that such a festive life Job's children also had lived; but they breathed an atmosphere of piety, guarded from guilt by their father's anxious care. They were cut off, but the children of the wicked live on in pleasure' (Peake).

12. *the timbrel and harp . . . the pipe.* The three musical instruments suggest the atmosphere of festivity in which the wicked spend their days and nights, singing gayly to the accompaniment of timbrel, harp and pipe. Rashi claims that *ugab*, pipe, is an expression for 'sensual laughter,' 'asbanayement' in his Old French rendering.

13 They spend their days in prosperity,
   And peacefully they go down to
   the grave.
14 Yet they said unto God: 'Depart
   from us;
   For we desire not the knowledge
   of Thy ways.
15 What is the Almighty, that we
   should serve Him?
   And what profit should we have,
   if we pray unto Him?'—
16 Lo, their prosperity is not in their
   hand;
   The counsel of the wicked is far
   from me.
17 How oft is it that the lamp of the
   wicked is put out?

יְבַלּ֣וּ בַטּ֣וֹב יְמֵיהֶ֑ם ◄
וּבְרֶ֗גַע שְׁא֥וֹל יֵחָֽתּוּ׃
וַיֹּאמְר֣וּ לָ֭אֵל ס֣וּר מִמֶּ֑נּוּ ◄
וְדַ֥עַת דְּרָכֶ֗יךָ לֹ֣א חָפָֽצְנוּ׃
מַה־שַּׁדַּ֥י כִּֽי־נַעַבְדֶ֑נּוּ
וּמַה־נּוֹעִ֗יל כִּ֣י נִפְגַּע־בּֽוֹ׃
הֵ֤ן לֹ֣א בְיָדָ֣ם טוּבָ֑ם 1
עֲצַ֥ת רְ֝שָׁעִ֗ים רָ֣חֲקָה מֶֽנִּי׃
כַּמָּ֤ה ׀ נֵֽר־רְשָׁ֘עִ֤ים יִדְעָ֗ךְ 1

v. 13. יכלו ק'   v. 17. קמץ בלא אס"ף

13. *peacefully they go down to the grave.*
A.V. and R.V.: 'and in a moment go
down to the grave (to Sheol).' A.J. gives
the right sense, in agreement with Rashi's
comment: 'And when the day of his
death arrives, he dies in a moment in
tranquillity without sufferings.' Job
contrasts the swift death for which he
longs with the protracted agony that has
been his reward for a righteous and un-
blemished life. The wicked, he says,
enjoy happiness and even festivity
throughout their lives, and then when
they die in old age (verse 7) they are
spared the anguish of a lingering illness.
Job's idyllic picture sharply compares
with that drawn by the friends who have
described the calamities of the wicked.

14. *yet they said unto God: 'Depart from
us.'* Although they openly flaunted
their irreligion, yet they were left undisturbed in their pleasure and prosperity.
For other examples of the irreligious,
sceptical temper to be found in Scripture, cf. Ps. lxxiii. 8f., 11; Mal. iii. 14.

15. *what is the Almighty, that we should
serve Him?* Coverdale (sixteenth-cen-
tury Bible translator) has a vigorous as
well as quaint rendering: 'What maner
of felowe is the Almightie that we shulde
serve Him?' One might call this the
'slot-machine' philosophy of religion.
The coin of faith demands the chocolate
bar of material benefit.

16. *lo, their prosperity is not in their hand.*
The prosperity enjoyed by the wicked
which I (Job) have described is not of
their own making. It comes from God
(Ibn Ezra). God must be held responsible for permitting the wicked thus to
prosper. Rashi, however, takes it as a
question: 'Is not all their good in their
hand?'

the counsel of the wicked is far from me.
Job disowns all sympathy with these
principles of the wicked. He repudiates
their view that their prosperity is their
own doing (cf. Deut. viii. 17). There
might have been ground for suspecting
that he shared their point of view after
his attractive picture of their well-being.
Cf. xxii. 18 where Eliphaz has the same
line.

17-21 CALAMITY RARELY OVERTAKES
THE WICKED

17. *how oft is it that the lamp of the
wicked is put out?* In xviii. 5 Bildad had
claimed that *the light of the wicked shall be
put out.* By his question Job means,
'What examples can you show in proof?'

that He distributeth pains in His anger.
Job alludes to the assertion of Zophar,
*He shall cast the fierceness of His wrath
upon him* (xx. 23). The word for *pains*
is *chebalim*, and Ibn Ezra renders:
'He sends upon them the *lines* of His
anger,' in contradistinction to *the lines*
(chebalim) *are fallen unto me in pleasant
places* (Ps. xvi. 6).

That their calamity cometh upon
them?
That He distributeth pains in His
anger?

18 That they are as stubble before
the wind,
And as chaff that the storm steal-
eth away?

19 'God layeth up his iniquity for
his children!'—
Let Him recompense it unto himself, that he may know it.

20 Let his own eyes see his destruction,
And let him drink of the wrath of
the Almighty.

21 For what pleasure hath he in his
house after him?
Seeing the number of his months
is determined.

וְיָבֹא עָלֵימוֹ אֵידָם
חֲבָלִים יְחַלֵּק בְּאַפּוֹ:

18 יִהְיוּ כְּתֶבֶן לִפְנֵי־רוּחַ
וּכְמֹץ גְּנָבַתּוּ סוּפָה:

19 אֱלוֹהַּ יִצְפֹּן־לְבָנָיו אוֹנוֹ
יְשַׁלֵּם אֵלָיו וְיֵדָע:

20 יִרְאוּ עֵינָו כִּידוֹ
וּמֵחֲמַת שַׁדַּי יִשְׁתֶּה:

21 כִּי מַה־חֶפְצוֹ בְּבֵיתוֹ אַחֲרָיו
וּמִסְפַּר חֳדָשָׁיו חֻצָּצוּ:

v. 20. עיניו ק'

---

18. *as stubble before the wind.* The question of Job continues: How often are the
wicked blown as straw before the wind
or as chaff before the storm? The
images are figurative for utter destruction (cf. Isa. xvii. 13; Ps. i. 4).

19. *'God layeth up his iniquity for his
children.'* Job is evidently quoting a
current adage. Buttenweiser translates:
'God layeth up for a man's children the
disaster due to him (is the saying): Let
Him pay it to the man himself that he
may feel it.' We may imagine the friends
interrupting to say, 'The wicked man's
sins are visited upon his children.' Job
replies, 'Justice requires that they should
be visited upon himself; he is unaffected
by what may happen to his children after
his death' (verses 20f.).

20. *his destruction.* The Hebrew word
kid is found nowhere else, and the Jewish
commentators admit that its meaning
has to be deduced from the context.
Modern scholars regard it as an error
for *pid* which occurs in xii. 5, but it may
be connected with the Arabic *kaid* 'war.'

let him drink of the wrath of the Almighty.
For this image, cf. Jer. xxv. 15; Ps. lxxv.9.

21. *for what pleasure hath he in his house
after him?* What interest does the sinner
have in his household once he is dead?
'Job's objection to the doctrine that a
man's iniquity is visited on his children
is that this is no punishment of the
wicked man himself, for he hath no concern in or knowledge of his children's
fate after his death (xiv. 21). From the
Prophetic Books of this age it appears
that the ancient doctrine of retribution,
the doctrine that the fathers have eaten
sour grapes, and the children's teeth are
set on edge (Ezek. xviii. 2), had begun to
awaken questionings (cf. Jer. xxxi. 28f.),
and in this Book such doubts are, naturally, brought to a point' (Davidson).

the number of his months is determined.
He cannot live for ever, and his span of
life is limited.

22-26 THE MYSTERY OF PROVIDENCE

22. *shall any teach God knowledge?* The
usual interpretation of this crucial verse
is that Job rebukes the friends for pre-
suming to force into the Procrustean bed
of their theology the cruel facts of human
experience. By insisting that their

22 Shall any teach God knowledge?
    Seeing it is He that judgeth those
       that are high.

23 One dieth in his full strength,
    Being wholly at ease and quiet;

24 His pails are full of milk,
    And the marrow of his bones is
       moistened.

25 And another dieth in bitterness
       of soul,
    And hath never tasted of good.

26 They lie down alike in the dust,
    And the worm covereth them.

הַלְאֵל יְלַמֶּד־דָּעַת
וְהוּא רָמִים יִשְׁפּוֹט׃
זֶה יָמוּת בְּעֶצֶם תֻּמּוֹ
כֻּלּוֹ שַׁלְאֲנַן וְשָׁלֵיו׃
עֲטִינָיו מָלְאוּ חָלָב
וּמֹחַ עַצְמוֹתָיו יְשֻׁקֶּה׃
וְזֶה יָמוּת בְּנֶפֶשׁ מָרָה
וְלֹא אָכַל בַּטּוֹבָה׃
יַחַד עַל־עָפָר יִשְׁכָּבוּ
וְרִמָּה תְּכַסֶּה עֲלֵיהֶם׃

principle of material retribution was
God's ordering of the universe, they were
trying to better God's own inscrutable
knowledge.

it is He that judgeth those that are high.
Commonly interpreted to refer to the
denizens of heaven (cf. iv. 18, *His angels*;
xv. 15, *His holy ones*; xxv. 2, *He maketh
peace in His high places*). Buttenweiser,
resting on Eliphaz's question in xxii. 13,
Thou sayest: '*What doth God know? Can
He judge through the dark cloud?* as well
as Ps. lxxiii. 11, *They say*: '*How doth
God know? And is there knowledge in the
Most High?*' obtains this illuminating
translation: 'Doth God practise discrimination? Doth He judge in His abode on
high?' It is Buttenweiser's contention
that later editors took umbrage at Job's
question, changing verse 22a but for-
tunately leaving xxii. 13 untouched. On
shall any teach God knowledge? Ibn Ezra
makes the significant comment: 'It is as
if the Omnipresent does not know what
He is doing!'

23. *one dieth in his full strength.* lit. 'in
his very perfection'; in the full enjoyment
of all that filled his cup of life to the
brim. 'This is the wicked,' remarks
Rashi.

24. *his pails are full of milk.* A.V., R.V.

translate 'his breasts'; but the R.V.
margin has 'milk pails' which is now
adopted. *Atinaw*, remarks Ibn Ezra, 'is
in Arabic the place upon which the
camels kneel for water.' In Rabbinic
Hebrew it denotes 'a vessel for olives.'

the marrow of his bones is moistened.
Figurative for well nourished and prosperous (cf. Prov. iii. 8).

25. *another dieth in bitterness of soul.*
'These are the high and holy ones'
(Rashi). Cf. Job's description of himself
in iii. 20, vii. 7.

26. *they lie down alike in the dust.* The
wicked and righteous share the same
fate (cf. Eccles. ii. 14ff.). 'After their
death persons cannot tell who was bad
and who was good, for the one is as the
other, *they lie down alike in the dust*'
(Rashi). 'It is noteworthy,' observes
Peake penetratingly, 'that here Job does
not mechanically reverse the doctrine of
his friends, and allot happiness to the
evil and calamity to the good. " He sees
life steadily and sees it whole" in these
few lines. Fate deals out its awards
irrespective of moral criteria. It is the
dissimilarity in the common human lot
that moves him, rather than its ethical
perversity.'

27 Behold, I know your thoughts,
  And the devices which ye wrong-
    fully imagine against me.

28 For ye say: 'Where is the house
    of the prince?
  And where is the tent wherein the
    wicked dwelt?'

29 Have ye not asked them that go
    by the way;
  And will ye misdeem their tokens,

30 That the evil man is reserved to
    the day of calamity,
  That they are led forth to the day
    of wrath?

31 But who shall declare his way to
    his face?
  And who shall repay him what he
    hath done?

32 For he is borne to the grave,
  And watch is kept over his tomb.

27 הֵן יָדַעְתִּי מַחְשְׁבוֹתֵיכֶם
וּמְזִמּוֹת עָלַי תַּחְמֹסוּ׃

28 כִּי תֹאמְרוּ אַיֵּה בֵית־נָדִיב
וְאַיֵּה אֹהֶל ׀ מִשְׁכְּנוֹת רְשָׁעִים׃

29 הֲלֹא שְׁאֶלְתֶּם עוֹבְרֵי דָרֶךְ
וְאֹתֹתָם לֹא תְנַכֵּרוּ׃

30 כִּי לְיוֹם אֵיד יֵחָשֶׂךְ רָע
לְיוֹם עֲבָרוֹת יוּבָלוּ׃

31 מִי־יַגִּיד עַל־פָּנָיו דַּרְכּוֹ
וְהוּא־עָשָׂה מִי יְשַׁלֶּם־לוֹ׃

32 וְהוּא לִקְבָרוֹת יוּבָל
וְעַל־גָּדִישׁ יִשְׁקוֹד׃

27-34 FATE OF THE EVIL MAN

27. *ye wrongfully imagine against me.*
From *chamas*, 'treat violently'; 'the devices wherewith ye do me violence' (Ibn
Ezra). Job let his friends know that he
understands the personal implications to
himself when they describe the fate of
the wicked man.

28. *the prince.* The rich oppressor.
Nadib usually means 'generous, princely,
noble' in a good sense. Here it indicates
'a wealthy man who is not righteous' (Ibn
Ezra), an exploiter of the poor (cf. xx. 19).
The question implies that his dwelling
has been swept away (cf. the threats
of the friends: Bildad in viii. 15, 22,
xviii. 15, 21, Eliphaz in xv. 34).

29. *have ye not asked them that go by the
way.* Travellers, with wider perspective,
knowing the happenings that transpire
in the world, will tell a different tale of
what happened to the wicked. They can
cite instances (*their tokens*) of how the
wicked man is spared in the day of
destruction.

30. *that the evil man is reserved to the day
of calamity.* Job means, of course, that
the evidence of world-travellers is that
the evil man is spared (*reserved*) in the

day of calamity and led away in safety
from the destroying wrath (cf. the use of
the verb in 2 Kings v. 20).

31. *who shall declare his way to his face?*
The reference is to the powerful but
wicked despot: who dare rebuke him
openly for his doings? This is the more
natural interpretation, although, as Ibn
Ezra comments, it may possibly be a
parenthetical sentence and refer to God:
who can declare unto Him His way since
He does as He pleases? Rashi also
believes the reference to be to God.
Modern scholars are agreed that the
language fits better the powerful irre-
sponsible oppressor before whom men
grovel.

32. *for he is borne to the grave.* Job
describes how the wicked tyrant is buried
in honour and his example widely followed. This is in direct opposition to
what the friends have asserted all along.

watch is kept over his tomb. The word
gadish occurs nowhere else in Scripture
in this sense. Ibn Ezra quotes Rab Hai
who defines it as 'the mausoleum (*kubba*,
"arched room") which is over the grave,
as is the custom in Arab lands.' Davidson
says that the word more literally means

33 The clods of the valley are sweet
    unto him,
  And all men draw after him,
    As there were innumerable be-
    fore him.

34 How then comfort ye me in vain?
  And as for your answers, there
    remaineth only faithlessness.

³ מָתְקוּ־לוֹ רִגְבֵי־נָחַל
וְאַחֲרָיו כָּל־אָדָם יִמְשׁוֹךְ
וּלְפָנָיו אֵין מִסְפָּר׃
³ וְאֵיךְ תְּנַחֲמוּנִי הָבֶל
וּתְשׁוּבֹתֵיכֶם נִשְׁאַר־מָעַל׃

22   CHAPTER XXII   כב

1 Then answered Eliphaz the Temanite, and said:

¹ וַיַּעַן אֱלִיפַז הַתֵּמָנִי וַיֹּאמַר׃

'his heap' as in v. 26 of a heap of sheaves, and adds that the word appears to be used in the wider sense of any sepulchral monument. This is watched against desecration. In the Sidonian inscription on the tomb of Eshmunazar, that monarch utters deep curses against any who shall violate his grave. Modern Hebrew philology distinguishes the two words although they appear identical, in agreement with two distinct Arabic nouns. It is clear that the wicked man, Job asserts, is buried in pomp and his tomb is carefully guarded.

33. *the clods of the valley are sweet unto him.* Valleys were commonly chosen for burial places. 'The description,' says Peake, 'fitly closes with the idyllic touch of perfect peace in the bosom of the fragrant earth. A life so full of unbroken happiness, lived out to its full measure, rounded off by sleep so sweet and grateful, was bound to attract many imitators, who, reversing Balaam's maxim, might say: Let me die the death of the wicked.' Buttenweiser has an interesting note on verses 32f. in which he shows how they throw light on the great gulf that existed between the few privileged and the masses. The common man often did not even have an individual grave in which he was buried.

all men draw after him. Influenced by his peaceful and honoured end after a wicked life, many follow his bad example.

34. *as for your answers, there remaineth only faithlessness.* Cf. xvi. 2. When the arguments of the friends are tested by experience, they are found to be void of reality.

With this address, the second cycle comes to an end.

CHAPTERS XXII-XXXI

THE THIRD CYCLE OF SPEECHES

THE third cycle of speeches, from the point of view of the faithful transmission of the text, presents almost insuperable difficulties. The pattern of the colloquies seems to have been disturbed. In the twenty-seventh chapter, verses 13-23 would come with greater appropriateness from Zophar (who fails to speak at all in the third round of the debate), or from Eliphaz, than from the mouth of Job. Not only is the careful reader aware of profound textual disturbance, such as creates the problem of chapter xxvii. He notices the unusual brevity of Bildad's speech in chapter xxv. The twenty-eighth chapter has likewise seemed to many scholars as a separate and independent poem in praise of 'Wisdom.'

2 Can a man be profitable unto God?
Or can he that is wise be profitable
unto Him?

2 הֲלְאֵל יִסְכָּן־גָּבֶר
כִּי־יִסְכָּן עָלֵימוֹ מַשְׂכִּיל׃

Nevertheless, without tampering with our received text, we are able to observe with sufficient clarity the forward march of the spiritual drama. We observe the friends now reduced in their argument to the only weapon left in their static theology. They turn finally from covert insinuation and veiled subterfuge to open accusation of Job. So far has their position deteriorated, that they must add flagrant insult to the injury of disappointment that Job has experienced when he first turned to them in his affliction. They are cruelly unsparing in heaping baseless and numberless sins upon his head.

Job does more than respond to these fanatical accusations. In xxvii. 1-6 and again in chapter xxxi we have his solemn asseveration of innocence and his great oath of clearance. But beyond this passionate affirmation of his moral integrity —the more dramatically moving since the reader, admitted into the true circumstances of Job's trial in the Prologue, finds it unnecessary—he advances to that far outpost of faith where he can transmute his grievous woe into the deepest wisdom of life. Although God's wonders remain beyond the boundaries of mortal understanding, he has come to rest in the fellowship of a righteous God and in the recognition that *the fear of the Lord, that is wisdom, and to depart from evil is understanding* (xxviii. 28).

CHAPTER XXII

THE THIRD SPEECH OF ELIPHAZ

WITH clear but cold logic, Eliphaz advances the argument that God has nothing personally to gain by afflicting Job. Since He can hardly be punishing him for his piety, it follows that his great wickedness must be the cause of his sufferings and misfortunes. Basing himself on this line of reasoning, Eliphaz

proceeds to impute to Job various sins, calculated to show him as a hard-hearted and inhuman hypocrite. Job has been guilty of more than oppression and wrong to his fellow-man. He has been impious besides, heretically questioning God's moral government. Eliphaz warns him against following the old path of ancient wicked men who renounced God, only in the end to be punished.

Let him return to God, casting away his unrighteousness; then once again will he have delight in the Almighty. He will not only enjoy spiritual fellowship; material blessings and the light of prosperity will shine upon his ways. Cf. Eliphaz's first speech, v. 17-27, Zophar's first speech, xi. 13-19.

2-20 JOB'S WICKEDNESS IS GREAT

2. *can a man be profitable unto God?* The verse has given translators and interpreters difficulty. A.V.: 'Can a man be profitable unto God, as he that is wise can be profitable unto himself?' R.V.: 'Can a man be profitable unto God? Surely he that is wise is profitable unto himself.' In both these renderings, the meaning is that a man's wisdom, his right and prudent conduct, does not affect God one way or another. It does, however, bring benefit to himself. A.J. brings out more directly the thought that God can gain no benefit from man's wise actions, and therefore has no purpose in afflicting punishment upon him if he has not done wrong. Berechiah understood the verse to mean: 'Can a man teach God? Is there a man who can teach God what he must do?' Similarly Buttenwieser who refers to the Targum: 'Can man teach God insight?' Rashi considers the two possibilities of the verb *yiskon*, from *sachan*, 'be of use, service, benefit': in the first line 'give pleasure to,' in the second 'to teach.' Even the first line, he holds, may mean 'teach': 'Can a man teach the Creator for His good or for His need as he teacheth the fool?' Ibn Ezra

115

3 Is it any advantage to the Almighty,
   that thou art righteous?
  Or is it gain to Him, that thou
   makest thy ways blameless?

4 Is it for thy fear of Him that He
   reproveth thee,
  That He entereth with thee into
   judgment?

5 Is not thy wickedness great?
  And are not thine iniquities without end?

6 For thou hast taken pledges of thy
   brother for nought,
  And stripped the naked of their
   clothing.

7 Thou hast not given water to the
   weary to drink,
  And thou hast withholden bread
   from the hungry.

הַחֵפֶץ לְשַׁדַּי כִּי תִצְדָּק
וְאִם־בֶּצַע כִּי־תַתֵּם דְּרָכֶיךָ׃
הֲמִיִּרְאָתְךָ יְכִיחֶךָ
יָבוֹא עִמְּךָ בַּמִּשְׁפָּט׃
הֲלֹא רָעָתְךָ רַבָּה
וְאֵין־קֵץ לַעֲוֺנֺתֶיךָ׃
כִּי־תַחְבֹּל אַחֶיךָ חִנָּם
וּבִגְדֵי עֲרוּמִּים תַּפְשִׁיט׃
לֹא־מַיִם עָיֵף תַּשְׁקֶה
וּמֵרָעֵב תִּמְנַע־לָחֶם׃

v. 6. דגש אחר שורק

weighs the interpretation of 'be profitable' (cf. xv. 3, *should he reason with
unprofitable talk*) against 'lean upon':
'Can a man in his deeds lean upon the
Omnipresent?' More probably, he contends, the meaning is 'argue, reason with':
'Can a man argue with God, or one that
is wise argue between them?'

3. *is it any advantage.* The same Hebrew
word as in *for what pleasure hath he*
(xxi. 21). 'Does God feel pleasure if
thou justifiest thy deeds in arguing before
Him, that He come unto thee to reprove
thy words? Or is it gain to Him if thou
makest thy ways blameless?' (Rashi).

4. *is it for thy fear of Him that He reproveth thee.* Eliphaz has used the word
yirah before in the sense of piety, religion
(see on iv. 6). Is it to be supposed that
God would afflict a man because he is
pious? The thought is preposterous.
Therefore, it must be because of his sins!
Eliphaz proceeds in the next verse to
make such open accusations. A.V.
rendered: 'Will He reprove thee for
fear of thee?' With this meaning in
mind, Metsudath David comments: 'Is
it from His fear of thee that thou shalt
not act wickedly that He reproves thee
and enters into judgment with thee?
What, then, would He do if thou actest
wickedly!'

5. *is not thy wickedness great?* The
accusations Eliphaz is about to make are
answered in Job's declaration of innocence (xxxi. 5ff.). The accuser, of course,
has no evidence, but imputes to Job the
misdeeds which are normally committed
by a person of influence and affluence.

6. *thou hast taken pledges . . . and stripped
the naked.* Eliphaz charges him with
violation of ancient Hebrew law which
protected the poor man, in case he was
forced to give his undergarment in
pledge. The creditor had to return it by
night-fall, so that the impoverished
debtor might at least have this one
covering against the cold of the night
(cf. Exod. xxii. 25f.; Deut. xxiv. 10ff.;
Amos ii. 8). When he uses the word
naked, Eliphaz infers that in his greed,
Job stripped his debtors until they were
practically reduced to nakedness (cf. the
emphatic denial in xxxi. 19-22).

7. *thou hast not given water to the weary.*
He is accused of neglecting the fundamental duties of hospitality and consideration for the wretched poor (cf. Isa.
lviii. 7, 10). Metsudath David suggests
that Eliphaz accuses Job of withholding
bread and water from those he had caused
to be imprisoned. But from his refuta-
tion in xxxi. 16f. it appears that the

8 And as a mighty man, who hath
the earth,
And as a man of rank, who dwelleth in it,

9 Thou hast sent widows away
empty,
And the arms of the fatherless
have been broken.

10 Therefore snares are round about
thee,
And sudden dread affrighteth
thee,

11 Or darkness, that thou canst not
see,
And abundance of waters cover
thee.

12 Is not God in the height of
heaven?
And behold the topmost of the
stars, how high they are!

8 וְאִישׁ זְרוֹעַ לוֹ הָאָרֶץ
וּנְשׂוּא פָנִים יֵשֶׁב בָּהּ׃

9 אַלְמָנוֹת שִׁלַּחְתָּ רֵיקָם
וּזְרֹעוֹת יְתֹמִים יְדֻכָּא׃

10 עַל־כֵּן סְבִיבוֹתֶיךָ פַחִים
וִיבַהֶלְךָ פַּחַד פִּתְאֹם׃

11 אוֹ־חֹשֶׁךְ לֹא־תִרְאֶה
וְשִׁפְעַת־מַיִם תְּכַסֶּךָּ׃

12 הֲלֹא־אֱלוֹהַ גֹּבַהּ שָׁמָיִם
וּרְאֵה רֹאשׁ כּוֹכָבִים כִּי־רָמּוּ׃

v. 12. בן"א המ' דגושה

accusation is that of indifference to the
wants of the needy.

8. *as a mighty man . . . and as a man of
rank.* lit. 'a man of arm . . . he whose
person is accepted,' i.e. one who is received with favour and respect because
of his wealth and rank. Eliphaz insin-
uates that Job, with the arrogance that
comes from power, had sought to eject
and dispossess his poorer neighbours (cf.
Isa. v. 8, *Woe unto them that join house to
house, that lay field to field*).

9. *thou hast sent widows away empty.*
Eliphaz now charges Job with heartless
treatment of widows, rejecting them
empty-handed. He also crushed the
arms of the orphans. Cf. Job's defence
against these false imputations in xxix.
12f., xxxi. 16f. To exploit the defenceless status of the widow and orphan was
regarded by the Hebrews as a most
heinous offence (cf. Deut. xxvii. 19;
Jer. vii. 6, xxii. 3).

10. *therefore snares are round about thee.*
In retribution for these offences, God
spreads about Job traps in which to
ensnare him, and terrifies him with
sudden dread to make him fall into them
from fright.

11. *or darkness, that thou canst not see.*
Better as R.V. margin: 'Or dost thou not
see the darkness, and the flood of waters
that covereth thee?' The point of the
question is: do you not understand the
true cause of the catastrophes which have
overwhelmed you? The expressions are
figurative for the crushing misfortunes
that have come upon Job.

12. *is not God in the height of heaven?*
Job is next accused of impiety. Eliphaz
may here imply that God is so lofty that
He can survey all that happens upon
earth (cf. Ps. xxxiii. 13f.). In the
next verse, however, Job is quoted as
arguing from the same fact that the
clouds and the great distance hide what is
done in the world from Him. Peake
therefore suggests this interpretation:
'Is not God exalted? Yes, too exalted,
you say, to mark man's ways.'

the topmost of the stars. Buttenwieser
renders the verse: 'Is not God exalted
even as the heavens? Behold the starry
dome, how high it is!' and states that
kochabim (*stars*) is descriptive genitive,
and *rosh* (*topmost*), lit. 'head,' like *polus* in
Latin and Greek, means, in the first
place, the vertex or axis of the (celestial)
sphere, then the 'sphere which revolves
on this axis,' i.e. 'the vault or dome of
heaven.'

13 And thou sayest: 'What doth God
    know?
    Can He judge through the dark
    cloud?

14 Thick clouds are a covering to
   Him, that He seeth not;
   And He walketh in the circuit of
   heaven.'

15 Wilt thou keep the old way
   Which wicked men have trodden?

16 Who were snatched away before
   their time,
   Whose foundation was poured
   out as a stream;

17 Who said unto God: 'Depart
   from us';
   And what could the Almighty do
   unto them?

18 Yet He filled their houses with
   good things—
   But the counsel of the wicked is
   far from me.

וְאָמַרְתָּ מַה־יָּדַע אֵל
הַבְעַד עֲרָפֶל יִשְׁפּוֹט׃
עָבִים סֵתֶר־לוֹ וְלֹא יִרְאֶה
וְחוּג שָׁמַיִם יִתְהַלָּךְ׃
הַאֹרַח עוֹלָם תִּשְׁמֹר
אֲשֶׁר דָּרְכוּ מְתֵי־אָוֶן׃
אֲשֶׁר־קֻמְּטוּ וְלֹא־עֵת
נָהָר יוּצַק יְסוֹדָם׃
הָאֹמְרִים לָאֵל סוּר מִמֶּנּוּ
וּמַה־יִּפְעַל שַׁדַּי לָמוֹ׃
וְהוּא מִלֵּא בָתֵּיהֶם טוֹב
וַעֲצַת רְשָׁעִים רָחֲקָה מֶנִּי׃

v. 15. חצי הספר בפסוקים

---

13. *and thou sayest: 'What doth God
know?'* See on xxi. 22. Not only the
vast distance, but also the dark cloud
which cuts off visibility of earth, hide
men's actions from Him.

the dark cloud. In which God is enveloped (cf. Exod. xx. 18; 1 Kings viii.
12; Ps. xviii. 10).

14. *He walketh in the circuit of heaven.*
i.e. 'the vault of the heavens.' That is
where God *walketh*, i.e. has His concerns,
not on earth. Buttenwieser explains this
verse as Eliphaz's sarcastic comment on
Job's question in xxi. 22 which he translates: 'Doth God practise discrimination?
Doth He judge in His abode on high?'

15. *wilt thou keep the old way.* Eliphaz,
with his fondness for tradition, now asks
whether Job intends to walk in the paths
of those sinners of old who were overwhelmed by the Flood. They defied
God and were swept away. Peake holds
that the reference may be to the Flood
story or to some tale no longer preserved,
such as the fate of the Nephilim (cf.
Gen. vi. 1-4).

16. *whose foundation was poured out as a
stream.* Their foundation gave way
beneath them and was poured away as
a flood, snatching them away. The
reference may be, says Rashi, to the
river of the Flood, or the brimstone and
fire of Sodom poured out upon their
foundation. Ibn Ezra and Metsudath
David are of the opinion that the generation of the Flood is meant.

17. *what could the Almighty do unto them?*
This and the next verse closely resemble
xxi. 14-16. R.V. renders: 'What can the
Almighty do for (or, to) us' and adds the
marginal note, 'Heb. them.' The meaning is: What can the Almighty do either
to benefit or to harm us? According to
M.T. the line is a comment by Eliphaz
on the impious remark of the ancient
sinners.

18. *yet He filled their houses with good
things.* Despite their wickedness, God
showered material blessings upon them.

but the counsel of the wicked is far from me.
Job had used the same words in xxi. 16.
Retaining the text, which some moderns

19 The righteous saw it, and were
   glad,
   And the innocent laughed them
   to scorn:

20 'Surely their substance is cut off,
   And their abundance the fire hath
   consumed.'

21 Acquaint now thyself with Him,
   and be at peace;
   Thereby shall thine increase be
   good.

22 Receive, I pray thee, instruction
   from His mouth,
   And lay up His words in thy
   heart.

19 יִרְאוּ צַדִּיקִים וְיִשְׂמָחוּ

וְנָקִי יִלְעַג־לָמוֹ:

20 אִם־לֹא נִכְחַד קִימָנוּ

וְיִתְרָם אָכְלָה אֵשׁ:

21 הַסְכֶּן־נָא עִמּוֹ וּשְׁלָם

בָּהֶם תְּבוֹאַתְךָ טוֹבָה:

22 קַח־נָא מִפִּיו תּוֹרָה

וְשִׂים אֲמָרָיו בִּלְבָבֶךָ:

regard as an interpolation, we follow the
line of interpretation of Driver and
Davidson: Eliphaz, like Job, takes occasion to disown all sympathy with the
principles of the wicked. But whereas
Job had stressed the worldly prosperity
of such wicked persons, despite their
ungodliness, Eliphaz lays emphasis upon
their certain destruction. Unlike Job,
the sincerely righteous joyfully acknowledge God's overthrow of the wicked, and
see in their downfall the proof of God's
righteous rule of the world.

19. *the righteous saw it, and were glad.*
Almost identical with Ps. cvii. 42a.
Metsudath David specifies Noah and his
sons (so too Berechiah). They were the
righteous who saw the downfall of the
wicked of their generation and rejoiced.
The classic illustration of these verses
seems to have been either the righteous
of the generation of the Flood or of
Sodom's destruction.

20. *surely their substance is cut off.* This
is what the righteous joyfully say when
they see the downfall of the wicked, but
the rendering of A.J. does not correspond to the Hebrew. *Kimanu* means
either 'our substance,' or, as R.V.: 'they
that did rise up against us.' The former
is preferable as having a true parallel in
their abundance; but the line should be
rendered: 'Indeed, our substance is not
cut off, but their abundance the fire hath
consumed.'

21-30 JOB URGED TO RETURN TO GOD

21. *acquaint now thyself with Him.* Eliphaz exhorts Job to reconcile himself
with God, promising him great spiritual
and material felicity in reward (cf.
v. 17-27, xi. 13-19). Peake notices that
no comforting prospect is held out in the
second cycle of speeches. The verb
acquaint is used in a now obsolete sense,
viz. 'acquiesce.' Rashi gives the true
sense, 'Learn to be at peace with Him.'
Davidson has observed that verses 21-30
consist of two parts: first, a series of
exhortations, each of which is accom-
panied by a promise (verses 21-25); and
second, a series of great promises simply
(verses 26-30).

shall thine increase be good. A.J. translates *teboathechah* as though it were
identical with *tebuathechah.* The Jewish
commentators construe as a verb: 'good
shall come to thee' (so A.V., R.V.).

22. *instruction.* This word Torah is
freighted with the most precious meanings of the Jewish Faith, and is defined
by *His words* in the parallel clause. It is
the only occurrence in this Book.

23. *if thou return to the Almighty, thou
shalt be built up.* Eliphaz promises Job
restoration (*be built up*), provided he
return to the Almighty against Whom,
in the opinion of the friends, he has
rebelled. Ralbag suggests that the phrase

23 If thou return to the Almighty,
   thou shalt be built up—
   If thou put away unrighteousness
   far from thy tents,

24 And lay thy treasure in the dust,
   And the gold of Ophir among
   the stones of the brooks;

25 And the Almighty be thy treasure,
   And precious silver unto thee;

26 Then surely shalt thou have thy
   delight in the Almighty,
   And shalt lift up thy face unto
   God;

27 Thou shalt make thy prayer unto
   Him, and He will hear thee,
   And thou shalt pay thy vows;

28 Thou shalt also decree a thing,
   and it shall be established unto
   thee,
   And light shall shine upon thy
   ways.

29 When they cast thee down, thou
   shalt say: 'There is lifting up';
   For the humble person He saveth.

אִם־תָּשׁוּב עַד־שַׁדַּי תִּבָּנֶה
תַּרְחִיק עַוְלָה מֵאָהֳלֶיךָ׃
וְשִׁית־עַל־עָפָר בָּצֶר
וּבְצוּר נְחָלִים אוֹפִיר׃
וְהָיָה שַׁדַּי בְּצָרֶיךָ
וְכֶסֶף תּוֹעָפוֹת לָךְ׃
כִּי־אָז עַל־שַׁדַּי תִּתְעַנָּג
וְתִשָּׂא אֶל־אֱלוֹהַּ פָּנֶיךָ׃
תַּעְתִּיר אֵלָיו וְיִשְׁמָעֶךָּ
וּנְדָרֶיךָ תְשַׁלֵּם׃
וְתִגְזַר־אֹמֶר וְיָקָם לָךְ
וְעַל־דְּרָכֶיךָ נָגַהּ אוֹר׃
כִּי־הִשְׁפִּילוּ וַתֹּאמֶר גֵּוָה
וְשַׁח עֵינַיִם יוֹשִׁעַ׃

be built up may imply not only restoration but that he will again have sons (cf. the use of the verb in Gen. xvi. 2).

24. *and lay thy treasure in the dust*. Job is no longer to make earthly treasure a matter of dominant concern to him. Let him toss it away to the dust or among the rocks of the wadis (see on vi. 15) as worthless. The word for *treasure* is literally 'ore' (that which is 'cut' out of the earth), and *the gold of Ophir* is literally simply 'Ophir.'

25. *and precious silver*. lit. 'silver of eminences.' The latter word is found again in Num. xxiii. 22, xxiv. 8, *the lofty horns of the wild-ox*, and Ps. xcv. 4, *the heights of the mountains*. Some authorities suggest that here the meaning is 'silver in bars.' Eliphaz exhorts Job to make God, not gold and silver, his treasure. Job makes a vigorous retort to this in xxxi. 24f., 28.

26. *shalt lift up thy face unto God*. Once restored to fellowship with God, Job will be able to turn to Him unabashed, knowing that when he petitions God for

his needs, he will have confidence that God will fulfil his requests. For 'lift up thy face,' see on xi. 15.

27. *thou shalt make thy prayer unto Him*. 'In making requests in prayer it was customary to make a vow to sacrifice or offer unto the Lord if the prayer was granted. Job shall have cause to fulfil his vows, his prayers being heard' (Davidson). Cf. Ps. lxvi. 13f., and the action of Jacob (Gen. xxviii. 20ff.).

28. *thou shalt also decree a thing*. When Job would determine in his mind upon a certain purpose and plan, God would see that it would stand. The light of success would shine upon Job's path.

29. *when they cast thee down, thou shalt say: 'There is lifting up.'* One interpretation of this difficult line is: When Job's path leads him downward into misfortune, he will be able to cheer himself with the thought that it will lead upward. Having known the experience of suffering, now, through penitent confession, he would have confidence of restoration. But the word rendered *there is lifting up*

30 He delivereth him that is inno-
　　cent,
　　Yea, thou shalt be delivered
　　through the cleanness of thy
　　hands.

30 יְמַלֵּט אִי־נָקִי
וְנִמְלַט בְּבֹר כַּפֶּיךָ׃

23　　　　　CHAPTER XXIII　　　　　כג

1 Then Job answered and said:

2 Even to-day is my complaint
　　bitter;
　　My hand is become heavy because
　　of my groaning.

1 וַיַּעַן אִיּוֹב וַיֹּאמַר׃
2 גַּם־הַיּוֹם מְרִי שִׂחִי
יָדִי כָּבְדָה עַל־אַנְחָתִי׃

---

properly means 'pride.' Accordingly
Driver translates: 'When they have
humbled thee, and thou sayest (i.e. com-
plainest), Pride, He will save him that
is lowly of eyes (i.e. Job himself).' The
intention is that so long as Job is humble,
God will come to his help when the
arrogant try to overthrow him.

30. *He delivereth him that is innocent.*
Again A.J. does not correspond to the
Hebrew. *Him that is innocent (i-naki)* is
taken, with the Targum, as an abbreviation of *ish naki*, which is highly improbable. The curious rendering of A.V.:
'He shall deliver the island (*i*) of the
innocent,' is derived from Ibn Ezra.
R.V. correctly reproduces the Hebrew:
'He shall deliver even him that is not
innocent; yea, he shall be delivered
through the cleanness of thine hands.'
On this rendering, *i* signifies 'not,' as in
i-chabod (1 Sam. iv. 21). What Eliphaz
promises is that for Job's merit even
sinners will experience the Divine salvation. Unconsciously he foretold what
was to happen to him and his two friends
(xlii. 8).

CHAPTERS XXIII-XXIV

JOB'S SEVENTH REPLY—TO ELIPHAZ

THE substance of Job's reply to Eliphaz
is that his tragic experience and his
observations of human society give him
no clear assurance of God's righteous
government. Chapter xxiii is concerned

with his personal search for God so that
He might establish his innocence; and
chapter xxiv deals with his indictment of
the high-handed oppression, crime and
poverty that are rampant in the world.

CHAPTER XXIII

1-7 JOB'S LONGING TO FIND GOD

2. *even to-day is my complaint bitter.* The
suggestion has been made that this
opening is an indication that the colloquy
between Job and the friends is conceived
of as extending over several days. In the
apocryphal *Testament of Job* the discourses are said to have lasted twenty-
seven days. Rashi's comment on *even
to-day* is: 'after all these consolations.'
As for the remainder of the line, Ibn
Ezra gives it the interpretation: 'My complaint is more bitter than all complaints.'
A.J. agrees with A.V., but perhaps preference should be given to R.V.: 'Even
to-day is my complaint rebellion', i.e.
either from his friends' standpoint—
they regard his complaint as rebellion,
or better from Job's own standpoint—he
refuses to accept any explanation which
is based on the assumption of his guilt.

*my hand is become heavy because of my
groaning.* His fight for self-vindication
has left him exhausted. An alternative
rendering is that of R.V. margin: 'is
heavy upon my groaning'; he does his
best to suppress his words which express
his feelings.

3 Oh that I knew where I might find
    Him,
    That I might come even to His
    seat!

4 I would order my cause before
    Him,
    And fill my mouth with arguments.

5 I would know the words which He
    would answer me,
    And understand what He would
    say unto me.

6 Would He contend with me in His
    great power?
    Nay; but He would give heed unto
    me.

7 There the upright might reason
    with Him;
    So should I be delivered for ever
    from my Judge.

8 Behold, I go forward, but He is
    not there,
    And backward, but I cannot per-
    ceive Him;

מִי־יִתֵּן יָדַעְתִּי וְאֶמְצָאֵהוּ ‪3‬

אָבוֹא עַד־תְּכוּנָתוֹ׃

אֶעֶרְכָה לְפָנָיו מִשְׁפָּט

וּפִי אֲמַלֵּא תוֹכָחוֹת׃

אֵדְעָה מִלִּים יַעֲנֵנִי

וְאָבִינָה מַה־יֹּאמַר לִי׃

הַבְּרָב־כֹּחַ יָרִיב עִמָּדִי

לֹא אַךְ־הוּא יָשִׂם בִּי׃

שָׁם יָשָׁר נוֹכָח עִמּוֹ

וַאֲפַלְּטָה לָנֶצַח מִשֹּׁפְטִי׃

הֵן קֶדֶם אֶהֱלֹךְ וְאֵינֶנּוּ

וְאָחוֹר וְלֹא־אָבִין לוֹ׃

3. *where I might find Him.* That He may
judge me (Rashi).

that I might come even to His seat. The
noun signifies 'fixed place', i.e. dwelling-
place, of God (BDB). Job longs to
appear before the Divine tribunal and
defend himself against any charges
levelled at him.

4. *I would order my cause before Him.*
A legal phrase: set out my case in defence.

5. *I would know the words which He would
answer me.* Then he would ascertain
what are the charges in the Divine
indictment of him, as distinct from the
innuendoes of his friends.

6. *but He would give heed unto me.* As
the verse is translated, the sense is that
could Job but find God, he feels sure that
He would no longer brow-beat him with
His might. He would listen attentively
to what Job has to say. But Eitan contends that in the second line, *yasim* (He
would give heed) is to be connected with
the Arabic root *sha'am*, 'to attack' (a
signification which he also finds in 1 Sam.

xv. 2; 1 Kings xx. 12; Ezek. xxiii. 24).
He renders the verse: 'Is it only by
means of His great power that He would
contend with me? Is He not only attacking me (without taking into account all
the arguments)?' That was the existing
situation; therefore Job wants to meet
God to obtain a true verdict from Him.

7. *there the upright might reason with Him.*
Most moderns understand *there* as 'in
such circumstances,' but Rashi's explanation 'in the place of our contest' is to be
preferred. 'There an upright man
would be disputing with him, i.e. before
such a tribunal it would soon appear
that it was an upright man (i. 1) who was
disputing with Him, and Job would
never again be arraigned before Him'
(Driver).

8-12 HIS HOPE TO MEET GOD IS FORLORN

8. *behold, I go forward, but He is not
there.* 'From this fascinating dream of a
Divine tribunal after the manner of that
of a human judge, Job awakens to
realize the actual circumstances in which
he is placed. God, everywhere present,

9 On the left hand, when He doth
　 work, but I cannot behold Him,
　 He turneth Himself to the right
　 hand, but I cannot see Him.

10 For He knoweth the way that I
　 take;
　 When He hath tried me, I shall
　 come forth as gold.

11 My foot hath held fast to His
　 steps,
　 His way have I kept, and turned
　 not aside.

12 I have not gone back from the
　 commandment of His lips;
　 I have treasured up the words of
　 His mouth more than my
　 necessary food.

13 But He is at one with Himself,
　 and who can turn Him?
　 And what His soul desireth, even
　 that He doeth.

9 שְׂמֹאול בַּעֲשׂתוֹ וְלֹא־אָחַז
יַעְטֹף יָמִין וְלֹא אֶרְאֶה:

10 כִּי־יָדַע דֶּרֶךְ עִמָּדִי
בְּחָנַנִי כַּזָּהָב אֵצֵא:

11 בַּאֲשֻׁרוֹ אָחֲזָה רַגְלִי
דַּרְכּוֹ שָׁמַרְתִּי וְלֹא־אָט:

12 מִצְוַת שְׂפָתָיו וְלֹא אָמִישׁ
מֵחֻקִּי צָפַנְתִּי אִמְרֵי־פִיו:

13 וְהוּא בְאֶחָד וּמִי יְשִׁיבֶנּוּ
וְנַפְשׁוֹ אִוְּתָה וַיָּעַשׂ:

v. 9. מלעיל

everywhere eludes him; he feels His
omnipotent power, but in vain seeks to
see His face. The words *forward, backward, the left hand, the right hand*, probably denote the points of the compass'
(Davidson). Both Rashi and Ibn Ezra
define *forward* and *backward* as east and
west.

9. *when He doth work*. Such a translation is hardly intelligible and Rashi offers
the forced explanation: 'When He
created it, He did not make the place of
His throne there that I should see Him
there.' Eitan relates the verb to an
Arabic root with the meaning 'to go to,
turn to,' and obtains the simple sense,
'When I turn to the left I do not see
Him.'

10. *for He knoweth the way that I take.*
The verse admits of two variant interpretations: God eludes my search because He knows the way I take, i.e. that
I am an innocent man (verses 10-12).
Nevertheless, He will not be diverted
from His hostility towards me (verses
13f.). Alternatively, in spite of God's
elusiveness, I feel that He is still watch-
ing me, and will in the end justify me.
When He has tested me, He will discover
no dross in me. In Job's present chastened mood, the latter seems the more
probable meaning.

11. *my foot hath held fast to His steps.*
Job's assurance is derived from his
conviction that he had always walked in
the godly path.

12. *I have not gone back from the commandment of His lips*. Eliphaz (xxii. 22)
had exhorted Job to *receive instruction
from His mouth, and lay up His words in
thy heart.* Job replies that he had always
so lived.

*I have treasured up . . . more than my
necessary food*. This rendering agrees
with Rashi who comments: 'More than
my sustenance I have been quick to
treasure up the words of His mouth.'
According to this translation *chukki* is
connected with *portion* (of food) in Gen.
xlvii. 22 and elsewhere. But the modern
commentators are probably right in
asserting that any mention of food here
is out of place. The literal meaning is
'my apportioning, decreeing,' i.e. 'more
than what I apportioned for myself have
I treasured up the words of His mouth.'
Job claims that he gave preference to
God's will above his personal inclinations.

13-17 GOD IS IMPLACABLE

13. *but He is at one with Himself*. lit. 'but
He (is) in one,' which A.V. and R.V.

14 For He will perform that which
    is appointed for me;
    And many such things are with
    Him.

15 Therefore am I affrighted at His
    presence;
    When I consider, I am afraid of
    Him.

16 Yea, God hath made my heart
    faint,
    And the Almighty hath affrighted
    me;

17 Because I was not cut off before
    the darkness,
    Neither did He cover the thick
    darkness from my face.

14 כִּי יַשְׁלִים חֻקִּי
וְכָהֵנָּה רַבּוֹת עִמּוֹ:

15 עַל־כֵּן מִפָּנָיו אֶבָּהֵל
אֶתְבּוֹנֵן וְאֶפְחַד מִמֶּנּוּ:

16 וְאֵל הֵרַךְ לִבִּי
וְשַׁדַּי הִבְהִילָנִי:

17 כִּי־לֹא נִצְמַתִּי מִפְּנֵי־חֹשֶׁךְ
וּמִפָּנַי כִּסָּה־אֹפֶל:

24   CHAPTER XXIV   כד

1 Why are times not laid up by the
    Almighty?

1 מַדּוּעַ מִשַּׁדַּי לֹא־נִצְפְּנוּ עִתִּים

---

incorrectly reproduce as 'but He is in
one (mind).' The phrase seems to intend, 'He is in a class by Himself.' The
Almighty is One, everlasting and immovable in His inscrutable purpose.
What His soul desires that He does;
unlike man, who being a frail creature of
emotion as well as of mind, may be
swayed by changing mood and caprice.

14. *for He will perform that which is
appointed for me.* 'He will fulfil the
resolve which He has decreed for me'
(Ibn Ezra). The phrase, *that which is
appointed for me*, is intentionally left
vague. 'Job means "his death" but we
must not tie him down to any one thought.
Rather he is oppressed with the inscrut-
ability of the Divine decrees. This is
the profound enigma of Job; but it is
far from being a solitary one: *many such
things are with Him*—the instance is but
one of many similar ones that happen
under God's rule of the world of mankind' (Davidson).

15. *therefore am I affrighted at His presence.* When Job considers God's mysterious dealings with him, he is dismayed
(cf. xxi. 6).

16. *God hath made my heart faint . . .
affrighted me.* The emphatic words are
God and *Almighty*. The thought that
God should inflict all this undeserved
misery upon him makes Job's heart
faint and fills him with terror.

17. *because I was not cut off before the
darkness.* A.J. has retained the translation of A.V. and R.V.; but a better sense
is given by R.V. margin: 'For I am not
dismayed because of the darkness, nor
because thick darkness covereth my face.'
Job contends that what has overwhelmed
him so completely is not the catastrophe
which has darkened his life, but the
consciousness that God has decreed it.

CHAPTER XXIV

1-12 GOD'S INDIFFERENCE TO INJUSTICE

1. *why are times not laid up by the
Almighty?* Thus far in his address, Job
has stated that he can find no marks of
a righteous providence in God's dealings
with himself. He reflects in this chapter

And why do not they that know
  Him see His days?

2 There are that remove the landmarks;
  They violently take away flocks,
  and feed them.

3 They drive away the ass of the
  fatherless,
  They take the widow's ox for a
  pledge.

4 They turn the needy out of the
  way;
  The poor of the earth hide themselves together.

5 Behold, as wild asses in the wilderness

וְיֹדְעָו לֹא־חָזוּ יָמָיו׃

2 גְּבוּלֹת יַשִּׂיגוּ
עֵדֶר גָּזְלוּ וַיִּרְעוּ׃

3 חֲמוֹר יְתוֹמִים יִנְהָגוּ
יַחְבְּלוּ שׁוֹר אַלְמָנָה׃

4 יַטּוּ אֶבְיוֹנִים מִדָּרֶךְ
יַחַד חֻבְּאוּ עֲנִיֵּי־אָרֶץ׃

5 הֵן פְּרָאִים ׀ בַּמִּדְבָּר

v. 1. וידעיו ק׳   v. 4. עניי ק׳

upon the problem in the world at large.
He now asks, 'Why is there no day of
reckoning for the ungodly? Why are
times of retribution not reserved for the
wicked?' Buttenwieser translates: 'Why
are not sessions of judgment set apart
by the Almighty?' and cites Ps. lxxv. 3f.
where the opposite is stated. The meaning may be: 'Why has God hidden His
purpose even from the pious?' Davidson
interprets *times* and *days* as diets of
assize for sitting in judgment and dis-
pensing right among men. Job complains that such times and days are not
appointed by the Judge of the world. He
fails to exercise a righteous rule; the
godly (*they that know Him*) look for the
manifestation of His righteousness in
vain.

2. *there are that remove the landmarks*.
Job illustrates his contention that observation of human society fails to disclose
the presence of God's righteous rule of
the world. On removing the landmarks,
note the law in Deut. xix. 14, and cf.
Isa. v. 8; Hos. v. 10.

and feed them. So indifferent are these
plunderers to law and order, that they
openly put out the stolen animals to
graze as though these were their lawful
property.

3. *the ass of the fatherless . . . the widow's
ox*. The orphan with his single ass and

the widow with her only ox are thus deprived of their means of sustenance and
reduced to abject penury.

4. *they turn the needy out of the way*. A
phrase denoting the wronging of the
poor, depriving them of their just rights
(cf. Amos iv. 1).

*the poor of the earth hide themselves
together*. 'Because they are afraid of
their oppressors' (Rashi). Job returns
to this thought in xxx. 6 where he describes the exploited as forced to live *in
the clefts of the valleys* and *in holes of the
earth*.

5. *as wild asses in the wilderness*. Many
modern scholars contend that Job here
describes a particular class of miserable
outcasts of society, perhaps some abori-
ginal dispossessed settlers whose lands
and homes had been seized by more
powerful marauding peoples. They
seem to be a nomadic group, outcasts on
'the open moor.' Buttenwieser, disputing this prevailing interpretation that a
lawless and outcast class living the life
of freebooters is intended, claims that
Job here describes the lot of the common
people. He writes, 'In the Orient and
Occident alike, the masses were ground
down by extortion and oppression into a
condition of hopeless degradation. The
Egyptian pyramids, which have endured
to this day, are the colossal monuments

They go forth to their work, seeking diligently for food;
The desert yieldeth them bread
for their children.

6 They cut his provender in the
field;
And they despoil the vineyard of
the wicked.

7 They lie all night naked without
clothing,
And have no covering in the cold.

8 They are wet with the showers of
the mountains,
And embrace the rock for want
of a shelter.

יֵצְאוּ בְּפָעֳלָם מְשַׁחֲרֵי לַטָּרֶף
עֲרָבָה לוֹ לֶחֶם לַנְּעָרִים:
בַּשָּׂדֶה בְּלִילוֹ יִקְצִירוּ ⁶
וְכֶרֶם רָשָׁע יְלַקֵּשׁוּ:
עָרוֹם יָלִינוּ מִבְּלִי לְבוּשׁ ⁷
וְאֵין כְּסוּת בַּקָּרָה:
מִזֶּרֶם הָרִים יִרְטָבוּ ⁸
וּמִבְּלִי מַחְסֶה חִבְּקוּ־צוּר:

v. 6. יקצורו ק׳

of the enslavement of the masses . . .
Even Plato held that the aristocratic
classes alone had a claim to human rights
and privileges, that the masses existed
for the sole purpose of toiling for the
comfort of the few. Job xxiv. 1-17, in
their indictment of these conditions, are,
barring the prophetic writings, without
parallel in ancient literature; more than
any other part of Job they strike a distinctly modern note. We cannot but
marvel at the keen analytic mind and the
rare human sympathy of the author whose
soul, twenty-three hundred years ago,
was stirred to passionate protest by the
contemplation of the wretched lot of the
poor. No wonder that these verses were
misunderstood. How could it be guessed
(such was the spirit of the times) that they
referred to the common people?'

6. *they cut his provender in the field.* The
word for *provender* is translated *fodder*
in vi. 5, and the change to the singular
from the plural denotes, 'They cut, each
one, his provender.' The poor have
to subsist on the kind of food given to
animals. Ibn Ezra, like the LXX,
understands *belilo* as 'that which is not
his,' i.e. 'they must harvest a field that
is not the possession of any of them.'
Rashi took the line to indicate that they
were compelled by hunger to steal the
produce from fields not their own.

they despoil the vineyard of the wicked.
R.V. renders: 'And they glean the
vintage of the wicked.' On this Driver

comments: 'They gather the late-ripe
fruit (i.e. the poorest and scantiest fruit
of the year) from the vineyard of the
wicked (i.e. probably, the hard-hearted
proprietor of the soil, who has evicted
them from their former homes).' Buttenwieser, who holds that these verses are a
description of the wretched misery and
exploitation of the poor, translates: 'They
must harvest fields that are not theirs, the
vineyard of the wicked they must pick
clean.' Perhaps we might think of them
as the poor outcasts, who live on the
provender intended for cattle, driven to
steal by night and pilfer the late-ripe
fruit of the vines.

7. *they lie all night naked without clothing.*
'They steal the clothes, and the one
robbed, because of his extreme poverty,
must remain thus naked, without covering, and he has nothing with which to
cover himself when it is cold' (Metsudath
David). Whether Job means some
particular class of outcasts, or the
wretched poor in general, he draws a
heart-breaking picture of human priva-
tion and suffering.

8. *they are wet with the showers of the
mountains.* 'Concerning the naked he
speaks who embrace the rock since they
have no shelter and are drenched with the
floods of rain that come down from the
mountains' (Ibn Ezra). Cf. Isa. xxv. 4
where the Hebrew for *showers* is translated *storm*.

9 There are that pluck the fatherless
from the breast,
And take a pledge of the poor;

10 So that they go about naked
without clothing,
And being hungry they carry the
sheaves;

11 They make oil within the rows of
these men;
They tread their winepresses,
and suffer thirst.

12 From out of the populous city
men groan,
And the soul of the wounded
crieth out;
Yet God imputeth it not for unseemliness.

9 יִגְזְלוּ מִשֹּׁד יָתוֹם

וְעַל־עָנִי יַחְבֹּלוּ׃

10 עָרוֹם הִלְּכוּ בְּלִי לְבוּשׁ

וּרְעֵבִים נָשְׂאוּ עֹמֶר׃

11 בֵּין־שׁוּרֹתָם יַצְהִירוּ

יְקָבִים דָּרְכוּ וַיִּצְמָאוּ׃

12 מֵעִיר מְתִים ׀ יִנְאָקוּ

וְנֶפֶשׁ־חֲלָלִים תְּשַׁוֵּעַ

וֶאֱלוֹהַּ לֹא־יָשִׂים תִּפְלָה׃

9. *there are that pluck the fatherless from the breast*. Job has described the helpless poor violently despoiled of their meagre possessions; other wretches, like scavengers, finding a miserable sustenance in the desert. Verses 9-12 depict still others in slavery, compelled to toil for harsh taskmasters. These heartless creditors even tear young children from their widowed mothers to be sold into slavery.

and take a pledge of the poor. An impossible translation. The Hebrew means either 'take a pledge (getting power) over the poor' (BDB), or better, as R.V. margin, 'take in pledge that which is on the poor,' their clothing, since it suits what follows in the next verse.

10. *being hungry they carry the sheaves*. Cf. Deut. xxv. 4 which forbade one to muzzle the ox when it treads out the corn so that it can feed while working. Here, the poor workmen, toiling amidst the abundant harvest of their masters, must go hungry, starving in the midst of plenty. Peake gives as an alternative that it may refer to 'the starving wretches, already described, who raid the sheaves of the rich, and press out oil and wine from their olives and grapes, and in their presses, of course by stealth.'

11. *they make oil within the rows of these men*. 'As it seems to me, they work the olives in rows in the building containing the olive-press, and the fresh oil flows between them' (Rashi). *Make oil* is more literally 'press out oil.'

they tread their winepresses, and suffer thirst. As in the preceding verse, we have the acute contrast between the surrounding abundance, in this case the fragrant, tempting aroma and mouth-watering sight of the luscious grapes, and the half-naked serfs panting with thirst.

12. *from out of the populous city men groan*. lit. 'from the city of men.' 'From out of the city men cry out because of the violence that is done unto them' (Ralbag).

yet God imputeth it not for unseemliness. The last word occurred in i. 22 and is here rendered by the Targum as 'guilt.' Ibn Ezra holds that *tiphlah* is comparable to the Hebrew *taphel*, 'tasteless, unseasoned.' It would accordingly mean something which lacks a right moral savour. Despite all the grave wrongs that Job has described, God does not treat it as anything morally anomalous. He takes no umbrage.

13 These are of them that rebel
    against the light;
    They know not the ways thereof,
    Nor abide in the paths thereof.

14 The murderer riseth with the
    light, to kill the poor and
    needy;
    And in the night he is as a thief.

15 The eye also of the adulterer
    waiteth for the twilight,
    Saying: 'No eye shall see me';
    And he putteth a covering on his
    face.

16 In the dark they dig through
    houses;
    They shut themselves up in the
    day-time;
    They know not the light.

הֵמָּה ׀ הָיוּ בְּמֹרְדֵי־אוֹר
לֹא־הִכִּירוּ דְּרָכָיו
וְלֹא יָשְׁבוּ בִּנְתִיבֹתָיו׃
לָאוֹר ׀ יָקוּם רוֹצֵחַ
יִקְטָל־עָנִי וְאֶבְיוֹן
וּבַלַּיְלָה יְהִי כַגַּנָּב׃
וְעֵין נֹאֵף ׀ שָׁמְרָה נֶשֶׁף
לֵאמֹר לֹא־תְשׁוּרֵנִי עָיִן
וְסֵתֶר פָּנִים יָשִׂים׃
חָתַר בַּחֹשֶׁךְ בָּתִּים
יוֹמָם חִתְּמוּ־לָמוֹ
לֹא־יָדְעוּ אוֹר׃

13-17 EVIL-DOERS ENUMERATED

**13. *these are of them that rebel against the
light.*** Job now particularizes other
wrong-doers: the murderer, adulterer,
and thief who violate the Sixth, Seventh
and Eighth Commandments. They are
those *that rebel against the light*, doing
their evil deeds under the cover of darkness. Ibn Ezra and Ralbag interpret
the phrase as 'that rebel against God Who
is the Light of the world.' It seems
however, that the *light* here signifies the'
light of day.

14. *the murderer riseth with the light.* The
first of these rebels against the light is
the murderer. Peake remarks that it is
surprising that he should kill *the poor
and needy*; 'he would prowl after more
profitable prey.' But the words probably denote the less affluent section of
society whose murder would not arouse
much notice, so that they were a safer
prey. Berechiah comments: 'Immediately, when the daylight has come, with
the rising of the dawn, as the caravans
set out, then he goes before them and
sits in ambush on the road. Therefore

it states, *he killeth the poor and needy*,
and takes away his property, which he
can do by violence only and openly.
And in the night, when he can take it in
secret, *he is as a thief* who ransacks houses
for the sake of money.'

**15. *the eye also of the adulterer waiteth
for the twilight.*** Cf. Prov. vii. 9. Ibn
Ezra notes that the thief is likened to the
adulterer because he too commits his
transgression in secret. It has been
suggested that the last line means that
the man covers himself with a woman's
veil to slip into the harem where he has
an assignation.

**16. *in the dark they dig through houses.*
** Cf. Exod. xxii. 1, *if a thief be found breaking in.* The Hebrew verb for *breaking in*
is the same as *dig through.* It is the
Hebrew term for 'burglary.' 'The houses
are often made of clay, so that the walls
can be dug through without much difficulty. An Eastern burglar would hesitate to break into a house through the
door because of the sanctity of the
threshold' (Peake).

17 For the shadow of death is to all
   of them as the morning;
   For they know the terrors of the
   shadow of death.

18 He is swift upon the face of the
   waters;
   Their portion is cursed in the
   earth;
   He turneth not by the way of the
   vineyards.

19 Drought and heat consume the
   snow waters;
   So doth the nether-world those
   that have sinned.

יִ כְּי יַחְדָּו ׀ בְּקֶר לָמוֹ צַלְמָוֶת 17
כִּי יַכִּיר בַּלְהוֹת צַלְמָוֶת׃

קַל־הוּא ׀ עַל־פְּנֵי־מַיִם 18
תְּקֻלַּל חֶלְקָתָם בָּאָרֶץ
לֹא־יִפְנֶה דֶּרֶךְ כְּרָמִים׃

צִיָּה גַם־חֹם יִגְזְלוּ מֵימֵי־שֶׁלֶג 19
שְׁאוֹל חָטָאוּ׃

17. *for the shadow of death is to all of them as the morning.* The phrase *shadow of death* is equivalent to 'midnight' (cf. iii. 5). 'For during the day they are shut up and at night they go forth to their burglary, and they are not at all afraid of the demons' (Rashi). 'What is the reward of these malefactors?' asks Ibn Ezra. 'God turns for them the morning into the shadow of death.'

they know the terrors of the shadow of death. i.e. they are familiar with these terrors; night is their day. Just as ordinary men might dread the thickest darkness of midnight, so these criminals fear the coming of day.

18-25 WHAT IS THE FATE OF THE EVIL-DOERS?

18. R.V. margin introduces at the beginning of the verse 'Ye say.' We have then to understand verses 18-21 as the view of the friends, in opposition to what Job has been maintaining. Job had described in verses 2-17 the oppressions and wrongs done in human society. The question arises: 'What is the fate of the evil-doers? Are they seized by the sudden judgments of God and delivered into the hand of their own transgression, as Bildad had asserted in viii. 4? Or, are they prolonged in their evil power, protected in their wickedness, and brought to a natural and peaceful end at last like men in general?' We thus have both answers in the concluding portion of this speech, so far as we can interpret the text before us. It is, however, possible with

Davidson, Driver and others to understand verses 18-24 as the answer of the friends, or of the common mind, introduced by Job with irony. The sinner, they say, is swift upon the face of the waters, i.e. rapidly borne away by the stream. Passers-by, as they behold his desolated homestead, utter a curse over it. The wicked man no more revisits the well-planted vineyards. As a *class* of persons is referred to, the singular *he*, denoting an individual representative of the class, and the plural *their*, are used indiscriminately.

he is swift upon the face of the waters. The wicked person is likened to a piece of flotsam carried along hopelessly by the current (cf. xx. 28; Hos. x. 7).

their portion is cursed. They find no enjoyment in it and derive no happiness from it.

he turneth not by the way of the vineyards. Either he is no longer able to visit his plantations because he has been deprived of them; or they have been cursed with barrenness and he no longer experiences pleasure in going to them.

19. *drought and heat consume the snow waters.* The verb *consume* is literally 'tear away, seize violently, rob'; here used figuratively of drying up the snow waters. As the snow dissolves and disappears in a hot and dry season, so does the wicked man vanish in Sheol. Job used the same metaphor in vi. 15ff. of his friends who abandoned him in his time of trouble.

20 The womb forgetteth him; the
   worm feedeth sweetly on him;
   He shall be no more remembered;
   And unrighteousness is broken
   as a tree.

21 He devoureth the barren that
   beareth not;
   And doeth not good to the widow.

22 He draweth away the mighty also
   by his power;
   He riseth up, and he trusteth not
   his own life.

23 Though it be given him to be in
   safety, whereon he resteth,
   Yet His eyes are upon their ways.

24 They are exalted for a little while,
   and they are gone;
   Yea, they are brought low, they
   are gathered in as all others,
   And wither as the tops of the ears
   of corn.

יִשְׁכָּחֵהוּ רֶחֶם ׀ מְתָקוֹ רִמָּה

עוֹד לֹא־יִזָּכֵר

וַתִּשָּׁבֵר כָּעֵץ עַוְלָה׃

רֹעֶה עֲקָרָה לֹא תֵלֵד

וְאַלְמָנָה לֹא יְיֵטִיב׃

וּמָשַׁךְ אַבִּירִים בְּכֹחוֹ

יָקוּם וְלֹא־יַאֲמִין בַּחַיִּין׃

יִתֶּן־לוֹ לָבֶטַח וְיִשָּׁעֵן

וְעֵינֵיהוּ עַל־דַּרְכֵיהֶם׃

רֹמּוּ מְעַט ׀ וְאֵינֶנּוּ

וְהֻמְּכוּ כַּכֹּל יִקָּפְצוּן

וּכְרֹאשׁ שִׁבֹּלֶת יִמָּלוּ׃

v. 24. ב"א רומו

---

20. *the womb forgetteth him; the worm feedeth sweetly on him.* He will be forgotten even by the mother who bore him. Only the worms, feeding upon his corpse, will find pleasure in him.

broken as a tree. Cf. xix. 10.

21. *he devoureth the barren that beareth not.* He deals mercilessly with the woman who has no sons to uphold her rights. The verse connects closely with the last phrase of verse 20.

22. *he draweth away the mighty also by his power.* In verses 18-21 Job had been recounting the popular theology touching the fate of the wicked. He now describes, in verses 22-24, reality as he has experienced it in bitter personal history. R.V. margin brings out the meaning more clearly: 'Yet God by His power maketh the mighty to continue; they rise up, when they believed not that they should live.' Even when they are sick and in despair of their life, God preserves with His power the tyrants and oppressors, restoring them again to life.

23. *yet His eyes are upon their ways.* Job

seems to be saying bitterly that God graciously watches over the wicked man with care, so that the place in which he lives is secure. To interpret the phrase in the meaning of punishment is out of harmony with the context.

24. Davidson translates: 'They are exalted: in a moment they are not; they are brought low, and gathered in as all others, and are cut off as the tops of the ears of corn.' Sinners must die, to be sure, as all other men. That is the inescapable human destiny. But they are also exalted, enjoy a long life, and at the end are cut off or wither like the tops of the ears of corn. They have a quick and painless death; cf. v. 26, xxi. 13. Peake contends that 'the immediate impression of the verse is that the prosperity of the wicked is brief, and if so the verse, since the contrary of what Job maintains, must be a mitigating gloss.' Ibn Ezra and Rashi seem so to understand the verse, i.e. the brief prosperity of the wicked. If this is correct, Job must be again giving expression to the commonly accepted belief. But the first-mentioned interpretation is preferable.

25 And if it be not so now, who will
    prove me a liar,
    And make my speech nothing
    worth?

25 וְאִם־לֹא אֵפוֹ מִי יַכְזִיבֵנִי
    וְיָשֵׂם לְאַל מִלָּתִי׃

25   CHAPTER XXV   כה

1 Then answered Bildad the Shu-
    hite, and said:

2 Dominion and fear are with Him;
    He maketh peace in His high
    places.

3 Is there any number of His armies?
    And upon whom doth not His
    light arise?

4 How then can man be just with
    God?

1 וַיַּעַן בִּלְדַּד הַשֻּׁחִי וַיֹּאמַר׃

2 הַמְשֵׁל וָפַחַד עִמּוֹ
  עֹשֶׂה שָׁלוֹם בִּמְרוֹמָיו׃

3 הֲיֵשׁ מִסְפָּר לִגְדוּדָיו
  וְעַל־מִי לֹא־יָקוּם אוֹרֵהוּ׃

4 וּמַה־יִּצְדַּק אֱנוֹשׁ עִם־אֵל

---

25. *and if it be not so now, who will prove me a liar.* Job boldly concludes his bitter indictment of the injustice of God's moral government of the world. He has pictured life without whitewashing its ugly anomalies. He ends by demanding: If the facts are not as I have described them, who will gainsay me and prove me a liar?

CHAPTER XXV
THE THIRD SPEECH OF BILDAD

THE reader cannot fail to be struck by the brevity of Bildad's speech. He does not answer Job: he cannot. Perhaps he feels that the debate has reached a deadlock. The argument has come to exhaustion. If we accept what stands before us in the text, we may say, with Davidson, that Bildad 'will not retire without at least uttering a protest against the spirit of his adversary and in behalf of reverential thought concerning God. Let the facts of history brought forward by Job be as they may, the spirit in which they are brought forward, and the conclusions in regard to God founded on them, must be for ever false.'

2. *dominion and fear are with Him.* God is the omnipotent Ruler over all. He alone possesses rulership. His majesty inspires terror.

He maketh peace in His high places. i.e. the heavenly spheres. The suggestion has been made that the idea of 'making peace in His high places' may have originated in observation of the atmospheric pheno-menon, the stilling of the warring ele-ments in the tempest on high. When God intervenes, the storm becomes a calm. The idea was then extended and the words may include reference to traditional discords among the heavenly hosts (cf. xxi. 22, xl. 9ff.; Isa. xxiv. 21).

3. *is there any number of His armies?* These are the numberless celestial hosts (cf. Isa. xl. 26). 'There was a tendency in Oriental thought to identify the angels with the stars, or at least to regard the stars as animated' (Davidson).

upon whom doth not His light arise? The words express God's universal beneficent rule. The light which emanates from God illumines the whole world and all in it; nothing can be concealed from Him.

4. *how then can man be just with God?* Verses 4-6 repeat, partly in similar lan-guage, the argument of Eliphaz in iv. 17, xv. 14-16. Beside the majesty and might of God, how can man presume to be righteous or just?

Or how can he be clean that is
born of a woman?

5 Behold, even the moon hath no
brightness,
And the stars are not pure in His
sight;

6 How much less man, that is a
worm!
And the son of man, that is a
maggot!

וּמַה־יִּזְכֶּה יְלוּד אִשָּׁה׃

הֵן עַד־יָרֵחַ וְלֹא יַאֲהִיל

וְכוֹכָבִים לֹא־זַכּוּ בְעֵינָיו׃

אַף כִּי־אֱנוֹשׁ רִמָּה

וּבֶן־אָדָם תּוֹלֵעָה׃

---

26   CHAPTER XXVI   כו

1 Then Job answered and said:

2 How hast thou helped him that is
without power!
How hast thou saved the arm that
hath no strength!

וַיַּעַן אִיּוֹב וַיֹּאמַר׃

מֶה־עָזַרְתָּ לְלֹא־כֹחַ

הוֹשַׁעְתָּ זְרוֹעַ לֹא־עֹז׃

---

how can he be clean that is born of a woman?
The human being, inheriting the weak-
nesses of the flesh and motived by the
urges of his body, cannot be faultless, as
is God. Bildad merely says in different
words the verdict of Eccles. vii. 20.

5. *even the moon hath no brightness.*
Eliphaz (xv. 15) had contrasted man and
the angels. Bildad here contrasts man
and the luminaries. Even the moon has
no brightness and the stars are dim in
comparison with God's dazzling radiance.
What, then, is man, a worm!

6. *a worm . . . a maggot.* The first word
denotes 'decay and corruption,' the
second 'utmost abasement and abjectness.'

CHAPTERS XXVI-XXXI

THE EIGHTH REPLY OF JOB—TO BILDAD

From chapter xxvi to chapter xxxi, as
the text stands, we have what purports
to be the final reply of Job. In its present
form, we are confronted with what
Montefiore describes as ' many strange
and heterogeneous passages.' The beautiful external symmetry of the cycles is
broken when Zophar does not appear to
speak in this third and last round of the
debate. It may be that the author intended thus forcibly to convey the confession of defeat and confusion on
Zophar's part. A grave difficulty arises,
nevertheless, when words are placed in
Job's mouth that seem contrary to and
inconsistent with the position which he
steadfastly maintained. Scholars will
long continue to be baffled by obscurities
in the passages we shall encounter and
shall seek, perhaps in vain, to find
natural and reasonable links of continuity
between the abrupt transitions. Despite
these textual enigmas, we shall meet here
in this most perplexing portion of the
Book some of the loftiest insights ever
revealed to the groping mind of man
concerning the limitless grandeur of
God's universe and the ultimate wisdom
by which man, hemmed in as he is with
infinite mystery, can achieve the good
life.

CHAPTER XXVI

2-4 JOB'S SARCASTIC RETORT TO BILDAD

2. *how hast thou helped him that is without power!* The sarcasm of Job, replying
to Bildad, is unmistakable. What a great
help he has been to his friend in his sore
trouble!

3 How hast thou counselled him that
hath no wisdom,
And plentifully declared sound
knowledge!

4 With whose help hast thou uttered
words?
And whose spirit came forth from
thee?

5 The shades tremble
Beneath the waters and the inhabitants thereof.

6 The nether-world is naked before
Him,
And Destruction hath no covering.

7 He stretcheth out the north over
empty space,

3 מַה־יָּעַצְתָּ לְלֹא חָכְמָה
וְתֻשִׁיָּה לָרֹב הוֹדָעְתָּ׃

4 אֶת־מִי הִגַּדְתָּ מִלִּין
וְנִשְׁמַת־מִי יָצְאָה מִמֶּךָּ׃

5 הָרְפָאִים יְחוֹלָלוּ
מִתַּחַת מַיִם וְשֹׁכְנֵיהֶם׃

6 עָרוֹם שְׁאוֹל נֶגְדּוֹ
וְאֵין כְּסוּת לָאֲבַדּוֹן׃

7 נֹטֶה צָפוֹן עַל־תֹּהוּ

3. *plentifully declared sound knowledge.*
The words are particularly biting after
Bildad's speech of only five verses. On
sound knowledge, see on v. 12 where it is
translated *substantial.* 'What sound
knowledge and wisdom hast thou plentifully declared to make known why one
wicked man dies in his full strength,
without mishap and sickness, and his seed
is established before him, who all his
days had been robbing, murdering and
committing adultery; while another,
equally wicked, dies in bitterness of
soul; and likewise, one who is perfectly
righteous? What hast thou answered
to this?' (Berechiah).

4. *with whose help hast thou uttered words?*
R.V. renders the line: 'To whom hast
thou uttered words?' expressive of Job's
disdain that Bildad should presume to
give him instruction concerning God's
rulership and awe.

spirit. Hebrew *neshamah,* defined as *the
lamp of the LORD* (Prov. xx. 27), i.e. 'the
Divine light illuminating *all the inward
parts,* all the organs of the body which
contribute to man's personality and
activity' (Cohen). Job speaks with irony:
'From whom hast thou received these
words that thou hast spoken?' (Ibn Ezra).
'Who does not know this?' (Rashi).

5-14 THE GREATNESS OF GOD

5. Job proceeds now to develop his
awareness of God's greatness, surely as
keen and profound as Bildad's. God's
presence and power reach to the nether-
world beneath and the star-studded
heavens above.

shades. Hebrew *rephaim,* 'the thin and
shadowy personalities of the dead'
(Davidson, *Old Testament Theology,*
p. 427).

*beneath the waters and the inhabitants
thereof.* Sheol was located in the bowels
of the earth, below the covering of the
seas. *The inhabitants* is doubtless an
allusion to the sea-monsters. Even
these tremble before the Divine might.

6. *naked before Him.* i.e. exposed to His
scrutiny.

Destruction. Hebrew *Abaddon,* a synonym
for Sheol, lit. '(a place of) perishing.'
(Cf. the same thought in *the nether-world
and Destruction are before the LORD,*
Prov. xv. 11.) These hold no secrets
from God.

7. *He stretcheth out the north over empty
space. The north,* Buttenwieser contends,
is the celestial pole, formed by the seven
stars of Ursa minor, from which the
movement of the universe was believed

And hangeth the earth over nothing.

8 He bindeth up the waters in His
thick clouds;
And the cloud is not rent under
them.

9 He closeth in the face of His
throne,
And spreadeth His cloud upon it.

10 He hath described a boundary
upon the face of the waters,
Unto the confines of light and
darkness.

11 The pillars of heaven tremble
And are astonished at His rebuke.

תֹּלֶה אֶרֶץ עַל־בְּלִימָה׃
צֹרֵר־מַיִם בְּעָבָיו
וְלֹא־נִבְקַע עָנָן תַּחְתָּם׃
מְאַחֵז פְּנֵי־כִסֵּה
פַּרְשֵׁז עָלָיו עֲנָנוֹ׃
חֹק חָג עַל־פְּנֵי־מָיִם
עַד־תַּכְלִית אוֹר עִם־חֹשֶׁךְ׃
עַמּוּדֵי שָׁמַיִם יְרוֹפָפוּ
וְיִתְמְהוּ מִגַּעֲרָתוֹ׃

v. 9. ה' במקום א'

to proceed. He beautifully translates:
'He hath arched the north over the void.'
Another interpretation is: the northern
region of the earth, known vaguely to the
Hebrews as the region of lofty and
massive mountains (cf. Isa. xiv. 13).

over nothing. Buttenweiser translates:
'He hath suspended the earth over the
vacuum' and comments: 'Our author,
though naturally ignorant of the law of
gravitation, had outgrown the naïve view
of his age about the universe, and conceived of the earth as a heavenly body
floating in space, like the sun, moon and
stars. It is not surprising to meet with
such a view in the Book of Job, when one
considers the advance astronomy had
made in Babylonia, Egypt and Greece.
As early as 540-510 B.C.E., Pythagoras of
Samos, on his travels in Egypt and the
East, acquired the knowledge of the
obliquity of the ecliptic and of the
earth's being a sphere freely poised in
space . . . xxxviii. 6 bears out rather than
contradicts the conclusion that the
writer of Job had attained a more advanced view of the universe, since the
question, "Whereon were its foundations
set?" shows that he no longer shared the
primitive notion that the earth was
resting on pillars erected in the sea.'

8. *He bindeth up the waters in His thick
clouds.* Job speaks here with awe of the
clouds, conceived as 'floating reservoirs
of water' which yet do not burst beneath

their weight (cf. xxxviii. 37; Prov.
xxx. 4).

9. *He closeth in the face of His throne.*
Above the solid firmament of heaven,
God's throne was conceived as ever enshrouded so that man might not behold
it. *The face of His throne* is the heavens,
in the meaning of Ps. ciii. 19, *The LORD
hath established His throne in the heavens*
(Ibn Ezra).

spreadeth. Hebrew *parshez;* 'it occurs
only here in Scripture and its meaning is
the same as *paras* "spreading" ' (Ibn
Ezra).

10. *a boundary upon the face of the waters.*
Cf. Prov. viii. 27. The earth is pictured
as a flat disc encircled by waters. God
has circumscribed a fixed boundary about
these waters, comparable to our thought
of a horizon, although for the ancients
fixed and immovable. The boundary
thus formed embraces the *confines* of
light and darkness. Within this dome
the heavenly bodies revolve. Outside
and beyond, all is darkness.

11. *the pillars of heaven tremble.* The
earth is called *pillars of heaven* (Metsudath David). Modern commentators
interpret the phrase as the distant
mountains on which the vault of heaven
was pictured as resting. At God's *rebuke,* i.e. the crashing peal of a thunderstorm, these supporting mountains quake
(cf. Ps. xviii. 14ff., xxix. 6, civ. 32).

12 He stirreth up the sea with His
   power,
   And by His understanding He
   smiteth through Rahab.

13 By His breath the heavens are
   serene;
   His hand hath pierced the slant
   serpent.

14 Lo, these are but the outskirts of
   His ways;
   And how small a whisper is heard
   of Him!
   But the thunder of His mighty
   deeds who can understand?

12 בְּכֹחוֹ רָגַע הַיָּם
וּבִתְבוּנָתוֹ מָחַץ רָהַב׃

13 בְּרוּחוֹ שָׁמַיִם שִׁפְרָה
חֹלֲלָה יָדוֹ נָחָשׁ בָּרִחַ׃

14 הֶן־אֵלֶּה ׀ קְצוֹת דְּרָכָו
וּמַה־שֵּׁמֶץ דָּבָר נִשְׁמַע־בּוֹ
וְרַעַם גְּבוּרֹתָו מִי יִתְבּוֹנָן׃

27   CHAPTER XXVII   כז

1 And Job again took up his parable,
  and said:

1 וַיֹּסֶף אִיּוֹב שְׂאֵת מְשָׁלוֹ וַיֹּאמַר׃

v. 12. ובתבונתו ק׳   v. 14. דרכיו ק׳   v. 14. גבורתיו ק׳

12. *He stirreth up the sea.* The verb *raga*
means 'disturb,' but as the R.V. margin
points out it may also signify the opposite
'stilleth.' The older Jewish commentators understood the verse to refer to the
miracle at the Red Sea when God
divided the waters and the Egyptian
hosts pursuing were destroyed. *Rahab*
is taken to mean Egypt (cf. Ps. lxxxvii. 4).
Driver holds that the exact meaning is
uncertain. Rahab more likely is here the
mythical monster-dragon of hoary antiquity, personifying the raging pride of
the sea (see on ix. 13). God first disturbs
by His power and then calms the stormy
deep. An alternative interpretation is:
An echo of the creation myth when God
triumphed over Rahab, identified with
Tiamat. Once subdued, the surging
waters were held within their limits (cf.
Isa. li. 9; Ps. civ. 7-9).

13. *the slant serpent.* Again in Isa.
xxvii. 1. This may be a continuation of
the mythical struggle alluded to in verse
12. As the result of the defeat of Tiamat
—the fleeing dragon or slant serpent—
darkness and chaos receded before light
and order. It may also be a poetical
description of how, after a storm, the
wind—God's *breath* (Isa. xl. 7)—clears
the darkened skies and makes the heavens
once more serenely bright. The *slant
serpent* was popularly supposed to cause
darkness at an eclipse. The sun's light
is restored when its power is broken.

14. Of this verse Davidson says, 'The
nervous brevity and sublimity of these
words are unsurpassable.' Buttenwieser,
with his inspired feeling for the grandeur
of the original Hebrew, nobly translates:
'Behold, these are but the outer edges of
His ways, only a whisper of Him do we
catch; who can perceive the thunder of
His Omnipotence?' Finite man, for all
the progress in science that he has
achieved, will ever be fringed in by the
larger mystery of God's infinite universe.
He may penetrate with mind and heart
the outer edges of the immense cosmic
enigma. He may hear the echo of the
rolling thunder of the Divine Omnipotence. But the final covert of God's
secret will elude him, and the absolute
solution of the problem of God's government of His world will for ever baffle
him until he rests in resignation upon the
everlasting arms. Job has reached here
a terminal peak in his metaphysical
struggle. He confesses that absolute
infinite wisdom is not within man's
power to attain. It belongs to God alone.

CHAPTER XXVII

WE expect Zophar to appear. He does

2 As God liveth, who hath taken
away my right;
And the Almighty, who hath dealt
bitterly with me;

3 All the while my breath is in me,
And the spirit of God is in my
nostrils,

4 Surely my lips shall not speak unrighteousness,
Neither shall my tongue utter deceit;

5 Far be it from me that I should
justify you;
Till I die I will not put away mine
integrity from me.

6 My righteousness I hold fast, and
will not let it go;
My heart shall not reproach me
so long as I live.

חַי־אֵל הֵסִיר מִשְׁפָּטִי
וְשַׁדַּי הֵמַר נַפְשִׁי:
כִּי־כָל־עוֹד נִשְׁמָתִי בִי
וְרוּחַ אֱלוֹהַּ בְּאַפִּי:
אִם־תְּדַבֵּרְנָה שְׂפָתַי עַוְלָה
וּלְשׁוֹנִי אִם־יֶהְגֶּה רְמִיָּה:
חָלִילָה לִּי אִם־אַצְדִּיק אֶתְכֶם
עַד־אֶגְוַע לֹא־אָסִיר תֻּמָּתִי מִמֶּנִּי:
בְּצִדְקָתִי הֶחֱזַקְתִּי וְלֹא אַרְפֶּהָ
לֹא־יֶחֱרַף לְבָבִי מִיָּמָי:

not come forward for the third encounter.
Job continues, solemnly asserting his
moral integrity before God.

1-6 JOB INSISTS HE SPEAKS THE TRUTH

1. *and Job again took up his parable.*
There does not appear to be anything
approaching a *parable* in the address
immediately following, and we would
expect a word like 'discourse' or 'address.' But the Hebrew term *mashal* has,
as Dr. Cohen shows in the Introduction
to *Proverbs*, a variety of meanings.
Sometimes, as in xxix. 1; Num. xxiii.
7, 18 it may mean an elevated, poetical
prophetic discourse in sententious mood.
Metsudath David finds the 'parable'
nature of Job's speech emerge in xxviii. 7,
That path no bird of prey knoweth.

2. *as God liveth.* Job, in a solemn oath,
affirms his innocence. It is striking to
observe that protesting the unjust treatment he has been meted out, he nevertheless cleaves to God and makes the
oath of clearance in His name. This
remarkable spiritual paradox did not
escape the Rabbis. Rashi comments:
'It is an oath, for in truth He hath taken
away my right; and from this R. Joshua
expounded that out of love Job served the
Omnipresent God, because no man makes
a vow by the life of the king unless he
loves the king.'

taken away my right. lit. 'my judgment.'
God has prejudiced him in the eyes of his
fellows by the imposition of afflictions.

3. *all the while my breath is in me.* 'As
long as I am permitted to live!' says Job.
Remembering how worn he must be
with the ravages of the disease, the words,
placed in parenthesis in R.V., add
strength to Job's oath.

4. *surely my lips shall not speak unrighteousness.* His contention is: 'My lips
do not speak unrighteousness.' Job
insists that all along he has spoken the
truth in defending his innocence.

5. *justify you.* i.e. 'that I should say the
right is with you to make me guilty'
(Rashi).

I will not put away mine integrity. 'I will
not confess to your words, saying that I
am not innocent' (Rashi). Job will never
abandon maintaining his integrity.

6. *my righteousness I hold fast.* Job
says that he will cling to, and never
surrender, the consciousness that he is
without guilt.

shall not reproach. R.V. margin: 'doth
not reproach me for any of my days.' He
can examine his conscience his
entire life; he has nothing to regret.
His record is an open book. For *heart*

7 Let mine enemy be as the wicked,
  And let him that riseth up against
  me be as the unrighteous.

8 For what is the hope of the godless, though he get him gain,
  When God taketh away his soul?

9 Will God hear his cry,
  When trouble cometh upon him?

10 Will he have his delight in the
   Almighty,
   And call upon God at all times?

11 I will teach you concerning the
   hand of God;
   That which is with the Almighty
   will I not conceal.

7 יְהִי כְרָשָׁע אֹיְבִי
וּמִתְקוֹמְמִי כְעַוָּל׃

8 כִּי מַה־תִּקְוַת חָנֵף כִּי יִבְצָע
כִּי יֵשֶׁל אֱלוֹהַּ נַפְשׁוֹ׃

9 הַצַעֲקָתוֹ יִשְׁמַע ׀ אֵל
כִּי־תָבוֹא עָלָיו צָרָה׃

10 אִם־עַל־שַׁדַּי יִתְעַנָּג
יִקְרָא אֱלוֹהַּ בְּכָל־עֵת׃

11 אוֹרֶה אֶתְכֶם בְּיַד־אֵל
אֲשֶׁר עִם־שַׁדַּי לֹא אֲכַחֵד׃

as 'conscience,' cf. 1 Sam. xxiv. 6. The sins and crimes of which the friends have shamefully accused him (Eliphaz, e.g. in xxii. 6-9) are without foundation.

7-23 JOB'S DETESTATION OF THE WICKED

7. *let mine enemy be as the wicked.* The spirit of this bitter utterance is not vindictiveness. ' The words express the speaker's abhorrence of the "wicked," they do not imprecate evil on his enemy. It is understood that he wishes his enemy ill, and he can wish him nothing worse than that he should be as the "wicked" —so much does he himself shrink from the thought of being as the wicked are' (Davidson).

8. *though he get him gain.* The verb *batsa* means 'cut off, break off' as well as 'gain by violence.' R.V. margin has: 'when God cutteth him off.' The impli-cation is: 'How could he, Job, ever have been tempted to do wrong when he knew so well the wretched, God-abandoned state of the godless!'

when God taketh away his soul. The verb *yeshal* is from *shalah*, 'draw out.' The word is unusual. It may possibly be related to *shalwah*, 'tranquillity': 'If God gives the hypocrite health and tranquil-lity, what is his hope when trouble cometh upon him?' (Kimchi, quoted by Berechiah).

9. *trouble.* The Hebrew *tsarah* means more sharply 'distress, straits.' The wicked person has cut himself off from fellowship with God. The Rabbis pictured the sinner building an impene-trable wall between himself and God through his sins.

10. *will he have delight in the Almighty.* Cf. xxii. 26a. The wicked man never knows the consolations and inward bliss that can support the righteous, pious man through the varied vicissitudes (*at all times*) of human experience.

11. *I will teach you concerning the hand of God.* Verses 11-23 have long been a source of difficulty to the commentators involving, as it seems, a contradiction and reversal of Job's previous position that an evil fate does *not* overtake the wicked. They who maintain the integrity of the text explain the passage as the triumph, if only temporary, of Job's deep-rooted faith over the bitter indictment of God's injustice as experienced by him. Altern-atively, it has been explained as Job's ironical presentation of his friends' doctrine, as in xxiv. It should be remem-bered that ancient writers used no punc-tuation marks, and the change of speaker was indicated by the inflection of the reader's voice. The latter interpretation is less probable here.

12 Behold, all ye yourselves have
   seen it;
   Why then are ye become altogether vain?
13 This is the portion of a wicked
   man with God,
   And the heritage of oppressors,
   which they receive from the
   Almighty.
14 If his children be multiplied, it is
   for the sword;
   And his offspring shall not have
   bread enough.
15 Those that remain of him shall be
   buried by pestilence,
   And his widows shall make no
   lamentation.
16 Though he heap up silver as the
   dust,
   And prepare raiment as the clay;
17 He may prepare it, but the just
   shall put it on,
   And the innocent shall divide the
   silver.
18 He buildeth his house as the
   moth,
   And as a booth which the keeper
   maketh.

הֵן אַתֶּם כֻּלְּכֶם חֲזִיתֶם
וְלָמָּה־זֶּה הֶבֶל תֶּהְבָּלוּ׃
זֶה ׀ חֵלֶק־אָדָם רָשָׁע ׀ עִם־אֵל
וְנַחֲלַת עָרִיצִים מִשַּׁדַּי יִקָּחוּ׃
אִם־יִרְבּוּ בָנָיו לְמוֹ־חָרֶב
וְצֶאֱצָאָיו לֹא יִשְׂבְּעוּ־לָחֶם׃
שְׂרִידָיו בַּמָּוֶת יִקָּבֵרוּ
וְאַלְמְנֹתָיו לֹא תִבְכֶּינָה׃
אִם־יִצְבֹּר כֶּעָפָר כָּסֶף
וְכַחֹמֶר יָכִין מַלְבּוּשׁ׃
יָכִין וְצַדִּיק יִלְבָּשׁ
וְכֶסֶף נָקִי יַחֲלֹק׃
בָּנָה כָעָשׁ בֵּיתוֹ
וּכְסֻכָּה עָשָׂה נֹצֵר׃

12. *all ye yourselves have seen it.* 'That
this is the portion of a wicked man'
(Rashi).

ye become altogether vain. You know
what the fate of the wicked is; why, then,
do you act thoughtlessly and foolishly,
by wickedly accusing me, so as to draw
down this fate upon your own heads
(Driver).

13. *this is the portion.* Almost identical
with Zophar's words in xx. 29.

14. *if his children be multiplied.* This is
the reverse of what Job had previously
maintained in xxi. 8.

15. *those that remain of him.* lit. 'his
survivors,' i.e. the children that are left
from the sword (Ibn Ezra).

by pestilence. lit. 'in death' (so R.V.);
but death here, as in Jer. xv. 2, xviii. 21,
means death by pestilence.

his widows shall make no lamentation.
Formal funeral rites, which included
wailing by women, are omitted in times
of disaster or pestilence. This line
occurs in Ps. lxxviii. 64b from which it
may be quoted. In contrast, note what
Job had said in xxi. 32 about the burial of
the wicked.

16. With this verse cf. Zech. ix. 3, *as
the clay* being paralleled by *the mire of the
streets*, a figure of abundance. Orientals
who could afford them delighted in
costly garments and used them as gifts
(cf. Gen. xxiv. 53).

17. *the innocent shall divide the silver.*
What the wicked accumulated will in the
end pass into the possession of the righteous.

18. *as the moth.* Cf. iv. 19. Some define
the word as 'spider.' Something flimsy
is intended.

19 He lieth down rich, but there
    shall be nought to gather;
    He openeth his eyes, and his
    wealth is not.

20 Terrors overtake him like waters;
    A tempest stealeth him away in
    the night.

21 The east wind carrieth him away,
    and he departeth;
    And it sweepeth him out of his
    place.

22 Yea, it hurleth at him, and
    spareth not;
    He would fain flee from its power.

23 Men shall clap their hands at
    him,
    And shall hiss him out of his
    place.

19 עָשִׁיר יִשְׁכַּב וְלֹא יֵאָסֵף
עֵינָיו פָּקַח וְאֵינֶנּוּ׃

20 תַּשִּׂיגֵהוּ כַמַּיִם בַּלָּהוֹת
לַיְלָה גְּנָבַתּוּ סוּפָה׃

21 יִשָּׂאֵהוּ קָדִים וְיֵלַךְ
וִישָׂעֲרֵהוּ מִמְּקֹמוֹ׃

22 וְיַשְׁלֵךְ עָלָיו וְלֹא יַחְמֹל
מִיָּדוֹ בָּרוֹחַ יִבְרָח׃

23 יִשְׂפֹּק עָלֵימוֹ כַפֵּימוֹ
וְיִשְׁרֹק עָלָיו מִמְּקֹמוֹ׃

| 28 | CHAPTER XXVIII | כח |

1 For there is a mine for silver,
    And a place for gold which they
    refine.

1 כִּי יֵשׁ לַכֶּסֶף מוֹצָא
וּמָקוֹם לַזָּהָב יָזֹקּוּ׃

פתח באתנח .v 21

---

a booth. The frail, impermanent hut in which the watchman of an orchard or vineyard took shelter. The winter winds and rain soon make a shambles of it.

19. *he lieth down rich.* The sense is obscure. Rashi interprets: 'He dies in his riches, and many a time there is none to gather him for burial.' As A.J. translates, the general sense seems to be that he goes to bed wealthy and wakes up dismayed to find that his wealth is no more. Verses 18f. speak of the sudden loss of home and fortune that awaits the wicked.

20. *terrors overtake him like waters.* Cf. xxii. 11.

in the night. As in verse 19, calamity befalls him when he is in bed.

21. *the east wind.* The violent, scorching sirocco from the desert (cf. xv. 2), used in Scripture as a destructive force.

22. *yea, it hurleth at him.* A.V. and R.V. render: 'For (God) shall hurl at him, and not spare; he would fain flee out of His hand.' There is no object to *hurl* as again in Num. xxxv. 20, but a deadly missile is to be understood.

23. *clap their hands . . . and shall hiss.* In derisive mockery and contempt (cf. Lam. ii. 15).

CHAPTER XXVIII

MAN CANNOT ATTAIN THE WISDOM OF GOD

THIS chapter is one of the deservedly celebrated portions of the Book and one of the incomparably great poems in the Bible, and indeed in world literature. The theme is at once the nature of and the quest for Wisdom: where shall it be found?

2 Iron is taken out of the dust,
  And brass is molten out of the
      stone.

3 Man setteth an end to darkness,

בַּרְזֶל מֵעָפָר יֻקָּח
וְאֶבֶן יָצוּק נְחוּשָׁה:
קֵץ | שָׂם לַחֹשֶׁךְ

By Wisdom is meant not the practical human gift, but the knowledge of those principles that control the Divine world economy. In the mysterious cosmic order of the physical universe, Wisdom plays its creative role (cf. Prov. iii. 19f.). In the domain of man, it consists of 'the knowledge of those truths which lead to the knowledge of God' (Maimonides).

Man can explore the hidden treasuries of the earth. He can range the vast wondrous arches of the starry sky. But the ultimate Divine knowledge will elude him. God alone possesses the key to unlock the gate of total understanding. Yet man can achieve a sufficient wisdom in the deep certainty rising from the earnest, questing soul that there is a Divine purpose in the human struggle. This man achieves by doing justly, loving mercy, and walking humbly with God (Mic. vi. 8). Only in the complete surrender to this moral law can man attain the highest level of spiritual perfection in the earthly pilgrimage. Man's realization of his destiny, the poet puts into the mouth of Job in these memorable climactic words: *And unto man He said:* '*Behold, the fear of the Lord, that is wisdom; and to depart from evil is understanding.*'

Many modern exegetes have concluded that this tremendous poem has no logical place in the Book, unless it be the conclusion of the confession in xlii. 1-6; but since its teaching corresponds to that of the author of the Book it may have been written by him. At least one modern Jewish scholar, however, has defended its integrity. Buttenweiser retains the poem as an integral portion of Job's utterance. 'The recognition,' he writes, 'of this eternal verity by Job (i.e. that *the fear of God is wisdom and to shun evil is understanding*) marks the highest of the many high points of the Book. It also marks the end of his titanic

conflict. Through adversity and suffering, through affliction and doubt, amidst darkness and the shadow of death, Job has wrestled for an explanation of God's ways with man, and now from the "still small voice" in his heart comes the only positive answer that the human soul may ever hope to receive, the enunciation of the moral law. . . . It is the one reality that constitutes human wisdom—it is the voice of God!'

Job wins his way out of rebellion against the dark cruelties and catastrophes of his fate to the calm serenity of reverent wonder on the endless mystery of the universe and humble dedication to the law of moral duty that ever challenges us within.

1-11 DESCRIPTION OF MINING

1. *for there is a mine for silver.* The difficulty of finding a logical sequence with what preceded has troubled the commentators. Many hold that text disturbances account for its place here. However that may be, the argument is: Other precious things have their abode in the physical universe. They appear inaccessible but men find their way. So, too, men may imagine that through skill and perseverance by means of which the precious metals or the fabulous jewels are uncovered from their secret retreat, they may at last achieve successfully the quest for Wisdom (Peake). Rashi connects the chapter with xxvii. 6, *My righteousness I hold fast*, etc.

2. *brass.* The Hebrew is more exactly defined as 'copper.'

3. *man setteth an end to darkness.* Here is vividly described how the miner with his lantern penetrates the darkest recesses of the earth. The shafts into the earth likewise bring the light of day.

And searcheth out to the furthest
bound
The stones of thick darkness and
of the shadow of death.

4 He breaketh open a shaft away
from where men sojourn;
They are forgotten of the foot that
passeth by;
They hang afar from men, they
swing to and fro.

5 As for the earth, out of it cometh
bread,
And underneath it is turned up as
it were by fire.

6 The stones thereof are the place of
sapphires,
And it hath dust of gold.

7 That path no bird of prey knoweth,
Neither hath the falcon's eye seen
it;

וּלְכָל־תַּכְלִית הוּא חוֹקֵר
אֶבֶן אֹפֶל וְצַלְמָוֶת:

4 פָּרַץ נַחַל ׀ מֵעִם־גָּר
הַנִּשְׁכָּחִים מִנִּי־רֶגֶל
דַּלּוּ מֵאֱנוֹשׁ נָעוּ:

5 אֶרֶץ מִמֶּנָּה יֵצֵא־לָחֶם
וְתַחְתֶּיהָ נֶהְפַּךְ כְּמוֹ־אֵשׁ:

6 מְקוֹם־סַפִּיר אֲבָנֶיהָ
וְעַפְרֹת זָהָב לוֹ:

7 נָתִיב לֹא־יְדָעוֹ עָיִט
וְלֹא שְׁזָפַתּוּ עֵין אַיָּה:

the shadow of death. A synonym for
'thick darkness,' here the darkness of the
mine (see on xxiv. 17).

4. *a shaft.* Hebrew *nachal.* The usual
meaning of this word is 'torrent.' Ibn
Ezra understood it as 'waters that are
poured down,' and so A.V. renders:
'The flood breaketh out from the inhabitant.' Modern commentators understand it as a technical term for 'a miner's
shaft.'

away from where men sojourn. The miner
it let deep down into the earth, far away
from the abode of men above.

they are forgotten of the foot. The miners,
deep down in their shafts, are forgotten
of the foot of those who walk overhead,
oblivious of them in the dark bowels of
the earth.

they hang afar from men. The image is
of miners, suspended from ropes, swing-
ing in the gloomy caverns, digging for
copper. Dr. Nelson Glueck's archæo-
logical discoveries in the Holy Land of
Solomon's copper mines have given
scientific corroboration to Deut. viii. 9,
*a land whose stones are iron, and out of
whose hills thou mayest dig brass.*

5. *as for the earth, out of it cometh bread.*

While on the surface the farmer peacefully works to grow his corn, below him
is a scene of upheaval and destruction
as though wrought by fire to bring up the
mineral treasures buried in the earth.
Some authorities explain *fire* as referring
to blasting operations.

6. *the stones thereof are the place of
sapphires.* The stones in the depths, to
be reached with such expenditure of
effort, are the place where sapphires are
to be obtained. The second line states
that the sapphire, which may be the
lapis lazuli, consists of particles that
glint like gold. Or it may mean that the
place where sapphires are produces
auriferous dust.

7. *that path no bird of prey knoweth.* In
the context the *path* appears to be that
of the miner, i.e. the shaft driven into
the earth. It is unseen by the keen eye
of the bird of prey. Some commentators
regard the line as parallel to verse 21 and
take it to mean the path of wisdom.

the falcon's eye. Rashi, following the
Talmudic sages, asserts that the falcon
can see farther than all other birds.
Tristram identifies the *ayyah* with the
'kite' (*Milvus regalis*) which, he says, is
common in Palestine in winter but scarcer
in summer.

8 The proud beasts have not trodden it,
    Nor hath the lion passed thereby.

9 He putteth forth his hand upon
   the flinty rock;
    He overturneth the mountains by
    the roots.

10 He cutteth out channels among
   the rocks;
    And his eye seeth every precious
    thing.

11 He bindeth the streams that they
   trickle not;
    And the thing that is hid bringeth
    he forth to light.

12 But wisdom, where shall it be
   found?
    And where is the place of under-
    standing?

13 Man knoweth not the price thereof;
    Neither is it found in the land of
    the living.

8 לֹא־הִדְרִיכֻהוּ בְנֵי־שָׁחַץ
לֹא־עָדָה עָלָיו שָׁחַל׃

9 בַּחַלָּמִישׁ שָׁלַח יָדוֹ
הָפַךְ מִשֹּׁרֶשׁ הָרִים׃

10 בַּצּוּרוֹת יְאֹרִים בִּקֵּעַ
וְכָל־יְקָר רָאֲתָה עֵינוֹ׃

11 מִבְּכִי נְהָרוֹת חִבֵּשׁ
וְתַעֲלֻמָהּ יֹצִא אוֹר׃

12 וְהַחָכְמָה מֵאַיִן תִּמָּצֵא
וְאֵי־זֶה מְקוֹם בִּינָה׃

13 לֹא־יָדַע אֱנוֹשׁ עֶרְכָּהּ
וְלֹא תִמָּצֵא בְּאֶרֶץ הַחַיִּים׃

8. *the proud beasts.* lit. 'sons of pride';
here the majestic, proud beasts; again in
xli. 26. Those powerful animals, in-
cluding even the lion, never tread the
path which is traversed by these under-
ground workers.

9. *he putteth forth his hand.* The verse
continues the account of mining operations which include breaking through the
hardest rocks. Even mountains are not
allowed to bar the miner's progress.

10. *he cutteth out channels among the rocks.*
The word for *channels* denotes the canals
cut out of the banks of the Nile. Here it
is probably a technical term for the
galleries hewn out of the rock. Others
explain it as channels to carry off water
collecting in the mine.

every precious thing. Describes the
object of all this arduous toil, precious
metal and stones.

11. *that they trickle not.* lit. 'from weeping.' The miner uses lime or clay to
prevent the water from seeping into the

mine. Davidson quotes from Cox,
Commentary on Job, 'The picturesque
phrase ("that they weep not") may have
been a technical term among the miners
in ancient times, just as our colliers name
the action of the water that percolates
through and into their workings *weeping*,
and our navvies call the fine sand which
percolates through the sides of a tunnel
crying sand.'

12-19 'WHERE SHALL WISDOM
BE FOUND?'

12. *but wisdom, where shall it be found?*
Man can unearth precious stones and
ores, bringing them to light from their
hidden places. But Wisdom, the absolute Wisdom of God in which He governs
the universe, eludes his search. Rashi
identifies Wisdom with Torah. The
second line repeats the question in the
first with different words.

13. *man knoweth not the price thereof.*
For *price* (*erkah*) the LXX reads 'the
way of it' (*darkah*) and so most moderns
emend; but the other ancient Versions

14 The deep saith: 'It is not in me';
And the sea saith: 'It is not with
me.'

15 It cannot be gotten for gold,
Neither shall silver be weighed
for the price thereof.

16 It cannot be valued with the gold
of Ophir,
With the precious onyx, or the
sapphire.

17 Gold and glass cannot equal it;
Neither shall the exchange thereof be vessels of fine gold.

18 No mention shall be made of
coral or of crystal;
Yea, the price of wisdom is above
rubies.

14 תְּהוֹם אָמַר לֹא בִי־הִיא
וְיָם אָמַר אֵין עִמָּדִי:

15 לֹא־יֻתַּן סְגוֹר תַּחְתֶּיהָ
וְלֹא יִשָּׁקֵל כֶּסֶף מְחִירָהּ:

16 לֹא־תְסֻלֶּה בְּכֶתֶם אוֹפִיר
בְּשֹׁהַם יָקָר וְסַפִּיר:

17 לֹא־יַעַרְכֶנָּה זָהָב וּזְכוֹכִית
וּתְמוּרָתָהּ כְּלִי־פָז:

18 רָאמוֹת וְגָבִישׁ לֹא יִזָּכֵר
וּמֶשֶׁךְ חָכְמָה מִפְּנִינִים:

corroborate M.T. *Price* must be understood in the sense that Wisdom is not
an article to be found among the mer-
chandise purchasable in a market-place.
The second line establishes this meaning. The question of 'value' is not
discussed until verse 15.

the land of the living. A common phrase
in Scripture for the inhabited earth (cf.
Ps. xxvii. 13, lii. 7).

14. *the deep . . . and the sea.* The *deep*
(*tehom*) is the great abyss of waters
beneath the earth. It was thought of as
the reservoir from which *the sea* drew
its supply of water. Rashi interprets that
they who go down to the sea for mer-
chandise will tell you that Wisdom *is
not with me.* They are not able to pur-
chase it as wares to give from their wealth
for a price.

15. *gold.* Hebrew *segor.* The word
occurs only here; it resembles a similar
word in 1 Kings vi. 20 and probably
means 'purified, fine' gold.

be weighed. In ancient times money was
weighed, not counted (cf. Gen. xxiii. 16;
Zech. xi. 12).

16. *be valued.* lit. 'be weighed, balanced

against,' i.e. estimated in the purest gold
of Ophir (cf. xxii. 24).

onyx. Hebrew *shoham*, a gem which
cannot be identified with certainty.
R.V. margin gives 'beryl.'

17. *glass.* The only direct reference to
glass in Scripture. It was manufactured
from early times, but it was rare and
expensive. It cannot *equal* Wisdom in
value and be bartered for it. Ibn Ezra
suggests that the word may here mean
some pure, clear gem.

vessels. The Hebrew word has many
meanings, like our 'article.' R.V. renders by 'jewels.'

18. *no mention shall be made.* i.e. as
regards worth they cannot be compared.

coral. *Ramoth*, again only in Ezek. xxvii.
16. A similar word occurs in Prov.
xxiv. 7, but probably with a different
meaning (see Cohen *ad loc.*).

crystal. *Gabish*, the only occurrence of
the word; but it is connected with *elga-
bish*, 'hail-stone.'

the price of wisdom is above rubies. The
translation is reminiscent of Prov. xxxi.
10; but the Hebrew is different and

19 The topaz of Ethiopia shall not
　　equal it,
　　Neither shall it be valued with
　　pure gold.

20 Whence then cometh wisdom?
　　And where is the place of under-
　　standing?

21 Seeing it is hid from the eyes of
　　all living,
　　And kept close from the fowls of
　　the air.

22 Destruction and Death say:
　　'We have heard a rumour thereof
　　with our ears.'

23 God understandeth the way
　　thereof,
　　And He knoweth the place there-
　　of.

24 For He looketh to the ends of the
　　earth,
　　And seeth under the whole
　　heaven;

25 When He maketh a weight for
　　the wind,
　　And meteth out the waters by
　　measure.

לֹא־יַעַרְכֶנָּה פִּטְדַת־כּוּשׁ
בְּכֶתֶם טָהוֹר לֹא תְסֻלֶּה׃
וְהַחָכְמָה מֵאַיִן תָּבוֹא
וְאֵי־זֶה מְקוֹם בִּינָה׃
וְנֶעֶלְמָה מֵעֵינֵי כָל־חָי
וּמֵעוֹף הַשָּׁמַיִם נִסְתָּרָה׃
אֲבַדּוֹן וָמָוֶת אָמְרוּ
בְּאָזְנֵינוּ שָׁמַעְנוּ שִׁמְעָהּ׃
אֱלֹהִים הֵבִין דַּרְכָּהּ
וְהוּא יָדַע אֶת־מְקוֹמָהּ׃
כִּי־הוּא לִקְצוֹת־הָאָרֶץ יַבִּיט
תַּחַת כָּל־הַשָּׁמַיִם יִרְאֶה׃
לַעֲשׂוֹת לָרוּחַ מִשְׁקָל
וּמַיִם תִּכֵּן בְּמִדָּה׃

means 'the acquisition of wisdom is above rubies,' i.e. rubies cannot buy it.

19. *the topaz.* This translation follows the LXX and Vulgate.

valued. See on verse 16.

20–28 'GOD KNOWETH THE PLACE THEREOF'

20. *whence then cometh wisdom?* The rhetorical question, repeated from verse 12, implies a negative answer. So far as man is concerned, the answer is 'no-where.'

21. *from the fowls of the air.* The language, says Metsudath David, is metaphorical. Even the birds, were they to soar aloft to the heavens, the fount of Wisdom, would not find it.

22. *destruction.* Hebrew *Abaddon*, see on xxvi. 6. The older Jewish commentators interpret *destruction and death* as the dead.

we have heard a rumour. Only a rumour, no more! They have no actual knowledge of it.

23. *God understandeth the way thereof.* The subject is emphatic, standing at the beginning of the verse. God alone knows the path that leads to Wisdom.

24. *for He looketh to the ends of the earth.* God, the Creator, surveys His entire universe, looking to the needs of all His creation. The pronoun *He* is emphatic.

25. *when He maketh a weight . . . wind . . . waters.* These two examples are offered as illustrations of God's providential care. God, alone in possession of Wisdom, carefully regulates the force of the winds and determines the amount of rainfall. As Rashi states, 'There are lands that are parched and need much rain, and there are lands that do not require it.' Driver declares that the verse becomes clearer rendered thus: 'In making a weight for the wind, and regulating the waters by measure.'

26 When He made a decree for the rain,

And a way for the storm of thunders;

26 בַּעֲשֹׂתוֹ לַמָּטָר חֹק

וְדֶרֶךְ לַחֲזִיז קֹלוֹת:

27 Then did He see it, and declare it;

He established it, yea, and searched it out.

27 אָז רָאָה וַיְסַפְּרָהּ

הֱכִינָהּ וְגַם־חֲקָרָהּ:

28 And unto man He said:

'Behold, the fear of the Lord, that is wisdom;

And to depart from evil is understanding.'

28 וַיֹּאמֶר ׀ לָאָדָם

הֵן יִרְאַת אֲדֹנָי הִיא חָכְמָה

וְסוּר מֵרָע בִּינָה:

29   CHAPTER XXIX   כט

1 And Job again took up his parable, and said:

1 וַיֹּסֶף אִיּוֹב שְׂאֵת מְשָׁלוֹ וַיֹּאמַר:

---

26. *when He made a decree for the rain.* The rain does not come by chance. God has carefully regulated the laws that govern its supply.

and a way for the storm of thunders. Hebrew *chaziz*, 'thunder-bolt, lightning-flash.' The line is repeated in xxxviii. 25 where it is translated *a way for the lightning of the thunder.*

27. *see . . . declare . . . established . . . searched it out.* The impressive array of verbs conveys the idea of God thoroughly examining and exploring Wisdom in all its manifold complexity as though it were a concrete object or idea with a separate task.

28. *the fear of the Lord, that is wisdom.* This is one of the great, climactic moments in the Book. God's absolute Wisdom, the moral order over which He rules, lies for ever hidden from man's finite mind. Man does have a wisdom that can guide him across the vicissitudes of the years: it is to stand in reverent awe of God and to shun evil. Of *fear* and *wisdom* Rashi remarks: 'The one stands in need of the other and there is no wisdom which is fair without fear.' It should be borne in mind that *fear* (*yirah*) does not convey the thought of dread. Rather does it connote humility and awe of God. The Rabbis of the Talmud have a profound aphorism: 'Everything is in the power of Heaven (God) save the fear of Heaven.' 'Holy Writ employs two terms for religion, both of which lay stress upon its moral and spiritual nature: *Yirath Elohim*—"fear of God" and *Daath Elohim*—"knowledge or consciousness of God." Whatever the fear of God may have meant in the lower stages of primitive religion, in the Biblical and Rabbinical conceptions it exercises a wholesome moral effect; it stirs up the conscience and keeps man from wrongdoing. Where fear of God is lacking, violence and vice are rife; it keeps society in order and prompts the individual to walk in the path of duty. Hence it is called the *beginning of wisdom* (cf. Ps. cxi. 10; Prov. ix. 10)' (Kohler, *Jewish Theology*, p. 29).

CHAPTERS XXIX-XXXI

THE SUMMING UP

THE cycle of debate is concluded. Job now, in language of literary and spiritual beauty, surveys his life. The three chapters before us give the retrospect of his past honour and happiness (xxix),

2 Oh that I were as in the months of
old,
As in the days when God watched
over me;

3 When His lamp shined above my
head,
And by His light I walked through
darkness;

4 As I was in the days of my youth,
When the converse of God was
upon my tent;

5 When the Almighty was yet with
me,
And my children were about me;

6 When my steps were washed with
butter,
And the rock poured me out rivers
of oil!

מִי־יִתְּנֵנִי כְיַרְחֵי־קֶדֶם

כִּימֵי אֱלוֹהַּ יִשְׁמְרֵנִי:

בְּהִלּוֹ נֵרוֹ עֲלֵי רֹאשִׁי

לְאוֹרוֹ אֵלֶךְ חֹשֶׁךְ:

כַּאֲשֶׁר הָיִיתִי בִּימֵי חָרְפִּי

בְּסוֹד אֱלוֹהַּ עֲלֵי אָהֳלִי:

בְּעוֹד שַׁדַּי עִמָּדִי

סְבִיבוֹתַי נְעָרָי:

בִּרְחֹץ הֲלִיכַי בְּחֵמָה

וְצוּר יָצוּק עִמָּדִי פַּלְגֵי־שָׁמֶן:

his present misery (xxx), and the solemn
oath and protest of his innocence (xxxi).

CHAPTER XXIX

1-20 JOB RECALLS HIS HAPPY PAST

1. *parable.* See on xxvii. 1.

2. *as in the months of old.* In language of
deep pathos Job draws a graphic picture
of his happy and honoured life before
disaster came upon him. At the outset
he attributes both his good and bad
times to Divine ordering.

3. *when His lamp shined.* In the past his
life had been illumined by the radiance
which issues from God (cf. the priestly
benediction, Num. vi. 25). Rashi finds
in *His lamp* 'an expression of light and
joy.'

by His light I walked through darkness.
The Hebrew has nothing to correspond
to *through*, but Ibn Ezra remarks that
the force is 'through darkness.' 'I was
wont to walk through all darkness and
difficulty that come to the world, but I
had light' (Rashi). 'When there was
darkness in the world, I walked by the
light which shone upon me from the
Omnipresent God' (Metsudath David).

4. *my youth.* The text employs the

unusual word *choreph* for *youth.* Its
ordinary meaning is 'harvest-time,
autumn,' in Arabic 'freshly gathered
fruit.' It denotes maturity rather than
youth; 'in the days of my autumn prime'
(BDB). R.V. has 'the ripeness of my
days.'

the converse of God. The Hebrew *sod*
has a variety of meanings; here friendly,
intimate converse (cf. xv. 8, xix. 19;
Ps. xxv. 14, lv. 15).

5. *the Almighty.* His awareness of
fellowship with God he places first, even
before the most intimate human companionship.

my children. The word may denote
'young men' (Gen. xxii. 3). Hence
Rashi's interpretation, 'my attendants.'
'My youths were about me to serve me'
(Metsudath David).

6. *when my steps were washed with butter.*
Metaphorical for overflowing abundance,
as in xx. 17.

the rock poured me out rivers of oil. 'An
expression of contentment of spirit and
every desire of the heart as smooth as
rivers of oil' (Rashi). The barren rock

7 When I went forth to the gate unto
the city,
When I prepared my seat in the
broad place,

8 The young men saw me and hid
themselves,
And the aged rose up and stood;

9 The princes refrained talking,
And laid their hand on their mouth;

10 The voice of the nobles was
hushed,
And their tongue cleaved to the
roof of their mouth.

11 For when the ear heard me, then
it blessed me,
And when the eye saw me, it gave
witness unto me;

12 Because I delivered the poor that
cried,

7 בְּצֵאתִי שַׁעַר עֲלֵי־קָרֶת
בָּרְחוֹב אָכִין מוֹשָׁבִי:

8 רָאוּנִי נְעָרִים וְנֶחְבָּאוּ
וִישִׁישִׁים קָמוּ עָמָדוּ:

9 שָׂרִים עָצְרוּ בְמִלִּים
וְכַף יָשִׂימוּ לְפִיהֶם:

10 קוֹל־נְגִידִים נֶחְבָּאוּ
וּלְשׁוֹנָם לְחִכָּם דָּבֵקָה:

11 כִּי אֹזֶן שָׁמְעָה וַתְּאַשְּׁרֵנִי
וְעַיִן רָאֲתָה וַתְּעִידֵנִי:

12 כִּי־אֲמַלֵּט עָנִי מְשַׁוֵּעַ

yielded unexpected blessings. 'The
allusion,' remarks Driver, 'is, probably,
partly to the fact that the olive flourishes
in rocky soil, partly to the fact that the
presses in which the oil was extracted
from the olive were commonly cavities
hewn out in the rock.' The line is also
metaphorically worded.

7. the city. The text has the poetical
word *kereth*, frequent in Aramaic, and
found in the place-name Carthage. Job
has now spoken of the three primary
sources of his former happiness: fellowship with God, the companionship of his
children, and the respect of the com-
munity. The elders of the city would
hold court at the city's gate (cf. Deut.
xxii. 15; Ruth iv. 1).

my seat in the broad place. By the city's
gate, in the broad market-place, the court
held its sessions and public meetings
took place (cf. Neh. viii. 1).

8. hid themselves. Apparently out of a
sense of reverence or, as Metsudath
David suggests, bashfulness to show
themselves before him.

the aged rose. Even the elders of the city,
seated in council, rose in respect and
stood until Job had sat down. Such was

their deference and esteem for this righteous man.

9. the princes refrained talking. His
arrival hushed the discussion already
going on, the assembly waiting to hear
his opinion.

10. was hushed. lit. 'hid.' Their voices
became 'veiled,' hushed in deferential
respect. They were unable to speak, as
though their tongues had become cleaved
to the roof of their mouth. This last
phrase is expressive of parched thirst
(cf. Lam. iv. 4), here of nervousness and
respect in the presence of an eminent
person.

**11. for when the ear heard me, then it
blessed me.** All this because of Job's
impeccable life. The ear that heard the
uprightness of his deeds praised him,
and the eye that saw the goodness of his
ways gave witness to his righteousness
(Metsudath David). An alternative
rendering suggested by Davidson reads:
'For the ear that heard of me blessed me,
and the eye that saw me gave witness
to me.'

12. because I delivered the poor that cried.
It was Job's outstanding benevolence and

The fatherless also, that had none to help him.

13 The blessing of him that was ready to perish came upon me; And I caused the widow's heart to sing for joy.

14 I put on righteousness, and it clothed itself with me; My justice was as a robe and a diadem.

15 I was eyes to the blind, And feet was I to the lame.

16 I was a father to the needy; And the cause of him that I knew not I searched out.

17 And I broke the jaws of the unrighteous, And plucked the prey out of his teeth.

18 Then I said: 'I shall die with my nest, And I shall multiply my days as the phoenix;

וְיָתוֹם וְלֹא־עֹזֵר לוֹ׃
בִּרְכַּת אֹבֵד עָלַי תָּבֹא
וְלֵב אַלְמָנָה אַרְנִן׃
צֶדֶק לָבַשְׁתִּי וַיִּלְבָּשֵׁנִי
כִּמְעִיל וְצָנִיף מִשְׁפָּטִי׃
עֵינַיִם הָיִיתִי לַעִוֵּר
וְרַגְלַיִם לַפִּסֵּחַ אָנִי׃
אָב אָנֹכִי לָאֶבְיוֹנִים
וְרִב לֹא־יָדַעְתִּי אֶחְקְרֵהוּ׃
וָאֲשַׁבְּרָה מְתַלְּעוֹת עַוָּל
וּמִשִּׁנָּיו אַשְׁלִיךְ טָרֶף׃
וָאֹמַר עִם־קִנִּי אֶגְוָע
וְכַחוֹל אַרְבֶּה יָמִים׃

v. 18. לנהרדעי וכחול בשורק

justice which had won him the profound regard of all (cf. Ps. lxxii. 12).

13. *the blessing of him that was ready to perish.* i.e. those brought to the brink of despair. Rashi gives the illustrations of a man who had died in his sins and (at the time of dying) was troubled about the fate of his family. Job would sustain his wife and children. To the widow he would lend his name, saying, 'She is my relative.' Cf. the protection that Boaz gave to Ruth (Ruth iv. 10).

14. *I put on righteousness.* So immersed was Job in righteousness and justice, that they were as a robe draped about him and as a diadem on his head, splendidly visible to all.

15. *I was eyes to the blind, and feet was I to the lame.* 'Whoever was blind or lame, unable to care for his needs because of his handicap, I did it for him and behold, it is as if I were his eyes and feet' (Metsudath David).

16. *I was a father to the needy.* The father was the provider for his family.

In that respect all in need were regarded by him as his children.

the cause . . . I searched out. The Hebrew is slightly ambiguous. It might mean, as R.V. margin, 'the cause which I knew not.' In this sense, Metsudath David comments: 'And when I did not know the true reasons of the quarrel, I would search to know them.' But A.J. seems preferable and tells that Job interested himself in the pleas for justice even of men who were strangers to him.

17. *the jaws.* The Hebrew word means 'teeth,' perhaps 'jaw-teeth' (cf. Prov. xxx. 14). As in Proverbs, the figure is that of a fierce beast of prey with its victims in its jaws.

18. *I shall die with my nest.* i.e. in his home surrounded by his children; they would bury him, not he them, as happened to him.

the phoenix. Hebrew *chol* normally means 'sand.' So R.V. which agrees with Metsudath David who interprets: 'My days shall be as numerous as the sands of the sea,' a hyperbolic expression.

19 My root shall be spread out to
the waters,
And the dew shall lie all night
upon my branch;

20 My glory shall be fresh in me,
And my bow shall be renewed in
my hand.'

21 Unto me men gave ear, and
waited,
And kept silence for my counsel.

22 After my words they spoke not
again;
And my speech dropped upon
them.

23 And they waited for me as for the
rain;
And they opened their mouth
wide as for the latter rain.

24 If I laughed on them, they believed it not;

19 שָׁרְשִׁי פָתוּחַ אֱלֵי־מָיִם

וְטַל יָלִין בִּקְצִירִי׃

20 כְּבוֹדִי חָדָשׁ עִמָּדִי

וְקַשְׁתִּי בְּיָדִי תַחֲלִיף׃

21 לִי־שָׁמְעוּ וְיִחֵלּוּ

וְיִדְּמוּ לְמוֹ עֲצָתִי׃

22 אַחֲרֵי דְבָרִי לֹא יִשְׁנוּ

וְעָלֵימוֹ תִּטֹּף מִלָּתִי׃

23 וְיִחֲלוּ כַמָּטָר לִי

וּפִיהֶם פָּעֲרוּ לְמַלְקוֹשׁ׃

24 אֶשְׂחַק אֲלֵהֶם לֹא יַאֲמִינוּ

But most modern scholars accept the
old Jewish tradition that the word means,
as Rashi asserts, 'a bird, whose name was
chol (phoenix) for whom death was not
decreed, since it did not taste of the tree
of knowledge; at the end of a thousand
years, it renews itself and returns to its
youth.' Driver and Davidson mention
the fable, current in Egypt, telling that
the phoenix was supposed to live five
hundred years, and to consume himself
and his nest with fire, only to arise anew
to life out of the ashes. Hence the name
became a proverb, expressing the highest
duration of life, 'to live as long as the
phoenix.'

19. *my root shall be spread out to the
waters*. As in viii. 16ff., the image is
that of a tree. The roots do not wither
and dry, and the dew upon the branches
keeps it green. Ibn Ezra calls attention
to the passage in Ps. lxxx. 12.

20. *my glory*. i.e. respect, rank. It
would continue undiminished.

my bow. A symbol of strength, as in
Gen. xlix. 24.

21-25 THE DEFERENCE JOB HAD ENJOYED
21. *unto me men gave ear*. Job returns,
in the conclusion of this chapter, to the

thought of the respect and confidence
which he had formerly known. Men
used to listen to his words, to follow his
advice.

22. *my speech dropped upon them*. The
figure is that of refreshing rain (cf. Deut.
xxxii. 2). His words had the effect of
encouraging those in despair and removing the doubts of the perplexed.

23. *the latter rain*. The eagerly awaited
malkosh, the 'spring-rain' which fell in
March-April and was of great importance
to the farmer for strengthening and
maturing his crops. For another instance of its metaphorical use, cf. Prov.
xvi. 15. In Deut. xi. 14 we have mentioned the contrasting *yoreh*, 'early rain'
which falls in Palestine from the end of
October until the beginning of December.
The autumn rain prepares the soil to
receive the seed.

24. *if I laughed on them, they believed it
not*. This translation accords with the
old Jewish commentators who interpreted the line in the sense that men had
so high a veneration and esteem for
Job's importance and dignity that they
could not believe it when he laughed

And the light of my countenance
they cast not down.

25 I chose out their way, and sat as
chief,
And dwelt as a king in the army,
As one that comforteth the
mourners.

וְאוֹר פָּנַי לֹא יַפִּילֽוּן׃
אֶבְחַר דַּרְכָּם וְאֵשֵׁב רֹאשׁ
וְאֶשְׁכּוֹן כְּמֶלֶךְ בַּגְּדוּד
כַּאֲשֶׁר אֲבֵלִים יְנַחֵֽם׃

30　　　　　CHAPTER XXX　　　　　ל

1 But now they that are younger
than I have me in derision,

Whose fathers I disdained to set
with the dogs of my flock.

2 Yea, the strength of their hands,
whereto should it profit me?

וְעַתָּה ׀ שָׂחֲקוּ עָלַי
צְעִירִים מִמֶּנִּי לְיָמִים
אֲשֶׁר־מָאַסְתִּי אֲבוֹתָם
לָשִׁית עִם־כַּלְבֵי צֹאנִֽי׃
גַּם־כֹּחַ יְדֵיהֶם לָמָּה לִּי

---

familiarly with them. It seemed so
strange to them. Modern scholars give
preference to R.V. margin: 'I smiled on
them when they had no confidence.'
Those who were troubled and despon-
dent found new encouragement through
Job's clear-sighted, buoyant counsel. In
contrast, the second line tells that the
gloom of others was never able to darken
his own cheerfulness.

25. *I chose out their way.* This probably
signifies that he took every opportunity
of associating with his fellow-men.
Rashi and Metsudath David understand
it in the sense that when men were
bewildered, seeking advice and the path
to follow, Job advised them, choosing
for them the road that they should take.

sat as chief. Job was recognized as their
leader, in their assemblies sitting as
chief and leading as a king leads his
troops.

as one that comforteth. Despite his high
station, he humbly and sympathetically
listened to the lowliest in his distress.

CHAPTER XXX
JOB'S PRESENT HUMILIATION
THE previous chapter described Job's

past happiness, to which the respect and
honour accorded him had greatly contributed. This chapter, in marked antithesis, pictures the contempt and ridi-
cule in which the lowest and vilest dregs
of society now hold him. He tells of the
indignities they heap upon him, then
turns to his own agony of body and mind,
and finally contrasts his present ruinous
state with the former joyous days when
life for him was as gay as the music of
harp and pipe.

1-8 EVEN OUTCASTS DESPISE HIM

1. *whose fathers . . . with the dogs of my
flock.* The contrast with the last lines
of chapter xxix is sudden and sharp.
From being accorded the honour of a
chief, Job complains that now even the
youth of families, so low and debased that
he would not have cared to set their
fathers with the dogs to guard his sheep,
mock and deride him. Formerly the
young had treated him with marked
respect (xxix. 8).

2. *ripe age.* See on v. 26. These
wretched men had come to old age
decrepit. Hence Job would find no use

Men in whom ripe age is perished.

3 They are gaunt with want and
    famine;
    They gnaw the dry ground, in the
    gloom of wasteness and desola-
    tion.

4 They pluck salt-wort with worm-
    wood;
    And the roots of the broom are
    their food.

5 They are driven forth from the
    midst of men;
    They cry after them as after a
    thief.

6 In the clefts of the valleys must
    they dwell,
    In holes of the earth and of the
    rocks.

7 Among the bushes they bray;

עֲלֵימוֹ אָבַד כָּלַח׃

3 בְּחֶסֶר וּבְכָפָן גַּלְמוּד
הַעֹרְקִים צִיָּה
אֶמֶשׁ שׁוֹאָה וּמְשֹׁאָה׃

4 הַקֹּטְפִים מַלּוּחַ עֲלֵי־שִׂיחַ
וְשֹׁרֶשׁ רְתָמִים לַחְמָם׃

5 מִן־גֵּו יְגֹרָשׁוּ
יָרִיעוּ עָלֵימוֹ כַּגַּנָּב׃

6 בַּעֲרוּץ נְחָלִים לִשְׁכֹּן
חֹרֵי עָפָר וְכֵפִים׃

7 בֵּין־שִׂיחִים יִנְהָקוּ

for them in his employment. Yet the children of such as these despised him.

3. they are gaunt. Through want and hunger they are stiff, lifeless. The word occurs in iii. 7, xv. 34 where it is translated *desolate*.

they gnaw. Descriptive of the scantiest subsistence. The verb occurs again only in verse 17.

gloom. The word *emesh* is normally translated 'yesterday' (A.V. 'in former times'); but though obscure, it admits of the meaning 'darkness.'

wasteness and desolation. The Hebrew phrase *shoah umeshoah*, which is vividly alliterative, appears again in xxxviii. 27, translated *desolate and waste*. It describes the ruin and waste of the desert.

4. salt-wort (malluach). Mallows, a plant growing in salt-marshes. Tristram describes this herb as having 'small, thick, sour-tasting leaves, which could be eaten, but it would be very miserable food.'

worm-wood (siach). The word is usually

translated 'bush' (A.V., R.V.), 'shrub' (Gen. ii. 5).

broom (rethamim). These wretched people must eat the roots of the broom-shrubs for food. 'Its roots are very bitter, but its softer portions might doubtless sustain life in extremity' (Tristram).

5. they are driven forth from the midst of men. These dregs of humanity could only exist by stealing (cf. xxiv. 6) and were consequently driven away when they approached inhabited places. The word for *midst* (gab) is an Aramaism.

6. clefts. Hebrew *aruts*, lit. 'dreadful'; 'in the (most) dreadful of ravines' (BDB), or 'in a place where a man would be afraid to descend' (Ibn Ezra). The word only occurs here. Nearly the same word in Arabic means a 'gully' or 'defile'; hence *clefts* (Driver).

7. they bray. Like wild asses (Ibn Ezra). To refined ears their raucous voices and uncouth speech sound repellent.

nettles (charul). 'I am inclined to believe that it designates the Prickly Acanthus (*Acanthus spinosus*), a very common and

Under the nettles they are gathered together.

8 They are children of churls, yea,
children of ignoble men;
They were scourged out of the
land.

9 And now I am become their song,
Yea, I am a byword unto them.

10 They abhor me, they flee far from
me,
And spare not to spit in my face.

11 For He hath loosed my cord, and
afflicted me,
And they have cast off the bridle
before me.

12 Upon my right hand rise the
brood;

תַּחַת חָרוּל יְסֻפָּחוּ׃

בְּנֵי־נָבָל גַּם־בְּנֵי בְלִי־שֵׁם
נִכְּאוּ מִן־הָאָרֶץ׃

וְעַתָּה נְגִינָתָם הָיִיתִי
וָאֱהִי לָהֶם לְמִלָּה׃

תִּעֲבוּנִי רָחֲקוּ מֶנִּי
וּמִפָּנַי לֹא־חָשְׂכוּ רֹק׃

כִּי־יִתְרוֹ פִּתַּח וַיְעַנֵּנִי
וְרֶסֶן מִפָּנַי שִׁלֵּחוּ׃

עַל־יָמִין פִּרְחַח יָקוּמוּ

v. 11. יתריק׳

troublesome weed in the Plains of
Palestine, and equally abundant among
ruins. We have often seen it in the Plain
of Esdraelon choking the corn and
reaching the height of six feet. Its sting
is most irritating and unpleasant, and
well supports the derivation of the
Hebrew word, "that which burns"'
(Tristram).

gathered together. The Hebrew verb
means more properly 'are huddled
together' (Driver). 'Their cries are like
those of the wild ass seeking for food
(vi. 5), and they throw themselves down
like wild beasts under the bushes in the
desert' (Davidson).

8. *ignoble men.* lit. 'of no name.' These
demoralized wretches are smitten outcasts of the land.

9-15 'I AM A BYWORD UNTO THEM'

9. *their song.* He has become the theme
of derisive verses (cf. Lam. iii. 14).

a byword unto them. 'It is not likely that
the dull outcasts described in the preceding verses composed and sang these
stinging lampoons about Job. It is the
base rabble that formed the lowest
stratum of the society in which Job lived,
sharp-witted in pungent satire as our
street-arabs, and as remorseless to their
butts' (Peake).

10. *they abhor me.* In xxiv. 4ff. Job had
spoken of these lowly wretches with
compassion and as illustration of the
injustices that prevail in human society.
Now he pictures them as utterly despis-
ing him, not even sparing him personal
affront and dreadful humiliation.

11. *for He hath loosed my cord.* A.J.
follows the *kerĕ*, while R.V. 'he hath
loosed his cord' agrees with the *kethib*,
i.e. God has aimed at him with His bow
(cf. xxix. 20b of which this is opposite
in meaning). Job may intend that God
has loosened the cord of his bow (the
symbol of his strength) with which he
held in restraint the forces that assailed
him.

the bridle. The rabble has cast off the
bridle of respect and now mock him.
Ibn Ezra suggests as illustration he had
heard, which he confesses may be far-
fetched, a horse grown old from which
they removed the bridle.

12. *upon my right hand rise the brood.*
The Hebrew for *brood, pirchach*, is only
found here. BDB define it as 'offshoot,
wretched crowd.' The older Jewish
commentators vary in their interpretations: 'little ones' (pygmies?) (Ibn Ezra);
'little sprouts' (Rashi); 'like flowers that

They entangle my feet,
And they cast up against me their
    ways of destruction.

13 They break up my path,
    They further my calamity,
    Even men that have no helper.

14 As through a wide breach they
    come;
    In the midst of the ruin they roll
    themselves upon me.

15 Terrors are turned upon me,
    They chase mine honour as the
    wind;
    And my welfare is passed away as
    a cloud.

16 And now my soul is poured out
    within me;
    Days of affliction have taken hold
    upon me.

רַגְלַי שִׁלֵּחוּ

וַיָּסֹלּוּ עָלַי אָרְחוֹת אֵידָם׃

13 נָתְסוּ נְתִיבָתִי

לְהַוָּתִי יֹעִילוּ לֹא עֹזֵר לָמוֹ׃

14 כְּפֶרֶץ רָחָב יֶאֱתָיוּ

תַּחַת שֹׁאָה הִתְגַּלְגָּלוּ׃

15 הָהְפַּךְ עָלַי בַּלָּהוֹת

תִּרְדֹּף כָּרוּחַ נְדִבָתִי

וּכְעָב עָבְרָה יְשֻׁעָתִי׃

16 וְעַתָּה עָלַי תִּשְׁתַּפֵּךְ נַפְשִׁי

יֹאחֲזוּנִי יְמֵי־עֹנִי׃

v. 13. לְהַוָּתִי ק

bloom forth all round a tree, so they
rise against me on all sides to laugh at
me' (Berechiah). It is clear from the
context that the word describes the
derisive rabble.

they entangle my feet. More lit. 'send on,
or, away,' perhaps 'push from place to
place.' Ibn Ezra renders: 'They place
thorns in my way.'

they cast up against me. Cf. xix. 12. The
image is of an army setting siege to a
fortress.

13. *they break up my path.* Cf. xix. 8.
They break up the path of life in which
Job has walked.

they further my calamity. By their
callous behaviour they intensify his
misfortunes.

even men that have no helper. Even such
as these, shunned and despised by the
mass of the people, insult him and heap
contumely upon his head.

14. *as through a wide breach they come.*
The image is of the furious onslaughts

of the invading army. Ibn Ezra understands the subject to be the calamities
that roll over Job, defenceless and helpless against them. Rashi pictures the
troops advancing stealthily, creeping
upon him to weary him so that he cannot
slip away from them.

15. *they chase mine honour as the wind.*
Cf. xvi. 12-14, xix. 12, where Job describes his afflictions. By *honour* he
means his former princely station and
fortune, his nobility of rank. 'The spirit
of nobility that rested upon me in the
past' (Rashi). In the words *as the wind*,
he has in mind the blowing away of chaff
on the ground; similarly has his dignity
been swept from him.

16-23 'I AM BECOME LIKE DUST AND
        ASHES'

16. *my soul is poured out within me.* Job
describes the spirit of despondency that
rises from his soul in tears and lamenta-
tions (cf. Ps. xlii. 5). The phrase is 'an
idiomatic expression by which an emotion is represented as acting upon the
person who is sensible of it' (Driver).

17 In the night my bones are pierced
   and fall from me,
   And my sinews take no rest.

18 By the great force [of my disease]
   is my garment disfigured;
   It bindeth me about as the collar
   of my coat.

19 He hath cast me into the mire,
   And I am become like dust and
   ashes.

20 I cry unto Thee, and Thou dost
   not answer me;
   I stand up, and Thou lookest at
   me.

21 Thou art turned to be cruel to
   me;
   With the might of Thy hand
   Thou hatest me.

22 Thou liftest me up to the wind,
   Thou causest me to ride upon
   it;
   And Thou dissolvest my substance.

לַיְלָה עֲצָמַי נִקַּר מֵעָלָי

וְעֹרְקַי לֹא יִשְׁכָּבוּן׃

בְּרָב־כֹּחַ יִתְחַפֵּשׂ לְבוּשִׁי

כְּפִי כֻתָּנְתִּי יַאַזְרֵנִי׃

הֹרָנִי לַחֹמֶר

וָאֶתְמַשֵּׁל כֶּעָפָר וָאֵפֶר׃

אֲשַׁוַּע אֵלֶיךָ וְלֹא תַעֲנֵנִי

עָמַדְתִּי וַתִּתְבֹּנֶן בִּי׃

תֵּהָפֵךְ לְאַכְזָר לִי

בְּעֹצֶם יָדְךָ תִשְׂטְמֵנִי׃

תִּשָּׂאֵנִי אֶל־רוּחַ תַּרְכִּיבֵנִי

וּתְמֹגְגֵנִי תֻּשִׁיָּה׃

v. 22. תשיה ק׳

17. in the night my bones are pierced. The tormenting pains, severest at night, make his bones seem pierced and as if corroded, dropping from off him.

my sinews. So Rashi and Ibn Ezra. For the word, cf. verse 3; lit. 'my gnawers.'

18. by the great force [of my disease] is my garment disfigured. Ibn Ezra comments: 'the great force of my affliction and pain,' supplying the words placed in parenthesis in A.J. Rashi understands garment as 'skin.' The verse is obscure, and an alternative rendering is R.V. margin: 'by (His) great force is my garment disfigured.' This may signify that in his writhing from pain sent by God his garment has been twisted out of shape, or the pus from his sores discolours and befouls it.

as the collar of my coat. It is doubtful whether this can mean that his outer garment clings to him like the neck of the close-fitting tunic as the effect of his emaciation. The shrinking of his body would result in his garment hanging loosely upon him. Perhaps he refers to the swelling of his body from his disease which makes the garment fit tightly.

19. he hath cast me into the mire. The verse seems to allude to Job's physical appearance because of his hideous affliction. It is as though God had plunged him into the mire.

dust and ashes. He has become as vile as the refuse amidst which he sits (ii. 8).

20. I stand up. Job may cry out seeking respite, but he meets with stony silence from God.

21. Thou hatest me. R.V.: 'persecutest me,' the same verb as in xvi. 9. 'As a man, whose enemy has fallen into his hand, and he does not want to kill him at once, but inflicts on him new punishments every day' (Berechiah).

22. Thou liftest me up to the wind. So that he is tossed about helplessly until flung to the ground a broken man.

Thou dissolvest my substance. R.V.: 'Thou dissolvest me in the storm.' Both meanings, lit. 'in the roar (of the storm)' or my substance, are possible. Job is destroyed in the whirlwind of his afflictions.

23 For I know that Thou wilt bring
me to death,
And to the house appointed for
all living.

24 Surely none shall put forth his
hand to a ruinous heap,
Neither because of these things
shall help come in one's
calamity,

25 If I have not wept for him that
was in trouble,
And if my soul grieved not for the
needy.

26 Yet, when I looked for good,
there came evil;
And when I waited for light,
there came darkness.

23 כִּי־יָדַעְתִּי מָוֶת תְּשִׁיבֵנִי
וּבֵית מוֹעֵד לְכָל־חָי׃

24 אַךְ לֹא־בְעִי יִשְׁלַח־יָד
אִם־בְּפִידוֹ לָהֶן שׁוּעַ׃

25 אִם־לֹא בָכִיתִי לִקְשֵׁה־יוֹם
עָגְמָה נַפְשִׁי לָאֶבְיוֹן׃

26 כִּי טוֹב קִוִּיתִי וַיָּבֹא רָע
וַאֲיַחֲלָה לְאוֹר וַיָּבֹא אֹפֶל׃

23. *the house appointed.* 'The place
which is appointed for all living, in the
grave' (Rashi). The Hebrew may be
translated, as R.V. margin, 'the house of
meeting for all living,' i.e. Sheol.

24-31 HIS DESPAIRING CRY IS
FORCED FROM HIM

24. *surely none shall put forth his hand
to a ruinous heap.* This verse has been
described as 'one of the most difficult
verses in the poem,' and a variety of
translations has been proposed. A.V.
and R.V. make God the subject of the
verb; i.e. although, as stated in verse 23,
Job is aware that God has determined
his death, surely He will not make the
end of *a ruinous heap*, such as he is, the
more painful by adding blow to blow.
R.V. margin and Davidson construe as a
question: 'Howbeit doth not one stretch
out his hand in his fall?' When a person
is in dire straits, does he not instinctively
cry out for help? It is as the effect of
this urge for self-preservation that Job
utters his cry for mercy to God.

*neither because of these things shall help
come in one's calamity.* The uncertainty
of interpretation continues. R.V.:
'though it be in his destruction, one may
utter a cry because of these things' is
as improbable as A.J., although the
rendering of *shua* by 'cry' is preferable
to *help*. R.V. margin and Davidson also

translate this line as a question; the
former as, 'Or in his calamity therefore
cry for help?' the latter as, 'When he is
destroyed doth he not because of this
utter a cry?' If this is accepted, Job
explains that his outburst is perfectly
natural and should not incur censure.

25. *if I have not wept.* Better, as A.V.,
R.V.: 'Did not I weep . . . was not my
soul grieved . . . ?' Job gives a reason for
his right to complain in his time of
anguish. He had formerly shown compassion for those in trouble (cf. xxix.
11-17).

him that was in trouble. lit. 'one whose
day (life) is hard.'

grieved. Hebrew *agam*, 'grieved,' in the
sense of 'be anxious, concerned.' The
word appears only here in Scripture.

26. *when I looked for good.* Job had a
claim to expect that his good fortune
would continue. But to his consterna-
tion, instead of good and light, he is
appalled by evil and darkness (cf. xxix.
18-20).

27. *mine inwards boil.* The Hebrew
word means the 'internal parts.' We
would say 'vitals,' a figurative expression
for the tumult of his emotions that rage
within him (cf. Lam. ii. 11).

27 Mine inwards boil, and rest not;
Days of affliction are come upon
me.

28 I go mourning without the sun;
I stand up in the assembly, and
cry for help.

29 I am become a brother to jackals,
And a companion to ostriches.

30 My skin is black, and falleth from
me,
And my bones are burned with
heat.

31 Therefore is my harp turned to
mourning,
And my pipe into the voice of
them that weep.

מֵעַי רֻתְּחוּ וְלֹא־דָמּוּ
קִדְּמֻנִי יְמֵי־עֹנִי׃
קֹדֵר הִלַּכְתִּי בְּלֹא חַמָּה
קַמְתִּי בַקָּהָל אֲשַׁוֵּעַ׃
אָח הָיִיתִי לְתַנִּים
וְרֵעַ לִבְנוֹת יַעֲנָה׃
עוֹרִי שָׁחַר מֵעָלָי
וְעַצְמִי־חָרָה מִנִּי־חֹרֶב׃
וַיְהִי לְאֵבֶל כִּנֹּרִי
וְעֻגָבִי לְקוֹל בֹּכִים׃

---

31   CHAPTER XXXI   לא

1 I made a covenant with mine eyes;
How then should I look upon a
maid?

בְּרִית כָּרַתִּי לְעֵינָי
וּמָה אֶתְבּוֹנֵן עַל־בְּתוּלָה׃

v. 31. בב"א הג' דגושה

---

rest not. 'They are unable to be still and
silent' (Rashi).

28. *I go mourning without the sun.* The
phrase *go mourning* usually denotes to
wear the squalid attire of a bereaved
person (cf. 2 Sam. xix. 25; Ps. xxxviii. 7);
but here it is better translated 'I go
blackened.' His swarthy appearance,
however, has not been caused by the
sun (cf. Cant. i. 6), but is the effect of
his disease.

in the assembly. Where a wronged person
pleads his cause.

29. *a brother to jackals.* The verse
amplifies *cry for help.* 'I make a wailing
like jackals; they are wild animals which
have a cry of desolation' (Ibn Ezra).
The mournful howling of the jackal is

mentioned in Mic. i. 8, which also refers
to the ostrich in the same connection.

30. *my skin is black.* Job refers again
to the fearful ravages of his disease.
And falleth is implied but not expressed
in the text.

with heat. More lit. 'from dryness.'
Burning dryness and feverish heat are
symptoms of his ailment.

31. *therefore is my harp turned to mourning.* A beautiful but pathetic contrast
between his former happy state and his
present misery and pain. *Turned* is
implied but not explicit in the Hebrew.

CHAPTER XXXI

JOB'S SOLEMN OATH OF CLEARANCE

THE lofty nobility of the ethical ideals

2 For what would be the portion of
  God from above,
  And the heritage of the Almighty
  from on high?

3 Is it not calamity to the unrighteous,
  And disaster to the workers of
  iniquity?

4 Doth not He see my ways,
  And count all my steps?

5 If I have walked with vanity,
  And my foot hath hasted to deceit—

‎2 וּמֶה ׀ חֵלֶק אֱלוֹהַּ מִמָּעַל
‎וְנַחֲלַת שַׁדַּי מִמְּרֹמִים׃
‎3 הֲלֹא־אֵיד לְעַוָּל
‎וְנֵכֶר לְפֹעֲלֵי אָוֶן׃
‎4 הֲלֹא־הוּא יִרְאֶה דְרָכָי
‎וְכָל־צְעָדַי יִסְפּוֹר׃
‎5 אִם־הָלַכְתִּי עִם־שָׁוְא
‎וַתַּחַשׁ עַל־מִרְמָה רַגְלִי׃

expressed in this chapter has won
universal admiration from modern
scholars. Job solemnly affirms that he
is conscious of no thought and act which
he has committed to deserve just visitation of woe as has befallen him. He has
never entertained or yielded to improper
sensual desire. He has abstained from
all dishonesty, untruthfulness and covet-
ousness. He has not been tempted to
adultery. Those dependent upon him
have been treated with patience and
consideration. He has never refused
help to those in need or want, nor taken
advantage of the weak and unprotected.
He has never put his trust in material
wealth or been lured from the worship
of the One and Only God to any false
worship. He has never rejoiced over the
misfortune of an enemy, never been
inhospitable, never a hypocrite. Could
any make such charges against him, Job
would fearlessly bring the false indictment before his Judge. His great estates
had been acquired honestly and justly.

This chapter is an amazing summary of
the ethics of the Bible, a dramatic
portrayal of the requirements for the
good life as taught in the Torah and by
the prophets of Israel.

1-4 HE HAD NOT SINNED WITH HIS EYE

1. *I made a covenant with mine eyes.* Job
had never let his eye, one of 'the agents of
sin' as the Rabbis called it, wander lust-

fully. The *covenant*, interprets Rashi,
was 'not to look upon a married woman.'
Bound by such a covenant and always
loyal to it, he had never been unlawfully
attracted to any woman.

2. *what would be the portion of God.* The
verses 2-4 state the considerations that
occupied Job's mind in the past, re-
straining him from such sin. The
thought of his responsibility to God and
His power to punish the sinner had been
a constant deterrent.

3. *is it not calamity to the unrighteous.*
That is how his mind had worked in the
past. Job contends that such calamity
and disaster might have been fitting for
the unrighteous and for the workers of
iniquity, but not to such a man as he.

4. *doth not He see my ways.* 'Here *ways*
and *steps* are said of things so slight as the
glance of the eye. These are "seen" and
"counted" by God. The thought of
God in these verses is as lofty as the
conception of morality is close and
inward' (Davidson).

5-8 HE HAD NOT BEEN GUILTY OF VANITY

5. *vanity.* The term *shaw* means what is
morally empty and unreal, insincerity
and falsehood (cf. Ps. xii. 3, xxvi. 4,
xli. 7). Both *vanity* and *deceit* are per-
sonified. Job has not walked with the
one nor hurried after the other.

6 Let me be weighed in a just balance,
   That God may know mine integrity—

7 If my step hath turned out of the
   way,
   And my heart walked after mine
   eyes,
   And if any spot hath cleaved to
   my hands;

8 Then let me sow, and let another
   eat;
   Yea, let the produce of my field be
   rooted out.

9 If my heart have been enticed
   unto a woman,
   And I have lain in wait at my
   neighbour's door;

10 Then let my wife grind unto another,
   And let others bow down upon
   her.

11 For that were a heinous crime;
   Yea, it were an iniquity to be
   punished by the judges;

יִשְׁקְלֵנִי בְמֹאזְנֵי־צֶדֶק
וְיֵדַע אֱלוֹהַּ תֻּמָּתִי:

אִם־תִּטֶּה אַשֻּׁרִי מִנִּי הַדָּרֶךְ
וְאַחַר עֵינַי הָלַךְ לִבִּי
וּבְכַפַּי דָּבַק מֻאוּם:

אֶזְרְעָה וְאַחֵר יֹאכֵל
וְצֶאֱצָאַי יְשֹׁרָשׁוּ:

אִם־נִפְתָּה לִבִּי עַל־אִשָּׁה
וְעַל־פֶּתַח רֵעִי אָרָבְתִּי:

תִּטְחַן לְאַחֵר אִשְׁתִּי
וְעָלֶיהָ יִכְרְעוּן אֲחֵרִין:

כִּי־הוא זִמָּה
וְהוּא עָוֹן פְּלִילִים:

א' בחה .7 v.   היא ק' .11 v.   והוא ק' .11 v.   במקצת ספרים בלא מ'

6. *let me be weighed.* The verse is parenthetical. Job solemnly calls upon God
to weigh his faults and his virtues in a
just balance. He is certain that his
integrity will tip the scales.

7. *out of the way.* From the path of
virtue (cf. xxiii. 11).

after mine eyes. Yielding to the lusts and
temptations of the eye (cf. Num. xv. 39).

any spot. Hebrew *mum*, 'a blemish.'
Ibn Ezra: 'the least thing'; Rashi: 'the
whisper of suspicion.' Job denies that
he has ever yielded to temptations that
would have left the least blemish on his
life.

8. *then let me sow.* He utters an imprecation upon himself if he is guilty.

the produce of my field. lit. 'my produce,
or, offspring'; here that which springs
out of what has been sown or planted by
him.

9-12 HE IS GUILTLESS OF ADULTERY

9. *have lain in wait at my neighbour's door.*
'For his wife' (Rashi). He solemnly
denies that he had ever broken the
Seventh Commandment.

10. *let my wife grind unto another.* 'Be
slave to another, the daily grinding of
corn at the handmill being the task of
the lowest slave-girl' (Driver). The
Rabbis interpreted it as euphemism for
intercourse. In fact, both senses may be
implied, because the female slave was
often the concubine of her master, and
so the curse means, Let my wife be the
slave (first clause) and the concubine
(second clause) of others (Davidson).

11. *for that were a heinous crime.* Zim-
mah, translated *enormity* in Hos. vi. 9.
Adultery was a capital crime (Deut.
xxii. 22).

to be punished by the judges. lit. 'for
judges, calling for judgment.'

12 For it is a fire that consumeth
　　unto destruction,
　　And would root out all mine in-
　　crease.

13 If I did despise the cause of my
　　man-servant,
　　Or of my maid-servant, when
　　they contended with me—

14 What then shall I do when God
　　riseth up?
　　And when He remembereth,
　　what shall I answer Him?

15 Did not He that made me in the
　　womb make him?
　　And did not One fashion us in
　　the womb?

16 If I have withheld aught that the
　　poor desired,
　　Or have caused the eyes of the
　　widow to fail;

12 כִּי אֵשׁ הִיא עַד־אֲבַדּוֹן תֹּאכֵל
וּבְכָל־תְּבוּאָתִי תְשָׁרֵשׁ׃

13 אִם־אֶמְאַס מִשְׁפַּט עַבְדִּי וַאֲמָתִי
בְּרִבָם עִמָּדִי׃

14 וּמָה אֶעֱשֶׂה כִּי־יָקוּם אֵל
וְכִי־יִפְקֹד מָה אֲשִׁיבֶנּוּ׃

15 הֲלֹא־בַבֶּטֶן עֹשֵׂנִי עָשָׂהוּ
וַיְכֻנֶנּוּ בָּרֶחֶם אֶחָד׃

16 אִם־אֶמְנַע מֵחֵפֶץ דַּלִּים
וְעֵינֵי אַלְמָנָה אֲכַלֶּה׃

12. *destruction.* Hebrew *abaddon* (see on
xxvi. 6). A fire so vehement as to burn to
the depths of the nether-world. The
figure is one of total destruction.

13-15 HE HAD BEEN A CONSIDERATE
MASTER

13. *despise the cause of my man-servant.*
With Job's wealth and power, he might
have treated his servants contemptuously
when they thought they had grievances
or a case to argue. Note Job's line of
reasoning: It is his deep understanding
that the One and Only God is the Creator
of all that makes him vividly aware of the
ethical claims and the spiritual reality
of human brotherhood. He regards
the servant not as a possession but as a
person with equal dignity and rights to
his own. Peake comments: 'For God
was the Maker of both, the right of the
slave was as much to Him as Job's right,
a most remarkable advance on the ethics
of antiquity, even in Israel.'

14. *what then shall I do when God riseth
up?* He kept the thought that his servants were also God's creatures for ever
in the focus of his consciousness. The

weakness from which they suffered would
be fortified by God when He came to
judge and champion their cause.

when He remembereth. The verb *pakad*
conveys the idea of 'to scrutinize, judge.'

15. *did not One fashion us.* 'One
God' (Ibn Ezra), 'One Creator' (Rashi).
Master and slave being created by God,
He is as concerned for the latter as the
former.

16-23 HE HAD BEEN BENEVOLENT

16. *if I have withheld aught.* R.V. reads:
'If I have withheld the poor from their
desire.' Both readings convey the
thought that Job had never refused help
to those in need.

caused the eyes of the widow to fail.
Looking vainly for aid in her distress
(cf. Ps. lxix. 4). Rashi remarks that
unfulfilled desire is called 'failing of the
eye.' Ibn Ezra comments: 'If I robbed
her and her eyes fail in longing after that
which I had robbed.' In xxix. 12ff. Job
claimed that his conduct had been such
as to free him from any accusation of
this kind.

17 Or have eaten my morsel myself
alone,
And the fatherless hath not eaten
thereof—

18 Nay, from my youth he grew up
with me as with a father,
And I have been her guide from
my mother's womb.

19 If I have seen any wanderer in
want of clothing,
Or that the needy had no covering;

20 If his loins have not blessed me,
And if he were not warmed with
the fleece of my sheep;

21 If I have lifted up my hand
against the fatherless,
Because I saw my help in the
gate;

22 Then let my shoulder fall from
the shoulder-blade,
And mine arm be broken from
the bone.

23 For calamity from God was a
terror to me,

וְאֹכַל פִּתִּי לְבַדִּי 1
וְלֹא־אָכַל יָתוֹם מִמֶּנָּה:

כִּי מִנְּעוּרַי גְּדֵלַנִי כְאָב 1
וּמִבֶּטֶן אִמִּי אַנְחֶנָּה:

אִם־אֶרְאֶה אוֹבֵד מִבְּלִי לְבוּשׁ 1
וְאֵין כְּסוּת לָאֶבְיוֹן:

אִם־לֹא בֵרֲכוּנִי חֲלָצָו 2
וּמִגֵּז כְּבָשַׂי יִתְחַמָּם:

אִם־הֲנִיפֹתִי עַל־יָתוֹם יָדִי 2
כִּי־אֶרְאֶה בַשַּׁעַר עֶזְרָתִי:

כְּתֵפִי מִשִּׁכְמָה תִפּוֹל 2
וְאֶזְרֹעִי מִקָּנֶה תִשָּׁבֵר:

כִּי־פַחַד אֵלַי אֵיד אֵל 2

v. 20. חלציו ק'

17. *or have eaten my morsel myself alone.*
Job anticipates the admonition of Josĕ,
the son of Jochanan, in Aboth i. 5, 'Let
thy house be open wide; let the poor be
the members of thy household.'

18. *from my youth he grew up with me.*
The verse is a parenthetical comment.
From childhood Job had reared the
fatherless and guided the widow (Ibn
Ezra). There is an obvious difficulty
in the statement that he had guided the
widow when he was an infant. Szold
construes the verse: 'For, from my youth
—yea, from my mother's womb—He
reared me that I should guide him (the
orphan) like a father.'

19. *any wanderer.* lit. 'perishing, ready
to perish' (cf. xxix. 13). The word
occurs in the same sense in, *A wandering
Aramean was my father* (Deut. xxvi. 5).

20. *his loins.* Metaphorical for the body
which had been clothed by Job's
benevolence.

the fleece of my sheep. Cf. *the lambs will
be for thy clothing* (Prov. xxvii. 26).

21. *because I saw my help in the gate.*
Job had not cruelly taken advantage of
the defenceless orphan, even though he
knew that were a charge of exploitation
brought against him before the judges in
the gate, his honoured status would
secure a verdict in his favour.

22. *let my shoulder fall.* The imprecation
follows the principle of measure for
measure. If his hand had been guilty of
oppression, may he be deprived of his
arm.

from the bone. Hebrew *kanah* conveys
the image of a 'tube.' A.V. margin has
'the chanel bone' which is an old term
for the collar-bone.

23. *calamity from God.* Job dreaded the
just retribution which he knew God
would exact of the wicked.

And by reason of His majesty I
could do nothing.

24 If I have made gold my hope,
And have said to the fine gold:
'Thou art my confidence';

25 If I rejoiced because my wealth
was great,
And because my hand had gotten
much;

26 If I beheld the sun when it
shined,
Or the moon walking in brightness;

27 And my heart hath been secretly
enticed,
And my mouth hath kissed my
hand;

28 This also were an iniquity to be
punished by the judges;
For I should have lied to God
that is above.

וּמִשְּׂאֵתוֹ לֹא אוּכָל׃

24 אִם־שַׂמְתִּי זָהָב כִּסְלִי
וְלַכֶּתֶם אָמַרְתִּי מִבְטַחִי׃

25 אִם־אֶשְׂמַח כִּי־רַב חֵילִי
וְכִי־כַבִּיר מָצְאָה יָדִי׃

26 אִם־אֶרְאֶה אוֹר כִּי יָהֵל
וְיָרֵחַ יָקָר הֹלֵךְ׃

27 וַיִּפְתְּ בַּסֵּתֶר לִבִּי
וַתִּשַּׁק יָדִי לְפִי׃

28 גַּם־הוּא עָוֹן פְּלִילִי
כִּי־כִחַשְׁתִּי לָאֵל מִמָּעַל׃

His majesty. The Hebrew suggests the
thought of 'loftiness' displayed in God's
judgment (cf. xiii. 11). Job felt himself
powerless to do wrong, restrained as he
was by his sense of awe before God's
majesty and fear of His judicial wrath.

24-25 HE HAD NOT ABUSED HIS WEALTH

24. *if I have made gold my hope.* He
denies that he had ever made material
wealth his hope or reliance.

25. *if I rejoiced because my wealth was
great.* He had not been carried away
by his large possessions to act with overweening pride or assert himself unduly.
He had not been spoilt by his good fortune.

26-28 HE HAD NOT BEEN
FAITHLESS TO GOD

26. *the sun.* lit. 'light'; 'the sun in the
course of its strength and brilliance'
(Rashi).

the moon walking in brightness. The full
moon (Ibn Ezra). The allusion is to
idolatrous worship of the two luminaries,
a lure which this belief exercised throughout antiquity even over the minds of

enlightened men. 'The moon moving in
stately splendour across the wonderful
Eastern sky is so majestic a spectacle
that the thrill of homage it inspired is
not hard to understand' (Peake). Job
never yielded even secretly to it.

27. *my heart hath been secretly enticed.*
'To the sun and moon to say, "These
are deities," like some of the idolaters'
(Rashi).

and my mouth hath kissed my hand. lit.
'and my hand hath kissed my mouth.'
Job denies that his hand ever touched
his mouth in homage to the sun and
moon. The worship of the heavenly
bodies was widespread in the East. The
prophets frequently inveighed against
such idolatry (cf. Jer. xlv. 17ff. against
adoration of *the queen of heaven*; Ezek.
viii. 16 against sun-worship). For kissing
as an act of worship, cf. 1 Kings xix. 18;
Hos. xiii. 2.

28. *an iniquity.* An act forbidden by
the Torah (cf. Deut. iv. 19, xvii. 3).

I should have lied to God. R.V. margin:
'I should have denied God.' By practis-
ing such secret idolatry, while ostensibly

29 If I rejoiced at the destruction of
  him that hated me,
  Or exulted when evil found him—

30 Yea, I suffered not my mouth to
  sin
  By asking his life with a curse.

31 If the men of my tent said not:
  'Who can find one that hath not
  been satisfied with his meat?'

32 The stranger did not lodge in the
  street;
  My doors I opened to the roadside.

33 If after the manner of men I
  covered my transgressions,
  By hiding mine iniquity in my
  bosom—

אִם־אֶשְׂמַח בְּפִיד מְשַׂנְאִי
וְהִתְעֹרַרְתִּי כִּי־מְצָאוֹ רָע:
וְלֹא־נָתַתִּי לַחֲטֹא חִכִּי
לִשְׁאֹל בְּאָלָה נַפְשׁוֹ:
אִם־לֹא אָמְרוּ מְתֵי אָהֳלִי
מִי־יִתֵּן מִבְּשָׂרוֹ לֹא נִשְׂבָּע:
בַּחוּץ לֹא־יָלִין גֵּר
דְּלָתַי לָאֹרַח אֶפְתָּח:
אִם־כִּסִּיתִי כְאָדָם פְּשָׁעָי
לִטְמוֹן בְּחֻבִּי עֲוֹנִי:

a worshipper of God, Job would have
been false to the One and Only God.

that is above. 'God is above the luminaries' (Ibn Ezra).

29-34 HIS BLAMELESS CONDUCT TOWARDS HIS FELLOWS

29. *the destruction.* Hebrew *pid*, i.e.
'ruin, disaster'; translated *calamity* in
xxx. 24.

of him that hated me. Note Job's generous
attitude towards his enemies, which was
in the true Hebraic spirit (cf. Exod.
xxiii. 4f.; Prov. xxiv. 17, xxv. 21).

evil. i.e. retribution, or misfortune.

30. *my mouth.* lit. 'my palate,' 'the
organ of taste; the suggestion is that the
cursing of a foe is a dainty delicious
morsel, but Job would not gratify his
palate with it' (Peake). This verse is
parenthetical.

with a curse. The ancient Hebrews believed in the potency of a curse; and
there is a Talmudical saying, 'Even the

curse of an ordinary person should not
be treated lightly' (B.K. 93a).

31. *who can find one.* The reference, as
both Rashi and Ibn Ezra point out, is to
Job's hospitality. He had practised it
in princely style. 'His servants (*the men
of my tent*) are represented as expressing
the wish that they could find any one
who has not yet (like others) been filled
from Job's rich table' (Davidson).

32. *to the roadside.* A.V. and R.V.: 'to
the traveller,' but A.J. is preferable, the
literal sense being 'way.' The doors of
his house were opened wide to the cross-
roads to welcome all who came. Job's
hospitality was wide and generous.

33. *after the manner of men.* 'As is the
way of men to hide their transgressions
from their fellow-men' (Ibn Ezra). 'The
verses mean that his life had been so
upright that he had nothing of which
to be ashamed or that might give him
just cause to dread the fury of the
populace. Hence he did not need to
keep close at home, but could fearlessly
mingle among men and look all his
fellows in the face' (Peake).

34 Because I feared the great multitude,
   And the most contemptible
   among families terrified me,
   So that I kept silence, and went
   not out of the door.

35 Oh that I had one to hear me!—
   Lo, here is my signature, let the
   Almighty answer me—
   And that I had the indictment
   which mine adversary hath
   written!

36 Surely I would carry it upon my
   shoulder;
   I would bind it unto me as a
   crown.

37 I would declare unto him the
   number of my steps;
   As a prince would I go near unto
   him.

34 כִּי אֶעֱרוֹץ ׀ הָמוֹן רַבָּה

וּבוּז־מִשְׁפָּחוֹת יְחִתֵּנִי

וָאֶדֹּם לֹא־אֵצֵא פָתַח:

35 מִי יִתֶּן־לִי ׀ שֹׁמֵעַ לִי

הֶן תָּוִי שַׁדַּי יַעֲנֵנִי

וְסֵפֶר כָּתַב אִישׁ רִיבִי:

36 אִם־לֹא עַל־שִׁכְמִי אֶשָּׂאֶנּוּ

אֶעֶנְדֶנּוּ עֲטָרוֹת לִי:

37 מִסְפַּר צְעָדַי אַגִּידֶנּוּ

כְּמוֹ נָגִיד אֲקָרְבֶנּוּ:

34. the great multitude. The general public.

the most contemptible among families. Had he ever done anything wrong, even the most despised and lowly would have filled him with dread (cf. xxx. 8). Fear of the contempt of the most abject of men would have deterred him from sin. Job lived in the broad day and fearlessly confronted all (xxix. 7). 'Job repudiates all hypocritical conduct or secret transgression. This was the charge his friends made against him. And this consciousness of purity of heart, struggling with false accusations of hypocrisy, forces from him a new appeal to God to make known to him the sins laid to his charge' (verses 35-37) (Davidson).

35-37 HIS PLEA TO GOD TO BE HEARD

35. Oh that I had one to hear me! Metsudath David interprets it of some human sympathetic ear. But the usual and probable interpretation, sustained by the third line, is that Job refers to God.

here is my signature. Hebrew *taw,* 'my

(written) mark (in attestation)' (BDB). Job fearlessly affirms that he had been innocent of all the sins he has recounted. The language is legal in phraseology, as we have noticed before. 'Here, he says, is my solemn signature to these protestations of innocence; let the Almighty refute them, and *answer me,* if He can' (Driver).

the indictment. lit. 'scroll,' here the legal document.

mine adversary. Job means God Himself. 'Defiant the tone may be, but why should the poet have shrunk from letting his hero brave God, in proud assurance of his integrity? It is no emasculated pietist whom he has chosen for his protagonist in this titanic struggle' (Peake). Bear in mind also that God, although unknown to Job, had paid high testimony to his character when addressing the Satan (i. 8).

36. as a crown. Job would proudly bear God's indictment as a king bears his crown, confident that it would contain nothing to incriminate him.

38 If my land cry out against me,
And the furrows thereof weep together;

אִם־עָלַי אַדְמָתִי תִזְעָק
וְיַחַד תְּלָמֶיהָ יִבְכָּיוּן :

39 If I have eaten the fruits thereof
without money,
Or have caused the tillers thereof
to be disappointed—

אִם־כֹּחָהּ אָכַלְתִּי בְלִי־כָסֶף
וְנֶפֶשׁ בְּעָלֶיהָ הִפָּחְתִּי :

40 Let thistles grow instead of wheat,
And noisome weeds instead of
barley.

The words of Job are ended.

תַּחַת חִטָּה ׀ יֵצֵא חוֹחַ
וְתַחַת־שְׂעֹרָה בָאְשָׁה
תַּמּוּ דִּבְרֵי אִיּוֹב :

---

37. *the number of my steps.* 'All my ways I would declare before Him' (Ibn Ezra). There is nothing in his past which he could wish to conceal.

as a prince. He would present himself before his Accuser with the proud bearing of a prince, seeing that his conscience was perfectly clear.

38-40 HE IMPRECATES HIMSELF IF HE BE GUILTY

38. Most modern scholars are of the opinion that these verses are out of place, and variously insert them after verses 8, 12, 15, 23, 25, 32, 34, the other passages where Job pronounces a curse upon himself if the allegations made against him be true. But the judgment of Davidson is, 'To modern feeling the passage would thus gain in rhetorical effect; but it is not certain that the author's taste would have coincided with modern feeling in this instance. . . . If the verses belong to the passage at all, which there is no reason to doubt, they seem to stand in the only place suitable for them.'

if my land cry out. The land would cry out in protest because it had been unjustly seized.

39. *the fruits thereof.* lit. 'its strength,' as in Gen. iv. 12.

the tillers thereof to be disappointed. lit. '(or if) the life of its (the land's) owners I have caused to breathe out' (BDB). 'The reference may be either to oppressions which brought the owners death (like the case of Naboth, 1 Kings xxi.), after which the land was seized without money, or to oppressive appropriation of the land so that the rightful owner was brought to death through penury and misery' (Davidson). Cf. Mic. ii. 2, 9.

40. *noisome weeds.* ' *Boshah* is derived from a root signifying to stink like carrion, and may, therefore, denote any noisome weeds or offensively smelling plant. There is a smut which attacks corn, and has a putrid smell, *Uredo fœtida*' (Tristram).

the words of Job are ended. Cf. Ps. lxxii. 20 for a similar editorial note. Davidson remarks: 'The concluding statement *the words of Job are ended* hardly belongs to the author of the Book. It is the remark of some editor or copyist, who drew attention to the fact that Job's connected discourses here come to an end. It is rather hazardous to draw any critical conclusion from it in reference to the immediately following speeches of Elihu.' The LXX connects the phrase with what follows: 'The words of Job were ended, so these three men,' etc.

1. So these three men ceased to answer Job, because he was righteous in his own eyes. 2. Then was kindled the wrath of Elihu the son

1 וַיִּשְׁבְּתוּ שְׁלֹשֶׁת הָאֲנָשִׁים הָאֵלֶּה
מֵעֲנוֹת אֶת־אִיּוֹב כִּי הוּא צַדִּיק
2 בְּעֵינָיו: וַיִּחַר אַף ׀ אֱלִיהוּא בֶן־

CHAPTERS XXXII-XXXVII

THE SPEECHES OF ELIHU

THE long and heated debate between Job and his friends has concluded, and a new personality is introduced at this point. He is described as a listener to the discussion, whose feelings had been so worked up by Job's defence of himself and the inadequacy of the friends' arguments, that he could not refrain from intervening.

It is accepted by modern exegetes that these chapters are a later interpolation and not part of the original version of the Book. This conclusion is based upon the following arguments: (i) Elihu is not mentioned in the Prologue and, more important still, in the Epilogue. God's rebuke is addressed only to the three friends (xlii. 7f.). (ii) His long tirade called forth no reply from Job, and it is deduced that he had not heard it. (iii) Unlike the friends, he frequently addresses Job by name, and he quotes the earlier chapters in such a way that the impression is created that he had *read* them. (iv) Chapter xxxviii, God's reply to Job, follows naturally on xxxi. and ignores Elihu's speeches. (v) The language of these chapters, as well as the style, differs from the rest of the Book, and reflects a later period of Hebrew. (vi) Elihu adds nothing new to the preceding discussion.

Davidson judiciously remarks that 'some of these arguments have little weight, while others are of considerable force.' The case is carefully weighed by Professor F. Godet, in his *Studies on the Old Testament* (The Expositor's Library), pp. 215ff., and his verdict is, 'Far from

being a mere by-play in the plan of the Book, this passage is an indispensable feature of it.'

Whereas the modern tendency is to belittle the value of this section contributed by Elihu and depreciate it in comparison with the rest of the Book, Maimonides described it as 'a profound and wonderful discourse' (*Guide*, III. 23) and detected therein new ideas not before expressed. Even a critical authority like Cheyne admits of Elihu's speeches, 'They are not without true and beautiful passages which, with all their faults of expression, would in any other book have commanded universal admiration' (*Job and Solomon*, pp. 90f.).

CHAPTER XXXII

1-5 ELIHU INTERPOSES

1. *righteous in his own eyes*. The friends abandon all further argument, seeing they cannot move Job from the assertion of his innocence and his insistence that God had afflicted him without just provocation.

2. *Elihu*. The name occurs elsewhere in Scripture of other men (cf. 1 Sam. i. 1; 1 Chron. xii. 21, xxvi. 7, xxvii. 18. It signifies 'my God is He.'

the son of Barachel the Buzite. He was related to Abraham, through his brother Nahor, *Uz his first-born and Buz his brother* (Gen. xxii. 21) and also related to Job (see on i. 1). Cf. Jer. xxv. 23 where Buz occurs with Tema (vi. 19) and included among the Arab tribes.

of Barachel the Buzite, of the family
of Ram; against Job was his wrath
kindled, because he justified himself
rather than God. 3. Also against his
three friends was his wrath kindled,
because they had found no answer,
and yet had condemned Job. 4. Now
Elihu had waited to speak unto Job,
because they were older than he.
5. And when Elihu saw that there
was no answer in the mouth of these
three men, his wrath was kindled.

6. And Elihu the son of Barachel
the Buzite answered and said:

בָּרַכְאֵל הַבּוּזִי מִמִּשְׁפַּחַת רָם בְּאִיּוֹב
חָרָה אַפּוֹ עַל־צַדְּקוֹ נַפְשׁוֹ מֵאֱלֹהִים:
וּבִשְׁלֹשֶׁת רֵעָיו חָרָה אַפּוֹ עַל אֲשֶׁר
לֹא־מָצְאוּ מַעֲנֶה וַיַּרְשִׁיעוּ אֶת־
אִיּוֹב: וֶאֱלִיהוּ חִכָּה אֶת־אִיּוֹב
בִּדְבָרִים כִּי זְקֵנִים־הֵמָּה מִמֶּנּוּ
לְיָמִים: וַיַּרְא אֱלִיהוּא כִּי אֵין מַעֲנֶה
בְּפִי שְׁלֹשֶׁת הָאֲנָשִׁים וַיִּחַר אַפּוֹ:
וַיַּעַן | אֱלִיהוּא בֶן־בַּרַכְאֵל הַבּוּזִי
וַיֹּאמַר

v. 3. תיקון סופרים

---

justified himself rather than God. Speaking out of his great pain, Job had condemned God's justice (cf. xl. 8), instead
of acknowledging that his affliction was
the effect of sin. 'God had afflicted Job,
and thus, in Job's view and the view of
the time, passed a verdict of wickedness
on him. Against this verdict Job re-
claims, God does him wrong in this.
This is the formal question of right between Job and God. But this naturally
goes back into the material question of
Job's past life. Elihu, defending the
righteousness of God, keeps before him
chiefly the formal question. He touches
little upon Job's life and history, differ-
ing in this entirely from the three friends.
He makes a general, abstract question out
of Job's complaints against God, which
he argues on general lines with almost
no reference to Job's particular case'
(Davidson).

3. *and yet had condemned Job.* Rashi
and Ibn Ezra mention that this is one of
the places in Scripture where we have
an emendation of a Biblical phrase
introduced by the Scribes (*tikkun Sophe-
rim*) to avoid an apparently irreverent
expression. The original reading, it is
alleged, was 'condemned God.' There
are eighteen such passages in Scripture

(cf. vii. 20). Note that Elihu does not
censure the friends for condemning Job.
He is aroused because they did not find
forcible arguments to refute him as he
deserved.

4. *had waited to speak.* lit. 'waited for
Job with words.'

because they were older than he. Elihu's
youth is given as the reason for his previous reticence.

5. *his wrath was kindled.* The phrase
has appeared three times in these five
verses, indicating how intensely he was
moved.

6-10 WISDOM IS NOT NECESSARILY
WITH THE OLD

Elihu lists the reasons that compel him
to join in the debate: Wisdom is not a
matter of years, but of the Divine
spirit which is accessible to all (6-10);
dissatisfaction with the arguments advanced by the three friends (11-14); and
because the friends are dumb, must he be
silent? His thoughts and emotions stir
and ferment within him like wine ready
to burst new wine-skins (15-22).

I am young, and ye are very old;
Wherefore I held back, and durst
not declare you mine opinion.

7 I said: 'Days should speak,
And multitude of years should
teach wisdom.'

8 But it is a spirit in man,
And the breath of the Almighty,
that giveth them understanding.

9 It is not the great that are wise,
Nor the aged that discern judgment.

10 Therefore I say: 'Hearken to me;
I also will declare mine opinion.'

11 Behold, I waited for your words,
I listened for your reasons,
Whilst ye searched out what to
say.

צָעִיר אֲנִי לְיָמִים וְאַתֶּם יְשִׁישִׁים
עַל־כֵּן זָחַלְתִּי וָאִירָא ׀
מֵחַוֺּת דֵּעִי אֶתְכֶם׃

7 אָמַרְתִּי יָמִים יְדַבֵּרוּ
וְרֹב שָׁנִים יֹדִיעוּ חָכְמָה׃

8 אָכֵן רוּחַ־הִיא בֶאֱנוֹשׁ
וְנִשְׁמַת שַׁדַּי תְּבִינֵם׃

9 לֹא־רַבִּים יֶחְכָּמוּ
וּזְקֵנִים יָבִינוּ מִשְׁפָּט׃

10 לָכֵן אָמַרְתִּי שִׁמְעָה־לִּי
אֲחַוֶּה דֵּעִי אַף־אָנִי׃

11 הֵן הוֹחַלְתִּי ׀ לְדִבְרֵיכֶם
אָזִין עַד־תְּבוּנֹתֵיכֶם
עַד־תַּחְקְרוּן מִלִּין׃

6. *wherefore I held back.* More lit.
'shrank back, crawled away.' Another
suggested translation, based upon the
cognate Arabic verb, is 'I sat in the
back.' Peake comments ironically:
'Elihu is little troubled by his modesty
in the sequel, he more than makes up
for his bashful silence.'

7. *I said: 'Days should speak.'* Owing to
his youth, he felt that he should keep
silent and allow older men, with their
ripe experience, to argue with Job.

8. *it is a spirit.* The Divine spirit or
breath (*ruach*) gives life and intelligence
to all (cf. xxvii. 3, xxxiii. 4). That is the
source of man's wisdom. Here Elihu
expresses a characteristically Hebrew
concept. As the effect of the in-breathing
by man of the *breath* (ruach) *of life* from
God, man became *a living soul* (Gen. ii.
7), which the Targum renders as 'a
speaking (i.e. rational) spirit.'

9. *the great.* i.e. 'great in age' as the
parallel line shows. The word *rab* is
used in this sense in Gen. xxv. 23.

10. *therefore I say.* Because wisdom de-
pends not on years but on the Divine
spirit in man, I claim the right to speak
although young in years. The verb
hearken is singular and is addressed to
Job. In the next section he turns to the
friends.

11-14 ANOTHER REASON FOR ELIHU'S
INTERVENTION

11. *I listened for your reasons.* He expresses his disappointment with the
arguments the three friends had advanced. He waited for other and more
cogent reasons for condemning Job than
they had advanced.

12 Yea, I attended unto you,
And, behold, there was none that
   convinced Job,
Or that answered his words,
   among you.

13 Beware lest ye say: 'We have
   found wisdom;
God may vanquish him, not
   man!'

14 For he hath not directed his
   words against me;
Neither will I answer him with
   your speeches.

15 They are amazed, they answer no
   more;
Words are departed from them.

16 And shall I wait, because they
   speak not,
Because they stand still, and
   answer no more?

17 I also will answer my part,
I also will declare mine opinion.

18 For I am full of words;

וְעָדֵיכֶם אֶתְבּוֹנָן
וְהִנֵּה אֵין לְאִיּוֹב מוֹכִיחַ
עוֹנֶה אֲמָרָיו מִכֶּם:
פֶּן־תֹּאמְרוּ מָצָאנוּ חָכְמָה
אֵל־יִדְּפֶנּוּ לֹא־אִישׁ:
וְלֹא־עָרַךְ אֵלַי מִלִּין
וּבְאִמְרֵיכֶם לֹא אֲשִׁיבֶנּוּ:
חַתּוּ לֹא־עָנוּ עוֹד
הֶעְתִּיקוּ מֵהֶם מִלִּים:
וְהוֹחַלְתִּי כִּי־לֹא יְדַבֵּרוּ
כִּי עָמְדוּ לֹא־עָנוּ עוֹד:
אַעֲנֶה אַף־אֲנִי חֶלְקִי
אֲחַוֶּה דֵעִי אַף־אָנִי:
כִּי מָלֵתִי מִלִּים

ע. 18. ‏חסר א'‏

12. *convinced.* An archaism for 'convicted' (Driver). Note how prolix
Elihu is in expressing his chagrin over the
shortcomings of the friends.

13. *beware lest ye say.* Elihu warns the
friends against excusing themselves from
having satisfactorily refuted Job on the
ground that he had a case which God
alone could answer. 'No,' he seems to
say, 'Job's wisdom is not as invincible
as it appears.'

14. *he hath not directed his words against
me.* This continues the thought of verse
13. Elihu, not too modestly, asserts that
he will offer a different and presumably
more effective argument.

*neither will I answer him with your
speeches.* Elihu undertakes to argue the
case on quite other lines. 'His promise
is ill-kept,' is Peake's comment.

15-22 ELIHU SOLILOQUIZES

15. *they are amazed.* This section
describes the state of Elihu's mind.

Though the friends are apparently dis-
comfited and silent, he cannot contain
himself. He seems, however, to spend
more of his energy on his own rage than
in getting down to the more difficult
task of finding an effective rebuke to Job.

words are departed from them. More lit.
'words have removed, are gone from
them.' R.V. paraphrases: 'They have
not a word to say.'

16. *and shall I wait.* He evidently feels
that he has waited too long already. Now
that they are silent, he must speak out.

17. *I also will answer.* The reader waits
impatiently for Elihu's revelation of
truth!

18. *for I am full of words.* It is difficult
to repress the thought of the unconscious
illumination of these words. As Peake
remarks, 'Elihu's conceit would be less
insufferable to an Oriental than to us;
but it goes far beyond anything in the
other speeches.'

The spirit within me constraineth
me.

19 Behold, mine inwards are as wine
which hath no vent;
Like new wine-skins which are
ready to burst.

20 I will speak, that I may find relief;
I will open my lips and answer.

21 Let me not, I pray you, respect
any man's person;
Neither will I give flattering titles
unto any man.

22 For I know not to give flattering
titles;
Else would my Maker soon take
me away.

הֲצִיקַתְנִי רוּחַ בִּטְנִי׃

19 הִנֵּה בִטְנִי כְּיַיִן לֹא־יִפָּתֵחַ
כְּאֹבוֹת חֲדָשִׁים יִבָּקֵעַ׃

20 אֲדַבְּרָה וְיִרְוַח־לִי
אֶפְתַּח שְׂפָתַי וְאֶעֱנֶה׃

21 אַל־נָא אֶשָּׂא פְנֵי־אִישׁ
וְאֶל־אָדָם לֹא אֲכַנֶּה׃

22 כִּי לֹא יָדַעְתִּי אֲכַנֶּה
כִּמְעַט יִשָּׂאֵנִי עֹשֵׂנִי׃

---

33   CHAPTER XXXIII   לג

1 Howbeit, Job, I pray thee, hear
my speech,
And hearken to all my words.

2 Behold now, I have opened my
mouth,
My tongue hath spoken in my
mouth.

1 וְאוּלָם שְׁמַע־נָא אִיּוֹב מִלָּי
וְכָל־דְּבָרַי הַאֲזִינָה׃

2 הִנֵּה־נָא פָּתַחְתִּי פִי
דִּבְּרָה לְשׁוֹנִי בְחִכִּי׃

---

within me. lit. 'of my belly' (cf. Prov.
xviii. 8), deep within me.

19. *like new wine-skins.* He compares the
tempest within him to the fermenting
wine within new wine-skins which must
get vent or burst.

20. *that I may find relief.* lit. 'that there
may be relief for me.' The image is still
of the fermenting wine which must find
an outlet.

21. *flattering titles.* He intends to be
candid and sincere, concerned solely
with the argument and not betrayed into
hypocrisy by deference to any one's rank
or titles.

22. *else would my Maker soon take me
away.* Elihu's piety would deter him, if
at all tempted, to seek to flatter anyone.
The modern reader is apt to be repelled
by what seems Elihu's flagrant lack of

modesty. Davidson comes to the defence
of the author by warning us against
applying our canons of good taste.
'There was nothing further from the
intention of the author of these chapters
than to make Elihu play a ridiculous part.
This speaker is meant to offer what the
writer judged a weighty contribution to
the discussion, and to the vindication
of the ways of God to man.'

CHAPTER XXXIII

1-7 ELIHU ADDRESSES JOB

1. *howbeit, Job.* Observe that Elihu
frequently addresses Job by name. The
friends had not done so. It may be that
we have here a sign of familiarity which
is natural in a blood-relation (see on
xxxii. 2).

2. *in my mouth.* lit. 'palate.' It is hard

3 My words shall utter the uprightness of my heart;
And that which my lips know they
shall speak sincerely.

4 The spirit of God hath made me,
And the breath of the Almighty
giveth me life.

5 If thou canst, answer thou me,
Set thy words in order before me,
stand forth.

6 Behold, I am toward God even as
thou art;
I also am formed out of the clay.

7 Behold, my terror shall not make
thee afraid,
Neither shall my pressure be heavy
upon thee.

8 Surely thou hast spoken in my
hearing,

3 יֹשֶׁר־לִבִּי אֲמָרָי
וְדַעַת שְׂפָתַי בָּרוּר מִלֵּלוּ׃

4 רוּחַ־אֵל עָשָׂתְנִי
וְנִשְׁמַת שַׁדַּי תְּחַיֵּנִי׃

5 אִם־תּוּכַל הֲשִׁיבֵנִי
עֶרְכָה לְפָנַי הִתְיַצָּבָה׃

6 הֵן־אֲנִי כְפִיךָ לָאֵל
מֵחֹמֶר קֹרַצְתִּי גַם־אָנִי׃

7 הִנֵּה אֵימָתִי לֹא תְבַעֲתֶךָּ
וְאַכְפִּי עָלֶיךָ לֹא־יִכְבָּד׃

8 אַךְ אָמַרְתָּ בְאָזְנָי

to avoid the feeling that the speaker is
pompously redundant and stilted.

3. *my words shall utter the uprightness of
my heart.* lit. 'uprightness of heart are
my words.' Elihu stresses his sincerity.
Job had asked for that from his three
friends (vi. 25); he will get it from him.

4. *the spirit of God.* Cf. xxxii. 8 to which
it belongs in thought. Elihu means to
say that like Job, he is a human being,
sharing in the Divine spirit that gives
life. Elihu claims no special endowment
above the others. 'The spirit of God
hath made me, and I am not stronger than
you' (Rashi).

5. *set thy words in order.* The image has
the smell of battle about it. 'Answer
the charge!' 'All that thou art able to
answer, say!' (Metsudath David).

6. *behold, I am toward God.* This line,
like verse 4, expresses the thought: 'I,
Elihu, am in the same relation to God
that thou art, Job; I am a man like thyself' (so Ibn Ezra). Rashi, translating
the first line more literally, 'I am like
thy mouth toward God,' explains: 'Since

thy mouth hath asked to argue with one
who will not terrify thee (xiii. 21), behold
I am in place of the Holy One, blessed be
He, and on His behalf to speak His
words.' This explanation underlies
A.V. and R.V. margin: 'Behold, I am
according to thy wish in God's stead.'

7. *behold, my terror.* Elihu takes up
Job's complaint that God's terror and
majesty would overpower him, making
it impossible for him to plead the justice
of his cause (cf. ix. 34, xiii. 21). 'You
need not be afraid of me,' he says, 'I am
a man like yourself.'

my pressure. The word *achpi* occurs
only here. LXX reads 'my hand (*kappi*)'
which is adopted by A.V. Rashi cites
Prov. xvi. 26, *For his mouth compelleth*
(akaph) *him.* Ibn Ezra interprets:
'something hard' quoting the Proverbs
passage.

8-11 ELIHU STATES JOB'S CLAIM
OF INNOCENCE

8. *surely thou hast spoken in my hearing.*
Though Job had not complained to him,
Elihu says that all the time the dialogue
had been proceeding, he was paying
attention to his words. And now, after

And I have heard the voice of thy
   words:

9 'I am clean, without transgression,
   I am innocent, neither is there
      iniquity in me;

10 Behold, He findeth occasions
   against me,
   He counteth me for His enemy;

11 He putteth my feet in the stocks,
   He marketh all my paths.'

12 Behold, I answer thee: In this
   thou art not right,
   That God is too great for man;

13 Why hast thou striven against
   Him?
   Seeing that He will not answer
   any of his words.

14 For God speaketh in one way,
   Yea in two, though man per-
   ceiveth it not.

וְקוֹל מִלֶּיךָ אֶשְׁמָע׃

9 זַךְ אֲנִי בְּלִי־פָשַׁע
חַף אָנֹכִי וְלֹא עָוֺן לִי׃

10 הֵן תְּנוּאוֹת עָלַי יִמְצָא
יַחְשְׁבֵנִי לְאוֹיֵב לוֹ׃

11 יָשֵׂם בַּסַּד רַגְלָי
יִשְׁמֹר כָּל־אָרְחֹתָי׃

12 הֶן־זֹאת לֹא־צָדַקְתָּ אֶעֱנֶךָּ
כִּי־יִרְבֶּה אֱלוֹהַּ מֵאֱנוֹשׁ׃

13 מַדּוּעַ אֵלָיו רִיבוֹתָ
כִּי כָל־דְּבָרָיו לֹא יַעֲנֶה׃

14 כִּי־בְאַחַת יְדַבֶּר־אֵל
וּבִשְׁתַּיִם לֹא יְשׁוּרֶנָּה׃

ח' זעירא v. 9.   מלרע באתנח v. 9.

the inflated and boastful introduction,
he addresses himself to Job's plea in
rebuke.

9. *I am clean.* Elihu quotes Job's
declaration in ix. 21, x. 7, xvi. 17, xxiii.
10ff., xxvii. 5f., xxxi. Peake points out
that Elihu is somewhat unfair in his
statement. Job had never claimed to be
perfect, without human frailty (cf. vii. 21,
xiii. 26).

I am innocent. Hebrew *chaph*, 'clean,'
occurs nowhere else.

10. *He findeth occasions against me.*
Hebrew *tenuoth*, rendered *occasions*, is
found again only in Num. xiv. 34, *dis-
pleasure.* A similar word occurs in
Judg. xiv. 4, *he sought* an occasion
against the Philistines. The word signifies 'a pretext for hostility.' Job had
made that charge against God in xix. 6.

He counteth me for His enemy. Cf.
xiii. 24, xix. 11, xxx. 21.

11. *He putteth my feet in the stocks.* Elihu
quotes Job's statement in xiii. 27.

12-28 GOD SPEAKS TO MAN IN
VARIOUS WAYS

12. *that God is too great for man.* So
many are the righteous deeds of God that
He does not have to stoop to petty scrutiny of man. He is above all arbitrary,
unreasoning hostility.

13. *why hast thou striven against Him?*
In line with God's greatness, He speaks
to man in many ways though He may
not answer when challenged as Job had
challenged Him (cf. xix. 7). Why is
Job so foolish as to attempt a futile
contest with God? He will not answer
you in the way you demand of Him. He
has His own way of answering, as Elihu
now proceeds to expound.

14. *for God speaketh in one way, yea in
two.* The soul of man gets more than
one chance to hear God's voice, but may
not perceive it. The first warning may
be reproof, the second punishment (Ibn
Ezra, Metsudath David). 'The meaning
may be that God's modes of revelation

15 In a dream, in a vision of the
   night,
   When deep sleep falleth upon
   men,
   In slumberings upon the bed;

16 Then He openeth the ears of men,
   And by their chastisement sealeth
   the decree,

17 That men may put away their
   purpose,
   And that He may hide pride from
   man;

18 That He may keep back his soul
   from the pit,
   And his life from perishing by
   the sword.

19 He is chastened also with pain
   upon his bed,
   And all his bones grow stiff;

20 So that his life maketh him to
   abhor bread,

בַּחֲלוֹם ׀ חֶזְיוֹן לַיְלָה
בִּנְפֹל תַּרְדֵּמָה עַל־אֲנָשִׁים
בִּתְנוּמוֹת עֲלֵי מִשְׁכָּב׃
אָז יִגְלֶה אֹזֶן אֲנָשִׁים
וּבְמֹסָרָם יַחְתֹּם׃
לְהָסִיר אָדָם מַעֲשֶׂה
וְגֵוָה מִגֶּבֶר יְכַסֶּה׃
יַחְשֹׂךְ נַפְשׁוֹ מִנִּי־שָׁחַת
וְחַיָּתוֹ מֵעֲבֹר בַּשָּׁלַח׃
וְהוּכַח בְּמַכְאוֹב עַל־מִשְׁכָּבוֹ
וְרִיב עֲצָמָיו אֵתָן׃
וְזִהֲמַתּוּ חַיָּתוֹ לָחֶם

ורוב ק׳ v. 19.

are invisible. The text is very elliptical.
The sense required seems to be that God
speaks in one way, and then if man does
not pay regard, He speaks in a second
way' (Peake).

15. *in a dream.* The first manner of
God's speaking to man is by dreams
when man is in a deep sleep. The lines
recall the view of Eliphaz as he describes
the way of God's revelation (iv. 13ff.).

16. *then He openeth the ears of men.* 'As
He did in the instance of Abimelech in a
dream of the night' (Gen. xx. 3) (Rashi).
Cf. I Sam. ix. 15, *Now the LORD had
revealed unto Samuel,* which is literally
'now the Lord had uncovered the ear of
Samuel.'

and by their chastisement sealeth the decree.
'He seals them and binds them with
chastisements because of their iniquities'
(Rashi). A.V. and R.V. render: 'and
sealeth their instruction,' i.e. He puts the
seal to, or confirms, their moral education
(viz. by dreams), so diverting a man
from his evil purpose, and warning
him of the consequences of persisting in
sin.

17. *that men may put away their purpose.*
i.e. their evil purpose. A.V. and R.V. read:
'That He may withdraw man from his
purpose.' Afflictions humble a man
and bring him down from pride.

that He may hide. Conceal pride, rid
man of this vice.

18. *from the pit.* Of destruction.

the sword. *Shelach* means 'missiles,
weapons' (again in xxxvi. 12). It is
figurative of God's retribution.

19. *pain upon his bed.* Another form of
God's speaking is the discipline of illness.
He mentions this as particularly applic-
able to Job's experience.

all his bones grow stiff. A doubtful
rendering. The *kerë* is to be translated
'while the multitude of his bones are
firm.' When illness is a visitation from
God it comes upon a man in the prime of
his life. R.V.: 'and with continual strife
in his bones,' which follows the *kethib*,
describes the torment of pain.

20. *his life.* Here, and again in xxxviii.
39, like its parallel *his soul,* in the sense
of 'appetite' (see on vi. 7).

And his soul dainty food.

21 His flesh is consumed away, that
it cannot be seen;
And his bones corrode to unsightliness.

22 Yea, his soul draweth near unto
the pit,
And his life to the destroyers.

23 If there be for him an angel,
An intercessor, one among a
thousand,
To vouch for man's uprightness;

24 Then He is gracious unto him,
and saith:
'Deliver him from going down to
the pit,
I have found a ransom.'

25 His flesh is tenderer than a
child's;

וְנַפְשׁוֹ מַאֲכַל תַּאֲוָה׃

21 יִכֶל בְּשָׂרוֹ מֵרֹאִי
וְשֻׁפִּי עַצְמוֹתָיו לֹא רֻאּוּ׃

22 וַתִּקְרַב לַשַּׁחַת נַפְשׁוֹ
וְחַיָּתוֹ לַמְמִתִים׃

23 אִם־יֵשׁ עָלָיו ׀ מַלְאָךְ
מֵלִיץ אֶחָד מִנִּי־אָלֶף
לְהַגִּיד לְאָדָם יָשְׁרוֹ׃

24 וַיְחֻנֶּנּוּ וַיֹּאמֶר
פְּדָעֵהוּ מֵרֶדֶת שָׁחַת
מָצָאתִי כֹפֶר׃

25 רֻטֲפַשׁ בְּשָׂרוֹ מִנֹּעַר

v. 21. א׳ דגושה ובק״ס הרי״ש דגושה   v. 21 ק׳ ושפר   .v. 21

---

maketh him to abhor. Hebrew *zaham*, occurring only here in the Piel conjugation with causative emphasis, 'be foul, loathsome'; 'his life maketh it, bread, loathsome to him' (BDB. Ibn Ezra calls attention to its Arabic derivation.

his soul dainty food. It is part of the symptom of sickness to feel loathing at the sight of food (cf. Ps. cvii. 18).

21. *his flesh is consumed.* His flesh wastes away until it cannot be seen. The language is hyperbolic. The text might be translated 'his flesh is consumed so as to lose its comeliness.'

his bones corrode to unsightliness. R.V.: 'And his bones that were not seen stick out.' The bones become pulled from their proper position, mis-shapen and unsightly.

22. *draweth near unto the pit.* His hold on life grows precarious in his bodily affliction.

the destroyers. 'The angels that kill' (Ibn Ezra). The expression has no exact parallel in Scripture; but references to

angels doing harm to men are found in 2 Sam. xxiv. 16; Ps. lxxviii. 49; 1 Chron. xxi. 15.

23. *if there be for him an angel.* Verses 23-25 probably mean: 'if there is an angel to interpret to the afflicted sinner the providential meaning of his sickness, and to lead him into the right way, and if God consequently has mercy upon him, and grants him a reprieve, then his health is restored' (Driver).

24. *then He is gracious.* viz. God, Who says to the intercessor, 'Deliver him' (Ibn Ezra). Others interpret the pronoun of the angel who, satisfied that the sufferer has learnt the lesson to be derived from his pains, becomes gracious towards him and prays to God on his behalf.

I have found a ransom. The *ransom* which is acceptable is the chastened mood of the afflicted person, induced in him by his experience.

25. *his flesh is tenderer than a child's.* Elihu describes the sufferer's recovery,

He returneth to the days of his
youth;

26 He prayeth unto God, and He is
favourable unto him;
So that he seeth His face with
joy;
And He restoreth unto man his
righteousness.

27 He cometh before men, and saith:
'I have sinned, and perverted
that which was right,
And it profited me not.'

28 So He redeemeth his soul from
going into the pit,
And his life beholdeth the light.

29 Lo, all these things doth God work,
Twice, yea thrice, with a man,

30 To bring back his soul from the
pit,
That he may be enlightened with
the light of the living.

יָשׁוּב לִימֵי עֲלוּמָיו׃

יֶעְתַּר אֶל־אֱלוֹהַּ ׀ וַיִּרְצֵהוּ

וַיַּרְא פָּנָיו בִּתְרוּעָה

וַיָּשֶׁב לֶאֱנוֹשׁ צִדְקָתוֹ׃

יָשֹׁר ׀ עַל־אֲנָשִׁים וַיֹּאמֶר

חָטָאתִי וְיָשָׁר הֶעֱוֵיתִי

וְלֹא־שָׁוָה לִי׃

פָּדָה נַפְשׁוֹ מֵעֲבֹר בַּשָּׁחַת

וְחַיָּתוֹ בָּאוֹר תִּרְאֶה׃

הֶן־כָּל־אֵלֶּה יִפְעַל־אֵל

פַּעֲמַיִם שָׁלוֹשׁ עִם־גָּבֶר׃

לְהָשִׁיב נַפְשׁוֹ מִנִּי־שָׁחַת

לֵאוֹר בְּאוֹר הַחַיִּים׃

v. 28. נפשו ק'   v. 28. וחיתו ק'

---

completely restored to the freshness of
childhood. A similar statement is made
of Naaman after he was cured of his
leprosy (2 Kings v. 14).

26. *he seeth His face with joy.* In addition to physical recovery, he also enjoys
restoration to God's favour. He is
admitted (in a spiritual sense) to God's
presence. This is the blessedness of
the righteous (cf. Ps. xi. 7).

27. *he cometh before men.* The verb
yashor translated *cometh* is uncertain.
R.V. has 'singeth,' the margin 'looketh
upon'; Ibn Ezra, 'go about.' Rashi
(having in mind the Talmudical passages
j.Yoma VIII, end 45c, b.Yoma 87a, 'let
him *form a line* of men and say, I have
sinned') interprets the word as the
Rabbis did to mean 'to form rows':
'Let him make rows of men, for he has
been snatched from his illness, and
confess to his Creator.' (This line of
thought, that sickness is punishment for
transgression, was the very doctrine
against which the genius who conceived
the Book of Job was protesting.)

I have sinned. The sinner, restored to
health, is pictured as giving public
expression to his gratitude by words of
confession and thanksgiving.

28. *his life beholdeth the light.* The light
of life, for God has saved him from the
darkness of the grave. The *kethib*,
adopted by R.V., reads 'my soul . . . my
life,' making the verse the assertion of
the recovered invalid. The *kerë* is
supported by the Targum and Vulgate.

29-30 THE DIVINE PURPOSE OF DISCIPLINE

29. *twice, yea thrice.* Rashi, quoting as
an example Amos i. 3, 6, etc., *for three
transgressions . . . yea, for four, I will not
reverse it*, remarks that God chastises a
man for his iniquities with sickness so
as not to destroy him. If, however, he
continues to provoke Him, he should be
gravely concerned with (the thought of)
Gehinnom and death., The warning of
God, *twice, yea thrice*, is taken literally
by Berechiah.

30. *the light of the living.* A phrase of the

31 Mark well, O Job, hearken unto
   me;
   Hold thy peace, and I will speak.

32 If thou hast any thing to say,
   answer me;
   Speak, for I desire to justify thee.

33 If not, hearken thou unto me;
   Hold thy peace, and I will teach
   thee wisdom.

הַקְשֵׁב אִיּוֹב שְׁמַע־לִי 31
הַחֲרֵשׁ וְאָנֹכִי אֲדַבֵּר׃

אִם־יֵשׁ־מִלִּין הֲשִׁיבֵנִי 32
דַּבֵּר כִּי־חָפַצְתִּי צַדְּקֶךָּ׃

אִם־אַיִן אַתָּה שְׁמַע־לִי 33
הַחֲרֵשׁ וַאֲאַלֶּפְךָ חָכְמָה׃

34   CHAPTER XXXIV   לד

1 Moreover Elihu answered and
   said:

2 Hear my words, ye wise men;
   And give ear unto me, ye that have
   knowledge.

3 For the ear trieth words,
   As the palate tasteth food.

וַיַּעַן אֱלִיהוּא וַיֹּאמַר׃ 1

שִׁמְעוּ חֲכָמִים מִלָּי 2
וְיֹדְעִים הַאֲזִינוּ לִי׃

כִּי־אֹזֶן מִלִּין תִּבְחָן 3
וְחֵךְ יִטְעַם לֶאֱכֹל׃

Psalmist (lvi. 14), beautiful in its suggestion of one's life illumined by the
Divine Presence, and striking in contrast
with the gloom of the grave.

31-33   JOB URGED TO LISTEN
TO WHAT FOLLOWS

31. *mark well, O Job.* As if Elihu said,
'I was quiet, Job, while you raged.
Now you listen to me!'

32. *if thou hast any thing to say.* Elihu
wants to be fair. If Job has an answer,
let him reply.

I desire to justify thee. The tone seems
to be piously, perhaps too piously, in-
gratiating. The friends, Elihu appears
to imply, have condemned you outright.
I would like, if at all possible, to show
that you are in the right.

33. *I will teach thee wisdom.* If the
wisdom that we finally extract from the

Elihu speeches could match the magnificence that we find elsewhere in this
immortal spiritual epic, we could listen
with better grace. As it is, the modern
reader bears with some impatience this
pompous and vainglorious teacher of
wisdom. It hardly probes deeper into the
mystery of human suffering than Job
and his friends have led us.

CHAPTER XXXIV

2-9   ELIHU SUMMARIZES JOB'S PLEA

2. *ye wise men.* Elihu addresses the
bystanders and appeals to their sense of
what is right (cf. verses 10, 34), as he is
about to take up Job's complaint that
God had dealt unjustly with him.

3. *the ear trieth words.* An echo of Job's
own words in xii. 11. The *ear* is the
faculty of human reason. It can judge,
even as the palate can taste food.

4 Let us choose for us that which is
    right;
    Let us know among ourselves
      what is good.

5 For Job hath said: 'I am righteous,
    And God hath taken away my
      right;

6 Notwithstanding my right I am
      accounted a liar;
    My wound is incurable, though I
      am without transgression.'

7 What man is like Job,
    Who drinketh up scorning like
      water?

8 Who goeth in company with the
      workers of iniquity,
    And walketh with wicked men.

9 For he hath said: 'It profiteth a
      man nothing
    That he should be in accord with
      God.'

10 Therefore hearken unto me, ye
      men of understanding:
    Far be it from God, that He
      should do wickedness;

4 מִשְׁפָּט נִבְחֲרָה־לָּנוּ

נֵדְעָה בֵינֵינוּ מַה־טּוֹב׃

5 כִּי־אָמַר אִיּוֹב צָדַקְתִּי

וְאֵל הֵסִיר מִשְׁפָּטִי׃

6 עַל־מִשְׁפָּטִי אֲכַזֵּב

אָנוּשׁ חִצִּי בְלִי־פָשַׁע׃

7 מִי־גֶבֶר כְּאִיּוֹב

יִשְׁתֶּה־לַּעַג כַּמָּיִם׃

8 וְאָרַח לְחֶבְרָה עִם־פֹּעֲלֵי אָוֶן

וְלָלֶכֶת עִם־אַנְשֵׁי־רֶשַׁע׃

9 כִּי־אָמַר לֹא יִסְכָּן־גָּבֶר

בִּרְצֹתוֹ עִם־אֱלֹהִים׃

10 לָכֵן ׀ אַנְשֵׁי לֵבָב שִׁמְעוּ לִי

חָלִלָה לָאֵל מֵרֶשַׁע

v. 5. פתח באתנח

4. *that which is right.* We must try to
determine whether Job has a just griev-
ance against God.

5. *for Job hath said.* Elihu, like one who
advances the rebuttal in a formal debate,
takes up Job's claim of innocence.

6. *notwithstanding my right.* Elihu is
still restating Job's challenge of God's
justice and his complaint that he is
considered a liar when he protests his
integrity.

my wound. Apparently lit. 'my arrow,'
and usually explained as metaphorical for
the wound inflicted by God's arrow
(cf. vi. 4, xvi. 13). Eitan, however,
connects *chets* with a corresponding
Arabic noun and translates 'my lot is
woeful.' The word for *woeful* is found
in that sense in Jer. xvii. 16.

7. *drinketh up scorning like water.*
Although Elihu piously claims that he
wishes to be fair, his abhorrence of

Job's heresies breaks out here. For the
image, cf. xv. 16. Note that Elihu has
plumed himself with Eliphaz's feathers.

8. *walketh with wicked men.* Cf. xxii.
15; Ps. i. 1. In giving expression to
his views, Job finds himself in bad
company.

9. *for he hath said.* Job had never said
precisely what Elihu attributes to him,
but the inference is not unfair on the
basis of such passages as ix. 22, 31f.,
x. 3, xxi. 7ff.

it profiteth a man nothing. 'It profiteth
not a man if his ways are pure' (Rashi).
In chapter xxxv Elihu will deal with this
charge. For the present, he is concerned
with the general impeachment of God's
justice.

10-15 GOD NEVER ACTS UNFAIRLY

10. *far be it from God.* Cf. Gen. xviii. 25.
See also Bildad's question in viii. 3.
Elihu echoes it in verses 10-12.

And from the Almighty, that He
should commit iniquity.

11 For the work of a man will He
requite unto him,
And cause every man to find
according to his ways.

12 Yea, of a surety, God will not do
wickedly,
Neither will the Almighty pervert justice.

13 Who gave Him a charge over the
earth?
Or who hath disposed the whole
world?

14 If He set His heart upon man,
If He gather unto Himself his
spirit and his breath;

15 All flesh shall perish together,
And man shall return unto dust.

16 If now thou hast understanding,
hear this;
Hearken to the voice of my
words.

וְשַׁדַּי מֵעָוֶל׃

11 כִּי פֹעַל אָדָם יְשַׁלֶּם־לֹו
וּכְאֹרַח אִישׁ יַמְצִאֶנּוּ׃

12 אַף־אָמְנָם אֵל לֹא־יַרְשִׁיעַ
וְשַׁדַּי לֹא־יְעַוֵּת מִשְׁפָּט׃

13 מִי־פָקַד עָלָיו אָרְצָה
וּמִי שָׂם תֵּבֵל כֻּלָּהּ׃

14 אִם־יָשִׂים אֵלָיו לִבֹּו
רוּחֹו וְנִשְׁמָתֹו אֵלָיו יֶאֱסֹף׃

15 יִגְוַע כָּל־בָּשָׂר יָחַד
וְאָדָם עַל־עָפָר יָשׁוּב׃

16 וְאִם־בִּינָה שִׁמְעָה־זֹּאת
הַאֲזִינָה לְקֹול מִלָּי׃

v. 14. למדנחאי ישיב כתיב ישים ק׳

11. *the work of a man.* ' Whether he be
good or evil' (Metsudath David).

12. *God will not do wickedly.* Elihu
maintains that the nature of God is such
that it excludes and is incompatible with
the concept of injustice. 'Elihu's argument in these verses is the truest answer
that can be given: injustice on the part
of God is inconsistent with the idea of
God' (Davidson).

13. *who gave Him a charge over the earth?*
God is supreme over all, not under the
direction of another.

who hath disposed the whole world? Who
created the universe and all in it ? (Ibn
Ezra). The question, rhetorical in
character, admits of only one reply:
no one but God Himself. He is the One
and Only Ruler of the world.

14. *upon man.* lit. 'upon him.' The
meaning may be: if God were to scrutin-

ize man, noticing minutely his every sin,
no one would live. Davidson is of the
opinion that the more probable interpretation is that if God were to think
only of Himself, and ceased to think of
all creatures with a benevolent consideration, giving them life and upholding them
by His spirit, all flesh would perish.

15. *all flesh shall perish together.* Cf.
Gen. iii. 19; Eccles. xii. 7. 'God supplies
to all men of His own spirit, and were
He a capricious or unrighteous Deity,
He might at any moment withdraw
the boon of life; that man still lives on
proves His benevolent care' (Peake).

16-20 UNTHINKABLE THAT THE WORLD'S
RULER IS UNJUST

16. *if now thou hast understanding.* Elihu
again addresses himself to Job. Rashi
parses *binah* here not as a noun but the
imperative of the verb; but this is
grammatically impossible.

17 Shall even one that hateth right
   govern?
   And wilt thou condemn Him that
   is just and mighty—

18 Is it fit to say to a king: 'Thou
   art base'?
   Or to nobles: 'Ye are wicked'?—

19 That respecteth not the persons
   of princes,
   Nor regardeth the rich more than
   the poor?
   For they all are the work of His
   hands.

20 In a moment they die, even at
   midnight;
   The people are shaken and pass
   away,
   And the mighty are taken away
   without hand.

21 For His eyes are upon the ways of
   a man,
   And He seeth all his goings.

22 There is no darkness, nor shadow
   of death,

17 הַאַף שׂוֹנֵא מִשְׁפָּט יַחֲבֹשׁ
וְאִם־צַדִּיק כַּבִּיר תַּרְשִׁיעַ׃

18 הַאֲמֹר לְמֶלֶךְ בְּלִיָּעַל
רָשָׁע אֶל־נְדִיבִים׃

19 אֲשֶׁר לֹא־נָשָׂא ׀ פְּנֵי שָׂרִים
וְלֹא נִכַּר־שׁוֹעַ לִפְנֵי־דָל
כִּי־מַעֲשֵׂה יָדָיו כֻּלָּם׃

20 רֶגַע ׀ יָמֻתוּ וַחֲצוֹת לָיְלָה
יְגֹעֲשׁוּ עָם וְיַעֲבֹרוּ
וְיָסִירוּ אַבִּיר לֹא בְיָד׃

21 כִּי־עֵינָיו עַל־דַּרְכֵי־אִישׁ
וְכָל־צְעָדָיו יִרְאֶה׃

22 אֵין־חֹשֶׁךְ וְאֵין צַלְמָוֶת

17. *shall even one that hateth right govern?*
Peake calls this way of arguing 'a strange
begging of the question,' and says, 'The
pious man may laudably assert the
righteousness of God's rule, but it is
out of place to assert it in an argument,
where it is the very point to be proved.'
Davidson defends Elihu on the ground
that he is dealing with principles, and
the fact that God of His own will made
the world and governs it creates a presumption, to say the least, that His
government is just.

18. *is it fit to say to a king: 'Thou art
base'?* On the surface, the argument is
not convincing. One thinks of the prophet Nathan doing that very thing to
king David (2 Sam. xii. 7). But he is not
thinking of a particular king who proved
himself base, but of kings in general.
If this is true of earthly rulers, how is it
possible to impute unfairness to the
Ruler of the universe?

19. *that respecteth not.* God is absolutely
impartial. All creatures are the work of

His hands, and the difference in their
stations does not count with Him.

20. *in a moment they die.* Elihu gives
this example of God's just rule against
wicked rulers and their followers.

even at midnight. i.e. suddenly and
unexpectedly (again in verse 25).

without hand. Through no human,
visible hand but by the unseen might of
God (cf. Lam. iv. 6; Dan. ii. 34, viii. 25).

21-30 GOD KNOWS ALL WHEN HE
CONDEMNS

21. *for His eyes are upon the ways of a
man.* To the human being with his
imperfect knowledge, God's judgments
may appear at times fallible; but He
knows all and His verdict is the consequence of His complete awareness of all
the circumstances.

22. *there is no darkness.* Cf. Ps. cxxxix.
12. Nothing can be hidden from God's
scrutiny.

Where the workers of iniquity
may hide themselves.

23 For He doth not appoint a time
unto any man,
When he should go before God
in judgment.

24 He breaketh in pieces mighty
men without inquisition,
And setteth others in their stead.

25 Therefore He taketh knowledge
of their works;
And He overturneth them in the
night, so that they are crushed.

26 He striketh them as wicked men
In the open sight of others;

27 Because they turned aside from
following Him,
And would not have regard to
any of His ways;

28 So that they cause the cry of the
poor to come unto Him,
And He heareth the cry of the
afflicted.

לְהִסָּתֶר שָׁם פֹּעֲלֵי אָוֶן׃

23 כִּי לֹא עַל־אִישׁ יָשִׂים עוֹד
לַהֲלֹךְ אֶל־אֵל בַּמִּשְׁפָּט׃

24 יָרֹעַ כַּבִּירִים לֹא־חֵקֶר
וַיַּעֲמֵד אֲחֵרִים תַּחְתָּם׃

25 לָכֵן יַכִּיר מַעְבָּדֵיהֶם
וְהָפַךְ לַיְלָה וְיִדַּכָּאוּ׃

26 תַּחַת־רְשָׁעִים סְפָקָם
בִּמְקוֹם רֹאִים׃

27 אֲשֶׁר עַל־כֵּן סָרוּ מֵאַחֲרָיו
וְכָל־דְּרָכָיו לֹא הִשְׂכִּילוּ׃

28 לְהָבִיא עָלָיו צַעֲקַת־דָּל
וְצַעֲקַת עֲנִיִּים יִשְׁמָע׃

23. *for He doth not appoint a time unto any man.* An improbable rendering. Rashi interprets the first line: 'For He doth not impose upon a man more (than his guilt deserves).' Continue with 'to proceed against God in judgment' and this yields a satisfactory sense. R.V. has: 'For He needeth not further to consider a man, that he should go before God in judgment,' i.e. He knows all the time what a man is doing and can punish him whenever He thinks fit without a formal inquiry.

24. *without inquisition.* God is omniscient. He needs no special investigation to remove the mighty when they act unjustly and put others in their place of rulership.

25. *He taketh knowledge of their works.* God's judgment unfailingly overtakes the powerful oppressor, and His punishment comes with unexpected suddenness (*in the night*).

26. *as wicked men.* lit. 'instead of' or 'in the place of wicked men.' The preposition is used here in the unusual sense of 'as if they were.' Although they are men of high station, they meet the fate of the common criminal.

in the open sight. lit. 'in the place of beholders'; 'in sight of all' (Rashi).

27. *because they turned aside.* Therefore they are punished, regardless of their eminence.

28. *they cause the cry of the poor to come unto Him.* Oppressors bring destruction upon themselves. The cry of the poor whom they exploit rises to God, and He comes to their rescue striking down the tyrants.

29. *when He giveth quietness.* The verse is difficult. The first line may mean; if God does not intervene to hinder wrong, man has no right to condemn Him.

29 When He giveth quietness, who
then can condemn?
And when He hideth His face,
who then can behold Him?
Whether it be done unto a nation,
or unto a man, alike;

30 That the godless man reign not,
That there be none to ensnare the
people.

31 For hath any said unto God:
'I have borne chastisement,
though I offend not;

32 That which I see not teach Thou
me;
If I have done iniquity, I will do
it no more'?

33 Shall His recompense be as thou
wilt? For thou loathest it,
So that thou must choose, and
not I;
Therefore speak what thou
knowest.

34 Men of understanding will say
unto me,
Yea, every wise man that heareth
me:

²וְהוּא יַשְׁקִט ׀ וּמִי יַרְשִׁעַ
וְיַסְתֵּר פָּנִים וּמִי יְשׁוּרֶנּוּ
וְעַל־גּוֹי וְעַל־אָדָם יָחַד׃

³מִמְּלֹךְ אָדָם חָנֵף
מִמֹּקְשֵׁי עָם׃

³כִּי־אֶל־אֵל הֶאָמַר נָשָׂאתִי
לֹא אֶחְבֹּל׃

³בִּלְעֲדֵי אֶחֱזֶה אַתָּה הֹרֵנִי
אִם־עָוֶל פָּעַלְתִּי לֹא אֹסִיף׃

³הַמֵעִמְּךָ יְשַׁלְמֶנָּה ׀ כִּי־מָאַסְתָּ
כִּי־אַתָּה תִבְחַר וְלֹא־אָנִי
וּמַה־יָדַעְתָּ דַבֵּר׃

³אַנְשֵׁי לֵבָב יֹאמְרוּ לִי
וְגֶבֶר חָכָם שֹׁמֵעַ לִי׃

when He hideth His face. Repeats the
meaning of He giveth quietness. Driver
suggests this interpretation: 'When God
giveth rest (from tyrannical rule), who
can condemn Him (for indifference or
injustice)? and when He hideth His face
(viz. from the deposed tyrant in dis-
pleasure), who can behold Him (i.e.
recover His favour)? Verse 30 then states
the object for which God interferes in
such ways.' God is both sovereign and
just over nations and individuals alike.

30. ensnare the people. For the phrase,
meaning to lure on to ruin, cf. 1 Sam.
xviii. 21.

31-37 JOB CRITICIZES GOD IN IGNORANCE

31. hath any said. Elihu, of course, has
Job in mind. Has any one had the
effrontery to complain to God that he has
been treated unjustly, and punished for
offences of which he has no knowledge?

32. that which I see not teach Thou me.
Cf. Job's words in xiii. 23. The com-
plainant is represented as pleading, 'Tell
me the sins of which I have no knowledge,' and once his offence is clear to
him, he will desist from it.

33. as thou wilt. Elihu scornfully asks,
'If Job presumes to dictate the Divine
government of recompense, let him propose a better economy of the moral order.
Job, who is dissatisfied, must suggest
the alternative, not I who am content
with God's government.'

therefore speak. Elihu challenges Job to
state a better system of providence.
What would Job propose?

34. men of understanding. Elihu, in verse
10, had made that appeal before. All
reasonable men will condemn Job for
complaining of God's rule of the world.

35 'Job speaketh without knowledge,
   And his words are without dis-
   cernment.'

36 Would that Job were tried unto
   the end,
   Because of his answering like
   wicked men.

37 For he addeth rebellion unto his
   sin,
   He clappeth his hands among us,
   And multiplieth his words against
   God.

35 אִיּוֹב לֹא־בְדַעַת יְדַבֵּר
   וּדְבָרָיו לֹא בְהַשְׂכֵּיל:

36 אָבִי יִבָּחֵן אִיּוֹב עַד־נֶצַח
   עַל־תְּשֻׁבֹת בְּאַנְשֵׁי־אָוֶן:

37 כִּי יֹסִיף עַל־חַטָּאתוֹ פֶשַׁע
   בֵּינֵינוּ יִסְפּוֹק
   וְיֶרֶב אֲמָרָיו לָאֵל:

CHAPTER XXXV

35

לה

1 Moreover Elihu answered and
   said:

2 Thinkest thou this to be thy right,
   Or sayest thou: 'I am righteous
   before God,'

1 וַיַּעַן אֱלִיהוּ וַיֹּאמַר:

2 הֲזֹאת חָשַׁבְתָּ לְמִשְׁפָּט
   אָמַרְתָּ צִדְקִי מֵאֵל:

v. 1. בנ״א אליהוא

---

35. *Job speaketh without knowledge.* Such,
contends Elihu, is the judgment of men
of understanding for inveighing against
the moral economy as ordained by God.

36. *would that Job were tried unto the end.*
Cf. Job's words in vii. 18. 'Elihu would
have kept Job on the rack till he changed
his tone. This verse and the following
seem to show that Elihu charges Job, as
the friends had done (*a*) with sin which
had caused his punishment (*b*) with rebellious language against God under his
punishment' (Peake).

37. *rebellion unto his sin.* Elihu, like
Eliphaz in xxii., charges Job's former life
with secret sin. His *rebellion* consists in
the defiant speeches he uttered against
God's justice.

clappeth his hands. An insulting gesture
(see on xxvii. 23). Job claps his hands
in open mockery of God's rule. 'Elihu's
position in this chapter is substantially
that of the friends. The Ruler of the
universe cannot be unjust . . . God's
omniscience had been confessed quite
freely by Job, but it made the problem
more difficult rather than more simple.
The exhortation to Job is conceived in
a spirit more reprehensible even than
that of the friends' (Peake).

CHAPTER XXXV

2-8 JOB'S CLAIM ANSWERED THAT RIGHTEOUSNESS IS UNAVAILING

2. *this.* Alluding to what follows in
verse 3. Job had maintained that to be
righteous was not advantageous to a man.

'*I am righteous before God.*' lit. 'from (or,
more than) God'; hence Ibn Ezra's
translation, 'my righteousness is greater
than (the righteousness of) God,' which
is followed by A.V. and R.V. An alternative rendering is: '(this is) my vindication against God,' referring again to the
question in the next verse.

3 That thou inquirest: 'What ad-
    vantage will it be unto Thee?'
   And: 'What profit shall I have,
    more than if I had sinned?'

4 I will give thee answer,
  And thy companions with thee.

5 Look unto the heavens, and see;
  And behold the skies, which are
    higher than thou.

6 If thou hast sinned, what doest
   thou against Him?
  And if thy transgressions be multiplied, what doest thou unto
   Him?

7 If thou be righteous, what givest
  thou Him?

כִּי־תֹאמַר מַה־יִּסְכָּן־לָךְ 3
מָה אֹעִיל מֵחַטָּאתִי:

אֲנִי אֲשִׁיבְךָ מִלִּין 4
וְאֶת־רֵעֶיךָ עִמָּךְ:

הַבֵּט שָׁמַיִם וּרְאֵה 5
וְשׁוּר שְׁחָקִים גָּבְהוּ מִמֶּךָּ:

אִם־חָטָאתָ מַה־תִּפְעָל־בּוֹ 6
וְרַבּוּ פְשָׁעֶיךָ מַה־תַּעֲשֶׂה־לּוֹ:

אִם־צָדַקְתָּ מַה־תִּתֶּן־לוֹ 7

3. *'what advantage will it be unto Thee?'*
Cf. xxxiv. 9 where the offending statement of Job is made. It is doubtful,
however, whether *Thee* refers to God.
In the context it reads more like a taunt
hurled by Job at one of his antagonists
in a moment of bitterness.

4. *I will give thee answer.* The personal
pronoun is emphatic in the Hebrew.

and thy companions with thee. 'Who are
silent at thy words'; so Rashi who understands the *companions* to be the three
friends. But modern scholars, like
Davidson, question whether Elihu has
reference to them. Eliphaz (xxii. 2) had
advanced substantially the same answer
to Job as here given. Even Job had
touched upon it, though with a different
purpose, in vii. 20. 'The words,' says
Kraeling, one of the latest scholars to
deal with Job, 'seem to imply that there
are people on Job's side. . . . Perhaps the
Elihu editor . . . is thinking of the fact
that there are wise men of a sceptical
turn of mind who take this same position,
and thus are "companions" of the hero.'
Davidson makes a similar conjecture.
Job may have been, he remarks, the
centre of a circle of persons who cherished
the same irreligious doubts in regard to
God's providence as he did.

5. *look unto the heavens, and see.* Cf.
Eliphaz's words in xxii. 12. 'Since He

is lofty and thou art low and He hath no
benefit in thy wickedness or righteousness, wherefore dost thou vaunt thyself
before Him with thy righteousness?'
(Rashi). Elihu argues that God is far too
lofty to be affected one way or another by
human conduct. It is consequently
only men themselves who are either
benefited by their righteousness, or injured by their sin. The argument as-
sumes that some one must be both
benefited by righteousness and injured
by sin (Driver).

and behold the skies. The heavens and
the skies are regarded as the infinitely
exalted abode of God. Our conduct is
no advantage or disadvantage to Him.
It is men themselves who are affected by
their own wickedness or righteousness.
Davidson reminds us that Job had risen
to the sublime height of resolving to
adhere to righteousness, though God and
men should show their indifference to it
(xvii. 9).

6. *if thou hast sinned.* Elihu is using
Eliphaz's argument in xxii. 2f. both
here and in verse 7. But compare Job's
own words in vii. 20.

7. *if thou be righteous, what givest thou
Him?* 'What is the thing that thou canst
give unto Him?' (Metsudath David).
Elihu seems to be making a different

Or what receiveth He of thy hand?

8 Thy wickedness concerneth a man
as thou art;
And thy righteousness a son of
man.

9 By reason of the multitude of
oppressions they cry out;
They cry for help by reason of the
arm of the mighty.

10 But none saith: 'Where is God
my Maker,
Who giveth songs in the night;

11 Who teacheth us more than the
beasts of the earth,
And maketh us wiser than the
fowls of heaven?'

12 There they cry, but none giveth
answer,
Because of the pride of evil men.

אוֹ־מַה־מִיָּדְךָ יִקָּח:

8 לְאִישׁ־כָּמוֹךָ רִשְׁעֶךָ
וּלְבֶן־אָדָם צִדְקָתֶךָ:

9 מֵרֹב עֲשׁוּקִים יַזְעִיקוּ
יְשַׁוְּעוּ מִזְּרוֹעַ רַבִּים:

10 וְלֹא־אָמַר אַיֵּה אֱלוֹהַּ עֹשָׂי
נֹתֵן זְמִרוֹת בַּלָּיְלָה:

11 מַלְּפֵנוּ מִבַּהֲמוֹת אָרֶץ
וּמֵעוֹף הַשָּׁמַיִם יְחַכְּמֵנוּ:

12 שָׁם יִצְעֲקוּ וְלֹא יַעֲנֶה
מִפְּנֵי גְּאוֹן רָעִים:

point which Peake expresses well: 'Self-interest is accordingly not present in God as a disturbing influence to entice Him from the path of justice. He must therefore treat men according to their deserts.'

8. *thy wickedness concerneth a man as thou art.* lit. 'to a man as thou art is thy wickedness.' Thy wickedness or right-eousness affects thee alone; it cannot touch God, exalted in the skies.

9-16 WHY THE INNOCENT CRY OUT IN THEIR SUFFERING

9. *the multitude of oppressions.* Elihu now tries to deal with the seeming anomaly that God often does not apparently answer the cry of the innocent when they are oppressed. The argument he advances on behalf of the Almighty is that they cry amiss. Their outburst is only the instinctive cry of pain. They make no true, pious appeal to heaven, really seeking help from God. Peake asks the embarrassing question, 'But if God's rule is righteous, why the cry of the oppressed?' The argument that God needs a pious petition to work His righteousness on earth is an illuminating

flash revealing the nature of the religious and spiritual horizon of the loquacious Elihu.

10. *where is God my Maker.* Elihu asserts that God enables those whom He has delivered to utter songs of thanks-giving in the night (cf. Ps. xlii. 9, xcii. 3). Peake movingly writes, 'The reason is that their cry is not the cry for God, but simply for relief. Suffering should send man to God. . . . Even in the dark hours of pain, God fills the sufferer with rap-ture, that bursts instinctively into songs of praise.'

11. *Who teacheth us more than the beasts.* 'God has given to men a higher wisdom than to the beasts, and communicates to them a continuous instruction through His fellowship and ways. Their appeal to heaven should not be the mere in-stinctive cry of suffering, but the voice of trust and submission' (Davidson).

12. *none giveth aswer.* lit. 'He answereth not.' In the context the meaning is that their cry is not answered by God because it is the cry of pride. Hence it is vain, lacking humility.

13 Surely God will not hear vanity,
Neither will the Almighty regard
it.

אַךְ־שָׁוְא לֹא־יִשְׁמַע | אֵל 13
וְשַׁדַּי לֹא יְשׁוּרֶנָּה:

14 Yea, when thou sayest thou canst
not see Him—
The cause is before Him; therefore wait thou for Him.

אַף כִּי־תֹאמַר לֹא תְשׁוּרֶנּוּ 14
דִּין לְפָנָיו וּתְחוֹלֵל לוֹ:

15 And now, is it for nought that
He punished in His anger?
And hath He not full knowledge
of arrogance?

וְעַתָּה כִּי־אַיִן פָּקַד אַפּוֹ 15
וְלֹא־יָדַע בַּפַּשׁ מְאֹד:

16 But Job doth open his mouth in
vanity;
He multiplieth words without
knowledge.

וְאִיּוֹב הֶבֶל יִפְצֶה־פִּיהוּ 16
בִּבְלִי־דַעַת מִלִּין יַכְבִּר:

36   CHAPTER XXXVI   לו

1 Elihu also proceeded, and said:

וַיֹּסֶף אֱלִיהוּא וַיֹּאמַר: 1

2 Suffer me a little, and I will tell
thee;
For there are yet words on God's
behalf.

כַּתַּר־לִי זְעֵיר וַאֲחַוֶּךָּ 2
כִּי־עוֹד לֶאֱלוֹהַּ מִלִּים:

---

13. *vanity.* i.e. lacking substance and
reality, only a cry of anguish (see on
verse 9), without the feeling of humble
trust in God (verses 10f.).

14. *thou canst not see Him.* Elihu recalls Job's outcries in xiii. 24, xxiii. 8f.,
xxx. 20. 'Even though thou art not able
to see the Omnipresent God, the cause is
before Him' (Ibn Ezra). Elihu appears
to admonish Job not to lose hope or
become impatient. Some scholars hold
that Elihu is not thinking of Job, but is
speaking in general terms. The verse is
somewhat obscure.

15. *arrogance.* Hebrew *pash,* 'folly'
(BDB). The word occurs nowhere else.
Because God seems to be slow to punish
wickedness, Job has drawn the conclusion that He is indifferent. Hence,
righteousness no more avails one than
wickedness.

16. *in vanity.* Hebrew *hebel,* the word
which occurs often in Ecclesiastes. The
meaning is 'emptiness.' Job has empty,
hollow complaints against God.

CHAPTERS XXXVI-XXXVII

GOD'S PROVIDENTIAL DEALINGS
WITH MEN

CHAPTER XXXVI

2-21   GOD'S DESIGN IN
HUMAN AFFLICTION

2. *suffer me.* Hebrew *kattar,* 'wait, I
pray' (as in Aramaic) (BDB). Ibn Ezra
points out the similarity of the unusual
word to the Hebrew *kether,* 'crown,' and
suggests as the meaning, 'Show me a
little honour.' Elihu still has important
arguments to advance to justify God's
ways with man.

3 I will fetch my knowledge from afar,
And will ascribe righteousness to my Maker.

4 For truly my words are not false;
One that is upright in mind is with thee.

5 Behold, God is mighty, yet He despiseth not any;
He is mighty in strength of understanding.

6 He preserveth not the life of the wicked;
But giveth to the poor their right.

7 He withdraweth not His eyes from the righteous;
But with kings upon the throne He setteth them for ever, and they are exalted.

8 And if they be bound in fetters,
And be holden in cords of affliction;

3 אֶשָּׂא דֵעִי לְמֵרָחוֹק
וּלְפֹעֲלִי אֶתֵּן־צֶדֶק:

4 כִּי־אָמְנָם לֹא־שֶׁקֶר מִלָּי
תְּמִים דֵּעוֹת עִמָּךְ:

5 הֶן־אֵל כַּבִּיר וְלֹא יִמְאָס
כַּבִּיר כֹּחַ לֵב:

6 לֹא־יְחַיֶּה רָשָׁע
וּמִשְׁפַּט עֲנִיִּים יִתֵּן:

7 לֹא־יִגְרַע מִצַּדִּיק עֵינָיו
וְאֶת־מְלָכִים לַכִּסֵּא
וַיֹּשִׁיבֵם לָנֶצַח וַיִּגְבָּהוּ:

8 וְאִם־אֲסוּרִים בַּזִּקִּים
יִלָּכְדוּן בְּחַבְלֵי־עֹנִי:

3. *I will fetch my knowledge from afar.* Ibn Ezra interprets *from afar* as 'from God' Who is far off above. It may also mean, he says, that he will lift up (so *fetch* lit.) his knowledge (his voice of knowledge) and it will be heard afar. Modern scholars interpret: He will deal with the subject comprehensively, embracing distant parts of his theme.

4. *one that is upright in mind.* Ibn Ezra understands this of God, and in fact a similar phrase is attributed to Him in xxxvii. 16. But the moderns agree with Rashi that Elihu, immodestly, is speaking of himself. R.V. renders: 'One that is perfect in knowledge is with thee.'

5. *God is mighty.* 'In wisdom and compassion' (Rashi).

He despiseth not any. The fact that God is mighty does not imply that He lacks justice and mercy. The lowliest is not beneath His notice. He has the strength of understanding to discriminate between the righteous and the wicked. Job had denied this in ix. 22ff.

strength of understanding. lit. 'of heart,' the seat of understanding. God's consideration for all His creatures is the effect of the 'might' of His *understanding*.

6. *He preserveth not the life of the wicked.* Job had contended that the tents of robbers prosper and that the wicked live and grow old in power (xii. 6, xxi. 7ff., xxiv. 1ff.). This is Elihu's answer to that allegation.

7. *He setteth them for ever.* God's providence is over all, especially watchful of the lowly righteous whom He has exalted (cf. Ps. cxiii. 6ff.). 'He exalts kings to a throne; and if they are proud, He humbles them' (Ibn Ezra).

8. *holden in cords of affliction.* Elihu is expounding his theory of affliction as God's discipline. It stirs the righteous from their lethargy. When they are afflicted, they think of their experience as a warning from God to scrutinize their actions and amend what is wrong.

9 Then He declareth unto them
their work,
And their transgressions, that
they have behaved themselves
proudly.

10 He openeth also their ear to discipline,
And commandeth that they return from iniquity.

11 If they hearken and serve Him,
They shall spend their days in
prosperity,
And their years in pleasures.

12 But if they hearken not, they shall
perish by the sword,
And they shall die without
knowledge.

13 But they that are godless in heart
lay up anger;
They cry not for help when He
bindeth them.

14 Their soul perisheth in youth,
And their life as that of the depraved.

15 He delivereth the afflicted by His
affliction,
And openeth their ear by tribulation.

וַיַּגֵּד לָהֶם פָּעֳלָם

וּפִשְׁעֵיהֶם כִּי יִתְגַּבָּרוּ׃

וַיִּגֶל אָזְנָם לַמּוּסָר

וַיֹּאמֶר כִּי־יְשׁוּבוּן מֵאָוֶן׃

אִם־יִשְׁמְעוּ וְיַעֲבֹדוּ

יְכַלּוּ יְמֵיהֶם בַּטּוֹב

וּשְׁנֵיהֶם בַּנְּעִימִים׃

וְאִם־לֹא יִשְׁמְעוּ בְּשֶׁלַח יַעֲבֹרוּ

וְיִגְוְעוּ בִּבְלִי דָעַת׃

וְחַנְפֵי־לֵב יָשִׂימוּ אָף

לֹא יְשַׁוְּעוּ כִּי אֲסָרָם׃

תָּמֹת בַּנֹּעַר נַפְשָׁם

וְחַיָּתָם בַּקְּדֵשִׁים׃

יְחַלֵּץ עָנִי בְעָנְיוֹ

וְיִגֶל בַּלַּחַץ אָזְנָם׃

---

9. *their work.* Their evil work. 'With
these afflictions He makes them know
that they have sinned before Him. All
the words of Elihu are perfect consolations and not reproaches, as if to say,
"Worry not about the afflictions if thou
art righteous, because they are for thy
good" ' (Rashi).

10. *discipline.* Hebrew *musar*, translated
instruction in Prov. i. 2. It is a crucial
word in the Book of Proverbs and in
Jewish ethical thought generally.

11. *hearken and serve Him.* The text
does not include *Him*, but it is to be
understood.

pleasures. Here in the sense of material
pleasures. In Ps. xvi. 6, 11 (here another
form of the noun) the word is used of
spiritual bliss.

12. *the sword.* Elihu had used the word
shelach in xxxiii. 18.

die without knowledge. Cf. Eliphaz's
words in iv. 21.

13. *godless in heart lay up anger.* The
godless do not accept God's affliction
in the right spirit as Divine discipline,
but cherish resentment at His dealings
with them.

they cry not for help. Being resentful,
they refuse to appeal to God in their
distress.

14. *their soul perisheth in youth.* They
die an early and shameful death.

depraved. lit. 'consecrated,' to depraved
rites in idolatrous worship (cf. Deut.
xxiii. 18; 1 Kings xv. 12).

15. *He delivereth the afflicted.* Elihu
returns to the general principle of affliction in God's hands which he has been

16 Yea, He hath allured thee out of
    distress
    Into a broad place, where there is
      no straitness;
    And that which is set on thy
      table is full of fatness;

17 And thou art full of the judgment
    of the wicked;
    Judgment and justice take hold
      on them.

18 For beware of wrath, lest thou be
    led away by thy sufficiency;
    Neither let the greatness of the
      ransom turn thee aside.

19 Will thy riches avail, that are
    without stint,
    Or all the forces of thy strength?

20 Desire not the night,
    When peoples are cut off in their
      place.

16 וְאַ֤ף הֲסִיתְךָ֨ ׀ מִפִּי־צָ֗ר
רַ֭חַב לֹא־מוּצָ֣ק תַּחְתֶּ֑יהָ
וְנַ֥חַת שֻׁלְחָנְךָ֗ מָ֣לֵא דָֽשֶׁן׃

17 וְדִין־רָשָׁ֥ע מָלֵ֑אתָ
דִּ֖ין וּמִשְׁפָּ֣ט יִתְמֹֽכוּ׃

18 כִּֽי־חֵ֭מָה פֶּן־יְסִֽיתְךָ֣ בְסָ֑פֶק
וְרָב־כֹּ֝֗פֶר אַל־יַטֶּֽךָּ׃

19 הֲיַעֲרֹ֣ךְ שׁ֭וּעֲךָ לֹ֣א בְצָ֑ר
וְ֝כֹ֗ל מַאֲמַצֵּי־כֹֽחַ׃

20 אַל־תִּשְׁאַ֥ף הַלָּ֑יְלָה
לַעֲל֖וֹת עַמִּ֣ים תַּחְתָּֽם׃

expounding. He now connects it with
Job's case in order to found an exhortation to him upon it, and to apply the
argument to him personally. 'Through
the tribulation that He brings upon him,
He opens his ear, saying, "Return unto
Me"' (Rashi).

16. *He hath allured thee out of distress.*
God had afforded Job an opportunity to
escape from the confinement of his
sufferings into relief (*a broad place*) and
to enjoy the evidence of His bounty.
But Elihu goes on to urge that in his
perversity Job had thrown the chance
away.

17. *judgment.* The term *din* occurs twice
in the verse, but in different senses. Job
has joined the wicked in their judgment
(*din*) of God, that He does not deal
justly. For this he has merited condemnation (*din*) and punishment. By
refusing to look upon his sufferings as a
Divine warning, they become a judgment
upon his wickedness.

18. *but beware of wrath.* Job is warned:
Beware lest thy wrath and resentment of
God's dealings with thee lead thee away
into mockery and rebellion against Him.

sufficiency. Hebrew *sephek* is of doubtful

significance. It is probably to be connected with the root meaning 'to clap
the hands' (in mockery, see on xxvii. 23);
and the rendering of R.V. margin is the
more acceptable: 'For beware lest wrath
lead thee away into mockery.'

the ransom. Elihu means Job's great
afflictions (cf. xxxiii. 24), the price at
which God will spare his life. Do not
let them torment and plague Job into
being led astray.

19. *will thy riches avail, that are without
stint.* Only remorse and repentance can
provide *the ransom* which God demands.
It cannot be paid in riches, however
abundant. The same thought is found
in Ps. xlix. 8f.

or all the forces of thy strength. Nor is
there any means of escape available in
the exercise of Job's personal efforts.

20. *desire not the night, when peoples are
cut off in their place.* Job is further
warned not to hope for an end to his
afflictions in a sudden calamity which,
overtaking a multitude, will include him.
Night is used of a time of sudden catastrophe (cf. xxxiv. 20, 25). *Peoples*
denotes many persons (as in Ps. vii.

21 Take heed, regard not iniquity;
   For this hast thou chosen rather
      than affliction.

22 Behold, God doeth loftily in His
      power;
   Who is a teacher like unto Him?

23 Who hath enjoined Him His way?
   Or who hath said: 'Thou hast
      wrought unrighteousness'?

24 Remember that thou magnify
      His work,
   Whereof men have sung.

25 All men have looked thereon;
   Man beholdeth it afar off.

26 Behold, God is great, beyond our
      knowledge;
   The number of His years is un-
      searchable.

21 הִשָּׁמֶר אַל־תֵּפֶן אֶל־אָוֶן
כִּי־עַל־זֶה בָּחַרְתָּ מֵעֹנִי׃

22 הֶן־אֵל יַשְׂגִּיב בְּכֹחוֹ
מִי כָמֹהוּ מוֹרֶה׃

23 מִי־פָקַד עָלָיו דַּרְכּוֹ
וּמִי־אָמַר פָּעַלְתָּ עַוְלָה׃

24 זְכֹר כִּי־תַשְׂגִּיא פָעֳלוֹ
אֲשֶׁר שֹׁרְרוּ אֲנָשִׁים׃

25 כָּל־אָדָם חָזוּ־בוֹ
אֱנוֹשׁ יַבִּיט מֵרָחוֹק׃

26 הֶן־אֵל שַׂגִּיא וְלֹא נֵדָע
מִסְפַּר שָׁנָיו וְלֹא־חֵקֶר׃

9). *Are cut off* is literally 'to go up'; (cf.
take me not away (lit. let me not go
up) *in the midst of my days*, Ps. cii. 25.
In their place, i.e. where they are, without
warning.

21. *regard not iniquity.* Better, 'turn
not to iniquity.' Turn not to the iniquity
of rebelling against God's chastening
hand. 'It is better for thee that thou
shouldest choose Him in the day of
affliction; then will God elevate thee' (Ibn
Ezra).

for this hast thou chosen. Elihu rebukes
Job that he has shown himself more
inclined to regard iniquity than to accept
God's discipline with pious submission.

22-33 GOD IS INFINITELY
GREAT AND WISE

22. *behold, God doeth loftily in His power.*
Elihu dwells on the incomparable majesty
of God to impress upon Job the futility
of his railing against Him and the
necessity to submit to Him.

a teacher. Cf. *I will instruct thee and*
teach thee in the way which thou shalt go
(Ps. xxxii. 8). Eitan proposes the translation 'ruler.'

23. *who hath enjoined Him His way?* God
is supreme in His might. Who dare pass
judgment upon His acts?

24. *whereof men have sung.* Rashi and
Ibn Ezra (followed by A.V.) interpret as
though the root meant 'behold,' citing
as example, *I behold him, but not nigh*
(Num. xxiv. 17). The rendering *sung* is
preferable: pious men have always
magnified and praised the work of God.

25. *man beholdeth it afar off.* So overpowering is the sense of awe which His
works arouse, that men can only contemplate them at a reverential distance
(cf. xxvi. 14). Another interpretation is:
Man is unable to comprehend God's
works completely. Finite mind can
never wholly grasp the range of the
infinite universe.

26. *beyond our knowledge.* God's greatness transcends man's knowledge.

27 For He draweth away the drops
   of water,
   Which distil rain from His
   vapour;

28 Which the skies pour down
   And drop upon the multitudes of
   men.

29 Yea, can any understand the
   spreadings of the clouds,
   The crashings of His pavilion?

30 Behold, He spreadeth His light
   upon it;
   And He covereth the depths of
   the sea.

31 For by these He judgeth the
   peoples;
   He giveth food in abundance.

32 He covereth His hands with the
   lightning,
   And giveth it a charge that it
   strike the mark.

27 כִּי יְגָרַע נִטְפֵי־מָיִם
   יָזֹקּוּ מָטָר לְאֵדֽוֹ׃

28 אֲשֶׁר־יִזְּלוּ שְׁחָקִים
   יִרְעֲפוּ עֲלֵי ׀ אָדָם רָֽב׃

29 אַף אִם־יָבִין מִפְרְשֵׂי־עָב
   תְּשֻׁאוֹת סֻכָּתֽוֹ׃

30 הֵן־פָּרַשׂ עָלָיו אוֹרוֹ
   וְשָׁרְשֵׁי הַיָּם כִּסָּֽה׃

31 כִּי־בָם יָדִין עַמִּים
   יִתֶּן־אֹכֶל לְמַכְבִּֽיר׃

32 עַל־כַּפַּיִם כִּסָּה־אוֹר
   וַיְצַו עָלֶיהָ בְמַפְגִּֽיעַ׃

the number of His years is unsearchable.
'The ancients speak the language of man'
(Ibn Ezra) in suggesting that years can
be attributed to God. For Him time
has neither beginning nor end.

27. He draweth away. Better, 'He maketh small.' A description of the formation of rain.

from His vapour. Better, 'His mist,' the
same term that we find in Gen. ii. 6.
Elihu is now proceeding to illustrate the
incomprehensible greatness of God as
demonstrated in the formation of rain,
and then in a thunderstorm.

28. upon the multitudes of men. The
rain falls upon the whole earth, benefit-
ing all mankind.

29. the crashings of His pavilion. Elihu
describes the marvel of the thunderstorm
beginning with the diffusion of the clouds
and heralded by the claps of thunder.
The magnificent imagery is perhaps

borrowed from Ps. xviii. 12, He made
darkness His hiding-place, His pavilion
round about Him. The thundercloud is
the pavilion wherein God is enshrouded.

30. He spreadeth His light ... He covereth
the depths. The first line describes the
bright halo which surrounds the dark
clouds. The second line suggests that
in a great storm, the black, heavily-laden
clouds are replenished with water drawn
from the 'roots of' (so lit.) the sea.

31. by these. God judges the peoples,
i.e. mankind, by the spreadings of the
cloud (verse 29). It is His means of
striking terror into them (cf. Ps. xviii. 15).

He giveth food. The rain-storm is also
His method of fertilizing the earth and
making it to yield food.

32. He covereth His hands with the light-
ning. The image appears to be that of
God represented poetically as plunging
His hands into the flood of light about
Him, taking lightning-bolts to hurl
against the mark.

33 The noise thereof telleth concerning it,
   The cattle also concerning the
   storm that cometh up.

יַגִּיד עָלָיו רֵעוֹ
מִקְנֶה אַף עַל־עוֹלֶה:

37   CHAPTER XXXVII   לז

1 At this also my heart trembleth,
  And is moved out of its place.

אַף־לְזֹאת יֶחֱרַד לִבִּי
וְיִתַּר מִמְּקוֹמוֹ:

2 Hear attentively the noise of His
  voice,
  And the sound that goeth out of
  His mouth.

שִׁמְעוּ שָׁמוֹעַ בְּרֹגֶז קֹלוֹ
וְהֶגֶה מִפִּיו יֵצֵא:

3 He sendeth it forth under the
  whole heaven,
  And His lightning unto the ends
  of the earth.

תַּחַת־כָּל־הַשָּׁמַיִם יִשְׁרֵהוּ
וְאוֹרוֹ עַל־כַּנְפוֹת הָאָרֶץ:

4 After it a voice roareth;

אַחֲרָיו | יִשְׁאַג־קוֹל

---

33. *the noise thereof telleth concerning it.*
Better, 'concerning Him' as R.V. The
noise of the thunder announces the
manifestation of God.

*the cattle also concerning the storm that
cometh up.* The line has been variously
translated. There is nothing in the
Hebrew corresponding to *the storm*. The
simplest rendering is: '(it telleth) the
cattle also concerning Him Who cometh
up (in the storm)'. Even the animals
in the field have an awareness of the
approaching storm. Rashi quotes an
ancient Rabbinic interpretation: 'the
kindling of (God's) anger against one
who is arrogant.' The obscurity of the
language is indicated by Peake's statement that 'more than thirty explanations
have been given of this verse.'

CHAPTER XXXVII

1-13 EFFECT OF GOD'S 'VOICE' IN NATURE

1. *and is moved.* Hebrew *yittar* (from
natar), 'spring, or start up'; 'yea, it (the

heart) starts up from its place' (BDB).
The verb is used in the sense 'to leap' in
Lev. xi. 21 (of locusts). Elihu describes
his heart as jumping with terror at the
lightning storm.

2. *the noise.* The word *rogez* is better
translated 'raging'; 'rumbling of His
voice' (i.e. thunder) (BDB). For thunder as the *voice* of God, cf. Ps. xviii. 14,
xxix. 3ff.

the sound. The 'rumbling, growling'
thunder which issues from God's mouth.

3. *He sendeth it forth.* This sense of the
verb is derived from the root-meaning
'loosen'. With greater probability Eitan
connects it with an Arabic root, 'to gleam,
flash.' Translate: 'He causes to flash.'

His lightning. lit. 'His light,' the illumination of the lightning-flash.

4. *after it a voice.* Elihu describes how
the streak of lightning is swiftly followed
by the roll of thunder. The antecedent
of *it* is not 'earth' but 'lightning' in
verse 3. As Rashi comments: 'after the
lightning.'

He thundereth with the voice of
His majesty;
And He stayeth them not when
His voice is heard.

יַרְעֵם בְּקוֹל גְּאוֹנוֹ
וְלֹא יְעַקְּבֵם כִּי־יִשָּׁמַע קוֹלוֹ׃

5 God thundereth marvellously with
His voice;
Great things doeth He, which we
cannot comprehend.

⁵ יַרְעֵם אֵל בְּקוֹלוֹ נִפְלָאוֹת
עֹשֶׂה גְדֹלוֹת וְלֹא נֵדָע׃

6 For He saith to the snow: 'Fall
thou on the earth';
Likewise to the shower of rain,
And to the showers of His mighty
rain.

⁶ כִּי לַשֶּׁלַג ׀ יֹאמַר הֱוֵא־אָרֶץ
וְגֶשֶׁם מָטָר וְגֶשֶׁם מִטְרוֹת עֻזּוֹ׃

7 He sealeth up the hand of every
man,
That all men whom He hath made
may know it.

⁷ בְּיַד־כָּל־אָדָם יַחְתּוֹם
לָדַעַת כָּל־אַנְשֵׁי מַעֲשֵׂהוּ׃

8 Then the beasts go into coverts,
And remain in their dens.

⁸ וַתָּבֹא חַיָּה בְמוֹ־אָרֶב
וּבִמְעוֹנֹתֶיהָ תִשְׁכֹּן׃

the voice of His majesty. Rather, 'with
His voice of majesty,' an idiom for 'His
majestic voice.' 'They are the lightnings and the thunders that bring the
rain' (Rashi).

He stayeth them not. God does not
restrain the lightnings. 'The words
describe the play of the lightning,
rapidly succeeding the thunder. When
God's presence is announced by His
terrible voice, there also are His awful
ministers, the lightnings, swift to do His
commandments against His adversaries
(xxxvi. 32)' (Davidson).

5. *great things doeth He.* Cf. v. 9, ix. 10.
Elihu's words seem to echo both Eliphaz
and Job. The verse provides Elihu with
a transition to another of God's wonders,
snow and frost. 'Further great things
doeth He which we cannot comprehend'
(Metsudath David).

6. *fall thou on the earth.* Hebrew *hewē*
(from *hawa* 'to fall'); 'for He saith to
the snow, Fall earthwards (an Arabizing
usage)' (BDB). The word only occurs
here.

the shower of rain. Better, 'bursts of rain.'
'The word (*geshem*) denotes not what we
call a "shower" but the heavy and
continued rain of an Eastern winter'
(Driver).

7. *He sealeth up the hand of every man.*
The verse speaks of the enforced seclu-
sion of the farmer who has to suspend
his labour in the fields when snow and
rain come through the winter season.
It is as though the 'hand of man' were
sealed up.

all men whom He hath made. lit. 'all the
men of His making.' A.V.: 'that all men
may know His work' follows the Peshitta
and Vulgate (adding a *mem* to *anshē* and
reading *anashim*). But Metsudath David,
and more recently Szold, understand the
phrase as elliptical for *anshē ma'aseh
ma'asehu*, 'that all men of work (farmers)
may know His work.'

8. *the beasts go into coverts.* During the
winter rains and snow, the beasts hiber-
nate.

9 Out of the Chamber cometh the
storm;
And cold out of the north.

10 By the breath of God ice is given,
And the breadth of the waters is
straitened.

11 Yea, He ladeth the thick cloud
with moisture,
He spreadeth abroad the cloud of
His lightning;

12 And they are turned round about
by His guidance,
That they may do whatsoever He
commandeth them
Upon the face of the habitable
world:

13 Whether it be for correction, or
for His earth,

מִן־הַחֶדֶר תָּבוֹא סוּפָה

וּמִמְּזָרִים קָרָה:

מִנִּשְׁמַת־אֵל יִתֶּן־קָרַח

וְרֹחַב מַיִם בְּמוּצָק:

אַף־בְּרִי יַטְרִיחַ עָב

יָפִיץ עֲנַן אוֹרוֹ:

וְהוּא מְסִבּוֹת ׀ מִתְהַפֵּךְ בְּתַחְבּוּלֹתָו

לְפָעֳלָם כֹּל אֲשֶׁר יְצַוֵּם ׀

עַל־פְּנֵי תֵבֵל אָרְצָה:

אִם־לְשֵׁבֶט אִם־לְאַרְצוֹ

v. 12. בתחבולתיו ק׳

9. *out of the Chamber.* It was thought
that there was a chamber or treasury
where storm-winds were stored, ready
for God's use when He required them
(cf. xxxviii. 22; Ps. cxxxv. 7). A.V. and
R.V., following Ibn Ezra, identify *the
Chamber* with *the chambers of the south*
(see on ix. 9); but Davidson questions
the assumption.

the storm. The Hebrew *suphah* denotes
'storm-wind'; render 'whirlwind.'

out of the north. Hebrew *mezarim* (from
zarah), lit. 'scatterers.' The reference is
to the icy winds which blow from the
north bringing cold. The Vulgate
translates the word as the constellation
Arcturus. Ibn Ezra, discussing various
interpretations of the unusual word, also
thinks that it refers to certain stars and
cites xxxviii. 32 (*Mazzaroth*).

10. *the breath of God.* A poetical expression for the wind, as the thunder is
described as His voice (cf. Isa. xl. 7).

is straitened. lit. 'in constraint,' descriptive of water when it freezes.

11. *His lightning.* lit. 'His light' as in
verse 3. Ibn Ezra alludes to the wonder
seen at times of rain falling while the sun
shines.

12. *and they are turned round about.* This
may refer either to the lightning or the
cloud; more probably the former since
the verb suits it better. It is used of the
flaming sword guarding the entrance to
the garden of Eden which *turned every
way* (Gen. iii. 24).

His guidance. lit. 'His steering,' the
term being connected with the Hebrew
word for 'sailor.'

habitable world. The phrase is met with
again only in Prov. viii. 31. Its literal
meaning is 'habitable world of the earth,'
i.e. 'the completed universe made fit as
the habitation of living creatures' (Cohen,
ad loc.). 'Though the forked lightning
seems to men's eyes wholly capricious
in its random movements, yet it does not
strike blindly, but is guided in every flash
by the counsels of God' (Peake).

13. *for correction.* lit. 'rod' (cf. xxi. 9).
God has a moral purpose in His guidance
of the lightning-clouds and the rains.
Correction and *mercy* refer to God's
intent with regard to men.

His earth. At times God sends rain to
parts of the world which are not inhabited by man (cf. xxxviii. 26).

Or for mercy, that He cause it to
come.

14 Hearken unto this, O Job;
Stand still, and consider the
wondrous works of God.

15 Dost thou know how God enjoineth them,
And causeth the lightning of His
cloud to shine?

16 Dost thou know the balancings of
the clouds,
The wondrous works of Him who
is perfect in knowledge?

17 Thou whose garments are warm,
When the earth is still by reason
of the south wind;

18 Canst thou with Him spread out
the sky,

אִם־לְחֶסֶד יַמְצִאֵהוּ׃

14 הַאֲזִינָה זֹּאת אִיּוֹב
עֲמֹד וְהִתְבּוֹנֵן ׀ נִפְלְאוֹת אֵל׃

15 הֲתֵדַע בְּשׂוּם־אֱלוֹהַּ עֲלֵיהֶם
וְהוֹפִיעַ אוֹר עֲנָנוֹ׃

16 הֲתֵדַע עַל־מִפְלְשֵׂי־עָב
מִפְלְאוֹת תְּמִים דֵּעִים׃

17 אֲשֶׁר־בְּגָדֶיךָ חַמִּים
בְּהַשְׁקִט אֶרֶץ מִדָּרוֹם׃

18 תַּרְקִיעַ עִמּוֹ לִשְׁחָקִים

14-24 APPEAL TO JOB TO LEARN THE
LESSON NATURE TEACHES

14. *consider the wondrous works of God.*
Being himself profoundly stirred by the
grandeur of Nature as the revelation of
God's majesty, Elihu strives to communi-
cate his own feelings to Job. The questions that follow have the purpose of
exposing Job's ignorance of how God
governs the physical world; would he,
then, presume to claim knowledge of
how He rules the life of man!

15. *how God enjoineth them.* 'How God
sets the clouds over men' (Ibn Ezra).
Elihu may be referring to all the phenomena he had described.

the lightning. See on xxxvi. 32. Let Job
ponder on such wonderful happenings in
the heavens.

16. *the balancings of the clouds.* The
word for *balancings* is met with nowhere
else in the Bible. The phenomenon of
the clouds poised in the sky, heavy with
rain, yet without support, is to be mar-
velled at (cf. Job's words in xxvi. 8).

17. *thou whose garments are warm.* The
verse is to be connected with what
follows. Elihu ironically emphasizes the
littleness of man. The meaning is:
'Canst thou, whose garments are hot and
dry, in the sultry stillness preceding a
sirocco (xv. 2) and who art thus shown to
be powerless against the operations of
Nature—canst thou, like God, spread out
the solid firmament of heaven?' (Driver).

when the earth is still. A graphic description of the stillness of the earth under the
sultry south wind (the sirocco) is given
by Thomson: 'There is no living thing
abroad to make a noise. The birds hide
in thickest shades, the fowls pant under
the walls with open mouth and drooping
wings, the flocks and herds take shelter
in caves and under great rocks, and
labourers retire from the fields and close
the windows and doors of their houses.
No one has energy enough to make a
noise, and the very air is too weak and
languid to stir the pendent leaves even of
the tall poplars. Such a south wind
with the heat of a cloud does indeed
bring down the noise and quiet the earth.'

18. *spread out.* The verb *raka* conveys
the idea of 'beat out' metal. The word
firmament (*rakia*) is derived from it
(Gen. i. 6). The firmament was pictured
as a firm, solid expanse, supporting
'waters' above it.

Which is strong as a molten mirror?

חֲזָקִים כִּרְאִי מוּצָק׃

19 Teach us what we shall say unto
Him;
For we cannot order our speech
by reason of darkness.

הוֹדִיעֵנוּ מַה־נֹּאמַר לוֹ
לֹא נַעֲרֹךְ מִפְּנֵי־חֹשֶׁךְ׃

20 Shall it be told Him that I would
speak?
Or should a man wish that he
were swallowed up?

הַיְסֻפַּר־לוֹ כִּי אֲדַבֵּר
אִם־אָמַר אִישׁ כִּי יְבֻלָּע׃

21 And now men see not the light
which is bright in the skies;
But the wind passeth, and cleans-
eth them.

וְעַתָּה ׀ לֹא־רָאוּ אוֹר
בָּהִיר הוּא בַּשְּׁחָקִים
וְרוּחַ עָבְרָה וַתְּטַהֲרֵם׃

22 Out of the north cometh golden
splendour,
About God is terrible majesty.

מִצָּפוֹן זָהָב יֶאֱתֶה
עַל־אֱלוֹהַּ נוֹרָא הוֹד׃

23 The Almighty, whom we cannot
find out, is excellent in power,
Yet to judgment and plenteous
justice He doeth no violence.

שַׁדַּי לֹא־מְצָאנֻהוּ שַׂגִּיא־כֹחַ
וּמִשְׁפָּט וְרֹב־צְדָקָה לֹא יְעַנֶּה׃

strong as a molten mirror. In ancient
times mirrors consisted of metal (cf.
Exod. xxxviii. 8). The cloudless sky, in
the shimmering heat of day, is compared
to burnished copper (Deut. xxviii. 23).
Man obviously cannot match God in His
marvels of the sky, is the point of the
question.

19. *teach us what we shall say unto Him,*
In face of these awesome acts, what can
the human being say to Him Who is
responsible for them?

we cannot order our speech. i.e. arrange
our thoughts in orderly phrases (cf.
xiii. 18).

by reason of darkness. What puny knowledge have we, in the darkness of our
ignorance (cf. Eccles. ii. 14)!

20. *shall it be told Him that I would speak?*
Elihu is aghast at the thought of appear-
ing before God to contend with Him,
being conscious of his insignificance and
His incomprehensible greatness. Yet
that is what Job wished to do.

*or should a man wish that he were swallowed
up?* If, however, any man had such a
thought in his mind, as Job had, he is
merely asking to be destroyed.

21. *and now men see not the light.* Man has
not the power to gaze upon the sun when
the wind has cleared away the clouds
after a storm. How, then, can he look
upon the dazzling majesty of God! The
same argument was used by a Rabbi in
the Talmud when a heathen asked to be
shown God.

22. *golden splendour.* lit. 'gold,' which
Ibn Ezra interprets as 'the golden splendour of the heavens.' 'The allusion may
be to the Aurora Borealis, the streaming
rays of which, mysteriously blazing forth
in the northern heavens, may well have
been supposed to be an effulgence from
the presence of God Himself' (Driver).

23. *excellent in power.* 'We know by His
works that He is surpassing in power and
surpassing in justice' (Ibn Ezra). 'Elihu
sums up his teaching regarding the
greatness of God, which is ever conjoined

24 Men do therefore fear Him;
   He regardeth not any that are
   wise of heart.

24 לָכֵן יְרֵאוּהוּ אֲנָשִׁים
   לֹא־יִרְאֶה כָּל־חַכְמֵי־לֵב׃

38   CHAPTER XXXVIII   לח

1 Then the LORD answered Job out
  of the whirlwind, and said:

1 וַיַּעַן־יְהֹוָה אֶת־אִיּוֹב
  מִן ׀ הַסְּעָרָה וַיֹּאמַר׃

v. 1. מן ק׳

with righteousness. It is befitting men,
therefore, not to judge Him, but to fear
Him, for He regards not them that are
wise in their own understanding' (Davidson).

He doeth no violence. Elihu denies what
Job had often alleged, that God violates
justice.

24. *men do therefore fear Him.* In
xxxvi. 5 Elihu had expressed the thought
that although God is mighty, yet is He
also merciful and just. He now concludes his address with the same admonition. Let Job desist from his presumptuous complaints, and in humility
join with the pious in reverent fear of
Him.

He regardeth not any that are wise of heart.
The context shows that Elihu means
this scornfully: wise in their own presumptuous thoughts. The words, of
course, have special reference to Job.

CHAPTERS XXXVIII-XLII. 6

GOD ANSWERS JOB OUT OF THE STORM

THIS section reaches dazzling heights of
poetic splendour. Job's passionate cry
that he might confront God is now
granted. He had asked to know the
reason for his suffering and sought to
discover God's charges against him.
Above all, he sought to have God vindicate his innocence and his spiritual
integrity. This, as xlii. 7f. shows, Job
achieves. The friends are rebuked and

Job's rectitude acknowledged. Before
Job and his companions, God unfolds
the vast panorama of creation. 'With His
ironical questions regarding the laws of
Nature and the conduct of the universe,
God takes up the thread where Job left
off, and brings into greater emphasis the
thought enunciated by Job, that absolute
wisdom is found with God alone, and
that man by reason of his finite intelligence cannot fathom the infinite wisdom
of God, or comprehend the mystery of
His rule' (Buttenwieser).

More profoundly than ever, Job is
now filled with an overpowering sense of
the immensity of the Divine grandeur
and mystery. He is humbled into more
vivid awareness of how futile it is for man
to think he can ever penetrate the insuperable mysteries of God's moral government of the universe. His tormenting
questions have not been answered. But
he has found peace. Out of sorrow and
suffering he has come to know God, not
only in His blazing majesty but in His
boundless love. Job's pride has vanished
and in the vision of God, affirming his
integrity, he attains spiritual victory and
triumphant faith.

'This is the end—the end of the conflict and the end of the Book; and what a
fitting end it is! It will be remembered
that it was on the basis of the invincible
power of the good that God had staked
His honour in the opening scene in
Heaven, and now, by this crowning
victory of Job's, His thesis is vindicated,
His confidence fulfilled. It is not merely
a victory of Job's; we are made to feel

2 Who is this that darkeneth counsel
  By words without knowledge?

3 Gird up now thy loins like a man;
  For I will demand of thee, and
    declare thou unto Me.

4 Where wast thou when I laid the
    foundations of the earth?
  Declare, if thou hast the under-
    standing.

5 Who determined the measures
    thereof, if thou knowest?
  Or who stretched the line upon it?

מִי זֶה | מַחְשִׁיךְ עֵצָה
בְמִלִּין בְּלִי־דָעַת:
אֱזָר־נָא כְּגֶבֶר חֲלָצֶיךָ
וְאֶשְׁאָלְךָ וְהוֹדִיעֵנִי:
אֵיפֹה הָיִיתָ בְּיָסְדִי־אָרֶץ ⁴
הַגֵּד אִם־יָדַעְתָּ בִינָה:
מִי־שָׂם מְמַדֶּיהָ כִּי תֵדָע ⁵
אוֹ מִי־נָטָה עָלֶיהָ קָּו:

it is God's victory—the triumph of the Eternal goodness that rules the world' (Buttenweiser).

CHAPTER XXXVIII

1-3 GOD INTERVENES

1. *then the LORD answered Job.* Observe that Elihu, who has been holding forth all this time (xxxii. 6-xxxvii. 24), is now completely ignored.

out of the whirlwind. 'The explanation of *out of the whirlwind* is that most of the marvels which God recounts are in the storms of the heavens; or it means that He spoke to Job in a whirlwind' (Ibn Ezra). The upheaval of Nature which is the setting for God's appearance height-ens the solemnity of the occasion and the impressiveness of the message He de-livers. For other Biblical instances, cf. Exod. xix. 16; 1 Kings xix. 11f.; Isa. vi. 4; Ezek. i. 4ff.

2. *that darkeneth counsel.* viz. regarding God's plan of world government. The words are a rebuke addressed to Job who had inveighed against Divine providence and brought a charge of injustice against God. 'He had spoken as though it was all a tangled riddle. Really there is in it a beautiful luminous order. It is very instructive to compare what the author of Ecclesiastes says on this point: God has ordered all things, and each falls in place in the Divine plan of the world, but man

cannot see the harmonious design, to him the world presents only a perplexing reign of caprice. But this is because God has deliberately willed that man shall not be able to find out His work; He has implanted the instinct for search, but doomed it to futility. Job has expressed the view that there is no moral order, Ecclesiastes affirms that there is an order, but God has made it impenetrable to man' (Peake).

3. *gird up now thy loins.* A preparation for strenuous action (cf. Exod. xii. 11; 1 Kings xviii. 46). Job had been longing to meet God in contest. Now he is to have his wish.

for I will demand of thee. More lit. 'ask thee.' Job had pleaded, *Call Thou, and I will answer* (xiii. 22). Accordingly, God interrogates him.

4-7 WHAT DOES JOB KNOW OF CREATION?

4. *where wast thou when I laid the founda-tions.* The ironic question may imply, 'Was it Job, then, who laid the founda-tions of the earth?' The series of ques-tions which expose Job's ignorance carry with them the logic that he is presump-tuous when he criticizes God's plan.

declare. Tell how it all was done. The reference is to the questions that follow.

5. *who determined the measures thereof.* Cf. Prov. xxx. 4 where, as here, the intent is to show up man's ignorance. *Measures*

6 Whereupon were the foundations
   thereof fastened?
  Or who laid the corner-stone
   thereof,

7 When the morning stars sang together,
  And all the sons of God shouted
   for joy?

8 Or who shut up the sea with doors,
  When it broke forth, and issued
   out of the womb;

9 When I made the cloud the garment thereof,
  And thick darkness a swaddling-
   band for it,

עַל־מָה אֲדָנֶיהָ הָטְבָּעוּ 6
אוֹ מִי־יָרָה אֶבֶן פִּנָּתָהּ:

בְּרָן־יַחַד כּוֹכְבֵי בֹקֶר 7
וַיָּרִיעוּ כָּל־בְּנֵי אֱלֹהִים:

וַיָּסֶךְ בִּדְלָתַיִם יָם 8
בְּגִיחוֹ מֵרֶחֶם יֵצֵא:

בְּשׂוּמִי עָנָן לְבֻשׁוֹ 9
וַעֲרָפֶל חֲתֻלָּתוֹ:

means 'boundaries' (Ibn Ezra). The point of the question, says Davidson, is: 'Was he (Job) present to see who fixed them and how they were fixed, so as to be able to speak with knowledge?'

the line. i.e. the measuring line used in the process of building (Jer. xxxi. 39).

6. *the foundations.* lit. 'sockets' of the pillars (ix. 6) which were believed to support the universe.

the corner-stone. The imagery under-lying the verse is that of rearing a stupendous edifice. The earth is con-ceived as resting on pillars sunk into their bases in the vast watery abyss (cf. Ps. xxiv. 2). The corner-stone of the cosmic edifice (in the middle of the sea, declares Rashi) is laid amid shouts of rejoicing from the heavenly hosts.

7. *the morning stars.* The stars were, so to speak, the first choir at the act of creation. The morning stars are the brightest and most glorious, heralding the earth as it rose into existence at the first dawn. 'The morning stars were seven ministering angels and they are called stars of light' (Ibn Ezra).

the sons of God. i.e. the angels (see on i. 6). 'Age-old mythology ultimately imported from the land of Shinar, rings through these last lines, for the singing morning stars, that are equated here with the sons of God, belong to a pan-

theon of star-gods that acclaimed the supreme Divinity on the completion of His creative achievements, as is the case in the Creation Epic of Babylon' (Kraeling). Stars and angels are found mentioned in combination in Ps. cxlviii. 2f.

8-11 WHO CONTROLLED THE PRIMEVAL WATERS?

8. *shut up the sea with doors.* Set a boundary to the waters (Gen. i. 9).

when it broke forth, and issued out of the womb. For the language, cf. Ps. xxii. 10. The poet hints at the immemorial myth of the sea, pictured poetically as an un-ruly oceanic babe, bursting forth from the womb of the deep abyss and with giant might menacing the security of the world. There is an echo of the Baby-lonian Tiamat monster mythology here (cf. vii. 12, xxvi. 12).

9. *a swaddling-band.* 'When I made cloud round about the ocean that encom-passes the world, and which clouds surround it as a garment' (Rashi). 'For the new-born child there must be a garment and a swaddling-band; these are the clouds, which seem to be wreathed about it on the horizon, or the mists with which it is at times covered' (Peake).

10 And prescribed for it My decree,
   And set bars and doors,

11 And said: 'Thus far shalt thou
   come, but no further;
   And here shall thy proud waves
   be stayed'?

12 Hast thou commanded the morning since thy days began,
   And caused the dayspring to know
   its place;

13 That it might take hold of the
   ends of the earth,
   And the wicked be shaken out of
   it?

14 It is changed as clay under the
   seal;
   And they stand as a garment.

15 But from the wicked their light is
   withholden,
   And the high arm is broken.

וָאֶשְׁבֹּר עָלָיו חֻקִּי
וָאָשִׂים בְּרִיחַ וּדְלָתָיִם׃

וָאֹמַר עַד־פֹּה תָבוֹא וְלֹא תֹסִיף
וּפֹא יָשִׁית בִּגְאוֹן גַּלֶּיךָ׃

הֲמִיָּמֶיךָ צִוִּיתָ בֹּקֶר
יִדַּעְתָּה שַׁחַר מְקֹמוֹ׃

לֶאֱחֹז בְּכַנְפוֹת הָאָרֶץ
וְיִנָּעֲרוּ רְשָׁעִים מִמֶּנָּה׃

תִּתְהַפֵּךְ כְּחֹמֶר חוֹתָם
וְיִתְיַצְּבוּ כְּמוֹ לְבוּשׁ׃

וְיִמָּנַע מֵרְשָׁעִים אוֹרָם
וּזְרוֹעַ רָמָה תִּשָּׁבֵר׃

v. 11. א׳ במקום ה׳   v. 12. ידעת השחר ק׳   v. 13. ע׳ תלויה   v.15. ע׳ תלויה

10. *and prescribed for it My decree.* Better,
'and broke for it My decreed limit' (cf.
Prov. viii. 29). The allusion is to rocks
and cliffs which form the coast.

11. *thus far shalt thou come.* 'Thus far
shall thy strength be stayed' (Ibn Ezra).
Davidson comments on how splendid
are these figures of the ocean pictured
at an infant giant. 'Finally,' he remarks,
'the new-born monster must be tamed by
an almighty power, and an impassable
bound set to its proud fury.'

12-15 WHO ORDAINED THE MORNING?
12. *since thy days began.* 'From the day
that thou wast born' (Rashi). Is Job
responsible for the regular daily appearance of the dawn? By implication the
question also suggests: is Job as old as the
phenomenon of the rising of the sun?
Cf. the sarcastic point made in verse 21.

the dayspring. The dawn that spreads
its glory over the earth.

13. *the wicked be shaken out of it.* A
vigorous poetical figure, describing how
the dawn detects and disperses evil-doers.

The earth is pictured as a vast coverlet;
and the dawn, which darts in a moment
from east to west (Ps. cxxxix. 9), seizes
this coverlet by its corners, brings to light
the wicked upon it, and shakes them
off it like dust (Driver). As Davidson
remarks, 'The dawn is not a physical
phenomenon merely, it is a moral agent,'
because evil-doers prefer the darkness of
night for their nefarious exploits.

14. *it is changed as clay under the seal.*
Another lovely image comparing the
earth, suddenly taking on distinct form
and shape under the light of dawn, to
the swift impression that the seal makes
upon the clay.

they stand as a garment. The sun-light
brings to view the many colours with
which the earth is tinged. They *stand*
out like the different hues of a variegated
garment.

15. *but from the wicked.* Cf. xxiv. 17.
The *light* of the wicked is darkness.

the high arm. Raised to commit violence.
The dawn has not only beauty but it
checks lawless action.

16 Hast thou entered into the
  springs of the sea?
  Or hast thou walked in the recesses of the deep?

17 Have the gates of death been revealed unto thee?
  Or hast thou seen the gates of the
  shadow of death?

18 Hast thou surveyed unto the
  breadths of the earth?
  Declare, if thou knowest it all.

19 Where is the way to the dwelling
  of light,
  And as for darkness, where is the
  place thereof;

20 That thou shouldest take it to the
  bound thereof,
  And that thou shouldest know
  the paths to the house thereof?

21 Thou knowest it, for thou wast
  then born,
  And the number of thy days is
  great!

16 הֲבָאתָ עַד־נִבְכֵי־יָם
וּבְחֵקֶר תְּהוֹם הִתְהַלָּכְתָּ׃

17 הֲנִגְלוּ לְךָ שַׁעֲרֵי־מָוֶת
וְשַׁעֲרֵי צַלְמָוֶת תִּרְאֶה׃

18 הִתְבֹּנַנְתָּ עַד־רַחֲבֵי־אָרֶץ
הַגֵּד אִם־יָדַעְתָּ כֻלָּהּ׃

19 אֵי־זֶה הַדֶּרֶךְ יִשְׁכָּן־אוֹר
וְחֹשֶׁךְ אֵי־זֶה מְקֹמוֹ׃

20 כִּי תִקָּחֶנּוּ אֶל־גְּבוּלוֹ
וְכִי־תָבִין נְתִיבוֹת בֵּיתוֹ׃

21 יָדַעְתָּ כִּי־אָז תִּוָּלֵד
וּמִסְפַּר יָמֶיךָ רַבִּים׃

16-18 HAS JOB PENETRATED THE DEPTHS
OF SEA AND EARTH?

16. *the springs of the sea.* i.e. the deep
passages by which the illimitable waters
of the abyss beneath the earth rise to
replenish the waters of the sea.

recesses of the deep. Hebrew *tehom* (cf.
the foundations of the great deep, Gen.
vii. 11).

17. *the gates of death.* The gates of
Sheol, deep down in the earth below the
seas, where thickest darkness reigns
(cf. x. 21f., xxvi. 5f.). 'The conception of
the gates of Sheol is a Babylonian one,
and is found in the famous poem of the
Descent of Ishtar' (Davidson).

18. *hast thou surveyed unto the breadths
of the earth?* If Job has not explored the
depths of the earth, has he surveyed its
vast surface and appreciated its dimensions?

19-21 DOES JOB KNOW THE SOURCE OF
LIGHT AND DARKNESS?

19. *where is the way to the dwelling of light.*
Cf. xxvi. 10. Light and darkness have
each its separate dwelling-place. Is Job
aware of its location?

20. *that thou shouldest take it to the bound
thereof.* That thou shouldest take each,
light or darkness, back to its mysterious
covert after its daily or nightly task was
done. 'Each of these has its own home,
remote and difficult to find, to which it
must return after it has sallied forth over
the earth. Sarcastically God remarks
that if Job really is the embodiment of
wisdom (which according to Prov. viii.
22f. is older than the creation of the
world), he must have been present when
these things were arranged' (Kraeling).

21. *thou knowest it, for thou wast then
born.* Cf. xv. 7. The words are acid in
their biting sarcasm. 'Thou knowest all
this for thou wast born when I created
them!' (Rashi).

22 Hast thou entered the treasuries
of the snow,
Or hast thou seen the treasuries
of the hail,

23 Which I have reserved against
the time of trouble,
Against the day of battle and
war?

24 By what way is the light parted,
Or the east wind scattered upon
the earth?

25 Who hath cleft a channel for the
waterflood,
Or a way for the lightning of the
thunder;

26 To cause it to rain on a land
where no man is,
On the wilderness, wherein there
is no man;

הֲבָאתָ אֶל־אֹצְרוֹת שָׁלֶג 22
וְאֹצְרוֹת בָּרָד תִּרְאֶה׃

אֲשֶׁר־חָשַׂכְתִּי לְעֶת־צָר 23
לְיוֹם קְרָב וּמִלְחָמָה׃

אֵי־זֶה הַדֶּרֶךְ יֵחָלֶק אוֹר 24
יָפֵץ קָדִים עֲלֵי־אָרֶץ׃

מִי־פִלַּג לַשֶּׁטֶף תְּעָלָה 25
וְדֶרֶךְ לַחֲזִיז קֹלוֹת׃

לְהַמְטִיר עַל־אֶרֶץ לֹא־אִישׁ 26
מִדְבָּר לֹא־אָדָם בּוֹ׃

22-23 HAS JOB INSPECTED THE
TREASURIES OF SNOW AND HAIL?

22. treasuries of the snow. The quaint
conception that underlies the verse is
that God has created snow and hail and
laid them up in great store-houses high
above the heavens, turning them loose
for His moral purposes (cf. the picture
of the cave of Æolus, Vergil, Æn. i. 52ff.).

**23. against the time of trouble . . . the
day of battle.** 'The chief emphasis is
on the hail, for its stones, which can be
of formidable size (cf. Benvenuto Cellini's account of his experience, Book II.
50), are on occasion used by God when
He wishes to intervene in wars here upon
earth to change the course of history
(Josh. x. 11; Isa. xxx. 30)' (Kraeling).

the time of trouble. e.g. against the five
kings in Gibeon (Josh. x. 11); **the day of
battle,** e.g. the war with Gog and Magog
(Ezek. xxxviii. 22) (Rashi).

24-30 CAN JOB ACCOUNT FOR LIGHT,
WIND, LIGHTNING, RAIN, DEW AND FROST?

24. by what way is the light parted. In
verse 19 the dwelling of light was mentioned. Now the phenomenon of the
distribution of the sun's rays over the
earth is included among the mysterious
processes of Nature.

the east wind. The Hebrew kadim, 'east,'
is understood by Ibn Ezra as ruach
kadim, elliptical for 'the east wind,' the
sirocco (xv. 2). Rashi, on the other
hand, explains it as 'the sun in the east.'
Davidson accepts the former and comments: 'More probably the reference is
to the wonderful diffusion of light over
the whole earth, and the query concerns
the way or path by which this takes
place. Such a path appears to lie in the
East, from whence also the stormy wind
spreads over the earth; hence the two are
brought into connection. Job, of course,
knows the way along which this diffusion
of light and wind takes place.'

25. a channel. Hebrew t'alah, a poetical
word for 'channel for rain' (cf. Isa. vii. 3,
conduit). The waterflood of rain is
pictured pouring down through a conduit from the reservoirs of water in the
skies. That is its appointed path.

a way for the lightning of the thunder.
Repeated from xxviii. 26.

26. on a land where no man is. God's
providence is wider than the care of man.
It extends to the wilderness where no
human being lives. Peake regards verses
26f. as very important for the poet's
attitude to the problem raised by Job.

27 To satisfy the desolate and waste
ground,
And to cause the bud of the tender herb to spring forth?

28 Hath the rain a father?
Or who hath begotten the drops
of dew?

29 Out of whose womb came the ice?
And the hoar-frost of heaven,
who hath gendered it?

30 The waters are congealed like
stone,
And the face ot the deep is frozen.

31 Canst thou bind the chains of the
Pleiades,
Or loose the bands ot Orion?

27 לְהַשְׂבִּיעַ שֹׁאָה וּמְשֹׁאָה
וּלְהַצְמִיחַ מֹצָא דֶשֶׁא׃

28 הֲיֵשׁ לַמָּטָר אָב
אוֹ מִי־הוֹלִיד אֶגְלֵי־טָל׃

29 מִבֶּטֶן מִי יָצָא הַקָּרַח
וּכְפֹר שָׁמַיִם מִי יְלָדוֹ׃

30 כָּאֶבֶן מַיִם יִתְחַבָּאוּ
וּפְנֵי תְהוֹם יִתְלַכָּדוּ׃

31 הַתְקַשֵּׁר מַעֲדַנּוֹת כִּימָה
אוֹ־מֹשְׁכוֹת כְּסִיל תְּפַתֵּחַ׃

'The fault of Job,' he observes, 'is that he is self-centred. The world is cruel, immorally governed, because he suffers. He widens his view and brings, as a further indictment against God, the misery of mankind. Beyond that he does not look. But God's concerns embrace far more than man.' But this contention, set against the total picture of Job, seems very forced (cf. his assertions in xii. 7-9, xxvi. 5-14).

27. *desolate and waste ground.* The Hebrew implies but does not express *ground.*

to cause the bud . . . to spring forth. lit. 'to make the growing-place of young grass to sprout.' The soil being there, God makes it productive although there is nobody to reap its harvest.

28. *hath the rain a father?* Is the rain due to any human agency? 'In Arabia, the south-west wind, which brings rain, is called "father of rain"' (Buttenweiser).

drops of dew. Can Job explain the origin of the rain and dew? Who begets these? Certainly not man!

29. *who hath gendered it?* i.e. given birth to it. Driver comments that *gendered* is ambiguous: the translation

goes back to Wycliffe from whose version of 1388 the rendering is derived. Verse 28 speaks of the father, verse 29 of the mother.

30. *are congealed.* lit. 'hide themselves'; 'by the frost which solidifies every drop upon them' (Rashi). The frost hardens the waters like stone. The comparison is to the hardness. Davidson and Peake comment that the phenomenon of ice, rare in the East, naturally appeared wonderful. But is it any less wonderful to us?

31-38 CAN JOB CONTROL THE HEAVENLY CONSTELLATIONS, CLOUDS AND LIGHTNING?

31. *the Pleiades . . . Orion.* See on ix. 9. 'The Pleiades are attractively compared to a chain of jewellery that God has wrought, and Orion ("the fool") is regarded as a Titan who absurdly rebelled against God in primeval times and was for ever bound to the sky by means of the three stars known as the "girdle"' (Kraeling). 'Perhaps the thought is that in spite of his (Orion's) turbulent character the Almighty relaxes his bands, because, however dangerous he may be, God can, when He will, contemptuously leave him at large. Job, if he could, would not dare to do this' (Peake).

32 Canst thou lead forth the Mazzaroth in their season?
Or canst thou guide the Bear with
her sons?

33 Knowest thou the ordinances of
the heavens?
Canst thou establish the dominion
thereof in the earth?

34 Canst thou lift up thy voice to the
clouds,
That abundance of waters may
cover thee?

35 Canst thou send forth lightnings,
that they may go,
And say unto thee: 'Here we
are'?

36 Who hath put wisdom in the inward parts?
Or who hath given understanding to the mind?

הֲתֹצִיא מַזָּרוֹת בְּעִתּוֹ
וְעַיִשׁ עַל־בָּנֶיהָ תַנְחֵם:
הֲיָדַעְתָּ חֻקּוֹת שָׁמָיִם
אִם־תָּשִׂים מִשְׁטָרוֹ בָאָרֶץ:
הֲתָרִים לָעָב קוֹלֶךָ
וְשִׁפְעַת־מַיִם תְּכַסֶּךָּ:
הַתְשַׁלַּח בְּרָקִים וְיֵלֵכוּ
וְיֹאמְרוּ לְךָ הִנֵּנוּ:
מִי־שָׁת בַּטֻּחוֹת חָכְמָה
אוֹ מִי־נָתַן לַשֶּׂכְוִי בִינָה:

32. *the Mazzaroth.* While the derivation and significance of the word are
unknown, it is clear from the context that
a star or group of stars is intended. Some
authorities regard it as another form of
Mazzaloth (rendered *constellations*) in
2 Kings xxiii. 5, which is thought to
indicate the signs of the Zodiac.

the Bear. See on ix. 9. 'The Mazzaroth (probably the northern constellation
Boötes) and Ayish with her young (i.e.
Aldebaran and the other six Hyades in
the head of Taurus) are regarded as
being led or sent forth by God like
domestic animals. It is manifest that the
wonderful order apparent in the entire
celestial sphere is due to commands that
have been laid down by a sovereign will,
and it is equally clear that the heavens
(as evidenced by the seasons, tides, etc.)
exercise an office of powerful control
over the earth. Can Job organize the
cosmos and make it do his will in this
fashion?' (Kraeling).

33. *the ordinances of the heavens.* The
laws which govern the movement of the
sun, moon and stars.

dominion . . . in the earth. The dominion of
the planets appointed to bring upon the
earth cold and heat, summer and winter.
Similarly the sun and moon were ordained *to rule the day . . . night* (Gen. i. 16).

34. *lift up thy voice.* The image under-
lying the ironical question is that of God
calling to the clouds to let loose their
abundance of rain. What could Job's
voice accomplish in this respect? The
second line is repeated from xxii. 11.

35. *here we are.* i.e. we have fulfilled thy
mission. 'They do not have to return
to their former place to report on their
mission since the Divine Presence is
everywhere' (Rashi). But the text
conveys the idea that the lightnings reported to God the accomplishment of
their task. Could Job get them to do so
for him?

36. *the inward parts . . . the mind.* This
translation does not fit the context. The
word *tuchoth* rendered *inward parts*
occurs in Ps. li. 8 in that sense, which is
derived from the root-significance 'to be
covered over.' The probable meaning
here is 'the cloud-layers' as dark, hidden
spaces (BDB). The second word *sechwi*
is also uncertain. In Rabbinical Hebrew
it denotes 'the cock.' If derived from the
root *sachah*, 'to look out,' it expresses the
idea of 'a heavenly phenomenon,' a cloud-
formation. 'In any case they possess
wisdom, either in the sense that men can
draw auguries from them, or that they
prognosticate the weather' (Peake).

37 Who can number the clouds by
    wisdom?
    Or who can pour out the bottles
    of heaven,

38 When the dust runneth into a
    mass,
    And the clods cleave fast to-
    gether?

39 Wilt thou hunt the prey for the
    lioness?
    Or satisfy the appetite of the
    young lions,

40 When they couch in their dens,
    And abide in the covert to lie in
    wait?

41 Who provideth for the raven his
    prey,
    When his young ones cry unto
    God,
    And wander for lack of food?

מִי־יְסַפֵּר שְׁחָקִים בְּחָכְמָה 37
וְנִבְלֵי שָׁמַיִם מִי יַשְׁכִּיב׃

בְּצֶקֶת עָפָר לַמּוּצָק 38
וּרְגָבִים יְדֻבָּקוּ׃

הֲתָצוּד לְלָבִיא טָרֶף 39
וְחַיַּת כְּפִירִים תְּמַלֵּא׃

כִּי־יָשֹׁחוּ בַמְּעוֹנוֹת 40
יֵשְׁבוּ בַסֻּכָּה לְמוֹ־אָרֶב׃

מִי יָכִין לָעֹרֵב צֵידוֹ 41
כִּי־יְלָדָו אֶל־אֵל יְשַׁוֵּעוּ
יִתְעוּ לִבְלִי־אֹכֶל׃

ילדיו ק׳ .v. 41

37. *who can number the clouds by wisdom?*
The meaning of the verb *number* is
determined by *He that bringeth out their
host* (the stars) *by number* (Isa. xl. 26).
Who but God has the wisdom to muster
the clouds in the exact number required
at any particular time?

the bottles of heaven. For the idea of rain
being contained in bottles, see on xxvi. 8.

38. *when the dust runneth into a mass.* A
vigorous description of the earth after a
downpour of rain.

39-41 WHO FEEDS THE LIONESS, YOUNG LIONS AND THE RAVEN?

39. *wilt thou hunt the prey.* Rather,
'Dost thou hunt the prey?' This marks
a new section and the chapter should
properly have begun here. The lioness
and her young, as well as man, are the
objects of God's loving care (cf. Ps. civ.
21). 'These brilliant pictures from the
animal world have the same purpose as
those given before (verses 4-38) from in-
animate nature; they make God to pass
before the eye of Job. They exhibit
the diversity of the animal creation,
the strange dissimilarity of instinct and
habit in creatures outwardly similar, the
singular blending together of contradic-
tory characteristics in the same creature,
and the astonishing attributes and powers
with which some of them are endowed;
and all combines to illustrate the re-
sources of mind and breadth of thought
of Him Who formed them and cares for
them, the manifold play of an immeasurable intelligence and power in the world'
(Davidson).

40. *when they couch in their dens.* Waiting for a passing prey. Would Job be
concerned to provide them with food as
God is?

41. *when his young ones cry unto God.*
God's concern is not only for the king
of beasts but also for one of the most
despised of birds. 'The raven is repeatedly cited as manifesting the goodness
and care of God for His lower creatures.
Not only is its home in desolate places,
but its food is scanty and precarious, and
must be sought over a wide extent of
country, as may be seen by its habit of
flying restlessly about in constant search
of food' (Tristram).

CHAPTER XXXIX

1 Knowest thou the time when the
wild goats of the rock bring
forth?
Or canst thou mark when the
hinds do calve?
2 Canst thou number the months
that they fulfil?
Or knowest thou the time when
they bring forth?
3 They bow themselves, they bring
forth their young,
They cast out their fruit.
4 Their young ones wax strong, they
grow up in the open field;
They go forth, and return not
again.
5 Who hath sent out the wild ass
free?
Or who hath loosed the bands of
the wild ass?
6 Whose house I have made the
wilderness,
And the salt land his dwelling-
place.

1 הֲיָדַעְתָּ עֵת לֶדֶת יַעֲלֵי־סָלַע
חֹלֵל אַיָּלוֹת תִּשְׁמֹר׃
2 תִּסְפֹּר יְרָחִים תְּמַלֶּאנָה
וְיָדַעְתָּ עֵת לִדְתָּנָה׃
3 תִּכְרַעְנָה יַלְדֵיהֶן תְּפַלַּחְנָה
חֶבְלֵיהֶם תְּשַׁלַּחְנָה׃
4 יַחְלְמוּ בְנֵיהֶם יִרְבּוּ בַבָּר
יָצְאוּ וְלֹא־שָׁבוּ לָמוֹ׃
5 מִי־שִׁלַּח פֶּרֶא חָפְשִׁי
וּמֹסְרוֹת עָרוֹד מִי פִתֵּחַ׃
6 אֲשֶׁר־שַׂמְתִּי עֲרָבָה בֵיתוֹ
וּמִשְׁכְּנוֹתָיו מְלֵחָה׃

v. 3. פתח באתנח וס״פ

CHAPTER XXXIX

1-4 DOES JOB KNOW THE HABITS OF THE
WILD GOATS?

1. *knowest thou the time when the wild
goats.* The meaning is: dost thou know,
or canst thou attend to and regulate, i.e.
ordain these laws of birth? The *wild
goats* are a kind of ibex or chamois, an
extremely shy animal.

2. *the months.* The time it takes for
them to carry and bring forth their
young.

3. *they bow themselves.* A revealing
description of the ease with which they
bring forth their young.

4. *their young ones wax strong.* The
verse describes the rapidity with which
these young wild animals develop and
become independent. Though wild,
God's care provides for them.

5-8 THE WILD ASS

5. *the wild ass.* There are two distinct
words in the Hebrew, *perĕ* and *arod.* The
latter is probably an Aramaic loan-word.

free. 'For no man can train a wild ass
and teach it the work of a beast of burden' (Rashi). 'Who gave the wild ass his
freedom and his indomitable love of
liberty—who scorns the noise of cities
and laughs at the shouts of the driver,
which his tame brother obeys? The
point of the questions lies not only in the
striking peculiarities of the beautiful
creature itself, but in the strange
contrast between it and the tame ass,
which in external appearance it resembles.
. . . The abode of the wild ass is in
deserts, untrodden by man (verse 6),
hence he is called "the solitary" (cf.
Hos. viii. 9)' (Davidson).

6. *the salt land.* 'The steppe and the
salt land are the extreme opposite of the
fruitful lands. The wild ass contrives
to live there, and must, if he would be
free from men. Salt is a welcome in-
gredient in its diet' (Peake).

7 He scorneth the tumult of the city,
  Neither heareth he the shoutings
    of the driver.

8 The range of the mountains is his
    pasture,
  And he searcheth after every green
    thing.

9 Will the wild-ox be willing to
    serve thee?
  Or will he abide by thy crib?

10 Canst thou bind the wild-ox with
    his band in the furrow?
  Or will he harrow the valleys
    after thee?

11 Wilt thou trust him, because his
    strength is great?
  Or wilt thou leave thy labour to
    him?

12 Wilt thou rely on him, that he
    will bring home thy seed,
  And gather the corn of thy
    threshing-floor?

13 The wing of the ostrich beateth
    joyously;
  But are her pinions and feathers
    the kindly stork's?

7 יִשְׂחַק לַהֲמוֹן קִרְיָה
  תְּשֻׁאוֹת נוֹגֵשׂ לֹא יִשְׁמָע׃

8 יְתוּר הָרִים מִרְעֵהוּ
  וְאַחַר כָּל־יָרוֹק יִדְרוֹשׁ׃

9 הֲיֹאבֶה רֵּים עָבְדֶךָ
  אִם־יָלִין עַל־אֲבוּסֶךָ׃

10 הֲתִקְשָׁר־רֵים בְּתֶלֶם עֲבֹתוֹ
  אִם־יְשַׂדֵּד עֲמָקִים אַחֲרֶיךָ׃

11 הֲתִבְטַח־בּוֹ כִּי־רַב כֹּחוֹ
  וְתַעֲזֹב אֵלָיו יְגִיעֶךָ׃

12 הֲתַאֲמִין בּוֹ כִּי־יָשׁוּב זַרְעֶךָ
  וְגָרְנְךָ יֶאֱסֹף׃

13 כְּנַף־רְנָנִים נֶעֱלָסָה
  אִם־אֶבְרָה חֲסִידָה וְנֹצָה׃

ישיב ק׳ v. 12.

7. *he scorneth the tumult of the city.* In its innate yearning for liberty, the wild ass instinctively avoids places inhabited by men.

8. *he searcheth after every green thing.* Refusing to be subservient to a human master, this animal has to roam over wide spaces in search of its food. It is, consequently, dependent upon what God provides.

9-12 THE WILD-OX

9. *the wild-ox.* Hebrew *rem* (more commonly *reëm*). Tristram identifies it with the Aureochs, a species of bison, distinguished by its mighty horns and enormous size. It is now extinct in the Holy Land. The same distinction noticed previously between the wild ass and domesticated ass is here drawn between the wild-ox and the tame ox. It, too, is not fed by man.

10. *will he harrow the valleys.* The tame ox was used for ploughing, but let man attempt to use the wild-ox for that purpose!

11. *wilt thou leave thy labour to him?* No farmer would dare!

12. *wilt thou rely on him.* 'Who is the author of this strange diversity of disposition in creatures so like in outward form?' (Davidson).

13-18 THE OSTRICH

13. *the ostrich.* Hebrew *renanim*, lit. '(bird of) piercing cries.' Proverbially cruel to its young (Lam. iv. 3). The ostrich was thought to be deficient in parental instinct and stupid (the Arabs have a proverb, 'More foolish than an ostrich'); yet she can outstrip the fleetest horseman (Driver).

the kindly stork's. The stork is called *kindly* because of its affection for its young, in contrast to the ostrich. Its name *chasidah* is derived from the noun *chesed*, 'loving-kindness.'

14 For she leaveth her eggs on the
　　earth,
　　And warmeth them in the dust,

כִּי־תַעֲזֹב לָאָרֶץ בֵּיצֶיהָ
וְעַל־עָפָר תְּחַמֵּם׃

15 And forgetteth that the foot may
　　crush them,
　　Or that the wild beast may
　　trample them.

וַתִּשְׁכַּח כִּי־רֶגֶל תְּזוּרֶהָ
וְחַיַּת הַשָּׂדֶה תְּדוּשֶׁהָ׃

16 She is hardened against her
　　young ones, as if they were not
　　hers;
　　Though her labour be in vain,
　　she is without fear;

הִקְשִׁיחַ בָּנֶיהָ לְּלֹא־לָהּ
לְרִיק יְגִיעָהּ בְּלִי־פָחַד׃

17 Because God hath deprived her
　　of wisdom,
　　Neither hath He imparted to her
　　understanding.

כִּי־הִשָּׁהּ אֱלוֹהַ חָכְמָה
וְלֹא־חָלַק לָהּ בַּבִּינָה׃

18 When the time cometh, she rais-
　　eth her wings on high,
　　And scorneth the horse and his
　　rider.

כָּעֵת בַּמָּרוֹם תַּמְרִיא
תִּשְׂחַק לַסּוּס וּלְרֹכְבוֹ׃

---

14. *she leaveth her eggs on the earth.* 'Some difficulties have been raised respecting the statement of the ostrich leaving its eggs on the ground, hatching them in the sand, and being cruel to its young. Now the ostrich is polygamous, and several hens deposit their eggs in one place—a hole scraped in the sand. The eggs are then covered over, and left during the heat of the day; but in the colder regions at any rate, as in the Sahara, the birds sit regularly during the night, and until the sun has full power, the male also incubating. But the ostrich lays an immense number of eggs, far more than are ever hatched, and round the covered eggs are to be found many dropped carelessly, as if she forgot that the frost might crack them, or the wild beast might break them. But most naturalists confirm the statement of the natives, that the eggs on the surface are left in order to afford sustenance to the newly hatched chicks, which could not otherwise find food at first in these arid regions. The passage in Job speaks evidently of some eggs warmed in the dust, and others left on the ground' (Tristram).

15. *forgetteth that the foot may crush them.* The poet cites this as illustrating her neglect. But Peake comments: 'Really the shells are very hard, so that there is little danger of their being crushed.'

16. *she is hardened against her young ones.* An illustration of her cruelty to her young (Ibn Ezra). *Young ones* means the unhatched eggs.

she is without fear. 'Though her labour, in laying and sitting on the eggs, be in vain, she is unconcerned about it' (Driver).

17. *deprived her of wisdom.* The lack of understanding of the ostrich is as proverbial as her cruelty.

18. *she raiseth her wings on high.* The verb *tamri*, which only occurs here, probably means 'flappeth (her wings).' The ostrich, though accused of cruelty and stupidity, yet can run at amazing speed. When pursued, she can outdistance horse and rider. 'This singular union of dissimilar qualities, as if it were the work of creative power at play, shows both the inconceivable freedom and resource of the Mind that operates in creation' (Davidson).

19 Hast thou given the horse his
  strength?
  Hast thou clothed his neck with
  fierceness?

20 Hast thou made him to leap as a
  locust?
  The glory of his snorting is
  terrible.

21 He paweth in the valley, and re-
  joiceth in his strength;
  He goeth out to meet the clash of
  arms.

22 He mocketh at fear, and is not
  affrighted;
  Neither turneth he back from the
  sword.

23 The quiver rattleth upon him,
  The glittering spear and the
  javelin.

24 He swalloweth the ground with
  storm and rage;
  Neither believeth he that it is the
  voice of the horn.

19 הֲתִתֵּן לַסּוּס גְּבוּרָה
  הֲתַלְבִּישׁ צַוָּארוֹ רַעְמָה׃

20 הֲתַרְעִישֶׁנּוּ כָּאַרְבֶּה
  הוֹד נַחְרוֹ אֵימָה׃

21 יַחְפְּרוּ בָעֵמֶק וְיָשִׂישׂ בְּכֹחַ
  יֵצֵא לִקְרַאת־נָשֶׁק׃

22 יִשְׂחַק לְפַחַד וְלֹא יֵחָת
  וְלֹא יָשׁוּב מִפְּנֵי־חָרֶב׃

23 עָלָיו תִּרְנֶה אַשְׁפָּה
  לַהַב חֲנִית וְכִידוֹן׃

24 בְּרַעַשׁ וְרֹגֶז יְגַמֶּא־אָרֶץ
  וְלֹא יַאֲמִין כִּי־קוֹל שׁוֹפָר׃

19-25 THE WAR HORSE

19. *the horse.* In the Bible the horse is
always referred to as an animal employed
in war.

fierceness. Hebrew *ra'amah* is of uncertain meaning. In form it is the feminine
of the word rendered *thunder* in verse 25.
R.V. has 'the quivering mane,' but
Davidson thinks that it probably describes the quivering of the neck, when
the animal is roused, which erects the
mane. The noun is found nowhere else.

20. *as a locust.* Cf. Joel ii. 4 where the
locust is compared to the horse. 'The
picture of the horse is taken at the
moment immediately preceding the onset,
and thus his "bounding" and "snorting"
are brought into connection' (Davidson).

21. *he paweth in the valley.* An amaz-
ingly vivid description of the eager
impatience of the war-horse before battle.

22. *he mocketh at fear.* 'He mocks at
something of which a man would be
afraid' (Ibn Ezra).

23. *the quiver rattleth upon him.* The
quiver of the rider, the clang of which
excites him (Davidson).

24. *neither believeth he.* He can hardly
trust his ears that the horn of battle has
in truth been sounded as the signal to leap
forward. An alternative rendering is:
'Neither standeth he still at the sound of
the trumpet' (R.V. margin). The
Hebrew verb admits of both possibilities,
but modern authorities give preference
to the latter.

25. *as oft as he heareth the horn.* The
signal for battle (Amos iii. 6). Eitan
connects *dĕ* with a similar word in
Arabic meaning 'quaking, roar, shout'
and translates, 'at the sound of the
trumpet.'

he smelleth the battle. Has Job created
this wonder of beauty and fierceness and

25 As oft as he heareth the horn he
   saith: 'Ha, ha!'
   And he smelleth the battle afar
   off,
   The thunder of the captains, and
   the shouting.

26 Doth the hawk soar by thy wisdom,
   And stretch her wings toward
   the south?

27 Doth the vulture mount up at thy
   command,
   And make her nest on high?

28 She dwelleth and abideth on the
   rock,
   Upon the crag of the rock, and
   the stronghold.

29 From thence she spieth out the
   prey;
   Her eyes behold it afar off.

30 Her young ones also suck up
   blood;
   And where the slain are, there is
   she.

בְּדֵי שֹׁפָר ׀ יֹאמַר הֶאָח
וּמֵרָחוֹק יָרִיחַ מִלְחָמָה
רַעַם שָׂרִים וּתְרוּעָה׃

הֲמִבִּינָתְךָ יַאֲבֶר־נֵץ
יִפְרֹשׂ כְּנָפָו לְתֵימָן׃

אִם־עַל־פִּיךָ יַגְבִּיהַּ נָשֶׁר
וְכִי יָרִים קִנּוֹ׃

סֶלַע יִשְׁכֹּן וְיִתְלֹנָן
עַל־שֶׁן־סֶלַע וּמְצוּדָה׃

מִשָּׁם חָפַר אֹכֶל
לְמֵרָחוֹק עֵינָיו יַבִּיטוּ׃

וְאֶפְרֹחָו יְעַלְעוּ־דָם
וּבַאֲשֶׁר חֲלָלִים שָׁם הוּא׃

v. 26. כנפיו ק׳ v. 30. ואפרחיו ק׳

endowed him with his extraordinary
qualities, which make him mingle in the
conflicts of men with a fury and a lust of
battle greater even than their own?'
(Davidson).

26-30 THE HAWK AND VULTURE

26. *doth the hawk soar by thy wisdom.*
The verse alludes to the southward
migration of the birds at the approach of
winter (cf. Jer. viii. 7 for the migration
of the stork, turtle, swallow and crane).
Is it Job's wisdom that causes this bird
to fly southward? 'We might translate,
"to the south wind," in which case the
reference would not be to the presage of
winter, but to the strength of wing that
enabled it to fly in the teeth of the
south wind' (Peake).

27. *the vulture.* Cf. ix. 26; the griffon.
make her nest on high. Was it Job who
endowed this bird with the instinct to
build her nest in an almost inaccessible
height? 'While the eagles and other

birds are content with lower elevations,
and sometimes even with trees, the
griffon alone selects the stupendous
gorges of Arabia Petraea, and of the
defiles of Palestine, and there in great
communities rears its young, where the
most intrepid climber can only with
ropes and other appliances reach its
nest' (Tristram).

28. *she dwelleth and abideth on the rock.*
A vigorous description of where the
griffon makes its home.

29. *she spieth out the prey.* 'Did he (Job)
bestow on her the penetrating vision,
which scans the wide expanse of country
and pierces into the deep ravine?'
(Davidson).

30. *suck up blood.* 'Did he (Job) endow
her with her terrible instincts that show
themselves at once in her young, which
suck up blood?' (Davidson). That these
birds display the instinct when quite
young is mentioned in Prov. xxx. 17.

40   CHAPTER XL   מ

1 Moreover the LORD answered Job, and said:

2 Shall he that reproveth contend with the Almighty?
He that argueth with God, let him answer it.

3. Then Job answered the LORD, and said:

4 Behold, I am of small account; what shall I answer Thee?
I lay my hand upon my mouth.

5 Once have I spoken, but I will not answer again;
Yea, twice, but I will proceed no further.

6. Then the LORD answered Job out of the whirlwind, and said:

1 וַיַּעַן יְהֹוָה אֶת־אִיּוֹב וַיֹּאמַר:

2 הֲרֹב עִם־שַׁדַּי יִסּוֹר
מוֹכִיחַ אֱלוֹהַּ יַעֲנֶנָּה:

3 וַיַּעַן אִיּוֹב אֶת־יְהֹוָה וַיֹּאמַר:

4 הֵן קַלֹּתִי מָה אֲשִׁיבֶךָּ
יָדִי שַׂמְתִּי לְמוֹ־פִי:

5 אַחַת דִּבַּרְתִּי וְלֹא אֶעֱנֶה
וּשְׁתַּיִם וְלֹא אוֹסִיף:

6 וַיַּעַן־יְהֹוָה אֶת־אִיּוֹב
מִן | סְעָרָה וַיֹּאמַר:

v. 6. מן ק'

CHAPTER XL

1-2 WILL JOB ARGUE WITH GOD ANY LONGER?

1. *moreover the LORD answered Job.* God continued to address him.

2. *shall he that reproveth contend with the Almighty?* Does Job, who has been critical of God, still wish to dispute with Him after all that he has heard?

let him answer it. By *it* God refers to all the glory of Creation, the display of Divine omnipotence, which He has set before Job in the preceding chapters.

4-5 JOB HUMBLY OWNS HE CAN MAKE NO REPLY

4. *behold, I am of small account.* Hebrew *kallothi*, lit. 'I am too slight,' of too little account, to say anything in reply. The verb, as Ibn Ezra comments, is related to the noun *kalon*, 'ignominy, dishonour.'

I lay my hand upon my mouth. The phrase denotes his surrender by maintaining silence (cf. xxi. 5; xxix. 9). 'Feeling his own insignificance in the presence of God and all the wonders of His universe, Job cannot any longer contend with God . . . For Job's *I am of small account* one might compare the very striking experience under an imperfectly given anæsthetic, in James, *Varieties of Religious Experience,* "And yet, on waking, my first feeling was, and it came with tears, '*Domine non sum digna,*' for I had been lifted into a position for which I was too small" ' (Peake).

5. *but I will proceed no further.* Rashi interprets: 'I have spoken a bit but I will not add any more. But some refer this back to Job's bold charge, *It is all one—therefore I say: He destroyeth the innocent and the wicked* (ix. 22), and alludes to his plea, *Yea, twice—Only do not two things unto me*' (xiii. 20). Job's brief reply reveals his resignation to his fate and the speechless wonder he feels before the majesty of God's creations.

6-14 JOB IRONICALLY INVITED TO RULE THE WORLD

6. This verse is repeated from xxxviii. 1 with the omission of the definite article, the literal translation being 'out of **a** whirlwind.'

7 Gird up thy loins now like a man;
I will demand of thee, and
declare thou unto Me.

8 Wilt thou even make void My
judgment?
Wilt thou condemn Me, that
thou mayest be justified?

9 Or hast thou an arm like God?
And canst thou thunder with a
voice like Him?

10 Deck thyself now with majesty
and excellency,
And array thyself with glory and
beauty.

11 Cast abroad the rage of thy wrath;
And look upon every one that is
proud, and abase him.

אֱזׇר־נָא כְגֶבֶר חֲלָצֶיךָ 7
אֶשְׁאׇלְךָ וְהוֹדִיעֵנִי׃

הַאַף תָּפֵר מִשְׁפָּטִי 8
תַּרְשִׁיעֵנִי לְמַעַן תִּצְדָּק׃

וְאִם־זְרוֹעַ כָּאֵל ׀ לָךְ 9
וּבְקוֹל כָּמֹהוּ תַרְעֵם׃

עֲדֵה־נָא גָאוֹן וָגֹבַהּ 10
וְהוֹד וְהָדָר תִּלְבָּשׁ׃

הָפֵץ עֶבְרוֹת אַפֶּךָ 11
וּרְאֵה כָל־גֵּאֶה וְהַשְׁפִּילֵהוּ׃

7. Repeated from xxxviii. 3 with the
absence of the conjunction *waw, for*.

8. *wilt thou even make void My judgment?*
God inquires of Job whether he would
discredit the Divine righteousness, i.e.
deny what is God's lawful due that He
rules the world justly (cf. xxxiv. 5).
'Wilt thou decide that thy words make
void My judgment and show that it is
perverse?' (Rashi). The Rabbis in their
total perspective of Job were inclined
to agree that his violent outbursts
against the inscrutable justice of God
called for His rebuke. They were particularly shocked by Job's statement,
to them blasphemous, that *He destroyeth
the innocent and the wicked* (alike) (ix. 22).
On the other hand, as Metsudath David
remarks, commenting on xlii. 7 and
quoting the Talmud (B.B. 16b): 'No
man is taken to account for what he
speaks in his distress; because of his dire
afflictions Job spoke as he did.'

9. *or hast thou an arm like God?* 'Job
has challenged God's righteousness. This
righteousness should find its sphere in the
control of the universe; Job has failed to
find it there. But who is he to pose as
God's critic? Could he take God's place?
For that he would need strength to crush
the proud and the wicked. For such a

task he is incompetent; but if he cannot
do God's work, what right has he to say
God does not do it well? He is a critic
from the outside; he needs a knowledge
of the conditions, such as can be gained
only through actual experience of the
task God has to accomplish. For such a
knowledge his human frailty for ever
excludes him; let him recognize the true
inference, that he can never have the
right to impugn God's actions. . . . The
point He makes against Job is simply
that it is foolish for him to find fault with
the course of the world, unless he is
competent to play Providence himself'
(Peake).

canst thou thunder. 'As God thunders
with the Voice of thunder' (Ibn Ezra).

10. *deck thyself now with majesty and
excellency*. In effect the words signify,
'Put thyself in My place Who am *clothed
with glory and majesty* (Ps. civ. 1)'. Job
is invited to imagine himself in control
of the universe.

glory and beauty. These are attributes of
God (Ps. xcvi. 6).

11. *cast abroad the rage of thy wrath*.
'Scatter the rage of thine anger and
indignation upon the wickedness of the

12 Look on every one that is proud,
and bring him low;
And tread down the wicked in
their place.

13 Hide them in the dust together;
Bind their faces in the hidden
place.

14 Then will I also confess unto
thee
That thine own right hand can
save thee.

15 Behold now behemoth, which I
made with thee;
He eateth grass as an ox.

12 רְאֵה כָל־גֵּאֶה הַכְנִיעֵהוּ
וַהֲדֹךְ רְשָׁעִים תַּחְתָּם:

13 טָמְנֵם בֶּעָפָר יָחַד
פְּנֵיהֶם חֲבֹשׁ בַּטָּמוּן:

14 וְגַם־אֲנִי אוֹדֶךָּ
כִּי־תוֹשִׁעַ לְךָ יְמִינֶךָ:

15 הִנֵּה־נָא בְהֵמוֹת אֲשֶׁר־עָשִׂיתִי עִמָּךְ
חָצִיר כַּבָּקָר יֹאכֵל:

people to punish them with the breath of thy lips; and look upon every one that is proud and abase him; that is to say, direct thine eyes upon him and humble him as is proper, but leave the righteous unharmed as is his due' (Metsudath David).

12. *look on . . . bring him low.* This line is practically the same as the second part of verse 11.

tread down. The root *hadach* only occurs here in the Bible; in Arabic it signifies 'to demolish' a building. The meaning is: 'If thou hast the strength, trample upon the arrogant.' 'Of the proud, God mentions two: *behemoth*, which is on dry land (verses 15ff.) and *leviathan* (verses 25ff.) that is in the sea' (Ibn Ezra). The challenge to Job is suffused with irony.

13. *hide them in the dust together.* Cf. Isa. ii. 10, but here the sense is: obliterate them completely so that they are removed from the sight of man.

in the hidden place. i.e. 'in the dust' (Ibn Ezra); 'in the grave' (Ralbag); 'shut them up in the darkness of the prison-house of Death' (Davidson).

14. *then will I also confess unto thee.* Ibn Ezra renders: 'I also will praise thee.' 'The turn of the phrase is unexpected . . . Is God thinking of Job's many proud boasts of innocence, culminating in the splendidly bold utterance with which his great self-vindication had drawn to its close? If you would abase the proud,

you must begin at home, then when you have subdued your own arrogance, I could praise you as able to save yourself. This self-salvation might be scornful irony, for the measure Job would mete out to the proud was no salvation, but a trampling into Sheol' (Peake). There are many instances in Scripture of allusion to God's own saving arm (cf. Isa. lix. 16; Ps. xcviii. 1). It may mean that then, if Job could abase these proud, God would praise his independence or laud him as a perfectly righteous man without faults (Metsudath David).

15-24 CAN JOB SUBDUE BEHEMOTH?

15. *behemoth.* i.e. the hippopotamus, from an assumed Egyptian *p-ehemau,* ox of the water (BDB); but this derivation is disputed by Cheyne and the Egyptologist, W. M. Müller. In all probability the word is the plural of *behemah,* the common Hebrew term for 'beast, cattle,' and the plural form denotes immensity of size. 'The hippopotamus was the largest beast known to the Jews, and this well merited the name *behemoth,* the beast *par excellence*' (Tristram). 'Scholars have been much divided in opinion as to whether behemoth and leviathan are to be understood as actual creatures or as beasts of fable. . . . Leviathan appears as a kind of supernatural enemy of God, but it is more natural in the passage before us to regard both behemoth and leviathan as actual animals. In late Jewish thought they play a decidedly

16 Lo now, his strength is in his
    loins,
And his force is in the stays of
    his body.

17 He straineth his tail like a cedar;
The sinews of his thighs are knit
    together.

18 His bones are as pipes of brass;
His gristles are like bars of iron.

19 He is the beginning of the ways
    of God;
He only that made him can make
    His sword to approach unto
    him.

20 Surely the mountains bring him
    forth food,
And all the beasts of the field
    play there.

הִנֵּה־נָא כֹחוֹ בְמָתְנָיו
וְאֹנוֹ בִּשְׁרִירֵי בִטְנוֹ:
יַחְפֹּץ זְנָבוֹ כְמוֹ־אָרֶז
גִּידֵי פַחֲדָו יְשֹׂרָגוּ:
עֲצָמָיו אֲפִיקֵי נְחֻשָׁה
גְּרָמָיו כִּמְטִיל בַּרְזֶל:
הוּא רֵאשִׁית דַּרְכֵי־אֵל
הָעֹשׂוֹ יַגֵּשׁ חַרְבּוֹ:
כִּי־בוּל הָרִים יִשְׂאוּ־לוֹ
וְכָל־חַיַּת הַשָּׂדֶה יְשַׂחֲקוּ־שָׁם:

v. 17. פתדין ק׳ 18. ד נ׳א בחושה

---

mythological part. So in Enoch lx. 7-9
they are parted in one day to dwell, the
one in the abyss of the sea, and the other
in the wilderness. In IV Ezra vi. 49-52
and Apoc. of Baruch xxix. 4 they are
represented as having been created on
the fifth day of Creation to be the food of
the righteous in Messianic times' (David-
son-Lanchester). Rashi hints similarly
when he comments on *behemoth*: 'prepared for the future.'

which I made with thee. This monster
was the creation of God equally with Job.

he eateth grass as an ox. 'The hippopotamus is strictly herbivorous, and makes
sad havoc among the rice fields and
cultivated grounds when at night he
issues forth from the reedy fens' (Tristram).

16. *his force. On* is a synonym for *koach*,
the more familiar word for *strength* which
occurs in the first line.

stays of his body. The first word, which is
unique, is explained as 'sinews, muscles'
(BDB).

17. *his tail like a cedar.* The language is,
of course hyperbolical. 'The great
strength of the animal may be inferred
from the muscular stiffness of the tail,

which bends like the branch or young
stem of a cedar' (Davidson).

18. *his gristles.* R.V. has 'limbs' and the
margin 'ribs.'

19. *the beginning.* i.e. the largest and
strongest. A.V. and R.V. render: 'the
chief.' Szold and Peake understand the
word as *beginning* and suggest that we
have here an allusion to the statement that
behemah (*cattle*) was created by God first
(Gen. i. 24).

He only that made him . . . unto him.
The line is difficult. The reference is
taken to be to the teeth or eye-tusks of
the hippopotamus, said to be two feet
long. He can use it to cut grass as with
a sword or sickle. The older Jewish
commentators (followed by Szold) interpret: such is the terrifying strength and
size of this beast, that God alone dare
face it in combat.

20. *the mountains bring him forth food.*
'He feeds on the dry land, though an
inhabitant of the waters, and searches
the rising grounds near the rivers for his
sustenance in company with the animals
of the land' (Tristram).

all the beasts of the field play there. Without fear, since the monster does not
attack them, feeding only on grass.

21 He lieth under the lotus-trees,
   In the covert of the reed, and
   fens.

22 The lotus-trees cover him with
   their shadow;
   The willows of the brook compass him about.

23 Behold, if a river overflow, he
   trembleth not;
   He is confident, though the
   Jordan rush forth to his mouth.

24 Shall any take him by his eyes,
   Or pierce through his nose with a
   snare?

25 Canst thou draw out leviathan
   with a fish-hook?
   Or press down his tongue with a
   cord?

21 תַּחַת־צֶאֱלִים יִשְׁכָּב
   בְּסֵתֶר קָנֶה וּבִצָּה׃

22 יְסֻכֻּהוּ צֶאֱלִים צִלֲלוֹ
   יְסֻבּוּהוּ עַרְבֵי־נָחַל׃

23 הֵן יַעֲשֹׁק נָהָר לֹא יַחְפּוֹז
   יִבְטַח ׀ כִּי־יָגִיחַ יַרְדֵּן אֶל־פִּיהוּ׃

24 בְּעֵינָיו יִקָּחֶנּוּ
   בְּמוֹקְשִׁים יִנְקָב־אָף׃

25 תִּמְשֹׁךְ לִוְיָתָן בְּחַכָּה
   וּבְחֶבֶל תַּשְׁקִיעַ לְשֹׁנוֹ׃

21. *the lotus-trees.* A low thorny shrub, bearing fruit similar to a date.

in the covert of the reed. 'The whole of the day is spent under the shady covert of the marshes, or sleeping and snorting in still water, and in the long reaches of rivers' (Tristram).

22. *compass him about.* He finds shade beneath the lotus-trees and willows.

23. *he trembleth not.* He is not disturbed if the waters of the river rise. Tristram thinks there may be an allusion to the annual rising of the Nile.

the Jordan. 'The Jordan is a weird stream. It twists and tears ever more swiftly downward in an almost incredibly sinuous manner from the sweet waters of the Lake of Galilee to the bitter wastes of the Sea of Salt or Dead Sea' (Glueck). The Hebrew word lacks the definite article and is perhaps to be translated 'a Jordan,' the poet using it here only as an example of a swift-flowing river.

24. *shall any take him by his eyes.* The question is understood by some as asked ironically: Can anyone capture him when he is aware of what they intend to do? But the parallel *through his nose* suggests rather a literal interpretation: Would anybody dare to confront such a

powerful monster and hunt it by attacking the eyes or piercing the nose with a hook?

XL. 25-XLI. 26 LEVIATHAN:
THE CROCODILE

25. In A.V. and R.V. chapter xli begins with this verse.

leviathan. In iii. 8 it is mythological or metaphorical (but see *ad loc.*). Modern scholars are in accord that here not a mythological creature is described but the crocodile, familiar on the Nile and also, apparently, at one time in Palestine.

with a fish-hook. The usual explanation is that the line asks the sarcastic question whether this gigantic sea-monster can be caught with a hook like one of the smaller fish. Tristram, however, holds that 'the reference is not to fishing, but to the keeping alive, in tanks, after the Egyptian fashion, fish not required for immediate use, secured by a hook through their gills.'

or press down his tongue with a cord. The entire description is dominated by the idea that the crocodile defies capture. However, the Egyptians were able to take it. This line seems to mean that

26 Canst thou put a ring into his
　　nose?
　　Or bore his jaw through with a
　　hook?

27 Will he make many supplications
　　unto thee?
　　Or will he speak soft words unto
　　thee?

28 Will he make a covenant with
　　thee,
　　That thou shouldest take him for
　　a servant for ever?

29 Wilt thou play with him as with
　　a bird?
　　Or wilt thou bind him for thy
　　maidens?

30 Will the bands of fishermen make
　　a banquet of him?
　　Will they part him among the
　　merchants?

31 Canst thou fill his skin with
　　barbed irons,
　　Or his head with fish-spears?

32 Lay thy hand upon him;
　　Think upon the battle, thou wilt
　　do so no more.

הֲתָשִׂים אַגְמֹן בְּאַפּוֹ 2
וּבְחוֹחַ תִּקֹּב לֶחֱיוֹ:

הֲיַרְבֶּה אֵלֶיךָ תַּחֲנוּנִים 2
אִם־יְדַבֵּר אֵלֶיךָ רַכּוֹת:

הֲיִכְרֹת בְּרִית עִמָּךְ 2
תִּקָּחֶנּוּ לְעֶבֶד עוֹלָם:

הַתְשַׂחֶק־בּוֹ כַּצִּפּוֹר 2
וְתִקְשְׁרֶנּוּ לְנַעֲרוֹתֶיךָ:

יִכְרוּ עָלָיו חַבָּרִים 3
יֶחֱצוּהוּ בֵּין כְּנַעֲנִים:

הַתְמַלֵּא בְשֻׂכּוֹת עוֹרוֹ 3
וּבְצִלְצַל דָּגִים רֹאשׁוֹ:

שִׂים־עָלָיו כַּפֶּךָ 3
זְכֹר מִלְחָמָה אַל־תּוֹסַף:

v. 32. פתח בס״פ

when you have taken the monster, can
you put a rope about his tongue and
lower jaw to lead him about? (Peake).

26. *a ring into his nose.* After you have
caught the crocodile, can you string it on
a line as the fisherman does with fish, to
keep it fresh?

27. *make many supplications . . . speak soft
words.* The questions are sarcastic. Will
the crocodile entreat to be spared or given
kind treatment?

28. *a servant for ever.* Will the crocodile
be willing to be tamed and bound in
perpetual servitude as a bondman?
(Rashi).

29. *wilt thou play with him as with a bird?*
Will you be able to make a pet of him in
the way that children make a pet of small
birds? (Rashi).

for thy maidens. To be treated as a
plaything by them.

30. *make a banquet of him.* In later Jewish
folk-lore, the banquet on the flesh of
leviathan is the feast in store for the
righteous in the Hereafter. Here the
image is that of the company of fishermen
trafficking with the merchants.

the merchants. lit. 'the Canaanites,'
Phœnician traders.

31. *barbed irons . . . fish-spears.* The
crocodile's skin, like armour, will turn
aside the harpoons aimed at him.

32. *lay thy hand upon him.* A grim,
ironic warning. If you dare to lay your
hand on him, beware! You will probably never be able to repeat the attempt!
(Ibn Ezra).

CHAPTER XLI

1 Behold, the hope of him is in vain;
Shall not one be cast down even at the sight of him?

2 None is so fierce that dare stir him up;
Who then is able to stand before Me?

3 Who hath given Me anything beforehand, that I should repay him?
Whatsoever is under the whole heaven is Mine.

4 Would I keep silence concerning his boastings,
Or his proud talk, or his fair array of words?

א הֵן־תֹּחַלְתּוֹ נִכְזָבָה
הֲגַם אֶל־מַרְאָיו יֻטָל:

ב לֹא־אַכְזָר כִּי יְעוּרֶנּוּ
וּמִי הוּא לְפָנַי יִתְיַצָּב:

ג מִי הִקְדִּימַנִי וַאֲשַׁלֵּם
תַּחַת כָּל־הַשָּׁמַיִם לִי־הוּא:

ד לֹא־אַחֲרִישׁ בַּדָּיו
וּדְבַר־גְּבוּרוֹת וְחִין עֶרְכּוֹ:

v. 2. יעורנו ק׳   v. 4. לו ק׳

CHAPTER XLI

1-4 IF NONE DARE FACE HIM, WHO CAN CONFRONT GOD?

1. *the hope of him is in vain.* This passage is difficult and obscure. The meaning of the verse seems to be that it is the height of folly to think that one can subdue this terrible monster. If any person entertains such a hope, it is in vain. Its very appearance would fill him with dismay.

2. *before Me.* Before God, the Maker of all these (behemoth and leviathan) (Rashi). This and the next verse, though obscure, appear to be a moralizing reflection of the poet, impressing the reason for elaborating the invincible strength of leviathan. 'If none dare stir up this creature, which God has made, who will stand before God Who created him, or venture to contend with Him?' (Davidson).

3. *who hath given Me anything beforehand.* Which human being can have any demand upon God? He owes man nothing, since everything is His. The verse is an indirect rebuke of Job who thought he had reason to assert a claim against God.

4. The verse is obscure. Attached to what precedes, its intention perhaps is: were a man to presume to make a demand of God (as Job has done), would He maintain silence against such effrontery? Most modern scholars prefer to connect the verse with what follows as a statement by God on three aspects of leviathan which are to be noted: (1) 'its limbs' (so translate for *his boastings*, as in xviii. 13), (2) 'the matter of (its) strength' (so instead of *his proud talk*) and (3) 'its incomparable status' (not *his fair array of words*) among other creatures.

5-16 DESCRIPTION OF THE LIMBS OF LEVIATHAN

5. *garment.* His armour of scales.

double bridle. His terrible jaws with their two formidable rows of teeth.

5 Who can uncover the face of his
   garment?
  Who shall come within his double
   bridle?

6 Who can open the doors of his
   face?
  Round about his teeth is terror.

7 His scales are his pride,
  Shut up together as with a close
   seal.

8 One is so near to another,
  That no air can come between
   them.

9 They are joined one to another;
  They stick together, that they cannot be sundered.

10 His sneezings flash forth light,
   And his eyes are like the eyelids
    of the morning.

11 Out of his mouth go burning
    torches,
   And sparks of fire leap forth.

מִי־גִלָּה פְּנֵי לְבוּשׁוֹ 5
בְּכֶפֶל רִסְנוֹ מִי יָבוֹא:
דַּלְתֵי פָנָיו מִי פִתֵּחַ 6
סְבִיבוֹת שִׁנָּיו אֵימָה:
גַּאֲוָה אֲפִיקֵי מָגִנִּים 7
סָגוּר חוֹתָם צָר:
אֶחָד בְּאֶחָד יִגַּשׁוּ 8
וְרוּחַ לֹא־יָבֹא בֵינֵיהֶם:
אִישׁ־בְּאָחִיהוּ יְדֻבָּקוּ 9
יִתְלַכְּדוּ וְלֹא יִתְפָּרָדוּ:
עֲטִישֹׁתָיו תָּהֶל אוֹר 1
וְעֵינָיו כְּעַפְעַפֵּי־שָׁחַר:
מִפִּיו לַפִּידִים יַהֲלֹכוּ 1
כִּידוֹדֵי אֵשׁ יִתְמַלָּטוּ:

6. *the doors of his face.* His mouth.

round about his teeth is terror. The jaws
of the crocodile are very extended; and
being bare of lips, the teeth, long and
pointed, present a terrifying sight.

7. *his scales are his pride.* Verses 7-9
describe his armour of scales, lit. 'channels of shields,' referring to the grooves
between the rows. Each scale is like a
curved shield, and they adhere to the
monster's body firmly and closely in rows.

8. *one is so near to another.* An elabora-
tion of verse 7 describing the closeness
with which scale is attached to scale so
as to leave no vulnerable place exposed
to attack.

9. *they are joined one to another.* Further
repetitious detail. This is obviously a

feature of the crocodile which particularly aroused the poet's wonder.

10. *his sneezings.* Hebrew *atishothaw*,
a good example of onomatopœia. The
spray forced through his nostrils appears
to flash light in the bright sun.

the eyelids of the morning. As in iii. 9.
In Egyptian hieroglyphs, the eye of the
crocodile represents the dawn. Its
reddish eyes are seen under the water
before it comes to the surface (Davidson).

11. *burning torches.* Verses 11-13 are
poetic hyperbole, describing the spray
expelled from the animal's nostrils, his
steaming breath. But as Peake remarks,
'The author may have embroidered his
picture with reminiscences of stories of
fire-breathing dragons.'

12 Out of his nostrils goeth smoke,
   As out of a seething pot and
   burning rushes.

13 His breath kindleth coals,
   And a flame goeth out of his
   mouth.

14 In his neck abideth strength,
   And dismay danceth before him.

15 The flakes of his flesh are joined
   together;
   They are firm upon him; they
   cannot be moved.

16 His heart is as firm as a stone;
   Yea, firm as the nether millstone.

17 When he raiseth himself up, the
   mighty are afraid;
   By reason of despair they are
   beside themselves.

18 If one lay at him with the sword,
   it will not hold;
   Nor the spear, the dart, nor the
   pointed shaft.

19 He esteemeth iron as straw,
   And brass as rotten wood.

מִנְּחִירָיו יֵצֵא עָשָׁן 12
כְּדוּד נָפוּחַ וְאַגְמֹן׃

נַפְשׁוֹ גֶּחָלִים תְּלַהֵט 13
וְלַהַב מִפִּיו יֵצֵא׃

בְּצַוָּארוֹ יָלִין עֹז 14
וּלְפָנָיו תָּדוּץ דְּאָבָה׃

מַפְּלֵי בְשָׂרוֹ דָבֵקוּ 15
יָצוּק עָלָיו בַּל־יִמּוֹט׃

לִבּוֹ יָצוּק כְּמוֹ־אָבֶן 16
וְיָצוּק כְּפֶלַח תַּחְתִּית׃

מִשֵּׂתוֹ יָגוּרוּ אֵלִים 17
מִשְּׁבָרִים יִתְחַטָּאוּ׃

מַשִּׂיגֵהוּ חֶרֶב בְּלִי תָקוּם 18
חֲנִית מַסָּע וְשִׁרְיָה׃

יַחְשֹׁב לְתֶבֶן בַּרְזֶל 19
לְעֵץ רִקָּבוֹן נְחוּשָׁה׃

12. out of his nostrils goeth smoke. Compare this lurid description with 2 Sam. xxii. 9; Ps. xviii. 9, of the Divine theophany.

13. his breath. Hebrew *naphsho*, lit. 'his soul.' 'The breath that comes out of his mouth' (Ibn Ezra).

14. danceth. The Hebrew root *duts* only occurs here. 'No dismay is before him; only strength and pride' (Ibn Ezra). The verse rather describes the creature's mighty neck which makes everyone jump with terror.

15. the flakes of his flesh. The underparts beneath the neck and belly are not soft as in other animals but muscular and firm.

16. the nether millstone. The poet compares the creature's heart, firm as the lower millstone which was always heavier than the upper millstone. It bears all the pressure and rests upon the solid earth (Ibn Ezra).

17-24 LEVIATHAN'S STRENGTH

17. when he raiseth himself up. Disporting himself in the sea, his monstrous appearance fills even the strong and brave with terror.

18. if one lay at him with the sword. Verses 18-21 depict his impenetrable armour against all weapons. *Lay at him* means to strike him with any of these weapons.

pointed shaft. Hebrew *shiryah*, which is not found elsewhere in Scripture. In Arabic the cognate word is the term for a short dart. A missile like the harpoon is evidently intended.

19. iron as straw. Hard metals glance from his flanks like straw or dead wood.

20 The arrow cannot make him flee;
   Slingstones are turned with him
   into stubble.

לֹא־יַבְרִיחֶנּוּ בֶן־קָשֶׁת
לְקַשׁ נֶהְפְּכוּ־לוֹ אַבְנֵי־קָלַע׃

21 Clubs are accounted as stubble;
   He laugheth at the rattling of the
   javelin.

כְּקַשׁ נֶחְשְׁבוּ תוֹתָח
וְיִשְׂחַק לְרַעַשׁ כִּידוֹן׃

22 Sharpest potsherds are under
   him;
   He spreadeth a threshing-sledge
   upon the mire.

תַּחְתָּיו חַדּוּדֵי חָרֶשׂ
יִרְפַּד חָרוּץ עֲלֵי־טִיט׃

23 He maketh the deep to boil like a
   pot;
   He maketh the sea like a seething
   mixture.

יַרְתִּיחַ כַּסִּיר מְצוּלָה
יָם יָשִׂים כַּמֶּרְקָחָה׃

24 He maketh a path to shine after
   him;
   One would think the deep to be
   hoary.

אַחֲרָיו יָאִיר נָתִיב
יַחְשֹׁב תְּהוֹם לְשֵׂיבָה׃

25 Upon earth there is not his like,
   Who is made to be fearless.

אֵין־עַל־עָפָר מָשְׁלוֹ
הֶעָשׂוּ לִבְלִי־חָת׃

26 He looketh at all high things;
   He is king over all the proud
   beasts.

אֶת־כָּל־גָּבֹהַּ יִרְאֶה
הוּא מֶלֶךְ עַל־כָּל־בְּנֵי־שָׁחַץ׃

---

20. *the arrow.* lit. 'son of the bow.'

21. *clubs.* Hebrew *tothach*, occurring only here, but the translation is supported by the Arabic equivalent.

he laugheth. The crocodile scorns the brandishing of the javelin.

22. *sharpest potsherds are under him.* The verse describes the mark which he leaves on the mud where he has lain, as if a threshing-sledge had been there.

23. *a seething mixture.* Hebrew *merkachah*, lit. 'an ointment pan.' A description of the commotion in the deep raised by the crocodile. He stirs up a white frothy foam like the foaming mixture in the ointment pan.

24. *the deep to be hoary.* He leaves a white furrow of foam as his shining track through the seas, comparable to the grayness of old age in the human being.

25-26 LEVIATHAN'S UNIQUENESS

25. *upon earth there is not his like.* Verses 25f. depict him as the unrivalled monster of the deep. 'God has made him not to know the meaning of fear' (Ibn Ezra).

26. *he looketh at all high things.* i.e. without fear. Rashi explains: 'he looks down upon all creatures in the world'; he is supreme above them.

the proud beasts. lit. 'the sons of pride,' as in xxviii. 8.

CHAPTER XLII

1. Then Job answered the LORD, and said:

2 I know that Thou canst do every thing,
And that no purpose can be withholden from Thee.

3 Who is this that hideth counsel without knowledge?
Therefore have I uttered that which I understood not,
Things too wonderful for me, which I knew not.

4 Hear, I beseech Thee, and I will speak;
I will demand of Thee, and declare Thou unto me.

5 I had heard of Thee by the hearing of the ear;
But now mine eye seeth Thee;

1 וַיַּעַן אִיּוֹב אֶת־יְהֹוָה וַיֹּאמַר׃

2 יָדַעְתָּ כִּי־כֹל תּוּכָל
וְלֹא־יִבָּצֵר מִמְּךָ מְזִמָּה׃

3 מִי זֶה ׀ מַעְלִים עֵצָה בְּלִי־דָעַת
לָכֵן הִגַּדְתִּי וְלֹא אָבִין
נִפְלָאוֹת מִמֶּנִּי וְלֹא אֵדָע׃

4 שְׁמַע־נָא וְאָנֹכִי אֲדַבֵּר
אֶשְׁאָלְךָ וְהוֹדִיעֵנִי׃

5 לְשֵׁמַע אֹזֶן שְׁמַעְתִּיךָ
וְעַתָּה עֵינִי רָאָתְךָ׃

v. 2. ידעתי ק׳

CHAPTER XLII

2-6 JOB'S SECOND REPLY TO GOD

2. *Thou canst do every thing.* There is no purpose that the Almighty cannot carry out; a confession of His power but also of His wisdom as manifested in Creation.

3. *who is this that hideth counsel without knowledge?* Cf. xxxviii. 2 in God's speech to Job. Driver maintains that Job repeats the question addressed to him for the purpose of admitting in the succeeding two lines the justice of the rebuke implied in it.

4. *I will demand of Thee, and declare Thou unto me.* This line is a repetition of xxxviii. 3. Davidson takes the verse not as a petition by Job for further instruction, but as closely connected with what follows.

5. *I had heard of Thee by the hearing of the ear.* Job confesses that hitherto his awareness of God had been only by hearsay and borrowed tradition. Now privileged to behold the Divine Splendour, he is humbled and penitent. 'The supreme lesson,' says Peake finely, 'of the Book. His previous knowledge of God was that given by the traditional theology, in which he had been trained. It left no room for the suffering of the righteous; if the righteous suffered, then the theology was false. Such an inference Job had been forced to draw. But now he has seen God, and all is changed. He knows that God is righteous, he knows that, though he suffers, he is righteous also. How these apparent contradictories can be intellectually reconciled he does not know. But he and God are again at one, a deeper fellowship is possible, untroubled by misgivings as to God's moral integrity. Happy, even in his pain, that he has found himself and his God, he would rather suffer, if God willed it, than be in health and prosperity. He knows that all is well, he and his sufferings have their place in God's inscrutable design; why should he seek to understand it? In child-like reverence he acknowledges it to be far beyond him. This mystical solution is the most precious thing the Book has to offer us.'

6 Wherefore I abhor my words, and
  repent,
  Seeing I am dust and ashes.

7. And it was so, that after the
LORD had spoken these words unto
Job, the LORD said to Eliphaz the
Temanite: 'My wrath is kindled
against thee, and against thy two
friends; for ye have not spoken of
Me the thing that is right, as My
servant Job hath. 8. Now therefore,
take unto you seven bullocks and
seven rams, and go to My servant
Job, and offer up for yourselves a
burnt-offering; and My servant Job
shall pray for you; for him will I
accept, that I do not unto you aught
unseemly; for ye have not spoken
of Me the thing that is right, as My

עַל־כֵּן אֶמְאַס וְנִחָ֑מְתִּי
עַל־עָפָ֥ר וָאֵֽפֶר׃

וַיְהִ֗י אַחַ֨ר דִּבֶּ֧ר יְהֹוָ֛ה אֶת־
הַדְּבָרִ֥ים הָאֵ֖לֶּה אֶל־אִיּ֑וֹב וַיֹּ֣אמֶר
יְהֹוָ֗ה אֶל־אֱלִיפַ֣ז הַתֵּימָנִי֮ חָרָ֣ה אַפִּ֣י
בְךָ֘ וּבִשְׁנֵ֣י רֵעֶ֒יךָ֒ כִּ֣י לֹ֧א דִבַּרְתֶּ֛ם אֵלַ֖י
נְכוֹנָ֥ה כְּעַבְדִּ֣י אִיּֽוֹב׃ וְעַתָּ֡ה קְחֽוּ־
לָכֶ֣ם שִׁבְעָֽה־פָרִים֩ וְשִׁבְעָ֨ה אֵילִ֜ים
וּלְכ֣וּ ׀ אֶל־עַבְדִּ֣י אִיּ֗וֹב וְהַעֲלִיתֶ֤ם
עוֹלָה֙ בַּֽעַדְכֶ֔ם וְאִיּ֣וֹב עַבְדִּ֔י יִתְפַּלֵּ֖ל
עֲלֵיכֶ֑ם כִּ֤י ׀ אִם־פָּנָיו֙ אֶשָּׂ֔א לְבִלְתִּ֕י
עֲשׂ֥וֹת עִמָּכֶ֖ם נְבָלָ֑ה כִּ֛י לֹ֥א דִבַּרְתֶּ֛ם

פתח באתנח v. 6.

---

6. *I abhor my words.* The Hebrew is
simply 'I abhor.' A.V. and R.V. supply
'myself,' but probably Job has in mind
the attitude he had previously adopted
and the words in which he had expressed
it.

dust and ashes. Cf. Gen. xviii. 27. Job
penitently and humbly acknowledges his
human limitations in face of the impenetrable mystery of God's ordering.

PART III.—THE EPILOGUE

7-9 GOD REBUKES JOB'S FRIENDS

7. *the LORD said to Eliphaz.* It is not
without significance that in the epilogue
Eliphaz and his two companions are
referred to but the text is silent about
Elihu. The three friends are publicly
rebuked by God. Their theology, that
suffering necessarily implies sin, is thus
censured by Him.

the thing that is right. Job received God's
commendation in the presence of his
friends. 'It is obvious that the three

friends spoke many just and profound
things concerning God, and that Job on
the other hand said many things that
were both blameworthy and false, things
for which he was both rebuked by the
Almighty, and expressed his penitence.
The reference cannot be to such things
as these. . . . The friends are blamed for
speaking in regard to God that which was
not right, or true, *in itself*; and the reference must be to the theories they put
forth in regard to God's providence and
the meaning of afflictions. On this point
the friends spoke in regard to God what
was not right, while Job spoke that which
was right' (Davidson).

My servant Job. God so acclaims him
in the end as in the beginning (i. 8).

8. *for him will I accept.* Once again God
stresses the integrity of Job, applauding
his intellectual honesty. Job is delineated
here as forgiving the friends, despite
their cruel conclusions of his wickedness
and their later fanaticism, interceding
for them. We have one more touch to
the portrait of a completely righteous
man.

servant Job hath.' 9. So Eliphaz the Temanite and Bildad the Shuhite and Zophar the Naamathite went, and did according as the LORD commanded them; and the LORD accepted Job. 10. And the LORD changed the fortune of Job, when he prayed for his friends; and the LORD gave Job twice as much as he had before. 11. Then came there unto him all his brethren, and all his sisters, and all they that had been of his acquaintance before, and did eat bread with him in his house; and they bemoaned him, and comforted him concerning all the evil that the LORD had brought upon him; every man also gave him a piece of money, and every one a ring of gold. 12. So the LORD blessed the latter end of Job more than his beginning; and he had fourteen thousand sheep, and six thousand camels, and a thousand yoke of oxen, and a thousand she-

9 אֵלַי נְכוֹנָה כְּעַבְדִּי אִיּוֹב: וַיֵּלְכוּ
אֱלִיפַז הַתֵּימָנִי וּבִלְדַּד הַשּׁוּחִי צֹפַר
הַנַּעֲמָתִי וַיַּעֲשׂוּ כַּאֲשֶׁר דִּבֶּר אֲלֵיהֶם
יְהוָה וַיִּשָּׂא יְהוָה אֶת־פְּנֵי אִיּוֹב:
10 וַיהוָה שָׁב אֶת־שְׁבִית אִיּוֹב
בְּהִתְפַּלְלוֹ בְּעַד רֵעֵהוּ וַיֹּסֶף יְהוָה
אֶת־כָּל־אֲשֶׁר לְאִיּוֹב לְמִשְׁנֶה:
11 וַיָּבֹאוּ אֵלָיו כָּל־אֶחָיו וְכָל־אַחְיוֹתָיו
וְכָל־יֹדְעָיו לְפָנִים וַיֹּאכְלוּ עִמּוֹ
לֶחֶם בְּבֵיתוֹ וַיָּנֻדוּ לוֹ וַיְנַחֲמוּ אֹתוֹ
עַל כָּל־הָרָעָה אֲשֶׁר־הֵבִיא יְהוָה
עָלָיו וַיִּתְּנוּ־לוֹ אִישׁ קְשִׂיטָה אֶחָת
12 וְאִישׁ נֶזֶם זָהָב אֶחָד: וַיהוָה בֵּרַךְ
אֶת־אַחֲרִית אִיּוֹב מֵרֵאשִׁתוֹ וַיְהִי־לוֹ
אַרְבָּעָה עָשָׂר אֶלֶף צֹאן וְשֵׁשֶׁת
אֲלָפִים גְּמַלִּים וְאֶלֶף צֶמֶד בָּקָר

v. 10. שבות ק

---

aught unseemly. Hebrew nebalah, 'contumely, disgrace,' i.e. deal out to you disgrace, expose you and punish you as churls because of your utterances about Me (BDB).

9. the LORD accepted Job. He heard Job's prayer on behalf of the friends and forgave them their presumption.

10-17 JOB'S REHABILITATION

10. changed the fortune. lit. 'turned the captivity,' a Hebrew idiom for 'restored to prosperity.' Ibn Ezra remarks that at this point Job was delivered out of the jurisdiction of the Satan.

11. did eat bread with him. The friendship, which had been interrupted during his time of calamity, was now resumed.

they bemoaned him, and comforted him. For the sorrow and pain he had endured in the past, but now happily over.

a piece of money. Hebrew kesitah, a piece of uncoined silver (Gen. xxxiii. 19). 'The presents were simply tokens of congratulation, not designed to enrich him, their value was too trifling' (Peake).

12. so the LORD blessed the latter end. Davidson finds it necessary to comment that the exact doubling of Job's former possessions shows that we are not reading literal history here. Cf. the Talmudic statement (B.B. 15a) of the Rabbi who remarked, 'Job never was and never existed, but is only a typical figure (to teach men the virtue of resignation)'. The figures given in the verse are double those mentioned in i. 3.

asses. 13. He had also seven sons and three daughters. 14. And he called the name of the first, [a]Jemimah; and the name of the second, [b]Keziah; and the name of the third, [c]Keren-happuch. 15. And in all the land were no women found so fair as the daughters of Job; and their father gave them inheritance among their brethren. 16. And after this Job lived a hundred and forty years, and saw his sons, and his sons' sons, even four generations. 17. So Job died, being old and full of days.

[a]That is, *Dove*.   [b]That is, *Cassia*.
[c]That is, *Horn of eye-paint*.

וְאֶלֶף אֲתוֹנֽוֹת׃ וַיְהִי־לוֹ שִׁבְעָנָה
בָנִים וְשָׁלוֹשׁ בָּנוֹת׃ וַיִּקְרָא שֵׁם־
הָאַחַת יְמִימָה וְשֵׁם הַשֵּׁנִית קְצִיעָה
וְשֵׁם הַשְּׁלִישִׁית קֶרֶן הַפּוּךְ׃ וְלֹא
נִמְצָא נָשִׁים יָפוֹת כִּבְנוֹת אִיּוֹב בְּכָל־
הָאָרֶץ וַיִּתֵּן לָהֶם אֲבִיהֶם נַחֲלָה
בְּתוֹךְ אֲחֵיהֶם׃ וַיְחִי אִיּוֹב אַחֲרֵי־
זֹאת מֵאָה וְאַרְבָּעִים שָׁנָה וַיִּרְאֶ אֶת־
בָּנָיו וְאֶת־בְּנֵי בָנָיו אַרְבָּעָה דֹרוֹת׃
וַיָּמָת אִיּוֹב זָקֵן וּשְׂבַע יָמִים׃

v. 16. וירֽאה ק׳

חזק

סכום פסוקי איוב אלף ושבעים. וסימנו וגליתי להם עֲתֶרֶת שלום
ואמת. וחציו אשר קמטו ולא עת. וסדריו שמונה. וסימנו אֲהַב
ה׳ שערי ציון׃

13. *he had also seven sons and three daughters.* 'While his possessions are doubled, it is a fine trait that the number of the children is the same as before. For us no child lost can be replaced' (Peake).

14. *and he called the name.* The names are an indication of their beauty.

15. *gave them inheritance.* The law in Num. xxvii. 1-11 allowed daughters to inherit only when there was no son. Job went beyond the ancient law. 'The disposition of his property made by Job would retain the sisters in the midst of their brethren even after marriage, and allow the affectionate relations existing among Job's children to continue' (Davidson).

16. *and after this.* Metsudath David interprets that Job lived this number of years after his restoration. The more natural way to understand the figure is the total of his years when he died.

17. *old and full of years.* This was similarly reported of Abraham (Gen. xxv. 8) and Isaac (Gen. xxxv. 29).

Authorities quoted

Terms and Abbreviations

Index

AUTHORITIES QUOTED

Aboth—*Pirke Aboth, Sayings of the Fathers :* Mishnaic tractate.

Baldwin, E. C. (Christian Scholar), *Types of Literature in the Old Testament.*

Berechiah (Mediæval French Rabbi), *Commentary on Job,* ed. W. A. Wright and S. A. Hirsch.

Bewer, J. A. (Christian Hebraist), *The Literature of the Old Testament in its Historical Development* (Revised edition, 1933).

Blake, William (English Poet and Artist), *Illustrations of the Book of Job* (L. Binyon and G. Keynes).

Brown, F., Driver, S. R. and Briggs, C. A., *Hebrew and English Lexicon of the Old Testament.*

Buttenweiser, M. (American-Jewish Scholar), *The Book of Job.*

Chase, M. E. (American Novelist and Scholar), *The Bible and the Common Reader.*

Cheyne, T. K. (Christian Hebraist), *Job and Solomon.*

Cohen, A. (Anglo-Jewish Scholar), Commentary on *Psalms* and *Proverbs* (Soncino Books of the Bible).

Davidson, A. B. (Christian Hebraist), *The Book of Job* (Cambridge Bible); also new edition adapted to the text of the R.V. with some supplementary notes by H. C. O. Lanchester.

Driver, S. R. (Christian Hebraist), *The Book of Job in the Revised Version; An Introduction to the Literature of the Old Testament.*

Eitan, I. (Jewish Orientalist), *A Contribution to Biblical Lexicography.*

Glueck, N. (American Bible Archæologist), *The River Jordan.*

Ibn Ezra, Abraham (1092-1167, Bible Commentator), *Commentary on Job.*

Jastrow, M. (American-Jewish Orientalist), *The Book of Job.*

Kent, C. F. (Christian Hebraist), *The Growth and Contents of the Old Testament.*

Kimchi, David (1160-1235, Bible Commentator).

Kohler, K. (American-Jewish Theologian), *Jewish Theology.*

Kraeling, E. G. (Christian Hebraist), *The Book of the Ways of God.*

Levine, I. (Anglo-Jewish Philosopher), *Faithful Rebels.*

Lindsay, A. D. (Master of Balliol College, Oxford), Prologue to *The Legacy of Israel.*

Lofthouse, W. F. (Christian Hebraist), *Commentary on Job* (Abingdon Bible Commentary).

Maimonides, Moses (1135-1204, Jewish Philosopher), *Guide for the Perplexed.*

Metsudath David ('Tower of David'), *Commentary on Job by* David Altschul, 17th century.

Midrash—Rabbinic homilies on the Pentateuch, etc.

Montefiore, C. G. (Anglo-Jewish Scholar), *The Bible for Home Reading.*

Moore, G. F. (Christian Hebraist), *The Literature of the Old Testament; Judaism.*

Moulton, R. F. (Professor of English), *The Literary Study of the Bible.*

Peake, A. S. (Christian Hebraist), *Commentary on Job* (The Century Bible).

Peshitta—Syriac translation of the Bible, 2nd century C.E.

Pfeiffer, R. H. (Christian Hebraist), *Introduction to the Old Testament.*

Ralbag (Rabbi Levi ben Gershon, 1288-1344, Bible Commentator and Philosopher), *Commentary on Job.*

Rashi (Rabbi Solomon ben Isaac, 1040-1105, Bible Commentator), *Commentary on Job.*

Saadia (882-942, Bible Exegete and Philosopher).

Septuagint—Greek translation of the Bible, begun in the third century B.C.E.

Sonne, I. (Jewish Scholar), in *Kiryath Sepher.*

Spiegel, S. (American-Jewish Scholar), *Noah, Daniel and Job touching on Canaanite Relics in the Legends of the Jews* (in Louis Ginzberg Jubilee Volume).

Szold, B. (American-Jewish Scholar), *Das Buch Hiob.*

Talmud—Corpus of Jewish Law and Thought (compiled at the end of the 5th century C.E.).

Targum—Aramaic Translation of the Bible (1st and 2nd centuries C.E.).

Thomson, W. M. (Christian Traveller), *The Land and the Book.*

Tristram, H. B. (Natural Scientist), *The Natural History of the Bible.*

Vulgate—Latin Translation of the Bible (4th century C.E.).

TERMS AND ABBREVIATIONS

ad loc.   At that place.

A.J.   American-Jewish translation of the Scriptures.

Apoc.   Apocalypse.

A.V.   Authorized Version.

B.B.   *Baba Bathra*, Talmudical tractate.

B.C.E.   Before the Christian era.

BDB   Brown, Driver and Briggs (see Authorities Quoted).

B.M.   *Baba Metsia*, Talmudical tractate.

C.E.   Common era.

cf.   Compare, refer to.

ch.   Chapter.

ed.   Editor, or edited by.

e.g.   For example.

f.   Following verse or chapter (plural ff.).

fem.   Feminine.

i.e.   That is.

kerĕ.   The Hebrew as it is to be read according to the Masoretes.

kethib.   The Hebrew as it is written according to tradition.

lit.   Literally.

LXX.   Septuagint (see Authorities Quoted).

M.   Mishnah.

masc.   Masculine.

M.K.   *Moed Katon*, Talmudical tractate.

MS.   Manuscript (plural MSS.).

M.T.   Masoretic text.

R.H.   *Rosh Hashanah*, Talmudical tractate.

R.V.   Revised Version.

Sanh.   *Sanhedrin*, Talmudical tractate.

sing.   Singular.

Tos.   Tosiphta.

viz.   Namely.

INDEX

I. NAMES AND SUBJECTS.

A

Adulterer, 128

Adultery, 158

Aged, not necessarily wise, 57, 166f.; wisdom of the, 74

Angels, 9, 16, 17, 19, 40, 75, 112, 131, 173, 197

Anger, effect of, 18, 187

Animals, God's care of, 203, 204f.

Arcturus, 192

Asps, 104

Ass, the wild, 23, 52f., 125, 204f.

Astronomical references, 40, 133, 201f.

Augustine, *quoted*, 100

B

Bear, the (constellation), 40, 202

Behemoth, 211ff.

Belt, 'loosening,' the, 59

Bildad, 7, 221; speeches of, 34-38, 89-93, 131f.

'Bottles of heaven,' 203

Brass, 140

Bribery, 79

Broom, the, 151

Butter, 146

C

Carlyle, T., *quoted*, xiii

Cellini, Benvenuto, *quoted*, 200

Chaldeans, the, 4

'Chambers of the south,' 40

Chase, M.E., *quoted*, xiii

Cheek, smiting the, 82

Cheese, 47

Chiquitilla, Moses Ibn, *quoted*, 88

Chrysostomus, J., *quoted*, 100

City, gate of, 147, 160

Clay, man formed from, 47, 170; the body 'a house of,' 17

Cloud, life compared to, 30

Clouds, the, 134, 189, 192, 193, 197, 202, 203

Coat, collar of, 154

Conscience, a bad, 76f.

Coral, 143

Cosmology, primitive, 39, 134, 197

Coverdale, M., *quoted*, 110

Crystal, 143

Curse, 162

D

Darkness, location of, 199; metaphor of calamity, 76, 77, 78, 88, 106, 117, 124; the land of, 49f.

Dawn, ordained by God, 198

Day, Hebraic concept of, 9; of wrath, 113

Death, 'first-born' of, 92; 'gates' of, 199; 'house' of, 155; knowledge ceases at, 71; life after, 69; longing for, 13; peace in, 12; 'shadow' of, 9, 49f., 60, 83, 199 (a term for darkness, 129, 141, 178); 'terrors' of, 106

Demons, 22

Desolate places, haunted, 77f.

Dew, 201

Dreams, 31, 172

E

Earth, 'pillars' of the, 39

Earthquake, 39

Ecclesiastes, compared with *Job*, 196

Eclipse of the sun, 11

Egypt, author's knowledge of, 36, 213

Eitan, I., *quoted*, 97, 107, 122, 123, 176, 188, 190, 207

Elders, humbled, 59

Elephantiasis, 6; symptoms of, 30, 31, 32, 98, 154, 156

Elihu, xvii, 165f.; speech of, 167-195

Eliphaz, 7, 220, 221; speeches of, 13-22, 72-79, 115-121

Enchanters, 10

Enemy, kind treatment of, 162

Envy, effect of, 18

Eshmunazar, 114

Ethiopia, 144

Eye, agent of sin, 156, 157

'Eyelids of the morning,' 11, 216

Euphemism, use of, 2, 3, 6, 7, 158

F

Face, spitting in the, 87, 152

Falcon, the, 141

Fatness, symbol of insensibility, 77

Flower, life compared to, 67

Fool, fate of the, 18; nature of the, 52f.

Frost, R., *quoted*, xiii.

G

Gabirol, Solomon Ibn, *quoted*, 85

Gall, 83, 104, 106

Gate, place of judgment, 18

Glass, 143

Glueck, N., *quoted*, 141, 213

Goat, the wild, 204

God, accused of injustice, 95, 124ff., 176; adversaries of, 96; and human suffering, 12f., 23; anger of, 15, 39, 41, 49, 69, 79, 82, 96, 101, 105, 111, 184, 220; answers Job, 196-218; 'archers' of, 83; 'arrows' of, 23; avenging sword of, 101; beyond human knowledge, 188, 191, 194; 'breath' of, 15, 135, 167, 170, 192;

II. HEBREW WORDS